Innovative Solutions and Applications of Web Services Technology

Liang-Jie Zhang
Kingdee International Software Group Co., Ltd., China

Yishuang Ning
Tsinghua University, China

A volume in the Advances in Web
Technologies and Engineering
(AWTE) Book Series

Published in the United States of America by
    IGI Global
    Engineering Science Reference (an imprint of IGI Global)
    701 E. Chocolate Avenue
    Hershey PA, USA 17033
    Tel: 717-533-8845
    Fax: 717-533-8661
    E-mail: cust@igi-global.com
    Web site: http://www.igi-global.com

Library of Congress Cataloging-in-Publication Data

Names: Zhang, Liang-Jie, editor. | Ning, Yishuang, 1986- editor.
Title: Innovative solutions and applications of web services technology /
  Liang-Jie Zhang and Yishuang Ning, editors.
Description: Hershey, PA : Engineering Science Reference, an imprint of IGI
  Global, [2019] | Includes bibliographical references and index.
Identifiers: LCCN 2018022050| ISBN 9781522572688 (hardcover) | ISBN
  9781522572695 (ebook)
Subjects: LCSH: Web services.
Classification: LCC TK5105.88813 .I5524 2019 | DDC 006.7/8--dc23 LC record available at
https://lccn.loc.gov/2018022050

This book is published in the IGI Global book series Advances in Web Technologies and Engineering (AWTE) (ISSN: 2328-2762; eISSN: 2328-2754)

British Cataloguing in Publication Data
A Cataloguing in Publication record for this book is available from the British Library.

All work contributed to this book is new, previously-unpublished material.
The views expressed in this book are those of the authors, but not necessarily of the publisher.

For electronic access to this publication, please contact: eresources@igi-global.com.

Advances in Web Technologies and Engineering (AWTE) Book Series

ISSN:2328-2762
EISSN:2328-2754

Editor-in-Chief: Ghazi I. Alkhatib, The Hashemite University, Jordan & David C. Rine, George Mason University, USA

MISSION

The **Advances in Web Technologies and Engineering (AWTE) Book Series** aims to provide a platform for research in the area of Information Technology (IT) concepts, tools, methodologies, and ethnography, in the contexts of global communication systems and Web engineered applications. Organizations are continuously overwhelmed by a variety of new information technologies, many are Web based. These new technologies are capitalizing on the widespread use of network and communication technologies for seamless integration of various issues in information and knowledge sharing within and among organizations. This emphasis on integrated approaches is unique to this book series and dictates cross platform and multidisciplinary strategy to research and practice.

The **Advances in Web Technologies and Engineering (AWTE) Book Series** seeks to create a stage where comprehensive publications are distributed for the objective of bettering and expanding the field of web systems, knowledge capture, and communication technologies. The series will provide researchers and practitioners with solutions for improving how technology is utilized for the purpose of a growing awareness of the importance of web applications and engineering.

COVERAGE

- Data analytics for business and government organizations
- Metrics-based performance measurement of IT-based and web-based organizations
- Knowledge structure, classification, and search algorithms or engines
- Information filtering and display adaptation techniques for wireless devices
- Software agent-based applications
- Web user interfaces design, development, and usability engineering studies
- Strategies for linking business needs and IT
- Integrated user profile, provisioning, and context-based processing
- Quality of service and service level agreement issues among integrated systems
- Human factors and cultural impact of IT-based systems

IGI Global is currently accepting manuscripts for publication within this series. To submit a proposal for a volume in this series, please contact our Acquisition Editors at Acquisitions@igi-global.com or visit: http://www.igi-global.com/publish/.

Titles in this Series

For a list of additional titles in this series, please visit:
https://www.igi-global.com/book-series/advances-web-technologies-engineering/37158

Dynamic Knowledge Representation in Scientific Domains
Cyril Pshenichny (ITMO University, Russia) Paolo Diviacco (Istituto Nazionale di Oceanografia e di Geofisica Sperimentale, Italy) and Dmitry Mouromtsev (ITMO University Russia)
Engineering Science Reference • ©2018 • 397pp • H/C (ISBN: 9781522552611) • US $205.00

Innovations, Developments, and Applications of Semantic Web and Information Systems
Miltiadis D. Lytras (American College of Greece, Greece) Naif Aljohani (King Abdulaziz University, Saudi Arabia) Ernesto Damiani (University of Milan, Italy) and Kwok Tai Chui (City University of Hong Kong, Hng Kong)
Engineering Science Reference • ©2018 • 473pp • H/C (ISBN: 9781522550426) • US $245.00

Handbook of Research on Biomimicry in Information Retrieval and Knowledge Management
Reda Mohamed Hamou (Dr. Tahar Moulay University of Saida, Algeria)
Engineering Science Reference • ©2018 • 429pp • H/C (ISBN: 9781522530046) • US $325.00

Global Perspectives on Frameworks for Integrated Reporting Emerging Research and ...
Ioana Dragu (Babes-Bolyai University, Romania) Adriana Tiron-Tudor (Babes-Bolyai University, Romania) and Szilveszter Fekete Pali-Pista (Babes-Bolyai University, Romania)
Business Science Reference • ©2018 • 160pp • H/C (ISBN: 9781522527534) • US $135.00

Novel Design and the Applications of Smart-M3 Platform in the Internet of Things Emerging ...
Dmitry Korzun (Petrozavodsk State University (PetrSU), Russia) Alexey Kashevnik (St. Petersburg Institute for Informatics and Automation of the Russian Academy of Sciences (SPIIRAS), Russia & ITMO University, Russia) and Sergey Balandin (FRUCT Oy, Finland & St. Petersburg State University of Aerospace Instrumentation (SUAI), Russia)
Information Science Reference • ©2018 • 150pp • H/C (ISBN: 9781522526537) • US $145.00

For an entire list of titles in this series, please visit:
https://www.igi-global.com/book-series/advances-web-technologies-engineering/37158

701 East Chocolate Avenue, Hershey, PA 17033, USA
Tel: 717-533-8845 x100 • Fax: 717-533-8661
E-Mail: cust@igi-global.com • www.igi-global.com

Table of Contents

Detailed Table of Contents

Chapter 1

　　　Yilong Yang, University of Macau, Macau

Notwithstanding the advancement of service computing in recent years, service composition is still a main issue in this field. In this chapter, the authors present an integrated framework for semantic service composition using answer set programming. Unlike the AI planning approaches of top-down workflow with nested composition and combining composition procedure into service discovery, the proposed framework integrates a designed service workflow with automatic nested composition. In addition, the planning is based on service signature while validating through service contract. Moreover, a unified implementation of service discovery, selection, composition, and validation is achieved by answer set programming. Finally, the performance of proposed framework is demonstrated by a travel booking example on QWSDataset.

Chapter 2

　　　Wei-Ho Tsai, National Taipei University of Technology, Taiwan
　　　Cin-Hao Ma, National Taipei University of Technology, Taiwan

Singer identification (SID), which refers to the task of automatically identifying the singer(s) in a music recording, is of great help in handling the rapid proliferation of music data on the internet and digital media. Although a number of SID studies from acoustic features have been reported, most systems are designed to identify the singer in recordings of solo performances. Very little research has considered a more realistic case, which is to identify more than one singer in a music recording. The research presented in this chapter investigates the feasibility of identifying singers in music recordings that contain overlapping (simultaneous) singing voices (e.g., duet or trio singings). This problem is referred to as overlapping singer identification (OSID). Several approaches to OSID are discussed and evaluated in this chapter. In addition, a related issue on how to distinguish solo singings from overlapping singing recordings is also discussed.

Existing technologies for web services have been extended to give the value-added customized services to users through the service composition. Service composition consists of four major stages: planning, discovery, selection, and execution. However, with the proliferation of web services, service discovery and selection are becoming challenging and time-consuming tasks. Organizing services into similar clusters is a very efficient approach. Existing clustering approaches have problems that include discovering semantic characteristics, loss of semantic information, and a shortage of high-quality ontologies. Thus, the authors proposed hybrid term similarity-based clustering approach in their previous work. Further, the current clustering approaches do not consider the sub-clusters within a cluster. In this chapter, the authors propose a multi-level clustering approach to prune the search space further in discovery process. Empirical study of the prototyping system has proved the effectiveness of the proposed multi-level clustering approach.

Many cyber-physical systems operate together with others and with humans in a joint physical space. Because of their operation in proximity to humans, they have to operate according to very high safety standards. This chapter presents a method for developing the control software of cyber-physical systems. The method is model-based and assists engineers with spatial and real-time property verification. In particular, the authors describe a toolchain consisting of the model-based development toolset Reactive Blocks, the spatial analyzer BeSpaceD in conjunction with the real-time model checkers UPPAAL and PRISM. The combination of these tools makes it possible to create models of the control software and, if necessary, simulators for the actual system behavior with Reactive Blocks. These models can then be checked for various correctness properties using the analysis tools. If all properties are fulfilled, Reactive Blocks transforms the models automatically into executable code.

Chapter 5
Angel Fernando Kuri-Morales, ITAM, Mexico

The exploitation of large databases implies the investment of expensive resources both in terms of the storage and processing time. The correct assessment of the data implies that pre-processing steps be taken before its analysis. The transformation of categorical data by adequately encoding every instance of categorical variables is needed. Encoding must be implemented that preserves the actual patterns while avoiding the introduction of non-existing ones. The authors discuss CESAMO, an algorithm which allows us to statistically identify the pattern preserving codes. The resulting database is more economical and may encompass mixed databases. Thus, they obtain an optimal transformed representation that is considerably more compact without impairing its informational content. For the equivalence of the original (FD) and reduced data set (RD), they apply an algorithm that relies on a multivariate regression algorithm (AA). Through the combined application of CESAMO and AA, the equivalent behavior of both FD and RD may be guaranteed with a high degree of statistical certainty.

Chapter 6
Yong Feng, Chongqing University, China
Heng Li, Chongqing University, China
Zhuo Chen, Chongqing University, China
Baohua Qiang, Guilin University of Electronic Technology, China

Recommender systems have been widely employed to suggest personalized online information to simplify users' information discovery process. With the popularity of online social networks, analysis and mining of social factors and social circles have been utilized to support more effective recommendations, but have not been fully investigated. In this chapter, the authors propose a novel recommendation model with the consideration of more comprehensive social factors and topics. To further enhance recommendation accuracy, four social factors are simultaneously injected into the recommendation model based on probabilistic matrix factorization. Meanwhile, the authors explore several new methods to measure these social factors. Moreover, they infer explicit and implicit social circles to enhance the performance of recommendation diversity. Finally, the authors conduct a series of experiments on publicly available data. Experimental results show the proposed model achieves significantly improved performance over the existing models in which social information have not been fully considered.

Chapter 7
Ehtesham Zahoor, National University of Computer and Emerging Sciences, Pakistan
Kashif Munir, National University of Computer and Emerging Sciences, Pakistan
Olivier Perrin, University of Lorraine, France
Claude Godart, University of Lorraine, France

Traditional business process specification approaches such as BPMN are procedural, as they require specifying exact and complete process flow. In contrast, a declarative process is specified by a set of constraints that mark the boundary of any solution to the process. In this chapter, the authors propose a bounded model-checking-based approach for the verification of declarative processes using satisfiability solving (SAT). The proposed approach does not require exponential space and is very efficient. It uses the highly expressive event calculus (EC) as the modeling formalism, with a sound and complete EC to SAT encoding process. The verification process can include both the functional and non-functional aspects. The authors have also proposed a filtering criterion to filter the clauses of interest from the large set of unsatisfiable clauses for complex processes. The authors have discussed the implementation details and performance evaluation results to justify the practicality of the proposed approach.

Chapter 8
Georgia Kapitsaki, University of Cyprus, Cyprus

Privacy protection plays a vital role in pervasive and web environments, where users contact applications and services that may require access to their sensitive data. The current legislation, such as the recent European General Data Protection Regulation, is putting more emphasis on user protection and on placing users in the center of privacy choices. SOAP (simple object access protocol)-based and RESTful services may require access to sensitive data for their proper functioning, but users should be able to express their preferences on what should and should not be accessed. In this chapter, the above issues are discussed and a solution is presented for reconciling user preferences expressed in privacy policies and the service data needs tailored to SOAP-based services. A use example is provided and the main open issues providing directions for future research are discussed.

Chapter 9

To migrate on-premises business systems to the cloud environment faces challenges: the complexity, diversity of the legacy systems, cloud, and cloud migration services. Consequently, the cloud migration faces two major problems. The first one is how to select cloud services for the legacy systems, and the second one is how to move the corresponding workload from legacy systems to cloud. This chapter presents a total cloud migration solution including cloud service selection and optimization, cloud migration pattern generation, and cloud migration pattern enforcement. It takes the pattern as the core, and unifies the cloud migration request, the cloud migration service pattern, and the cloud migration service composition. A cloud migration example of blockchain system shows that the proposed approach improves the cloud service selection, cloud migration service composition generation efficiency, migration process parallelization, and enables long transaction support by means of pattern reuse.

Preface

In recent years, with the rapid development of Web technologies and the popularity of online social networks, Web or Internet has become a huge platform for global information delivery and sharing. More and more Web applications have been established on the Internet, such as e-commerce, e-government or enterprise application integration. However, since these applications may be distributed in different geographical locations, and use different data organization forms and operating systems, how to centralize and fully utilize these highly distributed data becomes an urgent problem in many application scenarios.

With the emergence of cloud and mobile computing paradigms, Web services technology as a means of management has been actively deployed within many business environments (Abdullah et al., 2016). It is considered as the backbone technology to implement the service-oriented architecture (SOA; Bouguettaya et al., 2017; Amin, 2018) which is a widely accepted paradigm to facilitate distributed application integration and interoperability (Endrei et al., 2004). With the SOA approach, the service components can be developed into complex business processes and value-added applications independently (Liu et al., 2016). Currently, Web services technology covers the whole life-cycle of services innovation research that includes business componentization, services modeling, services creation, services realization, services annotation, services deployment, services discovery, services composition, services delivery, service-to-service collaboration, services monitoring, services optimization, as well as services management. For several years now, the trend of providing everything as a service (XaaS) has depicted a promising scenario where SOA supports developing and deploying software applications as services (Duan et al., 2016).

Web services have experienced an exponential increase in popularity and usage in the past few years. With the development of services computing (SC) technologies, large amounts of Web services have been released on the Internet. According to a statistics from seekda.com, there are 28606 Web services available on the Web offered by around 8000 providers (Sheng et al., 2014). The fast increasing number of Web services is on the one hand transforming the Web into a service-oriented repository, and poses a number of challenges on the other hand, including services interoperability, services management, quality of Web services (QoWS; Yu et al., 2008), and services security and privacy.

Web service is a new platform for building interoperable distributed applications. Good interoperability is a must for the Web applications to achieve satisfactory services for users. The most challenging issue for achieving the truly seamless interoperation is how to implement the semantic interoperability which deals with semantic properties of Web services (Yu et al., 2008). Reaching full semantic interoperability is one of the long-term objectives of the architectural design and construction industry of Web services, demanding new technologies to combine different information representations (Pauwels et al., 2016).

Another challenge is services management (Bouguettaya, 2017). For different application backgrounds, the application objects of Web services are also different. Web services that are widely used today can be classified into four categories: business-oriented services, consumer-oriented services, device-oriented services and system-oriented services (Yue et al., 2004). Since Web services applications are built based on heterogeneous systems in different ways, it is difficult for service providers to efficiently manage, analyze and visualize the tremendous issues of Web services. Therefore, how to integrate the heterogeneous services poses a key challenge of service composition.

There is also the challenge of providing satisfactory QoWS as a key concept in distinguishing between competing Web services. With the popularity of online social networks and the development of SC, there are increasingly more people who tend to share their daily experiences and interact with Web applications, thus leading to the explosive growth of data on the Internet. Since users usually have difficulty in precisely describing their demands, traditional keyword-based search engine methods are not efficient to fully meet the need of user information discovery and recommendation. Besides, the accuracy of recommendation is also a main concern for improving the QoWS.

The last but not the least challenge for Web service applications is security. Since the requests and responses of Web services are sent over the Internet, and modern enterprise applications demand data can be shared within or across organizations (Nepal et al., 2016), they are easy to subject to various security threats, such as information integrity, encryption and authentication, and confidentiality. When Web services are invoked in open environment such as cloud, it is especially important to give users the confidence that their data are safely handled without increasing data movement and computation costs (Nepal et al., 2016). Privacy is another major concern of Web services deployment (Yu et al., 2006). As seen in Chapter 4, privacy is viewed as "the ability of individual's control over the use and dissemination of sensitive information". Traditional technologies for preserving privacy in Web services include digital privacy credentials, data filters and mobile privacy preserving agents. However, there is still no guarantee that Web services applications can provide message protection through preventing unauthorized access of services.

OBJECTIVE OF THE BOOK

The objectives of this book are in two folds. One is to motivate innovative solutions to solve the challenges above, and the other is to promote high quality research by bringing together researchers and practitioners from both academia and industry. To rapidly respond to the changing economy, this book puts its focus on the industry-specific services and tries to attract researchers, practitioners, and industry business leaders in all the services sectors to help define and shape the modernization strategy and directions of the services industry.

ORGANIZATION OF THE BOOK

The book is organized into nine chapters. A brief description of each of the chapters is as follows:

The first chapter on "An Integrated Framework for Semantic Service Composition Using Answer Set Programming" presents an integrated framework for semantic service composition using answer set programming which integrates a designed service workflow with automatic nested composition. In this framework, service discovery, composition, selection, and validation are unified into one procedure to provide high interoperability. The authors achieve a unified implementation by answer set programming, and demonstrate the performance of the proposed framework by a travel booking example on QWSDataset.

The authors in the second chapter titled "Overlapping Singer Identification in Music Recordings" report a feasibility study of detecting and identifying singers with overlapping singings in a recording. In this chapter, the authors propose using parallel model combination technique to characterize the simultaneous voices of duet or trio singers based on the individual voices of each singer, and proposes a triangulation-based decision approach by exploiting the relationships between the combinations of singers to improve the interoperation performance. The results of the experiment conducted using a database of a cappella demonstrated feasibility of the approaches.

In the third chapter of the book on "Multi-Level Web Service Clustering to Bootstrap the Web Service Discovery and Selection", the authors present a multi-level web service clustering approach to bootstrap the web service discovery and selection. In this chapter, the features that are ranked according to the contribution in clustering process are selected in each level to cluster the services. The proposed method in this chapter significantly increases the performance of the service discovery and the selection which are key ingredients to the interoperation of Web services.

The fourth chapter of the book is about "Model-Based Development and Spatiotemporal Behavior of Cyber-Physical Systems". Web service management refers to the control and monitoring of Web service qualities and usage which generally includes control management and monitoring management. To tackle the control management issue, the authors introduce a safety modeling and verification tool chain for the model-based engineering of controllers in distributed embedded systems that have to fulfill certain spatial behavioral properties. It creates a library of reusable building blocks which support the pattern matching used by the tool coupling.

In the next three chapters, the authors propose different approaches to tackle the effectiveness and efficiency problem to improve the QoWS and user satisfactory. Detailed information can be found in the following.

In the fifth chapter titled "Minimum Data Base Determination and Preprocessing for Machine Learning", the authors present a methodology derived from the practical solution of an automated clustering process over large database from a real large sized (over 20 million customers) company. The authors of this chapter emphasize that they used statistical methods to reduce the search space of the problem as well as the treatment given to the customer's information stored in multiple tables of multiple databases.

In the sixth chapter on "Improving Recommendation Accuracy and Diversity via Multiple Social Factors and Social Circles", the authors propose a personalized PTIC model which uses four social factors including individual preference, interpersonal trust influence, interpersonal interest similarity and interpersonal closeness degree to improve the recommendation accuracy and diversity. The authors demonstrate that the proposed PTIC model achieves significantly reduced recommendation error over existing models in which social information have not been fully considered, and improves the performance of recommendation diversity through a series of experiments on the real life social rating data.

The seventh chapter titled "Verification of Service-Based Declarative Business Processes: A Satisfiability Solving-Based Formal Approach" is about improving user satisfactory of Web services. In this chapter, the authors propose a complete and consistent bounded model-checking based approach for the verification of declarative Web services composition processes using satisfiability solving (SAT).

The authors propose a SAT based bounded model checking approach, which does not require exponential space and is very efficient as the state space is searched in an arbitrary order.

The eighth chapter is on "Context and End-User Privacy Policies in Web Service-Based Applications". In this chapter, it outlines the content of the user privacy preferences providing extensions to the original content captured in Consumer Privacy Language version 2.0 (CPL-2.0). It also provides the structure of the management architecture for SOAP (Simple Object Access Protocol)-based services, and builds on recent advances in the field discussing open research directions offering thus, a current view of privacy protection for web service-based applications that require user context.

The authors in the ninth chapter titled "Pattern-Based Cloud Migration: Take Blockchain as a Service as an Example" present a clustering-based approach to select corresponding cloud services, and introduce a cloud layer based node merging and splitting approach to solve the problem that is difficult to quickly and automatically select cloud services for complex system migration out of a large number of cloud services. The authors also present a cloud migration service composition approach, which adopts pattern-based approach by classifying and analyzing of service composition approaches.

With the rapid development of service and mobile computing, big data (Zhang et al., 2015; Zhang et al., 2015), cloud computing (Sousa et al., 2016) and Internet of things (IOT; Zhang et al., 2017), a fast increasing number of Web services are released on the Internet, making it difficult to select appropriate services from various of application program interfaces (APIs). Besides, the security and privacy problem is also a main concern of SC. The primary organization of the contents in this book is based on the nine sections above, providing innovative solutions to these typical challenges and applications of Web services technologies. As a comprehensive collection of research on the latest methodologies, technologies and applications related to Web services, this book, *Innovative Solutions and Applications of Web Services Technology*, provides all audiences including researchers and practitioners from both academia and industry with a novel perspective of defining and shaping the modernization strategy and directions of the services industry.

Liang-Jie Zhang
Kingdee International Software Group Co., Ltd., China

Yishuang Ning
Tsinghua University, China

REFERENCES

Abdullah, A., & Li, X. (2016). An efficient similarity-based model for web service recommendation. *Services Transactions on Services Computing*, *4*(3), 15–28. doi:10.29268tsc.2016.4.3.2

Amin, A. (2018). *Evaluating the quality of integrated software systems based on service-oriented architecture* (Doctoral dissertation). Sudan University of Science & Technology.

Bouguettaya, A., Singh, M., Huhns, M., Sheng, Q. Z., Dong, H., Yu, Q., & Ouzzani, M. (2017). A service computing manifesto: The next 10 years. *Communications of the ACM*, *60*(4), 64–72. doi:10.1145/2983528

Duan, Y. C., Duan, Q., Sun, X. B., Fu, G. H., Narendra, N. C., Zhou, N., ... Zhou, Z. (2016). Everything as a service (XaaS) on the cloud: Origins, current and future trends. *Services Transactions on Cloud Computing*, *4*(2), 32–45. doi:10.29268tcc.2016.0006

Endrei, M., Ang, J., Arsanjani, A., Chua, S., Comte, P., Krogdahl, P., & Newling, T. (2004). *Patterns: service-oriented architecture and web services* (pp. 17–44). IBM Corporation, International Technical Support Organization.

Liu, Z., Wang, H., Xu, X., & Wang, Z. (2016). Web services optimal composition based on improved artificial bee colony algorithm with the knowledge of service domain features. *Services Transactions on Services Computing*, *4*(1), 27–38. doi:10.29268tsc.2016.4.1.3

Nepal, S., Friedrich, C., Wise, C., Sinnott, R. O., Jaccard, J. J., & Chen, S. P. (2016). Key management service: Enabling secure sharing and deleting of documents on public clouds. *Services Transactions on Cloud Computing*, *4*(2), 15–31. doi:10.29268tcc.2016.0005

Pauwels, P., Zhang, S., & Lee, Y. C. (2017). Semantic web technologies in AEC industry: A literature overview. *Automation in Construction*, *73*, 145–165. doi:10.1016/j.autcon.2016.10.003

Sheng, Q. Z., Qiao, X., Vasilakos, A. V., Szabo, C., Bourne, S., & Xu, X. (2014). Web services composition: A decade's overview. *Information Sciences*, *280*, 218–238. doi:10.1016/j.ins.2014.04.054

Sousa, E., Lins, F., Tavares, E., & Maciel, P. (2016). A Modeling strategy for cloud infrastructure planning considering performance and cost requirements. *Services Transactions on Cloud Computing*, *4*(1), 30–43. doi:10.29268tcc.2016.0003

Yu, Q., Liu, X., Bouguettaya, A., & Medjahed, B. (2008). Deploying and managing Web services: issues, solutions, and directions. *The VLDB Journal—The International Journal on Very Large Data Bases, 17*(3), 537-572.

Yue, K., Wang, X. L., & Zhou, A. Y. (2004). Underlying techniques for Web services: A survey. *Journal of Software.*

Zhang, L. J., & Chen, H. (2015). BDOA: Big data open architecture. *Services Transactions on Big Data, 2*(4), 24–48. doi:10.29268tbd.2015.2.4.3

Zhang, L. J., & Li, C. (2017). Internet of things solutions. *Services Transactions on Internet of Things, 1*(1), 1–22. doi:10.29268tiot.2017.1.1.1

Zhang, L. J., & Zeng, J. (2015). 5C, a new model of defining big data. *Services Transactions on Big Data, 2*(4), 10–23. doi:10.29268tbd.2015.2.4.2

Acknowledgment

The editors would like to thank IGI Global for providing this opportunity to publish this volume based on the selected papers submitted and published in the earlier issues of the year 2013-2017 of our journal, *International Journal of Web Services Research* (IJWSR). We are also grateful to all the members of IGI Global who have been providing help during the entire process of this project.

The editors are thankful to acknowledge the help of all the people involved in this project who have made valuable contributions by enhancing this book and, more specifically, to the authors regarding the improvement of quality, coherence, and content presentation of chapters. Our sincere gratitude goes to the chapter's authors who contributed their time and expertise to this book.

Liang-Jie Zhang
Kingdee International Software Group Co., Ltd., China

Yishuang Ning
Tsinghua University, China

Chapter 1

An Integrated Framework for Semantic Service Composition Using Answer Set Programming (SSC-ASP)

Yilong Yang
University of Macau, Macau

ABSTRACT

Notwithstanding the advancement of service computing in recent years, service composition is still a main issue in this field. In this chapter, the authors present an integrated framework for semantic service composition using answer set programming. Unlike the AI planning approaches of top-down workflow with nested composition and combining composition procedure into service discovery, the proposed framework integrates a designed service workflow with automatic nested composition. In addition, the planning is based on service signature while validating through service contract. Moreover, a unified implementation of service discovery, selection, composition, and validation is achieved by answer set programming. Finally, the performance of proposed framework is demonstrated by a travel booking example on QWSDataset.

DOI: 10.4018/978-1-5225-7268-8.ch001

INTRODUCTION

Describe the general perspective of the chapter. End by specifically stating the objectives of the chapter.

Service computing has been extensively studied in recent years, and it mainly touches issues including formalizing the specification of service, service discovery, selection, and composition (Rao & Su, 2005; Dustdar & Schreiner, 2005). There are two primary paradigms for service composition: top-down and bottom-up paradigms (Bartalos & Bielikova, 2011). For top-down paradigm, we can specify the complex service workflow manually. Nevertheless, the bottom-up paradigm can composite services automatically by AI planing. Furthermore, a mixture paradigm is proposed in the paper (Paik, Chen, & Huhns, 2014). In this mixture paradigm, HTN is utilized to plan service workflow instead of manually designing. Like top-down paradigm to discover services, if matching more than one service, the best service can be selected. Same as a bottom-up paradigm to automatically composite service, if no existed service is matched, the procedure of the nested composition will be triggered to assemble the target service. However, automatic approaches usually are not the best solution for world-wild problems. Especially for workflow planning, AI planning approach is not correct all the time. Even though nested composition compensates this deficiency when planning service is coarse-grained, it would be a failure when dependent services are decomposed incorrectly. Therefore, new mixture approach for service composition is required. Regularly, service discovery and composition are regarded as two separate processes (Syu, Ma, Kuo, & FanJiang, 2012). In (Ku ̈ster, Kö nig-Ries, Stern, & Klein, 2007), they proposed an approach to combining composition procedure into discovery process in compliance with multiple effects. However, the effects coverage must be computed foremost.

In order to address above issues, we propose an integrated framework for semantic service composition using answer set programming (SSC-ASP), which includes:

1. **A New Mixture Composition Paradigm:** Our approach combines top-down and bottom-up paradigms by designing a workflow for discovering and selecting service foremost, when no service is matched or discovered, a bottom-up nested composition procedure will be triggered.

2. **A Unified Procedure for Service Discovery and Composition (Using Simplified Service Description):** In order to boost planning and validation, we apply simplified service description to divide the target service (i.e., to discover and composite service) into the source and target services. Hence, service discovery and composition can be cooked in the identical procedure. The only difference is the length of composition chain. An outstanding advantage of this approach is not required to compute the multiple effects.

3. **On-the-Fly Service Planning and Validation by Answer Set Program:** Using interface variables for unified planning, and service contract (pre/post condition) for service validation. Our paper aims at employing answer set programming (ASP) (Brewka, Eiter, & Truszczyn´ski, 2011) for workflow planning, which is a declarative oriented programming towards to search problems. ASP allows for a unified representation of the problem including rules and constraints without requiring the solution algorithms, in terms of features such as solid logic foundations, high-expressiveness, nondeterminism and high-declaratively.

The remainder of this paper is organized as follows: Section 2 overviews SSC-ASP. Section 3 presents the formal specification of service as well as ASP implementation. Section 4 defines the service compositionality formally, and then Section 5 discusses unified service discovery, selection and composition and validation base on the formal specification. Section 6 shows the performance of SSC-ASP with a travel booking example. Section 7 discusses related work, and finally, Section 8 concludes this paper and outlines future work.

Overview

In this section, the informal definition of service is introduced first, and then the low-level composition methodology is discussed. Accordingly, the high-level mixture design paradigm and details of generation engine are presented.

To illustrate our framework, we choose the travel booking example from OMG BPMN 2.0 example[1] shown in Figure 1, which includes four sub-processes, six gateways, 18 activities and 26 events with error handling and compensation mechanisms. Thus, the complexity of this example is adequate for evaluating the performance of proposed framework.

This example provides travel booking services to clients. A client requires interacting with the system by following this process for his or her travel booking. The process includes four portions: 1) acquiring alternatives reservation, 2) making a decision, 3) providing credit card information and booking, and 4) charging the credit card. The detail information can be found in above OMG document. In the remain of this paper, we will show how to use modified mixture paradigm to composite this process and on-the-fly validate.

The Proposed Mixture Paradigm

In SSC-ASP, we introduce the mixture design paradigm which combines complex top-down paradigm and automatic bottom-up paradigm. For top-down paradigm, the

Figure 1. Travel booking workflow

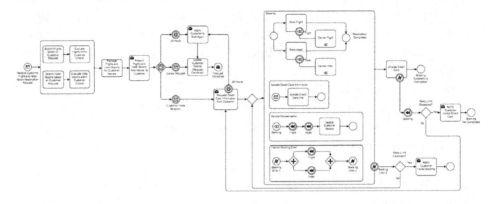

complex workflow is designed manually. Then all the un-matched services of the workflow are matching (i.e., service discovery) with services in the database. Once more than one services are founded, the best one will be selected. However, it would be failed if no one service is matched. For bottom-up paradigm, once providing the specification of the interface including service contract – pre and post conditions, un-matched services can be automatically generated by AI planning. Whereas this approach is time-consuming and has less accuracy. The better choice is to customize two paradigms first, and then combine both, so that we can not only make use of the advantage of automatic AI planning but also can obtain more complex and accuracy service than bottom-up methodology.

For customized bottom-up paradigm, the specification of target service such as domain, class, input and output variables are used for service composition, the contract of target service is used for validation. On-the-fly validation is hot-plug, and whether it is utilized or not is based on the requirements of time and accuracy. For top-down paradigm, an hot-plug validation layer is added. When the procedure is triggered by the services discovery, the correctness can be checked automatically.

The proposed mixture paradigm is shown in Figure 2:

- **Top Level:** Like top-down paradigm: designing workflow, discovering candidate services (*Service A, B, H, D*) and selecting best one (*Service A, B*).
- **Bottom Level:** If no service was discovered, customized bottom-up paradigm are used to composite services to fulfill the requirements (*Service G, H*).

Figure 2. The proposed mixture paradigm

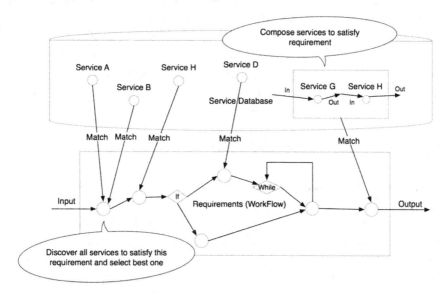

SSC-ASP Framework

SSC-ASP is a cloud-based framework shown in Figure 3. When you are a travel agency or even a traveler, in *client side*, you would like to find or develop a travel booking system. However, purchasing or developing a new system requires high expenditure. Once SSC-ASP is adopted, you can specify requirements as BPMN because BPMN can describe complex workflow with user-friendly interface and standardized specification. As a cloud client user in Figure 3, she can submit her requirement to the cloud. In the cloud side, the service crawler finds and downloads open services and partner services. Moreover, SSC-ASP transforms all service indexes to unified ASP service facts, which can be saved into service database. Here we use ASP to implements the proposed mixture paradigm as generation engine, in which all the services are denoted as ASP facts. The service can be any kind of WCF/ OSGI/COBRA/SOAP/RESTFul Services. Accordingly, the requirements of BPMN activities will be extracted and transformed to unmatched services (ASP goal facts).

Now we discuss *generation engine* shown in Figure 3. Based on the goal service (goal fact), service facts in database, all the pre-defined ASP rules, and constraints, the generation engine will take the actions for each goal service: *discover service* matched the functional requirements (for example, search flights: domain as travel, class as fights, input days and location, output available choices); select the best service with less cost of the non-functional requirements (such as price under $1000, time under 2 seconds), if more than one services were discovered; *composite services*, if no service was discovered, for example, booking service contains booking fight and hotel services; check correctness. After then, the result of composition (Answer Sets) with all matched services was produced by generation engine. Finally, SSC-ASP will transform it into an executable workflow (BPEL), and deploy it into workflow engine by returning a web service endpoint for agency or traveler for invoking. After using this service, agency or traveler can give the feedback to SSC-ASP for improving the accuracy of service generation engine.

ASP and SMT Solver for SSC-ASP

ASP (Answer Set Programming) can be used for realizing service discovery, service selection, and service composition. In this paper, we use Gringo as ASP grounder, Clasp as ASP solver (Gebser et al., 2010), and write the ASP code based on (Lifschitz, 2002). However, there are some disadvantages of Gringo and Clasp; they do not support set/list and its operations. Thus, more powerful ASP solver DLV-complex[2] can be taken into account which supports set/list and its operations. Also, it supports self-defined predicate which can invoke SMT solver for on-the-fly validation in ASP solver.

For SMT solver, we choose Z3[3], because Z3 is a high-performance theorem prover developed by Microsoft Research. Z3 supports linear real and integer arithmetic, fixed-size bit-vectors, extensional arrays, uninterpreted functions, and quantifiers.

Figure 3. The framework of generation engine

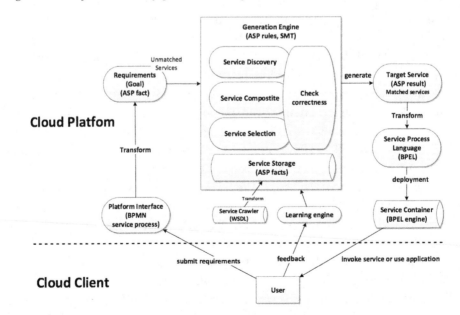

Z3 is integrated with some program analysis, testing, and verification tools from Microsoft Research. However, Z3 solver can only answer the satisfiable problem. A formula condition is valid if and only if its negation is un-satisfiable. If the running result of the Z3 solver is *unsat*, then the formula condition is valid. Hence, Z3 can be used to check the composability for service composition.

Service Specification

In this section, we will formally define SSC-ASP first, and then discuss how to implement SSC-ASP by the corresponding declarative ASP. Based on the formal defined service in logic tuples as well as composition tasks, we can transform them into ASP: the requirements and service description as ASP facts, and composition tasks as ASP rules. However, there is an assumption on a service contract for pre and post conditions in this work, which is that all constraints should be isolated. For example, $precondition : x > 0$ and $postcondition : y < 3$ are isolated, but $postcondition : x + y > 2$ is not isolated.

Usually, the semantic of services is defined by ontology and QoS tuples. Considering the efficiency and portability, the essential parts of OWL-S, WSMO, and QoS are used, we define Atomic Service as follows:

$$AS : \langle SDec, Spec, Sign, FuncR, NonFuncR \rangle$$

where

1. $SDec$: The *interface of service* is denoted as:, where the service with name of ServiceName with input variables in and output variables out, as well as their corresponding types of U and V.
2. $Spec$: Service contract is specified as Hoare Logic: $P \vdash R$.
3. $Sign : \langle PType, URL \rangle$, where
   a. Indicates the category of service vendor, could be provided by local, partner or open cloud as
   $PType \in \{LocalService, PartnerService, OpenService\}$
   b. URL denotes the service location address for invocation
4. $FuncR : \langle Desc, Class, Domain, In, Out \rangle$, where
   a. $Desc$: The human-readable functional description of service.
   b. $Class$: The catalog of service (e.g., hotel).
   c. $Domain$: Business domain of service (e.g., travel).
   d. $In : \{inX : U\}, Out : \{outY : V\}$: Input and output variables of service.

5.   *NonFuncR*   :
     $\langle Response\,Time,\ Availability,\ Throughput,\ Price, Rank,\ Privacy \rangle$,
     where

   a. $Response\,Time \in Float^+$: Response time is the duration time from sending a request to receiving a response with unit ms.

   b. $Availability \in [0,1]$: The number of successful invocations out of the total.

   c. $Throughput \in Integer^+$: The maximum number of service invocations for a given period such as 1 minute.

   d. $Price \in Float^+$: The price for invoking this service.

   e. $Rank \in Integer^+$: Customer satisfaction level.

   f. $Privacy \in \{OpenService, PartnerService, PrivateService\}$: Privacy level. Three levels are ordered with
        $OpenService \sqsubseteq PartnerService \sqsubseteq PrivateService$,
        which can be denoted as 0, 1, and 2, respectively. If Privacy equals 0, as *PartnerService* , only *Partner Service* and *Private Service* can be taken into account for matching procedure.

Note that web service usually consists of more than one services. Therefore, all services inside one web service have same non-functional properties.

An ASP example of atomic service *Search Flights* is shown in Listing 1. Its privacy attribute is open service; functional requirements are classified as flight, domain as travel, input variables are days and location, output variables are flights list, non-functional requirements are response time as 20 ms, availability as 98%, throughput as 1200, no price, rank 12. Therefore, ASP is tight and expressive technique. Here noted, *Spec* is string type in ASP, when invoking the SMT solver, it should be transformed to the corresponding language

Listing 1. Atomic service - search flights

```
atomService(
sdec(searchFlight),
```
$spec("days \in datatype \land location \in cities \vdash flights \neq \varnothing")\,,$
```
sign(openservice, "http://hostname/path"),
funcR({searchFlight}, {flight}, {travel},
in({var(days,data), var(location,string)}),
out({var(flights,list)}))),
nonFuncR("20","0.98","120","0.99","0.00","12","0")).
```

SERVICE COMPOSITION

Service composition is pivotal of generation engine. This section focuses on service composability. To unify service discovery, selection, nested composition into the same procedure, target and source services are introduced first.

EQUIVALENCE OF VARIABLES

Let var_1 and var_2 are two variables defined by $\langle Name_1, Type_1, Class_1, Domain_1 \rangle$ and $\langle Name_2, Type_2, Class_2, Domain_2 \rangle$. They are equivalence, denoted as $var_1 =_{eqv} var_2$, if and only if the following conditions hold:

1. $Type_1 = Type_2$
2. $Class_1 = Class_2$
3. $Domain_1 = Domain_2$

For instance, there are two variables: **variable location**, *type:string*, *class:hotel*, *domain:travel*, and **variable place**, *type:string*, *class:hotel*, *domain:travel*, they are equivalence because of the same type, class and domain.

COMPOSABILITY

Let A_1 and A_2 are services, they can be composited if the following conditions hold:

1. $\exists out \in A_1.FuncR.Out, in \in A_2.FuncR.In \cdot (out =_{eqv} in)$
2. $A_1.Spec.R \uparrow out \Rightarrow A_2.Spec.P \uparrow in$
3. $A_1.FuncR.Domain = A_2.FuncR.Domain$

where $Formula \uparrow VariableSet$ denotes the derived formula by removing all sub-formulas in $Formula$ which variables of $VariableSet$ do not appear. E.g., $(x > 1 \wedge y < 3) \uparrow \{x\} = (x > 1)$.

The conditions of *Composability* exhibit that the composable services must have the identical domain and output variables of service A_1 must have one variable which should be inside input variables of service A_2. In addition, the postcondition of A_1 should imply the precondition of A_2.

ATOMIC COMPOSITION

Let A_1 and A_2 are atomic services. If they are composable, composable variable set *Internel* can be defined as:

$$Internel = \{in \mid out \in A_1.FuncR.Out \wedge in \in A_2.FuncR.In \wedge in =_{eqv} out\}$$

The atomic composition of A_1 and A_2 can be denoted as $AC : A_1 >> A_2$, whose elements can be calculated as follows:

$$AC.SDec = A_1.SDec \char`\^ A_2.SDec$$
$$AC.Spec.p = A_1.Spec.p \uparrow \{A_1.FuncR.In\} \wedge A_2.Spec.p \uparrow \{A_2.FuncR.In - Internel\}$$
$$AC.Spec.R = A_1.Spec.R \uparrow \{A_1.FuncR.Out - Internel\} \wedge A_2.Spec.R \uparrow \{A_2.FuncR.Out\}$$
$$AC.FuncR.Desc = A_1.FuncR.Desc \cup A_2.FuncR.Desc$$
$$AC.FuncR.Class = A_1.FuncR.Class \cup A_2.FuncR.Class$$
$$AC.FuncR.Domain = A_1.FuncR.Domain$$
$$AC.FuncR.In = \{A_1.FuncR.In\} \cup \{A_2.FuncR.In - Internel\}$$
$$AC.FuncR.Out = \{A_1.FuncR.Out - Internel\} \cup \{A_2.FuncR.Out\}$$
$$AC.Sign.Type = \perp \{A_1.Sign.Type, A_2.Sign.Type\}$$
$$AC.NoFuncR.ResponseTime = Sum$$
$$AC.NoFuncR.Price = Sum$$
$$AC.NoFuncR.Others = LowValue$$
$$AC.NoFuncR.Privacy = \perp \{A_1.NoFuncR.Privacy, A_2.NoFuncR.Privacy\}$$

The result of service composition can be obtained by the conjunction of services without the composable variables, where function requirements are disjunction, the non-functional requirements are the sum of properties or lowest value except the attribute of *Privacy*.

COMPOSITION CHAINING

Let $S_1, S_2, \ldots, S_n$ are services. If they are composable, the outcome of the composition $S_1 >> S_2 >> \ldots >> S_n$ is:

$$\langle Services, CompositeResources, SoruceService, TargetService, CompositeRelations \rangle$$

1. *Services* is the collection of all the services participated in composition.
2. *CompositeResources* is the set of the composable variables.
3. *SoruceService* is the head service in chaining.
4. *TargetService* is the tail service in chaining.
5. *CompositeRelations* is the composite function:
   $$Services \times CompositeResources \rightarrow Services$$

Let us port the formal description to ASP in the following lists. Because of the advantage of declarative ASP and powerful ASP solver, we only need to define the problem and constraints. After then, ASP solver can recursively composite service as chaining, compute the cost, and finally select the best chaining after it terminates.

In Listing 2, lines 12-24 represent two services, lines 26-32 are for checking composibility. If they are composable, the composited service is expressed in lines 1-10. This rule will be invoked recursively by ASP solver. The ASP solver will terminate successfully if the corresponding constraints are satisfied.

UNIFY SERVICE DISCOVERY, SELECTION, COMPOSITION, AND VALIDATION

In this section, we present generation engine, and the algorithms of mixture diagram for service discovery, selection, composition, and validation. Moreover, then these algorithms are integrated into a unified procedure.

The pseudo codes in Algorithm 1 present the process of SSC-ASP. The code in line 2 extracts all atomic services from the submitted workflow. Afterward, for every service, Algorithm 2 of service composition will be invoked. In line 2 of algorithm 2, service discovery function is called for matching all the services to their functional requirements. If the result more than one, from line 3 to 5, service selection can be invoked to choose the best service according to non-function requirements, but if no service is matched, then in line 7, low level nested composition function will be triggered to composite services. In line 8 - 10, if the composition result contains more

Listing 2. ASP code for composition rule

```
1 % Composited service
2 atomService(sdec(cp(ServiceNameA, ServiceNameB)),
3 sign(#newType(TypeA, TypeB), #newUrl(new)),
4 funcR(#union(DescA,DescB),#union(ClassA,ClassB),
5 DomainA,in(CIN),out(COUT)),
6 nonFuncR(#sum(RTA,RTB),
7 #min(AvailabilityA, AvailabilityB),
8 #min(ThroughputA, ThroughputB),
9 #min(ReliabilityA, ReliabilityB),
10 #sum(PriceA, PriceB), #min(RankA, RankB)))
11
12% First service
13:- atomService(rdec(RDEC1),
14 sdec(ServiceNameA), sign(TypeA, URLA),
15 funcR(DescA, ClassA, DomainA,in(IN1), out(OUT1)),
16 nonFuncR(RTA, AvailabilityA, ThroughputA,
17 ReliabilityA, PriceA, RankA)),
18
19% Second service
20 atomService(rdec(RDEC2),
21 sdec(ServiceNameB), sign(TypeB, URLB),
22 funcR(DescB, ClassB, DomainB,in(IN2), out(OUT2)),
23 nonFuncR(RTB, AvailabilityB, ThroughputB,
24 ReliabilityB, PriceB, RankB)),
25
26% Check Compositibility:
27 #intersection(OUT1, IN2, INTERNEL), #difference(IN2, INTERNEL), CIN),
28 #union(#difference(OUT1, INTERNEL),
29 #typeOrder(goaltype, TypeA),
30 #typeOrder(goaltype, TypeB),
31 #card(INTERNEL) != 0,
32 DomainA == DomainB, ServiceNameA != ServiceNameB.
```

Algorithm 1. Generation engine

```
Require: Input workflow is valid ◁ Precondition
Ensure: Executable Workflow ◁ Postcondition
1: procedure GENERATIONENGINE(designwf)
2: services ← EXTRACT SERVICES(unworkflows)
3: for all s ∈ services do
4: SERVICECOMPOSITION(s)
5: end for
6: workflow ← GENERATIONWORKFLOW(services, designwf)
7: return workflow
8: end procedure
```

Algorithm 2. SSC-ASP composition

```
Require: Unmatched service ◁ Precondition
Ensure: Matched service ◁ Postcondition
1: function SERVICECOMPOSITION(unmservice)
2: rs ← SERVICE DISCOVERY(unmservice)
3: if lens(rs) > 1 then
4: bests ← SERVICE SELECTION(rs)
5: return bests
6: else if lens(rs) == 0 then
7: rnc ← NESTED COMPOSITION(service)
8: if lens(rnc) > 1 then
9: bestnc ← SERVICE SELECTION(rnc)
10: return bestnc
11: end if
12: else
13: return rs ◁ Return result
14: end if
15: end function
```

than one chains, the best one would be chosen. We find that both service discovery and composition need to select best one from candidate services or service chainings. Since selected one service can be regarded as a special chaining with the length 1. Thus, service discovery and composition can be unified into one procedure.

Unify Service Discovery and Composition

In order to unify, discovery or composition *goal service* is divided into two services. The first one is *source service* which only has output variables no input variables, the output is the same as input variables of goal service, and the other one is *target service* which only has input variables without output variables. The input variables of target service are the same as output variables of goal service, where

$$SourceService.FuncR.Out = GoalService.FuncR.In$$

$$SourceService.FuncR.In = \varnothing$$

$$SourceService.Spec.P = true$$

$$SourceService.Spec.R = GoalService.Spec.P$$

$$TargetService.FuncR.Out = \varnothing$$

$$TargetService.FuncR.In = GoalService.FuncR.Out$$

$$TargetService.Spec.P = GoalService.Spec.R$$

$$TargetService.Spec.R = true$$

Therefore, *SoruceService*, *TargetService,* and *Services* in service database are composited according to the composition rules. The positions are fixed: *Source Service* is the first one (head), *TargetService* is the last service (tail). The discovery or composition result is chaining revealed as follows:

$$Chaining : SoruceService >> S_1 >> S_2 >> \ldots >> S_n >> TargetService,$$

where $Chaining.FuncR.In = \varnothing \wedge Chaining.FuncR.Out \cap TargetService.FuncR.In = \varnothing$

Moreover, ASP snippet codes are shown in Listing 3.

Hence, the composition is satisfied if the composition service has no input variables and output variables without containing any input variable of TargetService. Composited chaining may provide more output variables. The required composition service GoalService is

$$S_1 >> S_2 >> \ldots >> S_n = \begin{cases} \text{service discovery} & \text{if } n = 1 \\ \text{service composition} & \text{if } n > 1 \\ \text{failures} & \text{if } n < 1 \end{cases}$$

Now, service discovery and composition are unified into one procedure.

Service Selection

Following unified service discovery and composition, service selection will make a global optimal decision. Nr_{target} and Nr_{chain} are non-functional requirements of *GoalService* and composition result, respectively. Service selection can be denoted as:

Listing 3. A snippet code for stop condition

```
33% Contrainst
34:- atomService(sdec(ServiceName), sign(Type, URL),
35 funcR(Desc, Class, Domain, in(IN), out(OUT)),
36 nonFuncR(RT, Availability, Throughput, Price,
37 Rank, Privacy)), #card(IN) == 0, #card(OUT) == 0.
```

$$Service = \underset{chain}{Min}\, Cost(W, Nr_{target}, Nr_{chain})$$

ASP implementation is shown in Listing 4.

Hence, the best chaining or service is chosen since it has the minimum cost to the target service. In this paper, the lease square cost is applied, and other standards could be chosen as well.

EVALUATION OF SSC-ASP

Preprocess for QWSDataset

The standard web service database with QoS attributes is QWSDataset[4], which can be used for travel booking example.

Nevertheless, QWSDataset was collected from the Internet in 2008, but it has not been updated from then on. Hence, all services must be pre-processed. The whole pre-process procedures are displayed in Table 1 and 2. QWSDataset includes 2507 entries (services), the Bash script downloads all services from the web, if the URL could be opened and connected, which are called downloadable with 1642 entries.

Afterward, the Bash script with Perl can check and transform downloadable original pages to standard form with QoS attributes, which only have 31 entries. Finally, Using Go language and Bash script transform standard web services to ASP. The number of services is 207.

Listing 4. A snippet code for composition rules

```
38% Compute Cost
39 composition(ServiceName, sign(Type, URL),
40 funcR(Desc, Class, Domain, in(IN), out(OUT)),
41 nonFuncR(RT, Availability, Throughput, Reliability,
42 Price, Rank), #costZZ(RT, Availability,
43 Throughput, Reliability, Price, Rank,
44 Type, rt, av, tr, re, pr, rank, goaltype))
45
46% Service Selction
47 resultcost(X):- #min{Cost, ServiceName:
48 composition(ServiceName, sign(Type, URL),
49 funcR(Desc, Class, Domain, in(IN), out(OUT)),
50 nonFuncR(RT, Availability, Throughput, Price,
51 Rank,Privacy),Cost)} = X.
```

Table 1. QWSDataset download

Codes	Descriptions	Num	Percents
N/A	All Entries	2507	100%
400	Bad Request	253	10.09%
403	Forbidden	145	5.78%
404	File Not Found	196	7.82%
502	Bad Gateway	45	1.79%
N/A	Timeout	128	5.11%
N/A	Unknown Host	143	13.65%
N/A	Downloadable	1642	65.50%

Table 2. QWSDataset transform

Descriptions	Num
Downloadable	1642
Empty File	246
Invalid File Format	967
Error Parsing	197
Invocation Target Exception	67
Databinding Exception	147
Pass Preprocess	31
Transformed	207

Evaluation ASP Performance on SSC-ASP

In this section, the evaluation result of compositing travel booking example on ASP-based SSC-ASP and QWSdataset is displayed in Table 3.

We pick up eight services in travel booking BPMN: SearchFights, SearchHotels, Package, Notifications, Book Fights, BookHotel, ChargeCard, and Booking. For example, Service Package is the package service for fights and hotels to users. Therefore, its length is 2. The length of chaining is denoted by clength. Because service discovery and composition is unified as one procedure, if $clength = 1$, it means that the service is discovered; if clength is more than 1, it means that serveral services should be composited. Similarly, nchain is the number of candidate composition chainings; rtime is the planning time; vtime is the validation time, and mcost and lcost are the min and max cost of candidate chainings. From the result,

Table 3. Travel Booking on QWSDataset

	Service Discovery/Composition				Service Selection		
	clength	nchain	rtime (ms)	vtime (ms)	mcost	lcost	rtime (ms)
Search Fights	1	4	12.1123	20.1252	20.12	234.32	2.2123
Search Hotels	1	2	50.0476	5.9384	9.0714	297.0923	4.2143
Package	2	3	87.9612	14.2721	128.2265	630.5455	5.2345
Notificafition	1	2	13.2342	23.1532	12.4123	51.2345	3.6438
Book Fights	1	4	23.4212	45.2435	53.4216	87.5425	6.1764
Book Hotel	1	6	15.3121	54.4342	98.5342	123.3234	9.4534
Charge Card	1	7	18.3418	34.5432	29.1942	44.5421	11.8745
Booking	4	5	112.3456	541.2978	102.1242	213.3122	20.1998

we can find that nested composition is much time consuming than service discovery, and selection time depends on the number of chaining.

RELATED WORK

Semantic Web Service

The primary issue of state-of-art semantic web service is too complicated to effectively composite service. SAWSDL (semantic annotations for WSDL and XML schema) is the first attempt to define semantic web service, which is extended from WSDL by adding some simple elements that denote the semantics of IO (input and output variables of service). The comparative research (Bouchiha, Malki, Djaa, Alghamdi, & Alnafjan, 2013) shows the effectiveness comparing this approach to other works. OWL-S (OWL for services) and WSMO (web service modeling ontology) are alternative techniques for semantic web service. OWL-S (Li, Zhang & Jiang, 2014) can delineate business process, functional requirement of service and QOS (quality of service) properties, nonetheless, it does not define how to map business process to a standard specification such as WSDL. WSMO is much flexible than OWL-S by allowing using expression of predicate logic. However, it has the same issue to OWL-S that can not map process to BPEL. Although the following works (Bordbar, Howells, Evans, & Staikopoulos, 2007; Le, Nguyen, & Goh, 2009) dissolve those issues, they only model the semantics of service and process, but not touch service validation. All the semantic web services techniques purposed for specific service composition, our tuples based and simplified formal description are much suitable.

Service Composition Framework

The comprehensive service composition are mentioned in composition survey (Jula, Sundararajan & Othman, 2014) (Garriga, Mateos, Flores, Cechich & Zunino. 2016). In (Rao & Su, 2005), a general framework is proposed based on workflow technique and AI planning. We refine and extend the abstract framework. For the top-down framework, the requester should build an abstract process model before the composition planning. The discovery and selection atomic web services can be processed automatically by the program. EFlow (Casati, Ilnicki, Jin, Krishnamoorthy, & Shan, 2000) uses a static workflow generation workflow method belonged to the top-down paradigm. All the services and execution dependency are described on the graph. Service discovery and selection can be done in a highly dynamic environment. Polymorphic process model (Schuster, Georgakopoulos, Cichocki, & Baker, 2000) combines the static and dynamic service composition based on a state machine. The process can consist of abstract subprocess (nested service composition). (Rodriguez-Mier, Pedrinaci, Lama, & Mucientes, 2016) proposed define a graph-based composition framework on the semantic input-output parameter of services. However, state machine and graph-based composition framework is not easy to use for normal user. That is the main reason that we use BPMN. For AI planning methods such situation calculus, PDDL, SWORD, SHOP2, they take service contract for planning, but time-consuming. Hence, we take mixture paradigm to deal with service composition. Applying service composition on cloud computing aslo a hot topic in recent year. In a typical cloud environment, existing service composition framework are not to provide the long-term QoS provision advertisements. Therefore, the paper (Ye, Mistry, Bouguettaya & Dong, 2016) propose a cloud service composition framework that selects the optimal composition based on an end user's long-term Quality of Service (QoS) requirements. The virtural machine is foundation techniques for the cloud platform. The paper (Singh, Juneja & Malhotra, 2017) proposes a new Agent-based Automated Service Composition (A2SC) algorithm not only for automated service composition but also considers reducing the cost of virtual machines.

Answer Set Programming for Service Composition

(Erdem, Gelfond & Leone, 2016) lists the application of answer set programming, which includes service composition. The related works about ASP-based service composition (Rainer, 2005; Dorn, Hrastnik, & Rainer, 2007) are the first two attempts using answer set programming to service composition. Furthermore, they won the first and second service composition competition. However, they only use the syntax information such as input and output variables for composition. Just like other bottom-up composition, the composition target is one service. Our approach treats this issue with the nested service composition. (Qian, Huang, & Zhao, 2011) presents the algorithm for translating semantic web service described by OWL-S to action language C, and then to answer set programming. Similar to the other AI planning approaches, they plan the service composition based on pre and post-conditions. However, there are two defects with them: one is the reasoning speed, and the other is most current practical services without condition description. In our approach, we take interface and domain information for reasoning with one option of pre and post conditions.

CONCLUSION AND FUTURE WORK

In this paper, we present an integrated framework for semantic service composition. To tackle the relevant issues in the same framework, all the portions of SSC-ASP are formally specified, in which each atomic service is specified by the service contract, which is a pair of pre and post conditions. We first revised the bottom-up paradigm, where the pre and post conditions are used for the validation of service composition rather than planing. After then, we nested the revised bottom-up paradigm into the top-down paradigm. Moreover, service discovery, composition, selection, and validation are unified into one procedure subsequently. Finally, an example of travel booking is used to evaluate the performance of SSC-ASP on QWSDataset.

In the future, we will improve the framework on without limitations, such as the constraints of pre and post conditions in the service contract, and integrate service composition into the prototype generation from requirements model.

ACKNOWLEDGMENT

The work presented in this paper was funded by project SAFEHR of Macao Science and Technology Development Fund ref. 018/2011/AI.

REFERENCES

Bartalos, P., & Bielikova, M. (2011). Automatic dynamic web service composition: A survey and problem formalization. *Computer Information*, *30*(4), 793–827.

Bordbar, B., Howells, G., Evans, M., & Staikopoulos, A. (2007). Model Transformation from OWL-S to BPEL Via SiTra. In D. Akehurst, R. Vogel, & R. Paige (Eds.), *Model Driven Architecture- Foundations and Applications* (Vol. 4530, pp. 43–58). Springer Berlin Heidelberg. doi:10.1007/978-3-540-72901-3_4

Bouchiha, D., Malki, M., Djaa, D., Alghamdi, A., & Alnafjan, K. (2013). Semantic Annotation of Web Services: A Comparative Study. In R. Lee (Ed.), *Software Engineering, Artificial Intelligence, Networking and Parallel/Distributed Computing* (Vol. 492, pp. 87–100). Springer International Publishing. doi:10.1007/978-3-319-00738-0_7

Brewka, G., Eiter, T., & Truszczyński, M. (2011). Answer set programming at a glance. *Communications of the ACM, 54*(12), 92–103. doi:10.1145/2043174.2043195

Casati, F., Ilnicki, S., Jin, L., Krishnamoorthy, V., & Shan, M. C. (2000). Adaptive and dynamic service composition in eFlow. *Advanced Information Systems Engineering*, 13–31.

Dorn, J., Hrastnik, P., & Rainer, A. (2007). Web service discovery and composition for virtual enterprises. *International Journal of Web Services Research, 4*(1), 23–39. doi:10.4018/jwsr.2007010102

Dustdar, S., & Schreiner, W. (2005). A survey on web services composition. *International Journal of Web and Grid Services, 1*(1), 1–30. doi:10.1504/IJWGS.2005.007545

Erdem, E., Gelfond, M., & Leone, N. (2016). Applications of Answer Set Programming. *AI Magazine, 37*(3), 53. doi:10.1609/aimag.v37i3.2678

Garriga, M., Mateos, C., Flores, A., Cechich, A., & Zunino, A. (2016). RESTful service composition at a glance: A survey. *Journal of Network and Computer Applications, 60*, 32–53. doi:10.1016/j.jnca.2015.11.020

Gebser, M., Kaminski, R., Kaufmann, B., Ostrowski, M., Schaub, T., & Thiele, S. (2010). A user's guide to gringo, clasp, clingo, and iclingo. University of Potsdam, Tech. Rep.

Jula, A., Sundararajan, E., & Othman, Z. (2014). Cloud computing service composition: A systematic literature review. *Expert Systems with Applications, 41*(8), 3809–3824. doi:10.1016/j.eswa.2013.12.017

Küster, U., König-Ries, B., Stern, M., & Klein, M. (2007). DIANE: an integrated approach to automated service discovery, matchmaking and composition. In *Proceedings of the 16th international conference on World Wide Web* (pp. 1033-1042). ACM. 10.1145/1242572.1242711

Le, D. N., Nguyen, V. Q., & Goh, A. (2009, September). Matching WSDL and OWL-S web services. In *Semantic Computing, 2009. ICSC'09. IEEE International Conference on* (pp. 197-202). IEEE. 10.1109/ICSC.2009.12

Li, H., Zhang, L., & Jiang, R. (2014). Study of manufacturing cloud service matching algorithm based on OWL-S. In *Control and Decision Conference (2014 CCDC), The 26th Chinese* (pp. 4155-4160). IEEE. 10.1109/CCDC.2014.6852909

Lifschitz, V. (2002). Answer set programming and plan generation. *Artificial Intelligence, 138*(1), 39–54. doi:10.1016/S0004-3702(02)00186-8

Paik, I., Chen, W., & Huhns, M. (2014). A scalable architecture for automatic service composition. *Services Computing. IEEE Transactions on, 7*(1), 82–95.

Qian, J., Huang, G., & Zhao, L. (2011). Semantic Web Service Composition: From OWL-S to Answer Set Programming. In *Computer Science for Environmental Engineering and EcoInformatics* (pp. 112–117). Springer Berlin Heidelberg. doi:10.1007/978-3-642-22691-5_20

Rainer, A. (2005). *Web service composition using answer set programming. In 19. Workshop" Planen, Scheduling und Konfigurieren*. Koblenz: Entwerfen.

Rao, J., & Su, X. (2005). A survey of automated web service composition methods. In *Semantic Web Services and Web Process Composition* (pp. 43–54). Springer Berlin Heidelberg. doi:10.1007/978-3-540-30581-1_5

Rodriguez-Mier, P., Pedrinaci, C., Lama, M., & Mucientes, M. (2016). An integrated semantic web service discovery and composition framework. *IEEE Transactions on Services Computing, 9*(4), 537–550. doi:10.1109/TSC.2015.2402679

Schuster, H., Georgakopoulos, D., Cichocki, A., & Baker, D. (2000). Modeling and composing service-based and reference process-based multi-enterprise processes. *Advanced Information Systems Engineering*, 247–263.

Singh, A., Juneja, D., & Malhotra, M. (2017). A novel agent based autonomous and service composition framework for cost optimization of resource provisioning in cloud computing. *Journal of King Saud University-Computer and Information Sciences*, *29*(1), 19–28. doi:10.1016/j.jksuci.2015.09.001

Syu, Y., Ma, S. P., Kuo, J. Y., & FanJiang, Y. Y. (2012). A survey on automated service composition methods and related techniques. In *Services Computing (SCC), 2012 IEEE Ninth International Conference on* (pp. 290-297). IEEE.

Ye, Z., Mistry, S., Bouguettaya, A., & Dong, H. (2016). Long-term QoS-aware cloud service composition using multivariate time series analysis. *IEEE Transactions on Services Computing*, *9*(3), 382–393. doi:10.1109/TSC.2014.2373366

ENDNOTES

[1]   http://www.omg.org/spec/BPMN/20100601/10-06-02.pdf
[2]   https://www.mat.unical.it/dlv-complex/dlv-complex
[3]   http://research.microsoft.com/en-us/um/redmond/projects/z3/
[4]   http://www.uoguelph.ca/~qmahmoud/qws/index.html

Chapter 2
Overlapping Singer Identification in Music Recordings

Wei-Ho Tsai
National Taipei University of Technology, Taiwan

Cin-Hao Ma
National Taipei University of Technology, Taiwan

ABSTRACT

Singer identification (SID), which refers to the task of automatically identifying the singer(s) in a music recording, is of great help in handling the rapid proliferation of music data on the internet and digital media. Although a number of SID studies from acoustic features have been reported, most systems are designed to identify the singer in recordings of solo performances. Very little research has considered a more realistic case, which is to identify more than one singer in a music recording. The research presented in this chapter investigates the feasibility of identifying singers in music recordings that contain overlapping (simultaneous) singing voices (e.g., duet or trio singings). This problem is referred to as overlapping singer identification (OSID). Several approaches to OSID are discussed and evaluated in this chapter. In addition, a related issue on how to distinguish solo singings from overlapping singing recordings is also discussed.

DOI: 10.4018/978-1-5225-7268-8.ch002

INTRODUCTION

Explosive growth in the Internet and digital media has motivated recent research on developing techniques for automatically extracting information from music for content-based retrieval (Michael *et al.*, 2008; Schedl *et al.*, 2014). In music recordings, the singing voice usually catches more of listeners' attention than other music attributes such as rhythm, tonality, or instrumentation. Therefore, extracting information on singers is essential to people for organizing, browsing, and retrieving music recordings, especially for singer identity information where it may be undocumented or difficult to find, such as cameo's or guest appearances in live concert recordings or a movie's musical interludes. In addition, singer information could enable rapidly scanning suspect websites for piracy, especially for bootleg concert recordings, in which the company will typically not have a copy of the original audio data for comparison.

Most people use singer's voice as a primary cue for identifying songs, and performing such a task is almost effortless. However, building a practicable automatic singer identification (SID) system (Tsai & Lin, 2011) is not an easy task for machine learning. One of the challenges lies in training the system to discriminate among the different sources of sounds intertwined in music recordings, which may include background vocal, instrumental accompaniment, background noise, and overlapping singings.

In the earlier period, a number of studies on SID focused on exploiting various musical features and combining them for SID (Kim & Whitman, 2002; Berenzweig *et al.*, 2002; Liu & Huang, 2002; Zhang, 2003; Bartsch & Wakefield, 2004; Tsai *et al.*, 2004; Maddage *et al.*, 2004; Fujihara *et al.*, 2005; Mesaros & Astola, 2005; Nwe & Li, 2007; Mesaros *et al.*, 2007; Nwe & Li, 2008). More recently, SID research has shifted the attentions to investigating the influence of background sounds on singer voice characterization, and several methods have been developed to reduce the interference of background sounds for SID (Tsai & Wang, 2006; Fujihara *et al.*, 2010; Tsai & Lin, 2011; Hu & Liu, 2015). However, very little research has considered the problem of automatically identifying more than one singer in a music recording.

Tsai & Wang (2004) investigated automatic detection and tracking of multiple singers in music recordings. However, the study only considered singing by multiple singers who performed in non-overlapping matters, that is, did not consider multiple voices singing simultaneously. By contrast, Tsai & Ma (2017) proposes a system to automatically identify multiple singers in a long audio stream that may have singing voices overlapping in time. The study explicitly discussed the problem of multiple voices singing simultaneously. In line with the research goal of Tsai & Ma (2017), the research presented in this chapter focuses on the problem of automatically identifying singers in music recordings that contain both simultaneous and non-simultaneous singings. We refer to this problem as overlapping singer identification (OSID). Other works related to OSID include speech overlapping (Okuno *et al.*, 1999; Shriberg *et al.*, 2001; Çetin & Shriberg, 2006; Yamamoto *et al.*, 2006; Boakye *et al.*, 2008) in multi-speakers environments and voice separation from music accompaniment (Li & Wang, 2007; Virtanen, 2007) in music recordings.

By intuition, one may consider applying any existing SID approaches on solo performances to OSID directly, i.e., segregating the simultaneous singing voices first, and then performing SID on the separated voices. However, while extracting the desired singing voice in a monaural recording from the other undesired sounds appears effortless to humans, the task turns out to be much more difficult for machines. To date, techniques for monaural sound separation, such as Li & Wang (2007) and Virtanen (2007), can only work on mixture of sound sources that have no correlation to the harmonics or other musical syntax. Moreover, when multiple singers perform the same tune and lyrics simultaneously, it becomes extremely difficult to segregate the singers' voices because their acoustic characteristics are intertwined on the signal level. Once the unique characteristics of individual voices cannot be extracted effectively, it is infeasible to perform SID.

Accordingly, design of an OSID system needs to consider the following factors and define the scope of applications.

- **Number of Singers:** A music recording may be classified as a pure instrumental, solo, duet, trio, band, or choral performance. In general, the complexity of the OSID problem grows as the number of simultaneous singers in a music recording increases.
- **Percentage of Overlapping Duration:** As multiple singers may not always perform simultaneously, an excerpt from a music recording can be a) an instrument-only segment, b) a solo-singing segment, or c) an overlapping-singing segment. An OSID system must be capable of distinguishing the three cases.
- **Ratio of Overlapping Energy:** In many bands, one or more musicians in addition to the lead singer often sing background vocal while they play their instruments. The audio signal energy of the background singer(s), therefore, may be very low compared to that of the lead singer. In such a case, identifying the background singers would be more difficult than identifying the lead singer.
- **Variations on Tune and/or Lyrics:** Multiple singers may sing together in a) exactly the same tune and lyrics, b) exactly the same tune but different lyrics, c) different tunes but exactly the same lyrics, or d) different tunes and different lyrics. The four cases would result in different OSID performances to each other.

- **With/Without Background Accompaniment:** Most popular music contains background accompaniment that inextricably intertwines singers' voice signals with a loud, non-stationary background music signal. The background accompaniment causes inevitable interference for OSID.

- **Open-Set/Close-Set Identification:** A close-set OSID, which identifies the singer(s) among a set of candidate singers, is considered easier than an open-set OSID, which has to further determine whether the singer(s) identified is/are among the candidate singers.

- **Signal Distortions:** Although most test recordings are taken from high quality sources such as CDs, many often undergo signal degradation due to audio filtering, encoding/decoding, or noise corruption. A successful OSID system should be robust against various signal distortions.

Study of Tsai & Ma (2017) focused on OSID for cappella vocal duets, i.e., at most two singing voices overlapping in time. For the scope of this chapter, we further investigate the problem of OSID on three singing voices overlapping in time, i.e., trios.

METHODOLOGY

As OSID differs from the conventional SID in the number of singers involved, the design approaches of an OSID system can be derived from two perspectives as follows.

Two-Stage OSID System

The approach begins with a solo/overlapping singing classification component, which determines if the test recording belongs to overlapping singing or not. If not, the problem becomes the conventional solo singer identification; otherwise, duet/trio singer identification component handles the case. As shown in Figure 1, the duet/trio singer identification component regards a recording as a mixture of two or three singers' voices. Thus, the possibilities of various combinations of different singers' voices must be evaluated.

Solo/Overlapping Singing Classification

The motivation behind the solo/overlapping singing classification is based on our observations on the distributions of solo and duet singings represented by Mel-scale frequency cepstral coefficients (MFCCs) (Davis & Mermelstein, 1980). Figure 2 shows a statistical result of the MFCCs for the singing recordings in our

Figure 1. Two-stage OSID system

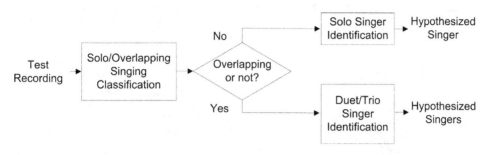

datasets detailed in the experiment section. For better visualization, only parts of the coefficients are shown. Each point in Figure 2 is plotted against the values of two coefficients computed for a frame of singing waveform, where the length of each frame is 20 ms. We can see that the distributions of MFCCs computed for solo singing and duet singing are different, though part of them are overlapping. This indicates that solo and overlapping singings could be distinguished in the MFCC domain using a stochastic classifier.

Figure 3 shows the block diagram of the solo/overlapping singing classification component. The component is divided into two phases: training and testing. During the training phase, two Gaussian mixture models (GMMs), λ^s and λ^o, are created, where λ^s represents the acoustic pattern of a solo singing passage while λ^o represents the acoustic pattern of an overlapping singing passage. Combinations of Gaussian densities generate a variety of acoustic classes, which, in turn, reflect certain vocal tract configurations. The GMMs provide good approximations of arbitrarily shaped densities of spectrum over a long span of time (Reynolds & Rose, 1995). Parameters of a GMM consist of means, covariances, and mixture weights. λ^s is generated from various solo singing passages and λ^o is generated from various overlapping singing passages. Then, prior to Gaussian mixture modeling, singing waveforms are converted into MFCCs. In the testing phase, an unknown test recording is converted into MFCCs and then tested for λ^s and λ^o. The results are based on likelihood probabilities, $\Pr(X|\lambda^s)$ and $\Pr(X|\lambda^o)$, where the recording is hypothesized as an overlapping singing passage (or a solo singing passage) if $\log\Pr(X|\lambda^o) - \log\Pr(X|\lambda^s)$ is larger (or smaller) than a pre-set threshold η.

Solo Singer Identification

Figure 4 shows the solo singer identification component. If there are N different candidates singers, then N GMMs, $\lambda_1, \lambda_2, \ldots, \lambda_N$, are created to represent the acoustic patterns of their singings. When an unknown test recording is received at the system

Figure 2. Statistical distributions of MFCCs computed for the solo and duet singings in our database, in which C0 represents the first coefficient, C1 represents the second coefficient, and so on

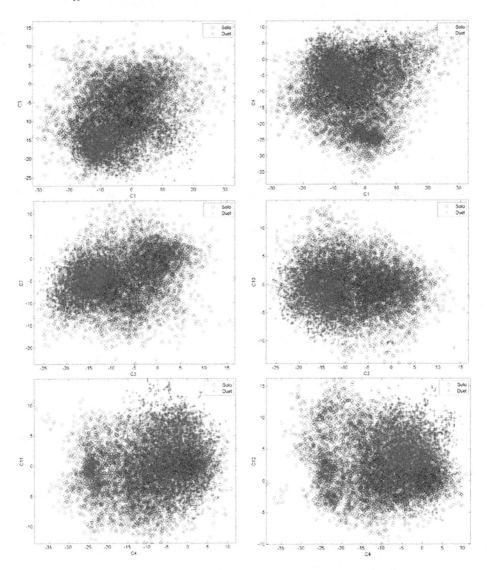

*For a more accurate representation see the electronic version.

Figure 3. Solo/overlapping singing classification

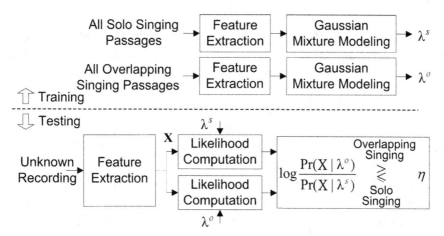

input, the component calculates and decides in favor of singer $I*$ when the condition in Eq. (1) is satisfied:

$$I^* = \arg\max_{1 \leq i \leq N} \Pr(X \mid \lambda_i), \tag{1}$$

where $\mathbf{X}$ is the MFCCs computed from the test recording.

Figure 4. The solo singer identification component

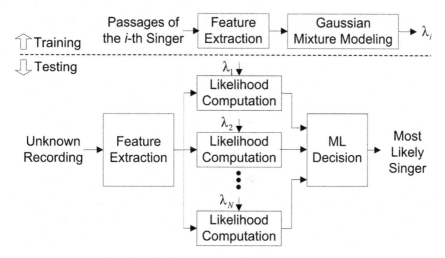

Duet/Trio Singer Identification

The duet/trio singer identification component is similar to the solo singer identification component. The only difference between the two is that the GMMs of solo singers are replaced with the GMMs of duet or trio singers. However, generating the GMMs of duet or trio singers is not as straightforward as generating the GMMs of solo singers, because it may be impractical to collect singing data from every possible combination of singers' voices. Hence, two approaches were taken to sidestep the collection of real simultaneous singing data. The first approach uses direct waveform mixing, which is shown in Figure 5.

In the training phase of this system, audio waveforms from every combination of two or three singers are mixed, based on roughly equal energies, to simulate real duet or trio singings. The resulting waveforms are then converted into MFCCs.

Figure 5. The duet/trio singer identification component using direct waveform mixing

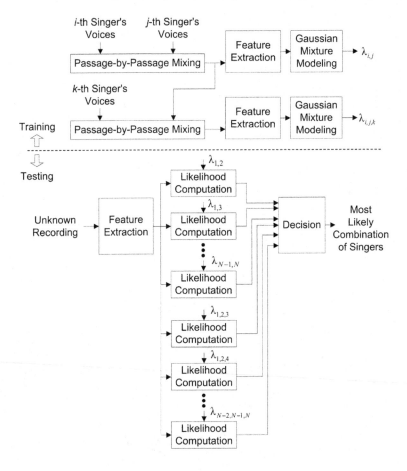

For each combination of singers, a GMM is built using these features. Hence, for a population of N candidate singers, a total of $C_2^N = N! / [2!(N-2)!]$ duet GMMs $\lambda_{i,j}$, $i \neq j$, $1 \leq i, j \leq N$ are created, and a total of $C_3^N = N! / [3!(N-3)!]$ trio GMMs $\lambda_{i,j,k}$, $i \neq j \neq k$, $1 \leq i, j, k \leq N$ are created. In the testing phase, an unknown audio recording is converted into MFCCs and then tested for each of the $(C_2^N + C_3^N)$ GMMs. The system then determines the most-likely combination of singers (I^*, J^*, K^*) performed in the recording based on the maximum likelihood decision rule:

$$(I^*, J^*, K^*) = \arg\max_{1 \leq i,j,k \leq N} \Pr(X \mid \lambda_{i,j,k}), \tag{2}$$

where $\lambda_{i,j,k}$ means duet GMM $\lambda_{i,j}$, if $j = k$, and $\lambda_{i,j,k}$ means duet GMM $\lambda_{i,k}$, if $i = j$. Likewise, the decision (I^*, J^*, K^*) represents duet singers (I^*, J^*), if $J^* = K^*$, and (I^*, J^*, K^*) represents duet singers (I^*, K^*), if $I^* = J^*$. And note that $\lambda_{i,i,i}$, $1 \leq i \leq N$, which means solo GMMs λ_i, are excluded in Eq. (2), since they have been included in the solo-singer identification component.

One shortcoming of the direct waveform mixing approach is that the training process can become very cumbersome if the number of candidate singers is large or if a new singer needs to be added. As an alternative to this problem, a second approach based on Parallel Model Combination (PMC) technique (Gales & Young, 1996) is used, as shown in Figure 6. Given a set of N solo singer GMMs, each GMM is used to generate C_2^N duet GMMs and C_3^N trio GMMs. Since duet and trio singing signals overlap in the time/frequency domain while the GMMs are in the cepstral/quefrency domain, the parameters of the GMMs need to be converted to the linear spectral/frequency domain before they can be added.

In addition, since two R-mixture GMMs would result in a large $R \times R$-mixture or $R \times R \times R$-mixture GMM, UBM-MAP (Reynolds *et al.*, 2000) is used to control the size of the resulting GMM R-mixture. The basic strategy of UBM-MAP is to generate a universal GMM using all solo singers' data, and then adapt the universal GMM

Figure 6. The training phase of the duet/trio singer identification component based on parallel model combination

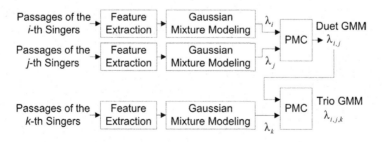

to each solo singer GMM based on maximum a posterior (MAP) estimation. Since all of the solo singer GMMs are adapted from the universal GMM, the mixtures of the GMMs are aligned. Thus, we do not need to consider the combination of the r-th Gaussian of one GMM with the ℓ-th Gaussian of another GMM, where $r \neq \ell$, but we only need to consider the case when $r = \ell$. For duet GMM $\lambda_{i,j}$, the combined mean and covariance of the k-th mixture is computed by

$$\boldsymbol{\mu}_{i,j}^{r} = \mathbf{D}\{\log\{\ \exp(\mathbf{D}^{-1}\boldsymbol{\mu}_{i}^{r}) + \exp(\mathbf{D}^{-1}\boldsymbol{\mu}_{j}^{r})\ \}\}, \tag{3}$$

$$\boldsymbol{\Sigma}_{i,j}^{r} = \mathbf{D}\{\log\{\exp[\mathbf{D}^{-1}\boldsymbol{\Sigma}_{i}^{r}(\mathbf{D}^{-1})'] + \exp[\mathbf{D}^{-1}\boldsymbol{\Sigma}_{j}^{r}(\mathbf{D}^{-1})']\}\}, \tag{4}$$

where $\boldsymbol{\mu}_{i}^{r}$ and $\boldsymbol{\Sigma}_{i}^{r}$ are the mean vector and covariance matrix of GMMs λ_{i}, respectively; $\mathbf{D}$ represents the discrete cosine transform matrix; prime ($'$) denotes the transpose. For trio GMMs $\lambda_{i,j,k}$, the combined mean and covariance of the r-th mixture is computed by

$$\boldsymbol{\mu}_{i,j,k}^{r} = \mathbf{D}\{\log\{\ \exp(\mathbf{D}^{-1}\boldsymbol{\mu}_{i,j}^{r}) + \exp(\mathbf{D}^{-1}\boldsymbol{\mu}_{k}^{r})\ \}\}, \tag{5}$$

$$\boldsymbol{\Sigma}_{i,j,k}^{r} = \mathbf{D}\{\log\{\exp[\mathbf{D}^{-1}\boldsymbol{\Sigma}_{i,j}^{r}(\mathbf{D}^{-1})'] + \exp[\mathbf{D}^{-1}\boldsymbol{\Sigma}_{k}^{r}(\mathbf{D}^{-1})']\}\}. \tag{6}$$

One-Stage OSID System

As an alternative approach, we present a second system that combines the three components in the two-stage OSID system. The system unifies the three components into a one-stage system, eliminating the stage of first determining if a test recording is a solo or overlapping singing performance. This is done by using the N solo-singer GMMs from the solo-singer identification and the $(C_{2}^{N} + C_{3}^{N})$ duet and trio GMMs from the duet/trio singer identification to build a unified classifier with $(N + C_{2}^{N} + C_{3}^{N})$ GMMs. In the testing phase, an unknown recording is converted into MFCCs and then tested for each of the $(N + C_{2}^{N} + C_{3}^{N})$ GMMs. Then, if we denote each solo-singer GMM λ_{i} as $\lambda_{i,i,i}$, and denote duet GMM $\lambda_{i,j}$ as $\lambda_{i,j,j}$, $1 \leq i, j \leq N$, the system should decide in favor of singer(s) (I^{*}, J^{*}, K^{*}) if the condition in Eq. (7) is satisfied.

$$(I^{*}, J^{*}, K^{*}) = \arg\max_{1 \leq i,j,k \leq N} \Pr(X \mid \lambda_{i,j,k}), \tag{7}$$

Again, if $I^* = J^* = K^*$, then the recording is hypothesized to be performed by a solo singer I^*; if $I^* \neq J^* = K^*$, then the recording is hypothesized to be performed by duet singers (I^*, K^*).

Triangulation-Based Decision

The testing phases of the OSID system could be further improved by applying the concept of the triangulation in trigonometry to the decision criteria. For example, suppose that a test singing clip $\mathbf{X}$ is performed by three singers, (s_1, s_2, s_3). Then, we can use models $\lambda_{1,m,n}$, $1 \leq m, n \leq N$, to examine if $\mathbf{X}$ contains voice from singer s_1, use models $\lambda_{2,m,n}$ to examine if $\mathbf{X}$ contains voice from singer s_2, and use models $\lambda_{3,m,n}$ to examine if $\mathbf{X}$ contains voice from singer s_3, This is because in general, $\Pr(\mathbf{X}|\lambda_{1,m,n})$ $> \Pr(\mathbf{X}|\lambda_{j,m,n})$, $\Pr(\mathbf{X}|\lambda_{2,m,n}) > \Pr(\mathbf{X}|\lambda_{j,m,n})$, and $\Pr(\mathbf{X}|\lambda_{3,m,n}) > \Pr(\mathbf{X}|\lambda_{j,m,n})$ for $4 \leq j \leq N$. In other words, besides likelihood probability $\Pr(\mathbf{X}|\lambda_{1,2,3})$ is a key to determining if $\mathbf{X}$ is performed by s_1, s_2 and s_3, likelihood probabilities, $\Pr(\mathbf{X}|\lambda_{1,m,n})$, $\Pr(\mathbf{X}|\lambda_{2,m,n})$, and $\Pr(\mathbf{X}|\lambda_{3,m,n})$, $1 \leq m, n \leq N$, are also helpful clues to inferring the singers of $\mathbf{X}$. Based on this concept, we can determine the most-likely singer pair (I^*, J^*, K^*) who performed in the singing clip using

$$(I^*, J^*, K^*) = \underset{1 \leq i,j,k \leq N}{\arg\max} \left[\sum_{m=1}^{N} \sum_{n=1}^{N} \Pr(X \mid \lambda_{i,m,n}) + \sum_{m=1}^{N} \sum_{n=1}^{N} \Pr(X \mid \lambda_{j,m,n}) + \sum_{m=1}^{N} \sum_{n=1}^{N} \Pr(X \mid \lambda_{k,m,n}) \right]$$
(8)

EXPERIMENTS

Data

Since no public corpus of music recordings meets the specific constraints of the OSID problem defined here, a small database of test recordings was created. The database contains vocal recordings by ten male amateur singers, aged between 20 and 35. Every singer was asked to perform 30 passages of Mandarin pop songs with a Karaoke machine. The duration of each passage ranges from 13 to 20 seconds.

The database was divided into two subsets, one for training the OSID system and the other for evaluating the system. The training subset consists of the first 15 passages, while the evaluation subset consists of the remaining 15 passages. Passages of the pop songs were recorded in a quiet room. The Karaoke accompaniments were output to a headset, and thus not recorded. All the passages were recorded at 22.05 kHz, 16 bits, in mono PCM wave.

Test recordings of duets were then obtained by mixing the wave files sung by a pair of singers. Two sets of recordings (i.e., for training and evaluation), sung by 45 ($C_2^{10} = 45$) different pairs of singers, were created. One set included 675 ($C_2^{10} \times 15 = 675$) recordings of duets sung in exactly the same tune and with the same lyrics; the other set included 4,725 ($C_2^{10} \times C_2^{15} = 4,725$) recordings of duets sung in different tunes and with different lyrics. To facilitate the discussions in the following sections, thereafter, recordings of duets sung in exactly the same tune and with the same lyrics are referred to as "STSL duet recordings." Similarly, recordings of duets sung in different tunes and with different lyrics are referred to as "DTDL duet recordings."

Test recordings of trios were obtained by mixing the wave files from three singers. Also, two sets of recordings (i.e., for training and evaluation), sung by 120 ($C_3^{10} = 120$) different couples of trio singers, were created. One set included 1,800 ($C_3^{10} \times 15 = 1,800$) STSL trio recordings; the other set included 54,600 ($C_3^{10} \times C_3^{15} = 54,600$) DTDL trio recordings.

Solo/Overlapping Singing Classification Experiments

The first experiment conducted examined the validity of the solo/overlapping singing classification component. There were 150 solo recordings and 61,800 (675 STSL duets + 4,725 DTDL duets + 1,800 STSL trios + 54,600 DTDL trios) overlapping singing recordings for testing. The classification accuracy was measured by

$$\frac{\#\text{Correctly} - \text{classified Recordings}}{\#\text{Testing Recordings}} \times 100\%.$$

Table 1 shows the classification results with respect to the different numbers of Gaussian mixtures in λ^s and λ^o. We can see that although the performance is not perfect, most of the overlapping singing recordings were correctly detected.

Table 1a. Solo/overlapping singing classification results: classification accuracy

No. of Mixtures	Accuracy
16	94.9%
32	93.1%
64	93.0%

Table 1b. Confusion matrix of the 16-mixture case

Classified	Actual	
	Solo	Overlapping
Solo	97.3%	5.4%
Overlapping	2.7%	94.6%

Solo-Singer Identification Experiments

For the purpose of comparison, experiments of the conventional SID for solo recordings were also conducted. The identification accuracy was measured by

$$\frac{\#\text{Correctly} - \text{identified Recordings}}{\#\text{Testing Recordings}} \times 100\%.$$

Table 2 shows the results of singer identification in 150 recordings sung by 10 different singers. As the singer population was small, the result obtained was almost perfect.

Duet-Singer Identification Experiments

Then, we examined the feasibility of OSID in the recordings that are duet only. In these experiments, test data consisted of 675 + 4,725 duet singing wave files, i.e., no solo or trio recordings were considered. Here the performances of the direct waveform mixing and the PMC methods of the duet/trio-singer identification component using Eq. (2) were evaluated. Depending on the context of application, the performance of OSID is evaluated differently. This study considers two types of OSID accuracy. The first one takes into account the number of *singer combinations* identified correctly. Specifically,

Table 2. Results of singer identification for solo recordings.

No. of Mixtures	SID Accuracy
16	96.7%
32	98.7%
64	100.0%

$$\text{Acc. 1 (in \%)} = \frac{\#\text{Correctly} - \text{identified Singer Combinations}}{\#\text{Testing Recordings}} \times 100\%.$$

The second one takes into account the number of *singers* identified correctly. Specifically,

$$\text{Acc. 2 (in \%)} = \frac{\#\text{Correctly} - \text{identified Singers}}{\#\text{Testing Singers}} \times 100\%.$$

For example, if a recording contains overlapping singings by two performers, s_1 and s_2, and the identified singers are s_1 and s_4, then #Correctly-identified Singer Combinations = 0 and #Correctly-identified Singers = 1. Consequently, Acc. 2 is always higher than Acc. 1.

Table 3 shows the OSID result obtained with direct waveform mixing methods. Here, the OSID results for four cases are presented: i) both training and testing data consist of STSL duet recordings; ii) training data consist of STSL duet recordings, while testing data consist of DTDL duet recordings; iii) training data consist of DTDL duet recordings, while testing data consist of STSL duet recordings; iv) both training and testing data consist of DTDL duet recordings.

It can be seen from Table 3 that OSID using STSL duet recordings for training always outperformed than those that using DTDL duet recordings for training. Similarly, the performance of OSID using STSL duet recordings for testing was always better than those that using DTDL duet recordings for testing. When both training and testing data consist of STSL duet recordings, we obtained the best OSID performance, showing that 85.0% of singer pairs or 92.5% of singers in the testing data can be correctly identified.

Table 4 shows the OSID result obtained with the PMC method. In this experiment, since no duet singing is required in the training process, we considered two cases: i) testing data consist of STSL duet recordings; ii) testing data consist of DTDL duet recordings. It can be observed in Table 4, that similar to the results in Table

Table 3a. Results of identifying duet recordings based on direct waveform mixing method. Both training and testing data consist of STSL duet recordings

No. of Mixtures	Acc. 1	Acc. 2
16	80.7%	90.1%
32	84.3%	92.1%
64	85.0%	92.5%

Table 3b. Training data consist of STSL duet recordings, while testing data consist of DTDL duet recordings

No. of Mixtures	Acc. 1	Acc. 2
16	67.9%	83.7%
32	69.8%	84.8%
64	73.6%	86. 7%

Table 3c. Training data consist of DTDL duet recordings, while testing data are STSL duet recordings

No. of Mixtures	Acc. 1	Acc. 2
16	77.3%	88.7%
32	78.4%	89.3%
64	80.7%	90.4%

Table 3d. Both training and testing data consist of DTDL duet recordings

No. of Mixtures	Acc. 1	Acc. 2
16	52.3%	75.8%
32	47.1%	73.4%
64	43.6%	71.6%

3, the performance of OSID was always better when STSL duet recordings were used for testing. Comparing Table 4 with Table 3 (a) and (b), it can also be found that the direct waveform mixing method was superior to the PMC method when STSL duet recordings were used for testing. However, the PMC method performed better than the direct waveform mixing method when DTDL duet recordings were used for testing. This indicates that the PMC method is not only better at scaling up the singer population, but it is also better at generalizing the singer identification problem than the direct waveform mixing method.

Singer Identification Experiments: Solo, Duet and Trio Recordings

Next, we considered a more complicated case that a test recording may be a solo singing, duet singing, or a trio recording. There were 150 solo recordings and 61,800 (675 STSL duets + 4,725 DTDL duets + 1,800 STSL trios + 54,600 DTDL trios)

Table 4a. Results of identifying duet recordings based on PMC method. Testing data consist of STSL duet recordings

No. of Mixtures	Acc. 1	Acc. 2
16	75.1%	87.1%
32	75.1%	87.3%
64	78.1%	88.7%

Table 4b. Testing data consist of DTDL duet recordings

No. of Mixtures	Acc. 1	Acc. 2
16	71.1%	85.0%
32	69.9%	85.0%
64	75.3%	87.6%

overlapping singing recordings for testing. The identification performance was characterized by Acc. 1 and Acc. 2, as before.

Table 5 shows the results obtained by the proposed two OSID systems, i.e., two-stage OSID system using Eq. (2) and one-stage OSID system using Eq. (7). The duet and trio GMMs used in this experiment were generated using the PMC method. The number of Gaussian mixtures was set to 64 for both solo singer and duet/trio GMMs. Compared to the results in Table 4, it is observed that while more uncertainties are added in the testing data, the resulting accuracies only decrease slightly. In addition, it is also found that the two-stage OSID system performed better than the one-stage OSID system. Our further analysis shows that many identification errors of the one-stage system arise from wrongly-identifying a solo-singer recording as an overlapping-singer recording or wrongly-identifying an overlapping-singer recording as a solo-singer recording. To illustrate this, Table 6 shows the confusion matrix of the one-stage OSID system. Compared to Table 1(b), we can see that the mis-classification errors of the one-stage OSID system are significantly higher than the solo/overlapping singing classification component. This indicates that although the one-stage OSID system takes advantage of the simplicity in design, it pays the loss of accuracy that can be achieved with the two-stage OSID system.

Lastly, we evaluated if the OSID performance can be further improved by using the triangulation-based decision in Eq. (8). Table 7 shows the OSID results obtained with and without the triangulation-based decision, in which two-stage OSID system was used. It can be seen from Table 7 that the triangulation-based decision improves the OSID performance noticeably. The Acc. 2 of 82.4% in Table 7 indicates that

Table 5. Results of identifying both solo and overlapping singing (duet/trio) recordings.

System	Acc. 1	Acc. 2
Two-Stage OSID System	69.2%	78.2%
One-stage OSID System	61.0%	72.6%

Table 6. Confusion matrix of the one-stage OSID system

Classified	Actual	
	Solo	Overlapping
Solo	89.6%	15.2%
Overlapping	10.4%	84.8%

Table 7. Results of identifying both solo and overlapping singing (duet/trio) recordings using the two-stage systems with and without triangulation-based decision.

System	Acc. 1	Acc. 2
Without triangulation-based decision	69.2%	78.2%
With triangulation-based decision	74.5%	82.4%

no matter the test recording belongs to solo, duet, or trio, 82.4% of the singer(s) involved in the recording can be identified correctly.

CONCLUSION

In contrast to most of the singer-identification systems proposed up to date, which only focus on identifying the singers in recordings of solo performances, this chapter reports a feasibility study of detecting and identifying singers with overlapping singings in a recording. The research extends previous works on solo singer identification to overlapping singer identification. The suggested approach consists of a solo/overlapping singing classification component that determines if a test music recording contains overlapping singing, followed by either a solo-singer identifier or a duet/trio singer identifier based on Gaussian mixture models. Recognizing that the combinations of singers can be vast in number, we proposed using parallel model combination technique to characterize the simultaneous voices of duet or trio singers based on the individual voices of each singer. In addition, to improve the OSID performance, this research proposed a triangulation-based decision approach by exploiting the relationships between the combinations of singers. The results of the experiment conducted using a database of a cappella demonstrated feasibility of the approaches.

The results we obtained at this pilot investigation are encouraging and lay a good foundation for the future development of a robust SID system. To maximize its practicability and applicability, we will relax the restriction of the OSID problem formulation step-by-step in the future. In particular, it is an imperative for our next step of research to investigate OSID for music data with background accompaniments, so that popular singer identification can be carried out. To this end, we are managing to build a large database of popular music recordings containing various simultaneous singers.

ACKNOWLEDGMENT

This research was supported in part by the Ministry of Science and Technology, Taiwan [Grant Number MOST-106-2221-E-027-125-MY2].

REFERENCES

Bartsch, M. A., & Wakefield, G. H. (2004). Singing voice identification using spectral envelope estimation. *IEEE Transactions on Speech and Audio Processing*, *12*(2), 100–109. doi:10.1109/TSA.2003.822637

Berenzweig, A., Ellis, D. P. W., & Lawrence, S. (2002). Using voice segments to improve artist classification of music. *Proc. Int. Conf. Virtual, Synthetic, and Entertainment Audio*.

Boakye, K., Trueba-Hornero, B., Vinyals, O., & Friedland, G. (2008). Overlapped speech detection for improved speaker diarization in multiparty meetings. *Proc. IEEE International Conference on Acoustics, Speech, and Signal Processing*. 10.1109/ICASSP.2008.4518619

Casey, M., Veltkamp, R., Goto, M., Leman, M., Rhodes, C., & Slaney, M. (2008). Content-Based Music Information Retrieval: Current Directions and Future Challenges. *Proceedings of the IEEE*, *96*(4), 668–696. doi:10.1109/JPROC.2008.916370

Çetin, Ö., & Shriberg, E. (2006). Speaker overlaps and ASR errors in meetings: effects before, during, and after the overlap. *Proc. IEEE International Conference on Acoustics, Speech, and Signal Processing*. 10.1109/ICASSP.2006.1660031

Davis, S. B., & Mermelstein, P. (1980). Comparison of Parametric Representations for Monosyllabic Word Recognition in Continuously Spoken Sentences. *IEEE Transactions on Acoustics, Speech, and Signal Processing*, *28*(4), 357–366. doi:10.1109/TASSP.1980.1163420

Fujihara, H., Goto, M., Kitahara, T., & Okuno, H. G. (2010). A modeling of singing voice robust to accompaniment sounds and its application to singer identification and vocal-timbre-similarity-based music information retrieval. *IEEE Transactions on Audio, Speech, and Language Processing*, *18*(3), 638–648. doi:10.1109/TASL.2010.2041386

Fujihara, H., Kitahara, T., Goto, M., Komatani, K., Ogata, T., & Okuno, H. G. (2005). Singer identification based on accompaniment sound reduction and reliable frame selection. *Proc. Int. Conf. Music Information Retrieval*.

Gales, M., & Young, S. (1996). Robust continuous speech recognition using parallel model combination. *IEEE Transactions on Speech and Audio Processing*, *4*(5), 352–359. doi:10.1109/89.536929

Hu, Y., & Liu, G. (2015). Separation of Singing Voice Using Nonnegative Matrix Partial Co-Factorization for Singer Identification, *IEEE/ACM Transactions on Audio. Speech, and Language Processing*, *23*(4), 643–653.

Kim, Y. E., & Whitman, B. (2002). Singer identification in popular music recordings using voice coding features. *Proc. Int. Conf. Music Information Retrieval*.

Li, Y., & Wang, D. L. (2007). Separation of singing voice from music accompaniment for monaural recordings. *IEEE Transactions on Audio, Speech, and Language Processing*, *15*(3), 1475–1487. doi:10.1109/TASL.2006.889789

Liu, C. C., & Huang, C. S. (2002). A singer identification technique for content-based classification of MP3 music objects. *Proc. Int. Conf. Information and Knowledge Management*. 10.1145/584792.584864

Maddage, N. C., Xu, C., & Wang, Y. (2004). Singer identification based on vocal and instrumental models. *Proc. Int. Conf. Pattern Recognition*. 10.1109/ICPR.2004.1334225

Mesaros, A., & Astola, J. (2005). The mel-frequency cepstral coefficients in the context of singer identification. *Proc. Int. Conf. Music Information Retrieval.*

Mesaros, A., Virtanen, T., & Klapuri, A. (2007). Singer Identification in polyphonic music using vocal separation and pattern recognition methods. *Proc. Int. Conf. Music Information Retrieval.*

Nwe, T. L., & Li, H. (2007). Exploring Vibrato-Motivated Acoustic Features for Singer Identification. *IEEE Transactions on Audio, Speech, and Language Processing, 15*(2), 519–530. doi:10.1109/TASL.2006.876756

Nwe, T. L., & Li, H. (2008). On fusion of timbre-motivated features for singing voice detection and singer identification. Proc. IEEE Int. Conf. Acoustics, Speech, and Signal Processing. doi:10.1109/ICASSP.2008.4518087

Okuno, H. G., Nakatani, T., & Kawabata, T. (1999). Listening to two simultaneous speeches. *Speech Communication, 27*(3-4), 299–310. doi:10.1016/S0167-6393(98)00080-6

Reynolds, D., Quatieri, T., & Dunn, R. (2000). Speaker verification using adapted Gaussian mixture models. *Digital Signal Processing, 10*(1-3), 19–41. doi:10.1006/dspr.1999.0361

Reynolds, D., & Rose, R. (1995). Robust text-independent speaker identification using Gaussian mixture speaker models. *IEEE Transactions on Speech and Audio Processing, 3*(1), 72–83. doi:10.1109/89.365379

Schedl, M., Gómez, E., & Urbano, J. (2014). Music Information Retrieval: Recent Developments and Applications. *Journal Foundations and Trends in Information Retrieval, 8*(2-3), 127–261. doi:10.1561/1500000042

Shriberg, E., Stolcke, A., & Baron, D. (2001). Observations on overlap: findings and implications for automatic processing of multi-party conversation. *Proc. European Conference on Speech Communication and Technology.*

Tsai, W. H., Liao, S. J., & Lai, C. (2008). Automatic Identification of Simultaneous Singers in Duet Recordings. *Proc. Int. Conf. Music Information Retrieval.*

Tsai, W. H., & Lin, H. P. (2011). Background Music Removal Based on Cepstrum Transformation for Popular Singer Identification. IEEE Trans. Audio, Speech, Lang. Process., 19(5), 1196-1205.

Tsai, W. H., & Ma, C. H. (2017). Automatic Identification of Simultaneous and Non-Simultaneous Singers for Music Data Indexing. *International Journal of Web Services Research, 14*(1), 29–43. doi:10.4018/IJWSR.2017010103

Tsai, W. H., Rodgers, D., & Wang, H. M. (2004). Blind clustering of popular music recordings based on singer voice characteristics. *Computer Music Journal, 28*(3), 68–78. doi:10.1162/0148926041790630

Tsai, W. H., & Wang, H. M. (2004). Automatic detection and tracking of target singer in multi-singer music recordings. *Proc. IEEE Conf. Acoustics, Speech, and Signal Processing (ICASSP).*

Tsai, W. H., & Wang, H. M. (2006). Automatic singer recognition of popular music recordings via estimation and modeling of solo vocal signals. *IEEE Transactions on Audio, Speech, and Language Processing, 14*(1), 333–341.

Virtanen, T. (2007). Monaural sound source separation by non-negative matrix factorization with temporal continuity and sparseness criteria. *IEEE Transactions on Audio, Speech, and Language Processing, 15*(3), 1066–1074. doi:10.1109/TASL.2006.885253

Yamamoto, K., Asano, F., Yamada, T., & Kitawaki, N. (2006). Detection of overlapping speech in meetings using support vector machines and support vector regression. *IEICE Trans. Fundamentals, 89*(8), 2158-2165.

Zhang, T. (2003). Automatic singer identification. Proc. IEEE Int. Conf. Multimedia Expo. doi:10.1109/ICME.2003.1220847

Chapter 3
Multi–Level Web Service Clustering to Bootstrap the Web Service Discovery and Selection

Banage T. G. S. Kumara
Sabaragamuwa University of Sri Lanka, Sri Lanka

Incheon Paik
University of Aizu, Japan

Koswatte R. C. Koswatte
Sri Lanka Institute of Information Technology, Sri Lanka

ABSTRACT

Existing technologies for web services have been extended to give the value-added customized services to users through the service composition. Service composition consists of four major stages: planning, discovery, selection, and execution. However, with the proliferation of web services, service discovery and selection are becoming challenging and time-consuming tasks. Organizing services into similar clusters is a very efficient approach. Existing clustering approaches have problems that include discovering semantic characteristics, loss of semantic information, and a shortage of high-quality ontologies. Thus, the authors proposed hybrid term similarity-based clustering approach in their previous work. Further, the current clustering approaches do not consider the sub-clusters within a cluster. In this chapter, the authors propose a multi-level clustering approach to prune the search space further in discovery process. Empirical study of the prototyping system has proved the effectiveness of the proposed multi-level clustering approach.

DOI: 10.4018/978-1-5225-7268-8.ch003

INTRODUCTION

Service Oriented Architecture (SOA) has been a widely accepted paradigm to facilitate distributed application integration and interoperability (Endrei, Ang et al., 2004). Web services are the backbone technology that can be used to implement SOA. The technology allows users to publish software applications as universally accessible and programmable services. Users can use service composition techniques to combine the existing services as components to create a value-added services to solve complex problems (Paik, Chen et al., 2014). Service composition consists of four major stages: planning, discovery, selection, and execution. However, Web service discovery and selection are becoming a challenging and time-consuming task that require considerable efforts because of unnecessary similarity calculations in the matchmaking process within repositories such as Universal Description, Discovery and Integrations (UDDIs) and Web portals., especially with the continuously increase of Web services. Thus, researchers intensively studied to increase the performance of the service discovery and the selection by clustering Web services into similar groups to reduce the search space (Wu, Chen et al., 2014). Then, many unnecessary similarity calculations in the matching process can be avoided.

Current research studies on the Web service clustering is mainly focusing on two main approaches: functional based clustering and quality-of-service (QoS) based clustering. The functional based approaches are clustering services based on functional attributes such as *input*, *output*, *precondition* and *effect* (Dasgupta, Bhat et al., 2011; Nayak & Lee, 2007). The QoS based clustering approaches are based on QoS properties such as *cost* and *reliability* (Xia, Chen et al., 2011). The functional based clustering are mainly used to bootstrap the discovery process (Elgazzar, Hassan et al., 2010) and QoS based clustering approaches are used to reduce the search space in selection phase (Karthiban, 2014). Apart from these two categories, there are some other clustering approaches based on social properties of the services such as sociability (Chen, Paik et al., 2013) and users (Zheng, Xiong et al., 2013). In this paper, we mainly focused on the functional based clustering.

A principal issue for the clustering is computing the semantic similarity between services. First, the clustering method computes the similarity of features (*SoFs*) of the services. Then, the similarity of services (*SoS*) is computed as an aggregate of the individual *SoF* values. Several matrix-based methods have been used to compute the *SoFs* in current functional based clustering approaches, such as those using string-based cosine similarity (Platzer, Rosenberg et al., 2009), the one-to-one matching of features such as the *service name*, matching of service signatures such as the *messages* (Elgazzar, Hassan et al., 2010), the corpus-based normalized Google distance (NGD) (Liu & Wong 2009; Elgazzar, Hassan et al., 2010), knowledge-based ontology methods (Wagner, Ishikawa et al., 2011; Wen, Sheng et al., 2011; Xie,

Chen et al., 2011). However, string-based one-to-one matching, structure matching or a vector-space model may not accurately identify the semantic similarity among the terms because of the heterogeneity and independence of service sources. These methods consider the terms only at the syntactic level. Furthermore, the Information retrieval based (IR) techniques such as cosine similarity usually focus on plain text, whereas the Web services contain much more complex structures, often with very little textual description. In the Search Engine based (SEB) similarity-measuring methods such as NGD, there is no guarantee that all the information needed to measure the semantic similarity between a given pair of words is contained in the top-ranking snippets. On the other hand, although ontologies help to improve semantic similarity, defining high-quality ontologies is a major challenge. Developing the ontology by obtaining assistance from domain expertise is a time-consuming task that requires considerable human effort. Further, the lack of standards for integrating and reusing existing ontologies also hampers ontology-based semantics matching. Thus, we proposed the hybrid term similarity (HTS) based clustering approach in our previous work (Kumara, Paik et al., 2014) to overcome the above issues. In this approach first, we use an ontology-learning method to build an ontology for service set. If the generated ontology fails to calculate the similarities, we then use an IR-based method. Our ontology learning uses the Web service description language (WSDL) documents to generate the ontologies by examining the hidden semantic patterns that exist within the complex terms used in service features. In IR method, we use both thesaurus-based and SEB term similarities. This paper is an extended version of the paper (Kumara, Paik et al., 2014).

In the HTS method, we extracted *service name*, *operation*, *domain name*, *input* and *output messages* as the service features from WSDL documents and calculated the individual feature similarities. Next, *SoFs* were integrated to calculate the *SoS*. However, contribution of the features in clustering the services is different from each other. Some futures show higher contribution and some features give low contribution. So, if we consider the all features equally in the feature integration, then it may be affected to the overall quality of clustering results. Further, in HTS method, the services are clustered according to the general domains such as *Vehicle* and *Food*. But, when we were analyzing the services in a particular domain, we could identify some sub categories under that domain. Thus, we can cluster services within a cluster to identify sub clusters. With this sub clustering method, we can reduce the search space more to increase the performance of service discovery. In this paper, multi-level clustering approach is proposed to identify the sub clusters. First, the features are ranked according to the contribution in clustering process. Then, the features are selected in each level according to the rank to cluster the services.

The remainder of this paper is organized as follows. Section 2 describes the motivation examples and proposed approach. Section 3 provides the summary of HTS method. Section 4 describes our proposed multi-level clustering approach. Section 5 discusses our experiments and their evaluation. In section 6, we present the related work. Finally, section 7 concludes the study.

MOTIVATION EXAMPLES AND PROPOSED APPROACH

In this section, we present motivating scenarios for ontology learning approach in HTS method and multi-level clustering. In addition, the architecture of proposed multi-level clustering approach is described.

Motivating Example for Ontology Learning

Consider the calculation of similarity between *ScienceFictionNovel* and *RomanticNovel* services. To calculate the similarity, we first tokenize the complex terms and calculate pair similarities (e.g., (*Science, Romantic*), (*Science, Novel*), (*Fiction, Romantic*)). Existing approaches consider only the distance between pairs of tokenized terms and cannot catch completely the semantics of the complex term. But, when we analyze the complex terms, hidden semantic patterns that exist between tokenized terms in the complex terms (e.g., *RomanticNovel* is a subclass of *Novel*) can be identified. This semantic pattern can be used to generate ontologies for the service domain. Figure 1 shows the generated ontology for the above two services. Figure 2 shows the extended ontology with more services.

Motivating Example for Multi-Level Clustering

Table 1 shows the similarity values between *service names*, *inputs* and *output*s of six service pairs. Here, we calculated the similarity values using HTS method.

Figure 1. Ontology for two web services

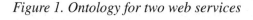
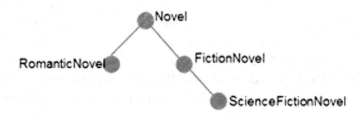

Figure 2. Extended ontology

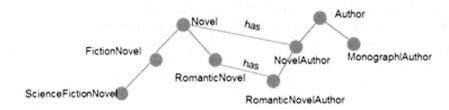

Table 1. Sample similarity values of service features

Service 1	Service 2	Similarity Service Name	Similarity Input	Similarity Output
VehiclePrice	*CarthrewwelTechnology*	0.68	0.70	0.40
NovelpersonPrice	*NovelPublisher*	0.87	0.74	0.35
EmergencyPhysian	*HospitalInvestigatingaddress*	0.89	0.75	0.35
BicyclecarPrice	*MonographPrice*	0.18	0.19	1.00
FourwheeledcarPrice	*ButterRecommendedprice*	0.47	0.16	1.00
CarPricequality	*TitleFilmrecommendedprice*	0.48	0.45	0.85

According to the values in Table 1, first three pairs obtained higher similarity values for the *service name* and *input*. Further, two services of each pair are from same domain. *VehiclePrice* and *CarthrewwelTechnology* services are from *Vehicle domain*. *NovelpersonPrice* and *NovelPublisher* services are from *Book* domain and *EmergencyPhysian* and *HospitalInvestigatingaddress* are from *Medical* domain. But, in each case similarity values of *output* are lower values. If we analyzed the WSDL documents of the *VehiclePrice* and *CarthrewwelTechnology,* then we observed that the services have different outputs. *VehiclePrice* service has *Price* as the output and *CarthrewwelTechnology* has *Technology* as the *output*. Further, output of *NovelpersonPrice* and *NovelPublisher* services are *Price* and *Publisher* respectively. So, we can determine that there are sub clusters like *Price* and *Technology* within a *Vehicle* cluster. On the other hand, if we consider the last three service pairs, similarity values of output obtained higher values compare to *service name* and *input*. Services in the each pair are from different domains. For an example, *BicyclecarPrice* service is from *Vehicle* domain and *MonographPrice service* is from *Book* domain. But, similarity value of the outputs of the services is 1.0. The same result can be observed for the *FourwheeledcarPrice* and *ButterRecommendedprice* services also. Thus, if we consider the output for the final similarity value in this case, then it will be affected to the clustering results. So as we mentioned, the contribution of features in clustering the services is different from each other. It is very important to identify the real contribution to obtain the high quality cluster.

Proposed Multi-Level Clustering Approach

The overview of the proposed multi-level clustering approach is illustrated in Figure 3. We use WSDL files to cluster the services. First, the WSDL documents are mined to extract the features that describe the functionality of the service. Then, we calculate the *SoFs* using HTS method (Kumara, Paik et al., 2014). Figure 4 illustrated the architecture of HTS unit. In the ontology-learning phase of the HTS unit, ontology learning method is used to generate ontologies for all of the extracted features. We then compute the *SoFs* in the similarity-calculation phase using the generated ontology and IR based term similarity. If we consider the Figure 3 again, after calculating the *SoFs,* features are ranked according to the contribution. Then, the top ranking features are selected for the top level clustering and *SoFs* are integrated to get the final similarity values. Next, in the clustering phase, an agglomerative clustering algorithm is used to cluster the services. After the first level clustering, we consider cluster by cluster for the second level clustering. Here, we select the bottom level features and apply the clustering process as in top level clustering.

HYBRID TERM SIMILARITY APPROACH

In this section, first we explain the feature extraction process. Then, the ontology learning method and the ontology learning algorithms are presented. Next, the IR-Based term similarity method is described. End of this section, we explain about the filters that are used in similarity calculating process.

Feature Extraction

We use *service name*, *operation name*, *input,* and *output* as the. Selected features of a WSDL file describe and reveal the functionality of its Web service. Operations give an abstract description of the actions supported by the service, which are listed in the main element *<portType>* of the WSDL document. We extract *operation name* as a feature. Message elements describe the data being exchanged between the Web service providers and consumers. Messages are composed of *part* elements, one for each parameter of the Web service's function. We consider the *part* elements for measuring the similarity of *input* and *output* messages. Multiple part names are used in the messages when the message has multiple logic units. For example, a

Figure 3. Overview of the multi-level clustering approach

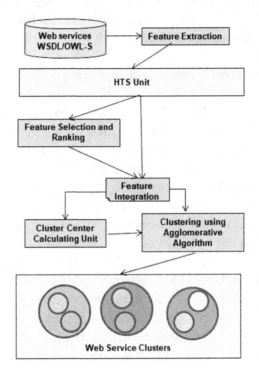

Figure 4. Overview of the HTS unit

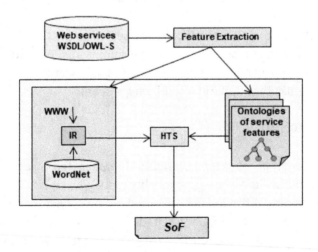

get_Book_PriceResponse output message in an *AuthorBook-price* service would have *Book* and *Price* part elements. Then the average similarity value for the input or output messages is calculated as follows:

$$Sim_m(S_i, S_j) = \sum_{p=1}^{k} \sum_{q=1}^{n} \frac{\max\_sim(s_p, r_q)}{(k+n)}$$

Here, s_p and r_q denote the individual part elements of input or output messages in services S_i and, S_j respectively. Parameters k and n are the number of part elements in input or output messages.

After extracting the features, we generate the ontologies from service documents. Here, ontologies are generated for each service feature type (*service name*) separately. Following sub section describes the ontology learning method.

Ontology Learning Method

HTS approach was presented in more details in our previous paper (Kumara, Paik et al., 2014). Here, we are presenting a brief description about the method. We proposed an ontology learning method that analyzes service features to recognize their semantics more precisely. We use the complex terms used in service features and their underling semantics to generate the ontologies automatically. First, the relevant feature (e.g., *service name*) is extracted from the service data set. If the feature is a complex term, then we split it into individual terms based on several assumptions. For example, the *ComedyFilm* name would be divided into two parts (*Comedy, Film*) based on the assumption that the capitalized characters indicate the start of a new word. Stop-word filtering is then performed to remove any stop words (e.g., of, the). In the next step after this preprocessing, we calculate the TF–IDF values of all the tokenized words. The terms are ranked according to their TF–IDF values, with the highest-ranking word having the highest TF–IDF value and a threshold TF–IDF value is defined. This is because we need to identify only the service-specific terms relevant to the service domain and the more meaningful terms in generating the upper-level concepts.

Ontology is an explicit specification of a conceptualization. Relations describe the interactions between the concepts or a concept's properties. We consider two types of relations, namely the concept hierarchy (Subclass–Superclass) and the triples (Subject–Predicate–Object). Let C be a set of concepts $\{C_1, C_2, \ldots, Cn\}$ in the ontology. Here, C_i represents S_iF, which is a feature F (e.g., *service name*) of service S_i. LSC(C_i) is the set of least specific concepts (direct children) C_x of C_i. That is, C_x is an immediate sub-concept of C_i in the concept hierarchy. LGC(C_x)

is the set of least generic concepts (direct parents) C_i of C_x. PROP(C_i) is the set of properties of concept C_i.

Definition 1 (Subclass–Superclass Relationship): *If $C_i \in LSC(C_j) \wedge C_j \in LGC(C_i)$, then there exists a Subclass–Superclass relationship between concepts C_i and C_j.*

Concept C_i can be an individual term (*Employee*) or a complex term (*OrganizationEmployee*). If a concept is a complex term, then its rightmost term is the head of the concept (*Employee*) and the element to the left is the modifier term of the concept (*Organization*).

Rule 1 (Head–Modifier Relation Rule): *Heads and modifiers express Subclass–Superclass relations between lexical items. This identifies a set of terms related through hyponymy with the head of the compound constituting the hypernym (Hippisley, Cheng et al., 2005).*

We consider two types of properties, namely *data* and *object* in this research. The *data* property refers to the *data* in a concept (*Organization name*). The *object* property is used to relate a concept to another concept (*Organization* has *Organization Employee*).

Definition 2 (Property Relationship): *If there exists $C_j \in PROP(C_i)$, then C_j has a property relation (triple relation) with C_i. Here, the target entity of the property could be either an object or data.*

Definition 2.1 (Data Property Relationship): *If $p_i \in PROP(C_j)$ and p_i is data in concept C_j, then there exists a data property relationship between p_i and concept C_j.*

Rule 2 (Compound Noun Rule): *If the individual terms in complex term t are nouns and if there is no concept in the ontology that is equal to head term H_t and if there is a concept that is equal to modifier term M_t, then there exists a data property relationship between concept M_t and data t.*

Definition 2.2 (Object Property Relationship): *If($C_i \in PROP(C_j)) \wedge (C_j \in PROP(C_i))$, then there exists an object property relationship between concepts C_i and C_j.*

Rule 3 (Concept and Modifier Rule): *If concept C_i is equal to a modifier term of concept C_j, then there exists an object property relationship between C_i and C_j.*

Rule 4 (Modifier Only Rule): *If a modifier term of concept C_i is equal to a modifier term of concept C_j and if there is no concept in the ontology that is equal to that modifier term, then there exists an object property relationship between C_i and C_j*

Ontology Construction Algorithm

Algorithm 1 in Table 2 describes the ontology-construction process for complex service terms. Concepts and the relationships between the concepts are generated using the TF–IDF value ranking and rules that were described in previous sub section. Word with the highest rank is selected and the concept for that term is generated. We then select all the complex terms that make use of that word to build the complex term by taking it as its head. All levels in the subsumption hierarchy of the complex term as show in Figure 5 are considered. Concepts for all levels of the particular complex term are generated (Lines 3–7). Then, Rule 1 is applied to generate a Subclass–Superclass relation (Line 8). This process is repeated for all tokenized words that have TF–IDF values greater than the defined threshold value. Next, we generate a data property relation by applying Rule 2 (Lines 11–17). Finally, Rules 3 and 4 are applied to generate object property relations (Lines 18–23).

IR-Based Term Similarity

As IR-based term-similarity methods, two approaches, namely thesaurus-based term similarity and SEB term similarity are used.

- **Thesaurus-Based Term Similarity:** This method can be considered as a knowledge-rich similarity-measuring technique. We use WordNet as the knowledge base. To calculate the semantic similarity of two terms, an edge-count-based approach (Qu, Sun et al., 2009) is used.
- **SEB Term Similarity:** One main issue for the above method is that some terms used in Web services may not be included in the thesaurus. We may therefore fail to obtain a reasonable similarity value for features (e.g., *"IphonePrice"* and *"NokiaPrice"*). However, the SEB method can overcome this problem because it analyzes Web-based documents. Further, it can identify the latent

Figure 5. Hierarchy of the complex term

Level 1 Organization

Level 2 EducationalOrganization

Level 3 HigherEducationalOrganization

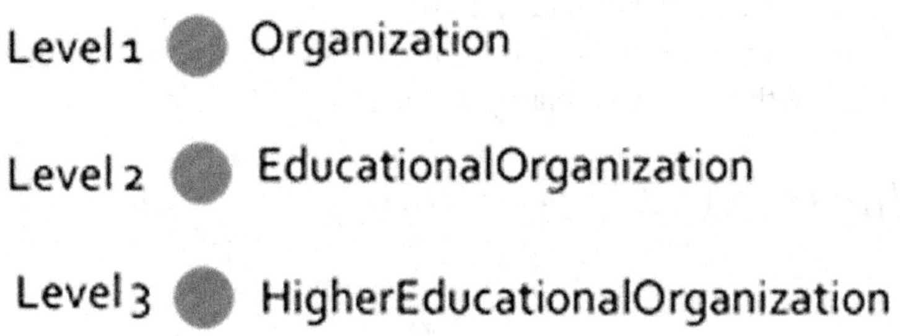

Table 2. Ontology Construction algorithm

Algorithm 1 Ontology Construction.	
Input T_c: Array of complex terms **Input** T_t: Array of tokenized terms **Input** 、 : Threshold TF–IDF value **Output** O: Ontology	
1:	**for** each tokenized term t_i, where TF–IDF value > 、 in T_t **do**
2:	generateConcept(t_i);
3:	**for** each complex term t in T_c **do**
4:	H_t = getHeadTerm(t);
5:	**if**(t_i.equals(H_t))
6:	generateConceptsforAllLevel-ComplexTerms(t);
7:	**end**
8:	generateSubSuperRelationship(); // By Rule 1.
9:	**end-for**

10:
11:
12:
13:
14:
15:
16:
17:
18:
19:
20:
21:
22:
23:
	end-for
	for each complex term t in T_c **do**
	H_t = getHeadTerm(t);
	M_t = getModifierTerm(t);
	If (H_t is not a concept and M_t is a concept)
	    generateDataProperty(); //By Rule 2.
	end
	end-for
	for each concept C_i **do**
	for each concept C_j **do**
	    generateObjectPropertyforConceptModifier(); // By Rule 3.
	    generateObjectPropertyforModifierOnly(); //By Rule 4.
	  end-for
	end-for

semantics in the terms (e.g., the semantic similarity between "*Apple*" and "*Computer*").

We consider three algorithms called Web-Jaccard, Web-Dice and Web-PMI, as described in (Bollegala, Matsuo et al., 2007).

First, we compute the pair similarity of the individual terms used in complex terms to calculate the feature similarity as follows:

$$Sim\left(T_1, T_2\right) = \alpha Sim_T\left(T_1, T_2\right) + \beta Sim_{SE}\left(T_1, T_2\right)$$

Here, $Sim_T\left(T_1, T_2\right)$ is the thesaurus-based term-similarity score and $Sim_{SE}\left(T_1, T_2\right)$ is the SEB similarity score. Parameters α and β .are real values between 0 and 1, with $\alpha + \beta = 1$.

Then feature similarity value is calculated as follows:

$$Sim_F\left(S_i, S_j\right) = \sum_{p=1}^{l}\sum_{q=1}^{m}\frac{\max\_ sim(x_p, y_q)}{(l + m)}$$

where x_p and y_q denote the individual terms, with l and m being the number of individual terms in a particular feature of services S_i and S_j. respectively.

Similarity Computation

To calculate the similarity of two Web services, first the relevant feature is extracted from two WSDL files. We do not split the complex terms as in usual literature, but consider the ontologies that generated by ontology learning method for those complex terms to check for the existence of concepts. If there are any concepts that relate to service features in the same ontology, then we compute the degree of semantic matching for the given pair of service features by applying different filters. We use the *Exact, Plug-in* and *Subsumes* filters defined in (Klusch, Fries et al., 2006). If one concept is a property of another concept, then those concepts are semantically closer to each other. We therefore proposed three filters, namely *Property-&-Concept, Property-&-Property* and *Sibling*, in previous paper (Kumara, Paik et al., 2014). .

Filters are applied in the following order, based on the degree of strength for logic-based matching: *Exact* > *Property-&-Concept* > *Property-&-Property* > *Plug-in* > *Sibling* > *Subsumes* > *Logic Fail* > *Fail*.

If there is an *Exact* match between two concepts, then the similarity is equal to the highest value 1. If the matching filter is *Property-&-Concept, Property-&-Property, Sibling, Plug-in, Subsumes, or Logic Fail*, then we calculate the similarity as follows:

$$Sim\left(C_i, C_j\right) = W_m + W_e Sim_E\left(C_i, C_j\right).$$

Here, W_m and W_e are weights for matching filter and edge-base similarity respectively, with $W_m + W_e = 1$. . $Sim_E\left(C_i, C_j\right)$ is the edge-based similarity and calculated by using following equation (Zhang, Jing et al., 2007).

$$Sim_E\left(C_i, C_j\right) = -\log \frac{d\left(C_i, C_j\right)}{2D}$$

Here, $d\left(C_i, C_j\right)$. is the shortest distance between concepts C_i and C_j .and parameter D is the maximum depth of the ontology.

If two concepts are in heterogeneous ontologies (the services fail to match using any matching filter except *Fail*), then the IR-based term-similarity method is used to calculate the feature similarity.

MULTI-LEVEL CLUSTERING

Feature Selection and Ranking

As we mentioned, the contribution of the features in clustering the services is different from each other. Some features give higher contribution and some features give low contribution. In HTS method, we integrated individual feature similarity values of all the features by assigning weight values to get the final *SoS*. Weight values were assigned manually considering the contribution. To evaluate the contribution, we implemented a program that returned a list of similar Web services for a given input Web service. This aimed to evaluate the strength of individual extracted features by measuring the Web service similarity. According to the result of that experiment, service *name* and *input message* obtained the higher precision values overall, whereas *operation name*, and *output message* obtained lower values (Kumara, Paik et al., 2014).

But in this paper, we use different method to identify the contribution of the features more accurately. In data mining, feature selection methods can be mainly divided into two types: filter and wrapper approaches. Filter method calculates the contribution of features by looking only at the intrinsic properties of the data. Further, the method is independent of the data mining algorithm to be applied. On the other hand, wrapper approach uses the result of the data mining algorithm to determine the contribution of features (Beniwal & Arora, 2012). In this paper, we apply filter techniques to evaluate the features.

Filter feature selection methods use a statistical measures such as Chi squared test and information gain to assign a scoring to each feature. The features are ranked by the score obtained by the filter. The methods consider the feature independently, or with regard to the dependent variable. Here, we consider Information Gain (IG) filter, correlation coefficient scores and Relief-f as the filters. Similarity values of each features between services are considered as attribute values. IG filter is ranking features based on high information gain entropy in decreasing order. Correlation-based feature selection filter evaluates and ranks the relevance of features by measuring correlation between features and classes and between some features and other features. Relief-f calculates the contribution of features according to how well its values distinguish the sampled instance of the same class and opposite class (Adel, Omar et al., 2014). After ranking the features by each filters, rank list is finalized by considering the majority select principle. We define the majority select rule as follows;

Rule 5 (Majority select rule): *If service feature f_i is selected by m number of filters and service feature f_j is selected by n number of filters for the rank r, and if (m >n), then f_i is the service feature for the rank r in the rank list.*

Clustering

After ranking the service features, we select two top ranking features for top level clustering. Other two features are selected for the second level clustering. Here, we consider only two levels. Then, the final service similarity value $Sim_s\left(S_i, S_j\right)$ to be used for service clustering is calculated by integrating the feature-similarity values for Web services S_i and S_j as follows:

$$Sim_s\left(S_i, S_j\right) = 0.5 * Sim\left(feature1_i, feature1_j\right) + 0.5 * Sim(feature2_i, feature2_j)$$

Here, feature1 and feature2 are top ranking features in the feature list.

After calculating the similarity values between the services, Affinity matrix is generated as shown in Table 3. Here, S_i represents the i-th service. Value of S_iS_j position represents the affinity value between service S_i and S_j.

Then, agglomerative clustering algorithm in Table 4 is used to identify the top level clusters. The algorithm can handle any form of similarity or distance easily and has a low computation cost. This bottom-up hierarchical clustering method starts by assigning each service to its own cluster (Lines 1 in Algorithm 2). It then starts merging the most similar clusters, based on proximity of the clusters at each iteration, until the stopping criterion is met (e.g., number of clusters) (Lines 4–10 in Algorithm). Several methods have been used to merge clusters, such as single-link and complete-link. We proposed novel cluster center identification approach in previous paper (Kumara, Paik et al., 2014). It is centroid-based method.

Table 3. Affinity matrix

	S_1	S_2	S_3	S_4	S_5
S_1	-	0.33	0.87	0.21	0.11
S_2	0.33	-	0.42	0.55	0.84
S_3	0.87	0.42	-	0.34	0.74
S_4	0.21	0.55	0.34	-	0.88
S_5	0.11	0.84	0.74	0.88	-

Table 4. Agglomerative clustering algorithm

Algorithm 2 Clustering Algorithm.	
Input S: Affinity matrix **Input** n: Number of required clusters **Output** C: Service clusters	
1:	Let each service be a cluster;
2:	ComputeProximityMatrix(S);
3:	k=NoOfServices;
4:	**while** k !=n **do**
5:	Merge two closest clusters;
6:	k=getNoOfCurrentClusters();
7:	Calculate center value of all services in all clusters;.
8:	Select service with highest value of each cluster as cluster centers;
9:	UpdateProximityMatrix();
10:	**end while**

After the top level clustering, we extract cluster by cluster for the next level clustering. Here also same equation is used to calculate the final similarity value as above. In this case, *feature1* and *feature2* represent the reaming two features (3rd and 4th ranking features in the feature list). Finally, same clustering algorithm is used to second level clustering.

EXPERIMENTS AND EVALUATION

The experiments were conducted on a computer running on Microsoft Windows 10, with an Intel core i7-4702MQ, a 2.20 GHz CPU and 8 GB RAM. Java was used as the programming language to implement the program, and the Jena Framework was used to build the ontologies. The Jena framework provides a collection of tools and Java libraries for developing ontologies. For the feature selection Weka attribute selection classifier was used. Weka is a collection of machine learning algorithms for data mining tasks (https://www.cs.waikato.ac.nz/ml/weka/). WSDL documents were gathered from real-world Web service repositories, and the OWL-S (http://projects. semwebcentral.org/projects/owls-tc/) test collection to act as the services dataset.

HTS Based Cluster Evaluation

In this paper, we presented limited number of evaluation about the HTS approach. We presented detail evaluation of the approach in our previous paper (Kumara, Paik et al., 2014). We performed a manual classification to categorize the Web service data set for comparison purposes. The categories identified were *Book, Medical, Food, Film* and *Travel*. Purity and entropy were used to evaluate the cluster quality. Purity determines how pure each of the clusters is and is defined as:

$$Purity = \frac{1}{n} \sum_{j=1}^{k} \max_{c} \left\{ n_j^i \right\}$$

Here, n is the total number of services and n_j^i is the number of services in cluster j belonging to domain class i.

Entropy measures how the various semantic classes are distributed within each cluster. Smaller entropy values indicate better clustering solutions. The entropy of a cluster is given by:

$$E\left(C_r \right) = -\frac{1}{\log q} \sum_{i=1}^{q} \frac{n_r^i}{n_r} \log \frac{n_r^i}{n_r}$$

Here, q is the number of domain classes in the data set, n_r^i is the number of services of the ith domain class that were assigned to the rth cluster and n_r is the number of services in cluster r. The entropy of the entire cluster is:

$$Entropy = \sum_{r=1}^{k} \frac{n_r}{n} E\left(C_r \right)$$

We implemented a clustering approach using only the edge-count-based method that uses WordNet to calculate similarities for comparison. Figure 6 shows the purity and entropy values for the two approaches with respect to the number of services.

According to the results, purity decreases and entropy increases when increasing the number of services in both approaches. However, our approach obtained lower entropy and higher purity values throughout. Moreover, the rate of entropy increase is greater in the edge-count-based method and the rate of purity-value decrease is smaller in the HTS approach. According to these results, we can see that our HTS approach improves the clustering performance.

Feature Ranking

Objective of this step is to rank the features according to their contribution. First, we selected 100 pair of services. Two services in some of pairs are from same domain, e.g., *VehiclePrice – FastcarPricereport* (both services are from *Vehicle* domain) and two services in remaining pairs are from different domains, e.g., *CoconutPrice - EmergencyPhysian* (services are from *Food* and *Medical* domains). Then, similarity values of individual features of each pair were calculated using HTS method. Next, we represented information of each pair using vectors to prepare the input dataset for filters, i. e., $P_i = \{\ S_i, S_j, SimSN_{ij}, SimON_{ij}, SimIN_{ij}, SimOP_{ij}, Class_{ij}\}$ Here, $SimSN_{ij}$, $SimON_{ij}$, $SimIN_{ij}$ and $SimOP_{ij}$ are similarity values of *service name, operation name input and output* of the service i and j. If two services are from same domain, then the value of $Class_{ij}$ is T otherwise value is F.

After preparing the dataset, IG, correlation coefficient scores and Relief-f filters were used to rank the features. Table 5 shows the output of each filter.

According to the table, the all three filters gave the same results. *Service name* obtained the rank one and *operation name* was the rank four. Further, when we analyzed the results of correlation ranking filter, we observed that correlation scores

Figure 6. Cluster performance with HTS approach

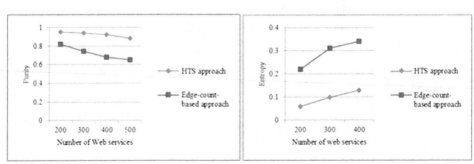

Table 5. Ranking output of each filter

Attribute Evaluator	Rank of the Feature			
	Service Name	Operation Name	Input	Output
Information Gain Ranking Filter	1	4	2	3
Correlation Ranking Filter	1	4	2	3
Relief-F Ranking Filter	1	4	2	3

of *service name, input, output* and *operation name* were 0.79, 0.78. 0.30 and 0.28 respectively. So, we can conclude that *service name* and *input* contribute more to calculating Web service similarity than do other features.

Evaluation of Multi-Level Clustering

In the top level, we clustered the services into main domains such as *Book* and *Film*. For the second level clustering, *output* and *operation name* were selected as features. Then, we extracted cluster by cluster to cluster the service. Let us consider the results of *Book* domain. We obtained three sub clusters from *Book* domain after applying the second level clustering. Cluster 1 contained services related to author and writer such as *SciencefictionNovelAuthor*. Cluster 2 contained services related to publishing such as *NovelPublisher*. Finally, Cluster 3 contained price related services such as *BookRecommendedPrice*. Following Table 6 shows part of clustering results.

As additional evaluation criteria, we used precision, recall and F-measure. Precision is the fraction of a cluster that comprises services of a specified class. Recall is the fraction of a cluster that comprises all services of a specified class. The F-measure measures the extent to which a cluster contains only services of a particular class and all services of that class. Here also, we performed a manual classification to categorize the Web service data set for comparison purposes. Table 7 shows the results of this step.

According to the experimental results in Table 7, cluster 3 obtained highest precision value and cluster 2 obtained highest recall value. However, precision value of cluster 1 is 76.2%. When we analyzed the WSDL documents, we observed that some services in the cluster had *Price* also as output. For example, *NovelAuthorPrice* service has two outputs (*Author* and *Price*). So, it shows the characteristics of both cluster 1 and 2. Here, it was placed in cluster1.

Next, let us consider *Travel* cluster. We obtained three sub clusters from *Travel* domain after applying the second level clustering. Cluster 1 contained services related to geographical location and weather such as *Geographical-regionLightning* and *Geographical-regionWeatherseason*. Cluster 2 contained services related to *Hotel*

Table 6. Sample output of sub clusters in Book cluster

Cluster	Services
C1 [*Author, Writer*]	*SciencefictionNovelAuthor* *NovelPerson* *PersonMonograph* *NovelPersonWriter* *NovelAuthorTime* *NovelUserreviewAuthor*
C2[*Publisher, Publication, ISBN, Search*]	*NovelPublisher* *SciencefictionBookPublisher* *Publication-numberCurrencyPublication* *MonographPublisher* *TitleBookFinderService* *IsbnPublicationPublisher* *TitleBookSearching*
C3[*Price, Max_Price, Recommended Price, Tax_price*]	*AuthorPublicationPrice* *AuthorBookTaxedPrice* *AuthorMonographMaxPrice* *BookReviewPrice* *NovelPersonPrice* *BookRecommendedPrice* *PersonbookOptiopnalPrice*

Table 7. Performance measures of sub clusters in Book cluster

Sub-Clusters of *Book* **cluster**	Precision %	Recall %	F-Measure %
C1[*Author, Writer*]	76.2	84.2	80.0
C2[*Publisher, Publication, ISBN, Search*]	86.4	95.5	90.7
C3[*Price, Max_Price, Recommended Price, Tax_price*]	97.0	91.4	94.1

such as *CountrycityHotel* and *VillageHotel*. Finally, Cluster 3 contained Activity related services such as *ActivityTown* and *SightseeingTown*. Following Table 8 shows part of clustering results.

According to the experimental results in Table 9, cluster 3 obtained highest precision value and also cluster 3 obtained highest recall value. It contains services related to various activities like sports and hiking.

DISCUSSION AND CONCLUSION

Clustering Web services into functionally similar clusters is a very efficient approach to increase the performance of service discovery. Computing semantic similarity

Table 8. Sample output of sub clusters in Travel cluster

Cluster	Services
C1 [*geographical location, weather*]	*Geographical-regionDrought* *Municipal-unitLightning* *Geopolitical-entityWeatherseason* *Geographical-regionLightning* *Municipal-unitWeatherseason* *Geopolitical-entityLightning*
C2[*Hotel*]	*CountrycityHotel* *TowncountryHotel* *VillageHotel* *CityLuxuryhotel* *DurationcountrycityHotel* *Postal-addresscityHotel*
C3[Activity: *Surfing, Hiking, Sports*]	*HikingNationalpark* *AdventureUrbanarea* *ActivityBeach* *SurfingRuralarea* *SportsFarmland SightseeingTown*

Table 9. Performance measures of sub clusters in Travel cluster

Sub-Clusters of *Book* cluster	Precision %	Recall %	F-Measure %
C1 [*geographical location, weather*]	82.8	83.3	83.0
C2[*Hotel*]	92.6	95.5	94.0
C3[*Activity: Surfing, Hiking, Sports*]	100	95.6	97.8

is the main issue in service clustering. To address the issues in current clustering approaches, we proposed HTS approach in previous work. Most of the current clustering approaches focus only top level clusters. But, we can identify sub clusters within clusters. Further, according to results of our previous paper, we observed that contribution of features in clustering process is different from each other. In this paper, first we applied three feature selection filters for ranking the features. *Service name* and *input* obtained rank one and two with all the filters. Then, multi-level clustering process was applied using feature ranks and HTS method. Experimental results showed that the our multi-level clustering approach performed efficiently.

In future work, experiments will be carried out to improve the performance of Web service discovery and selection. Further, we are planning to conduct more experiments to evaluate our approach.

RELATED WORK

In this section, we discuss work related to the Web service clustering. Calculating the semantic similarity between services has been a critical issue for functional based service clustering. Over recent decades, several approaches have been developed for the improved measurement of service similarity. The similarity methods such as keyword-matching (Elgazzar, Hassan et al., 2010; Liu & Wong, 2009), IR methods (Platzer, Rosenberg et al., 2009; Chen, Yang et al., 2010) and Ontology based methods (Wagner, Ishikawa et al., 2011; Xie, Chen et al., 2011) are the mainly used methods in literature. The approach taken has also affected the service clustering performance. These approaches have problems that include a lack of semantic characteristics. This results in a loss of semantic information caused by the shortage of proper ontologies. Thus, we proposed our HTS approach to address the issues.

As we mentioned, researchers proposed clustering approaches to reduce the search space. (Du, Zhang et al., 2013) proposed a semantic approach to cluster and Web service discovery. WordNet was used to calculate the semantic similarity. Further, they have proposed concept position vector model to refine the clusters by removing the services that do not completely match the user request. Further, (Gao, Wang et al., 2014) proposed a hierarchical clustering method for semantic Web service discovery. They tried to improve the accuracy and efficiency of the service discovery using vector space model. Web service was converted into a standard vector format through the Web service description document with the help of WordNet. Then, a semantic analysis was conducted to reduce the dimension of the term vector and to make semantic expansion to meet the user's service request. However, WordNet is a fixed knowledge base. So, lack of up-to-date information is one main issue in this kind of methods. In our HTS method, we addressed the issue using SEB methods.

(Skoutas, Sacharidis et al., 2010) proposed a Web service ranking and clustering approach based on dominance relationships. They proposed an approach to rank the relevant Web services for a given request by introducing objective measures based on dominance relationships defined among the services. In that work, they applied multiple matching criteria without aggregating the match scores of individual service parameters as in usual literature. To improve the performance of discovery, (Surianarayanan, Ganapathy et al., 2016) presented a clustering based approach. They used two similarity models namely, Output similarity model and total similarity model. (Huynh, Quan et al., 2017) proposed a quality-controlled logic-based clustering approach for web service composition and verification. In the approach, Web service was represented as a logical expression. Then, Web services were grouped into clusters based on the calculation of the similarity between their logical expressions. Finally, they combined hierarchical agglomerative clustering and k-means to ensure the quality of generated clusters. (Zhou, Liu et al., 2015) proposed heterogeneous service network clustering framework. They, integrated multiple types of entities, attributes and links with different semantics into a unified random walk distance model. Unified distance measure based on the neighborhood random walk model was proposed to integrate various types of link information in that work. Another clustering approach proposed an approach to cluster the Web services using relational database approach (Liu, Liu et al., 2015). Self-join operation in relational database was used to improve the efficiency and accuracy of service clustering. They have designed relational database table to store information about *input, output, precondition*, and *effect* of Web services.

However, the above methods only focused on single level clustering. Further, most of the current approaches did not evaluate the strength of the features. But, in this paper we proposed a multi-level clustering approach to reduce the search space more and filters were used to select the features. HTS approach was used as the foundation for the method.

REFERENCES

Adel, A., Omar, N., & Al-Shabi, A. (2014). A comparative study of combined feature selection methods for Arabic text classification. *Journal of Computational Science*, *10*(11), 2232–2239. doi:10.3844/jcssp.2014.2232.2239

Beniwal, S., & Arora, J. (2012). Classification and feature selection techniques in data mining. *Int J Eng Res Technol*, *1*(6), 2278–2284.

Bollegala, D., Matsuo, Y., & Ishizuka, M. (2007). Measuring Semantic Similarity between Words using Web Search Engines. *Proceeding of the 16th International World Wide Web Conference*, 757-766.

Chen, L., Yang, G., Zhang, Y., & Chen, Z. (2010). Web services clustering using SOM based on kernel cosine similarity measure. *Proceeding of the 2nd International Conference on Information Science and Engineering*, 846–850. 10.1109/ICISE.2010.5689254

Chen, W., Paik, I., & Hung, P. C. K. (2014). Constructing a Global Social Service Network for Better Quality of Web Service Discovery. *IEEE Transactions on Services Computing*, *26*(5), 1466–1476.

Dasgupta, S., Bhat, S., & Lee, Y. (2011). Taxonomic clustering and query matching for efficient service discovery. *Proceeding of the 9th IEEE International Conference on Web Services*, 363–370. 10.1109/ICWS.2011.112

Du, Y. Y., Zhang, Y. J., & Zhang, X. L. (2013). A semantic approach of service clustering and web service discovery. *Inf Technol J, 12*(5), 967–974. doi:10.3923/itj.2013.967.974

Elgazzar, K., Hassan, A. E., & Martin, P. (2010). Clustering WSDL Documents to Bootstrap the Discovery of Web Services. *Proceeding of the 8th IEEE International Conference on Web Services*, 147-154. 10.1109/ICWS.2010.31

Endrei, M., Ang, J., Arsanjani, A., Chua, S., Comte, P., Krogdahl, P., Luo, M., Newling, T. (2004, April). Patterns: Service-Oriented Architecture and Web Services. *IBM Redbooks*.

Gao, H., Wang, S., Sun, L., Nian, F., Liu, K., Gulliver, S., . . . Yu, C. (2014). Hierarchical clustering based web service discovery. Berlin: Springer.

Hippisley, A., Cheng, D., & Ahmad, K. (2005). The head-modifier principle and multilingual term extraction. *Natural Language Engineering, 11*(2), 129–157. doi:10.1017/S1351324904003535

Huynh, K. T., Quan, T. T., & Bui, T. H. (2017). A quality-controlled logic-based clustering approach for web service composition and verification. *International Journal of Web Information Systems, 13*(2), 173–198. doi:10.1108/IJWIS-12-2016-0068

Karthiban, R. (2014). A QoS-Aware Web Service Selection Based on Clustering. *International Journal of Scientific and Research Publications, 4*(2).

Klusch, M., Fries, B., & Sycara, K. (2006). Automated semantic Web service discovery with OWLS-MX. *Proceeding of the 5th International Conference on Autonomous Agents and Multi-Agent Systems*, 915-922. 10.1145/1160633.1160796

Kumara, B. T. G. S., Paik, I., Chen, W., & Ryu, K. (2014). Web Service Clustering using a Hybrid Term-Similarity Measure with Ontology Learning. *International Journal of Web Services Research, 11*(2), 24–45. doi:10.4018/ijwsr.2014040102

Liu, J. X., Liu, F., Li, X. X., He, K. Q., Ma, Y. T., & Wang, J. (2015). Web Service Clustering Using Relational Database Approach. *International Journal of Software Engineering and Knowledge Engineering, 25*(8), 1365–1393. doi:10.1142/S021819401550028X

Liu, W., & Wong, W. (2009). Web service clustering using text mining techniques. *International Journal of Agent-oriented Software Engineering, 3*(1), 6–26. doi:10.1504/IJAOSE.2009.022944

Nayak, R., & Lee, B. (2007). Web service discovery with additional semantics and clustering. *IEEE/WIC/ACM International Conference on Web Intelligence*, 555–558. 10.1109/WI.2007.82

Paik, I., Chen, W., & Huhns, M. N. (2014). A scalable architecture for automatic service composition. *IEEE Transactions on Services Computing*, *7*(1), 82–95. doi:10.1109/TSC.2012.33

Platzer, C., Rosenberg, F., & Dustdar, S. (2009). Web service clustering using multidimensional angles as proximity measures. *ACM Transactions on Internet Technology*, *9*(3), 1–26. doi:10.1145/1552291.1552294

Qu, X., Sun, H., Li, X., Liu, X., & Lin, W. (2009). WSSM: A WordNet-Based Web Services Similarity Mining Mechanism. *Proceeding of the Future Computing, Service Computation, Cognitive, Adaptive, Content, Patterns, 2009. COMPUTATIONWORLD '09. Computation World*, 339–345. 10.1109/ComputationWorld.2009.96

Skoutas, D., Sacharidis, D., Simitsis, A., & Sellis, T. (2010). Ranking and clustering web services using multicriteria dominance relationships. *IEEE Transactions on Services Computing*, *3*(3), 163–177. doi:10.1109/TSC.2010.14

Surianarayanan, C., & Ganapathy, G. (2016). An Approach to Computation of Similarity Inter-Cluster Distance and Selection of Threshold for Service Discovery using Clusters. *IEEE Transactions on Services Computing*, *9*(4), 524–536. doi:10.1109/TSC.2015.2399301

Wagner, F., Ishikawa, F., & Honiden, S. (2011). QoS-aware Automatic Service Composition by Applying Functional Clustering. *Proceeding of the 9th IEEE International Conference on Web Services*, 89–96. 10.1109/ICWS.2011.32

Wen, T., Sheng, G., Li, Y., & Guo, Q. (2011). Research on Web service discovery with semantics and clustering. *Proceeding of the 6th IEEE Joint International Information Technology and Artificial Intelligence Conference*, 62–67. 10.1109/ITAIC.2011.6030151

Wu, J., Chen, L., Zheng, Z., Lyu, M. R., & Wu, Z. (2014). Clustering web services to facilitate service discovery. *Knowledge and Information Systems*, *38*(1), 207–229. doi:10.100710115-013-0623-0

Xia, Y., Chen, P., Bao, L., Wang, M., & Yang, J. (2011). A QoS-Aware Web service selection algorithm based on clustering. *IEEE International Conference on Web Services*, 428-435. 10.1109/ICWS.2011.36

Xie, L., Chen, F., & Kou, J. (2011). Ontology-based semantic Web services clustering. *Proceeding of the 18th IEEE International Conference on Industrial Engineering and Engineering Management*, 2075–2079.

Zhang, X., Jing, L., Hu, X., Ng, M., & Zhou, X. (2007). A comparative study of ontology based term similarity measures on PubMed document clustering. *Proceeding of the 12th International Conference on Database Systems for Advanced Applications*, 115-126. 10.1007/978-3-540-71703-4_12

Zheng, K., Xiong, H., Cui, Y., Chen, J., & Han, L. (2012). User clustering based web service discovery. *2012 Sixth International Conference on Internet Computing for Science and Engineering*, 276–279.

Zhou, Y., Liu, L., Pu, C., Bao, X., Lee, K., Palanisamy, B., ... Zhang, Q. (2015). Clustering Service Networks with Entity, Attribute, and Link Heterogeneity. *2015 IEEE International Conference on Web Services*, 257-264. 10.1109/ICWS.2015.43

Chapter 4
Model–Based Development and Spatiotemporal Behavior of Cyber–Physical Systems

Peter Herrmann
Norwegian University of Science and Technology, Norway

Jan Olaf Blech
Altran, Germany

Fenglin Han
Norwegian University of Science and Technology, Norway

Heinz Schmidt
RMIT University, Australia

ABSTRACT

Many cyber-physical systems operate together with others and with humans in a joint physical space. Because of their operation in proximity to humans, they have to operate according to very high safety standards. This chapter presents a method for developing the control software of cyber-physical systems. The method is model-based and assists engineers with spatial and real-time property verification. In particular, the authors describe a toolchain consisting of the model-based development toolset Reactive Blocks, the spatial analyzer BeSpaceD in conjunction with the real-time model checkers UPPAAL and PRISM. The combination of these tools makes it possible to create models of the control software and, if necessary, simulators for the actual system behavior with Reactive Blocks. These models can then be checked for various correctness properties using the analysis tools. If all properties are fulfilled, Reactive Blocks transforms the models automatically into executable code.

DOI: 10.4018/978-1-5225-7268-8.ch004

INTRODUCTION

In safety critical domains like aviation, automotive and robotics, autonomous cyber-physical systems interact with each other and with humans in the same physical space. To avoid damage of machine equipment and injuries of humans, the control software of these systems has to guarantee spatiotemporal properties like collision avoidance or the reliable cooperation of several units that carry a heavy workpiece together. A popular way for the creation of functionally correct and safe system software is the application of integrated modeling and verification tools like MATLAB/Simulink (Tyagi, 2012). Our contribution is the combination of such a tool with efficient provers allowing engineers to verify that the coordinated behavior of multiple controlled cyber-physical systems fulfills relevant spatial safety properties. We introduce a toolchain combining the model-based engineering tool-set Reactive Blocks (Kraemer, Slåtten, & Herrmann, 2009) with the verification tool BeSpaceD (Blech & Schmidt, 2013). In particular, we use a development workflow starting with the collection of requirements for a cyber-physical system and its architecture followed by the steps 1 to 7 below:

1. Spatiotemporal properties of components are described in the input language of BeSpaceD.
2. A model of the system controller is created in Reactive Blocks. We compose it with a simulator model of the continuous system parts which is engineered using the BeSpaceD model developed in step 1.
3. The built-in model checker of Reactive Blocks is used to check the combined controller and simulator model for general design errors, (Kraemer, Slåtten, & Herrmann, 2009).
4. If the checks in step 3 are passed, the software model is transformed into the input language of BeSpaceD.
5. Assuming certain maximum reaction times of the discrete controller, the resulting model is now verified with BeSpaceD to check whether it fulfills the required spatiotemporal properties defined in step 1.
6. One of the model checkers UPPAAL (Bengtsson, et al., 1996) and PRISM (Kwiatkowska, Norman, & Parker, 2009) is now applied to prove that the real-time properties assumed in the proofs of step 5 are preserved by the Reactive Blocks model created in step 2 (Han & Herrmann, 2013), (Han, Herrmann, & Le, 2013).
7. By using the code generator from Reactive Blocks (Kraemer & Herrmann, 2007), (Kraemer, Herrmann, & Bræk, 2006), executable Java code of the controller and, if needed, of the simulator of the continuous behavior is created.

The generated code can be deployed on the system components running the control software of the embedded system.

Our approach has to guarantee that a model developed with Reactive Blocks indeed fulfills the desired safety properties if the verifications in steps 5 and 6 succeed. Formally, that proof is merely trivial: Let S be the logical formula corresponding to a system model in Reactive Blocks according to (Kraemer & Herrmann, 2010), P the conjunction of spatial behavioral properties to be fulfilled by S, and $R(t)$ a statement describing that the controller always guarantees a maximum reaction time t. Using BeSpaceD, we verify in step 5 that the system fulfills the safety properties if t is kept, i.e., $S \wedge R(t) \Rightarrow P$. If we use UPPAAL in step 6, we prove that the system guarantees the maximum reaction time, i.e., $S \Rightarrow R(t)$. PRISM does not give us this proof explicitly but is able to verify that $S \Rightarrow R(t)$ holds with a certain probability, e.g., 99.999999%. It is evident that the combination of the two proofs implies $S \Rightarrow P$ such that the Reactive Blocks model created in step 2 effectively fulfills the spatial properties defined in step 1, at least with an acceptable likelihood.

Further, we have to argue whether our model is a correct abstraction of the real physical system in which the generated code of the controller shall be used. In particular, it is important to understand if and under which conditions the real system may violate P even if the two proof steps succeed. Preserving safety properties throughout refinement and reuse of verification results achieved on abstract models has been studied in the past, e.g., (Loiseaux, Graf, Sifakis, Bouajjani, & Bensalem, 1995) and is especially important in the context of model checking. When regarding space, we distinguish here between the following:

- **Overapproximation of Spatial Behavior:** For instance, the size of a spatial area occupied by a unit can be extended for proving the absence of collisions. This enables us to reuse previous spatial proofs if the sizes of a physical model do not exceed the overapproximated ones taken as a basis in the former proof.
- **Underapproximation of Spatial Behavior:** Just as the overapproximations, we can, for example, underapproximate sensor ranges that allow the detection of other units, such that established properties can be reused in later development stages.
- **Overapproximation of Maximum Reaction Times:** The BeSpaceD verifications in step 5 are valid if we assume greater or equal reaction times than those guaranteed by the controller, the sensors and actuators in the worst case.

Figure 1. Layout of the moving robot

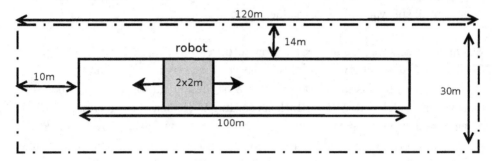

Guiding Example: Moving Robot

We intend to protect maintenance personnel in a factory hall against collisions with a fast moving robot transporting goods. The layout of the scenario is depicted in Figure 1. The robot has a size of up to 2 x 2 meters and moves on a straight line in the center of the room covering a distance of 100 m. Since it reaches a speed of up to 10 m/s, a collision with a human may lead to fatal injuries. The hall is equipped with sensors observing if a human approaches the robot and we shall design a safety controller which may stop the robot in due time. The robot can be operated in three different modes depending on its distance to humans in the hall:

- **Green Mode:** If no human is closer than 25 m to the robot, the robot increases its speed with an acceleration of 5 m/s^2 until reaching 10 m/s. After 87 m, the speed of the robot is reduced with an acceleration of -5 m/s^2 until it amounts to 1 m/s which is kept until the robot reaches the buffer stop at the endpoint.
- **Yellow Mode:** If a human is detected within a distance of less than 25 m but more than 10 m, the robot is slowed down with a deceleration of 10 m/s^2 until reaching a speed of 2 m/s (resp. 1 m/s if more than 87 m are passed).
- **Red Mode:** If the distance between the robot and a human is less than 10 m, the robot stops with a deceleration of 15 m/s^2.

For the mode changes, we assume a latency of 500 ms at maximum reflecting that there will be communication delays between the physical components as well as processing times of the robot controller. Of course, the main spatial proof task is to find out if the selected behavior of the safety control ensures that the robot is sufficiently slow or already stopped when a human reaches it. An aggravating fact is that the sensor may detect humans only if they are in the hall but that the face side is only 10 m and the long side 14 m from the path of the robot.

Synopsis

This chapter is an extension of (Herrmann, Blech, Han, & Schmidt, 2016): Our workflow and verification include now also probabilistic reasoning and the workflow makes use of the probabilistic model checker PRISM. First, we outline the first three steps of the workflow, in particular, the engineering of controllers with Reactive Blocks. Thereafter, step 5, i.e., the proof of spatial properties with BeSpaceD, is discussed followed by an introduction of step 4, the coupling between Reactive Blocks and BeSpaceD. Finally, we describe the use of UPPAAL and PRISM to verify real-time properties in step 6. After reflecting on related work, we then conclude the chapter.

MODELING CONTROLLERS AND CONTINUOUS BEHAVIOR

The input of BeSpaceD can be either direct logical terms or a Scala program generating the terms. For the moving robot example, we started the workflow with a Scala program modeling the spatial behavior of the robot and the human. Here, for instance the speed that the robot shall carry in the green mode can be described by the following code snippet:

```
if (mode == 3) { // green
     if (d <= 870) {
          if (speed < 10) {
                    speed += 0.0005 * timeraster; } }
               else {
               if (speed > 1) {
                         speed -= 0.0005 * timeraster; }
} }
```

For step 2, we apply the engineering tool Reactive Blocks (Kraemer, Slåtten, & Herrmann, 2009) that allows the model-based development of reactive systems all the way from abstract behavioral specifications to executable code. It enables to specify sub-functions of an application in separate models that we call building blocks. Using synchronous coupling, building blocks can be further composed to system models. An advantage of this proceeding is that a functionality recurring in several applications is specified once as a building block that can be reused in various models (Kraemer & Herrmann, 2009). The behavior of a building block is specified as a UML 2 activity while its behavioral interface is described by a so-called External State Machine (ESM) (Kraemer & Herrmann, 2009). Reactive

Blocks uses a formal semantics (Kraemer & Herrmann, 2010) such that in step 3 of our workflow the activities can be model checked for design properties, e.g., compliance of an activity with the ESM of its building block (Kraemer, Slåtten, & Herrmann, 2009). System models can be automatically transformed to executable Java code (Kraemer & Herrmann, 2007), (Kraemer, Herrmann, & Bræk, 2006) which corresponds to step 7 of the workflow.

Figure 2 depicts a UML activity modeling the behavior of a building block. Similarly to Petri nets, behavior is expressed as tokens passing via the edges of a graph towards its vertices which may be flow control units like forks duplicating tokens or timers as well as operations containing Java methods (e.g., *computeMode*). Further, an activity may contain call behavior actions like *Timer Periodic 2* referencing other building blocks. The interaction of the activity describing the behavior of a building block *B* with the one including a call behavior action referencing *B*, is modeled by pins and parameter nodes. The parameter nodes are described as little squares at the edges of the activity, e.g., *new1* in Figure 2, while the pins are similar symbols at the edges of the call behavior actions (e.g., *tick* in *Timer Periodic 2*). The pins at a call behavior action of a building block are identical to the parameter nodes of its activity.

In Reactive Blocks, we follow run-to-completion semantics modeling that tokens flow via several edges and nodes in a single atomic step, a so-called *activity step*, until they have to wait for other behaviors like receiving an event from another station or a timeout (Kraemer & Herrmann, 2010). An activity step may encompass several activities since the ``hop'' of a token between two activities via pins and parameter nodes is carried out synchronously.

Figure 2. UML activity of building block ControlTwoElements

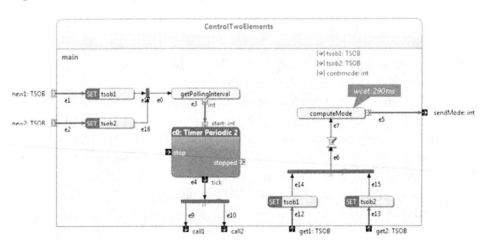

The UML activity in Figure 2 models the behavior of the building block *ControlTwoElements* that we use to specify the safety controller in our example. It is a feedback controller that polls the sensors of the the robot as well as the human and uses the sensor data to compute the correct control mode of the robot. The activity is initiated by two simultaneously arriving data tokens via the parameter nodes *new1* and *new2* containing location information about the robot and the human at system start. The corresponding time, location and speed data is defined by the Java class *TSOB* which is the type of both parameter nodes. In the same activity step, the two data tokens are stored in the variables *tsob1* and *tsob2* and the two tokens are joined to one passing operation *getPollingInterval*. This operation refers to a Java method that reads out a parameter of the building block which describes the time interval between two polls of the sensors (5 *ms* in the example). Thereafter, the token is forwarded starting the building block *Timer Periodic 2* that will periodically issue timeouts according to the value of the parameter.

A timeout is modeled by a token arriving through pin *tick* of block *Timer Periodic 2* that is duplicated in the succeeding fork and outputted via the parameter nodes *call1* and *call2*. Assuming that the drivers of the sensors rest in the same physical component as the controller, we can model that the sensor data arrives still in the same activity step through the pins *get1* and *get2*.

The data units are stored in the variables *tsob1* and *tsob2* followed by a join towards a flow breaker. That is a timer without a waiting time which sole purpose is to separate two activity steps.

In a new activity step, the token leaves the flow breaker and causes the execution of the Java method *computeMode* which takes the sensor data from the variables *tsob1* and *tsob2* and computes in which of the modes *green, yellow,* or *red* the robot has to operate. The mode values are typified by integer values that are outputted via parameter node *sendMode*.

In Figure 3, we point out the ESM of building block *ControlTwoElements*. The markings[1] at the edges of the state machine refer to the parameter nodes and model which parameter nodes are passed by tokens in a certain activity step. For instance, in the activity step leading from the initial node of the ESM to state *active*, tokens pass through both parameter nodes *new1* and *new2*. In state *active*, a transition may be executed which leads towards ESM state *computing*. It models the polling of sensor data and refers to the parameter nodes *call1* and *call2* followed by an immediate reaction via *get1* and *get2*. In state *computing*, a transition consisting of a flow via parameter node *sendMode* is allowed reflecting the transmission of new control modes. This transition sets the ESM back to state *active*. By the symbol / in the transition markings one expresses if a transition is triggered by the activity in a building block or by its environment.

Figure 3. The RTESM (ESM) of building block ControlTwoElements

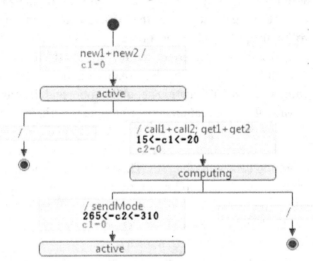

The overall system consists of twelve building blocks and, due to the similarity with Java, we profited from the Scala code created in step 1 of the workflow. For instance, the code snippet shown above was copied and pasted into an operation of building block *ContinuousStepRobot* that specifies the robot behavior in the Reactive Blocks model.

PROVING SPATIAL PROPERTIES WITH BESPACED

We implemented BeSpaceD (Blech & Schmidt, 2013), a tool for the specification and checking of spatial behavior of cyber-physical systems, in the programming language Scala. The description language of BeSpaceD allows us to define abstract datatypes that indicate spatial availability, interaction or occupation in areas in a coordinate system for time intervals or timepoints. BeSpaceD specifications are not limited to verification, but can also serve as basis for testing (Liu, Blech, Duckham, & Schmidt, 2017) and for decision making in adaptive systems, see (Svae, Taherkordi, Herrmann, & Blech, 2017), (Taherkordi, Herrmann, Blech, & Férnandez, 2017), (Blech, Fernando, Foster, Abilash, & Sudarsan, 2016), and (Herrmann, Svae, Svendsen, & Blech, 2016). As mentioned above, we can also use Scala code to generate BeSpaceD specifications. The language allows us to specify physical system behavior on various abstraction levels reaching from simple models regarding only distinct availability areas at certain time intervals or timepoints to complete behavioral models. In particular, we can describe the space covered by a system at a certain timepoint in form of rectangles and other shapes. Further, we can constrain the coordination of different systems by allowing interaction only if their locations are within a certain distance. To give a look and feel, the following code segment points out an extract of the moving robot behavior:

```
AND (
        AND (
                AND (
                        IMPLIES (TimeStamp (410),
    OccupyBox (160, 139, 182, 161)),
                        IMPLIES (TimeStamp (411),
                                OccupyBox (161, 139, 183,
161)))),
                IMPLIES (TimeStamp (412),
                        OccupyBox (161, 139, 183, 161))),
        IMPLIES (TimeStamp (413),
                OccupyBox (162, 139, 184, 161)));
```

The logical formula expresses that the robot covers a rectangle defined by the corner points (160 x 139) and (182 x 161) at the timepoint 410 which describe coordinates in the hall in decimeters. At the next timepoint the robot moved a decimeter to the right covering the box between (161 x 139) and (183 x 161) etc. Spatial verification with BeSpaceD can be difficult, if moving objects show excessive non-deterministic behavior since that multiplies the scenarios to be checked. In the example, we are able to specify the robot behavior exactly and use it for verification purposes. The human, however, can freely change speed and direction showing a high degree of non-deterministic behavior. Two solutions exist to cope with this kind of non-determinism: We can describe the non-deterministic behavior in a more abstract way, such that the number of verification scenarios is reduced. For instance, we can express the behavior of humans by rectangles describing all places, they may have reached at a certain timepoint. This may have the disadvantage, that scenarios are too coarse-grained, so that important safety properties cannot be verified even if they hold in reality, e.g., the rectangles modeling the possible position of a human will gradually grow until they cover the whole factory hall. Alternatively, we can select a set of worst-case scenarios and check only those. For a given case study, however, we have to argue why the chosen set of worst-case scenarios is indeed sufficient. No general solution exists so far for the automatic selection of worst-case scenarios.

For the most important proof of step 5 in our workflow, i.e., the robot runs only very slowly or already stands when it is reached by a human, we chose the second solution. Due to the basic laws of kinematics, we could restrict us to two worst-case scenarios, i.e., running from the door on the face side of the room (see Figure 1) against the moving direction of the robot, resp. entering the room through the door on the long side and running in a right angle towards its path. In these scenarios, we considered both, the highest possible approximation speed between robot and human and the situations in which the human is closest to the robot when the sensor detects an approximation. Since the robot needs 12.6 *s* for the overall run if it is in normal mode and we assume 5 *ms* between two timepoints, its behavior can be described by altogether 2520 timepoints. To be sure that by discretizing the robot behavior we did not overlook unsafe situations, we overapproximated the rectangle of the robot and assumed that it covers 2.2 x 2.2 *m*. As the human may enter the room any time, we created for each of the two scenarios 2520 variants such that the human may start its run at any of the timepoints defining the current robot location.

In the verification process, specifications realizing a verification scenario are given in the BeSpaceD language and are broken down to expressions containing geometrical information. Yet another automatic transformation breaks these geometric expressions down to representations that are suitable for solving algorithms and special solvers like SMT[2] and SAT[3]. Further, we use a simpler and faster hashset-based implementation for a subclass of SAT problems that checks possible collisions between two entities, each one defined by multiple points in space and time. The overall 5040 runs of the two scenarios could be proven by this refined prover within five minutes on a standard PC.

For the human in the model, we assumed a maximum speed of 10 *m/s* causing a relative speed of up to 20 *m/s* if the user enters the room from the face side. In spite of that and a distance of only 9.8 *m* between the door and the final position of the robot, this scenario was verified as safe for all starting points of the human since the robot already stands at the time of impact. The reason for that is that the robot is either sufficiently far from the human when the latter enters the room such that the controller has enough time to react, or it is already slowing down approaching its final point such that the breaking distance is shorter.

The problem in the other scenario is that the robot may be in full speed while the human enters the room from the side in a distance as close as 13.8 *m*. Indeed, if the human enters the room when the robot is about 9.5 *m* before the point of impact, it can be reached before having completely stopped. Simulating this case with the program generated from Reactive Blocks, we found out that the maximum speed of the robot at the time of impact is at most 0.625 *m/s*. It has to be decided if the risk of such an encounter, which is unlikely since the speed of 10 *m/s* can only be reached by few athletes and depending on the physics of the robot might not cause severe injuries as the robot is nearly standing at the time of impact, can be beard or if the control software resp. the environment have to be changed.

COMPOSING REACTIVE BLOCKS AND BESPACED

We use two different ways to compose the model-based engineering tool set Reactive Blocks with the spatiotemporal verification tool BeSpaceD, see also (Hordvik, Øseth, Svendsen, Blech, & Herrmann, 2016).

One possibility to combine the two tools, is to use simulator runs to achieve step 4 of the workflow (Han, Blech, Herrmann, & Schmidt, 2014), (Hordvik, Øseth, Svendsen, Blech, & Herrmann, 2016): The Reactive Blocks model of the simulator is amended by operations writing the positions of the robot and the human at each time point as an IMPLIES statement into files that formed the input for BeSpaceD. An apparent disadvantage of this coupling method is that the need to perform simulator runs for all scenarios can be rather time-consuming. So, assuming 12.6 seconds for the run of each of the altogether 5040 variants to be checked in the two scenarios, the simulator has to be executed nearly 18 hours just to generate the BeSpaceD input data. Further, by this kind of integration, we limit ourselves to purely scenario-based proofs in BeSpaceD. In particular, the verifications are not exhaustive, and we only guarantee that the properties for the simulated cases are preserved.

The other way to combine the two tool sets, is to exploit the ability of BeSpaceD to use Scala files as input and to copy the Java code that in a Reactive Blocks model realizes the controller and simulator, directly into the corresponding Scala files. As discussed above, compiling Java into Scala is nearly trivial since the syntaxes of the operations in both languages are identical and only the variable declarations have to be adjusted by the transformation tool.

The main problem of an automatic transformation from Reactive Blocks to BeSpaceD is to find out where the relevant code segments reside in an arbitrary Reactive Blocks model. To solve this, we utilize the property that Reactive Blocks models can be composed from reusable building blocks (Kraemer & Herrmann, 2009). We created a new library of building blocks for the domain of cyber-physical systems. That does not only help to create the controller and simulator models in step 2 of our workflow but can also be used as starting point for graphical pattern detection in order to find code segments to be transformed to BeSpaceD. Up to now, the library contains building blocks for several types of controllers, a block *ContinuousStep* to create various simulators, and *TimeStampOccupyBoxManager* managing the instances of type *TSOB* containing spatiotemporal information that can directly be handled by BeSpaceD.

The transformation tool searches a Reactive Blocks model for the occurrence of these blocks. This is basically achieved in three steps:

1. An instance of block *TimeStampOccupyBoxManager* contains the interval between two time points as a parameter that can be directly used in the Scala input file of BeSpaceD to compute the intervals between two timepoints.
2. The movement and speed of a physical unit depending on its current execution mode (e.g., *green, yellow,* or *red* in the robot system) are computed by an operation in the direct environment of block *ContinuousStep* that can be retrieved by the transformation tool and copied into the Scala program.
3. The execution mode of a unit is computed in a certain operation of its controller block. For example, in building block *ControlTwoElements* (see Figure 2) that is operation *computeMode*, the content of which is also copied into the Scala program.

The first and second transformation steps are carried out for each physical component of the system and the third one for each controller component used.

Of course, to guarantee the correctness of the transformations, the composition of the building blocks needs to fulfill certain properties: For instance, the interval between two simulator steps has to be in accordance with the parameter defined in block *TimeStepOccupyBoxManager*. Otherwise, BeSpaceD would possibly use a wrong assignment between time stamps and positions of the geospatial objects. Further, an operation mode computed in a controller block must be directly forwarded to block *ContinuousStep*. This is analyzed by the transformation tool using graph transformation techniques (Han & Herrmann, 2012). A practical limitation of this approach is that one rarely performs a development from scratch but mostly use already existing legacy code which mostly does not follow the specification limitations discussed above. In this case, it is often too laborious to redevelop a model from scratch and one has to use the simulation-based approach, see (Hordvik, Øseth, Svendsen, Blech, & Herrmann, 2016).

VERIFYING REAL-TIME PROPERTIES

To achieve step 6 of our workflow, we extend the interface descriptions of Reactive Blocks by using Real-Time ESMs (RTESMs) resp. Probabilistic Real-Time ESMs (PRTESMs). In an RTESM (Han & Herrmann, 2013), (Han, Herrmann, & Le, 2013), we can specify that a building block may only rest in a certain state for a maximum period of time before a transition has to be fired. RTESMs extend the ESMs with time variables, so-called clocks, as well as a set of labels expressing clock reset, state invariants and guard conditions. In the RTESM of building block *ControlTwoElements* in Figure 3, the state invariants are marked in black and the clock resets in red. Moreover, one can annotate the various vertices of an activity by worst case execution time attributes (Han & Herrmann, 2013). For instance, in the activity of block *ControlTwoElements* we assigned 290 *ms* to operation *computeMode* (see annotation in Figure 2). For some activity vertices, we further assume certain default delays, e.g., 2 *ms* for writing and reading variables as well as for the start of a new activity step.

A PRTESM (Han, Blech, Herrmann, & Schmidt, 2014) is an extension of an RTESM that allows us to model probabilistic real-time behavior, in particular, discrete probability distributions. PRTESMs make the straightforward transformation into Probabilistic Timed Automata (PTA) (Kwiatkowska M., Norman, Sproston, & Wang, 2005) possible that can be directly model checked by PRISM, see (Kwiatkowska, Norman, & Parker, 2011), (Kwiatkowska, Norman, & Parker, 2009).

In the following, we show the verification of our moving robot example with both UPPAAL and PRISM.

Real-Time Verification With UPPAAL

As explained in (Han & Herrmann, 2013), (Han, Herrmann, & Le, 2013), the RTESM and the activity of a building block are automatically transformed to Timed Automata (Alur & Dill, 1990) in which the real-time annotations introduced above are considered. Thus, one can use the model checker UPPAAL (Bengtsson, et al., 1996) to prove timed properties expressed in Timed-CTL (TCTL) (Laroussinie, Markey, & Schnoebelen, 2004) and to verify whether the activity indeed fulfills the RTESM of its block. The TCTL formulas are also automatically generated.

The approach is highlighted with our moving robot example. Table 1 describes the minimum resp. maximum execution times that we assume for the various tasks of the control cycle in our example. The sum of the worst case execution times (*wcet*) of all four steps is exactly the 500 *ms* assumed in the BeSpaceD proof shown above. The transition from state *active* to state *computing* in the RTESM models the fetching of sensor data which includes the time between two polling calls. We expect that this task is handled within 15 to 20 *ms* which is expressed by clock $c1$

Table 1. Maximum and minimum execution times of different tasks of the robot control system

Component	min. time	max. time
Time to fetch sensor data including polling delay	15 *ms*	20 *ms*
Processing time recognition unit	250 *ms*	290 *ms*
Communication time recognition unit to robot	15 *ms*	20 *ms*
Internal robot processing time and actuator reaction	150 *ms*	170 *ms*

in the RTESM enforcing that the transition is executed within this time interval. For the latency in state *computing*, we model by means of clock *c2* between 265 and 310 *ms* which corresponds to the sum of the image processing time in the controller and the communication delay towards the robot controller. In a similar way, we defined the RTESMs of the other building blocks forming our example system. The operation *computeMode* in the activity of block *ControlTowElements* (Figure 2) is annotated with a *wcet* of 290 *ms* since it contains the code to process the execution mode from the sensor inputs. Likewise, we annotated the other activities by suitable *wcet* attributes.

A critical element for the proof that building block *ControlTwoElements* fulfills its RTESM, is the flow breaker ahead of operation *computeMode*. During the execution of the activity step leading towards the flow breaker, other activity steps may be added to the execution queue such that they are carried out earlier than the one leaving the flow breaker. Considering the time guarantees of the environment as defined in the RTESM and the *wcets* of the other activity steps, the waiting time until the activity step being triggered from the flow breaker is at most 8 *ms*. Thus, together with the *wcet* of 290 *ms* defined for operation *computeMode*, the building block will stay at most 298 *ms* in its RTESM state *computing* which is lower than the 310 *ms* guaranteed by the RTESM.

The Timed Automaton transformed from the RTESM of block *ControlTwoElements* is depicted in Figure 4. For the communication between a Timed Automaton representing an RTESM and the one of the activities of its building block resp. its environment, we use synchronization channels (e.g., *new1*). Here, RTESM transitions with multiple parameters are expressed by interleaving (e.g., from state *_initial* to *active* in Figure 4). UPPAAL can now use the Timed Automata to prove whether the real-time properties are fulfilled. For instance, the proof discussed above is carried out by checking if the Timed Automaton of the RTESM receives signal *sendMode* from

Figure 4. Timed automata of RTESM for block ControlTwoElement

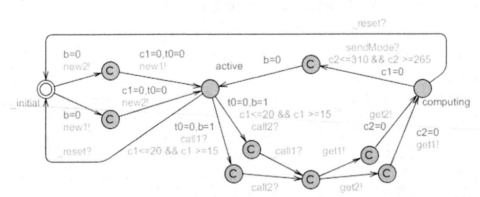

the one modeling the activity within 310 *ms* guaranteeing that the state invariant of this state is fulfilled. This corresponds to proving the TCTL formula $A[]$ (*external. computing imply c2≤310*). Altogether, we executed 22 UPPAAL proofs which were completed within some milliseconds each. This is due to a relatively small number of states in all Timed Automata effectively exploiting the compositional structure of the Reactive Blocks models (see Kraemer et al., 2009).

Probabilistic Real-Time Verification With PRISM

In the UPPAAL-based approach, we conducted our proofs based on a number of minimum and maximum execution times described in Table 1. By conducting practical tests, see (Hordvik, Øseth, Svendsen, Blech, & Herrmann, 2016), (Svae, Taherkordi, Herrmann, & Blech, 2017), one can also get more accurate real-time values including probabilities that they are actually met. Table 2 lists the accumulative likelihoods that the sub-tasks of our example are carried out within certain time intervals. For example, the probability that the sensor data can be fetched within 15 *ms* is only 10%, while they are read in 40% within 17 *ms* and in 85% within 18 *ms*. Further, we guarantee that the reading is always completed within 20 *ms*. The values used in Table 2 do not correspond to a factual system but represent data points, one might expect in typical field-bus based systems.

In practice, one cannot give axiomatic guarantees of real-time properties since a control system is always subject to external influences like a failure of the computer hardware running it. Nevertheless, to come to meaningful probability estimations, we decided to ignore these external errors in our models. In this respect, one should mention that our approach should not be seen as a replacement but only as an extension of traditional hazard analysis for safety-critical systems, see also (Hordvik, Øseth, Svendsen, Blech, & Herrmann, 2016).

From the data in Table 2, we can produce Probabilistic Real-Time ESMs (PRTESMs), see (Han, Blech, Herrmann, & Schmidt, 2014). The one for the building block realizing the communication between the controller and the robot is listed in Figure 5. This block is reached from the block *ControlTwoElements* (see Figure 2) via its parameter node *sendMode*. In Figure 5, the values *r1, r2, r3, r4,* and *r5* stand for the probabilities of the same names depicted in Table 2. To make the transformation into PTAs (Kwiatkowska M., Norman, Sproston, & Wang, 2005) possible, each PRTESM has an initial state *initial* that represents both, the initial and final state of the corresponding ESM. Further, a PRTESM may contain states expressing probabilistic system behavior as well as synchronization semaphores and timed constraints specifying real-time properties. In Figure 5, the timed constraints such as *c_c2 <= 150* specify values measured in 100 *ms*. The states *green, yellow,* and *red* refer to the three main system states introduced above. The states *s5* to *s9* express the probabilities that one of the rows *r1* to *r5* in Table 2 holds while *s11* describes that the data transfer is completed.

A PTA is computed from a PRTESM by transforming the PRTESM transitions to new states and transitions expressing probabilities. The PTAs form the input of the PRISM tool while the verification goals are expressed by the Probabilistic Timed Temporal Logic (PTCTL) (Kwiatkowska M., Norman, Segala, & Sproston, 2002). We verified a set of probabilities expressed in PTCTL as follows:

$$P_{=?}\left[F_{\leq T} \text{ " } target \text{ "}\right]\left(T \in \left[0.0,\ldots,0.5\right]\right)$$

Table 2. Accumulative likelihood distribution of the execution times if the robot

Component	Maximum Time	Accumulative Probability	Terms used in Figure 5
Time to fetch sensor data including polling delay	15 *ms*	10%	
	17 *ms*	40%	
	18 *ms*	85%	
	19 *ms*	99.998%	
	20 *ms*	100%	
Processing time recognition unit	250 *ms*	10%	
	260 *ms*	30%	
	270 *ms*	60%	
	280 *ms*	90%	
	285 *ms*	99%	
	290 *ms*	100%	
Communication time recognition unit to robot	15 *ms*	80%	r1
	16 *ms*	98%	r2
	16.5 *ms*	99.5%	r3
	16.9 *ms*	99.99999995%	r4
	20 *ms*	100%	r5
Internal robot processing time and actuator reaction	150 *ms*	5%	
	159 *ms*	90%	
	160 *ms*	95%	
	165 *ms*	99.9995%	
	170 *ms*	100%	

Here, the operator *F* is a path operator that is equal to *eventually* in Linear-time Temporal Logic (LTL), see, e.g., (Lamport, 2002), and can be used inside the operator *P*. The pattern $F_{\leq T}$ .defines the property *within* T *time units*. Inside the PTA models, the expression *target* models that the parallel composed real-time probabilistic actions are indeed executed. Altogether, the formula expresses the probability that the labeled actions are achieved within *T* time units.

Now, we can use PRISM to verify that a control cycle is finished within a certain time, with a certain reliability, i.e., with a minimal high likelihood. For instance, if we set $T = 0.46\,s$. the robot reacts with a likelihood of at least *99.99874114988752%*. This corresponds to an upper probability cap for failure-on-demand between 0.0001 (so-called 4 nines reliability) and 0.00001 (5 nines reliability) and therefore falls into the class of SIL 4 (Safety Integrity Level 4) according to the IEC 61508 functional safety standard (International Electronical Commission, 2010) and is hence equivalent to a risk reduction factor of 10,000 to 100,000 (4 powers of 10 to 5 powers of 10). While this reliability may be insufficient for very-high speed mobility with moderate to large number of humans continuously exposed to risks, such as in high-speed trains, buses and automobiles, in this particular case, the robot will be quite slow (less than 0.125 *m/s* according to our simulations) and the active safety mechanisms kick in on-demand, when humans are detected. Therefore, assuming this low-demand mode of operation, SIL 4 is providing relatively high safety.

Figure 5. Timed automata of the PRTESM for the block realizing the communication with the robot

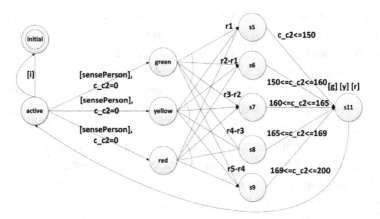

RELATED WORK

Work relevant to this paper has been done in areas such as formal logic and process algebras, hybrid-systems, robotics and formal methods for component-based software engineering.

The Duration Calculus (Chaochen, Hoare, & Ravn, 1991) and timed Durational Action Timed Automata (Guellati, Kitouni, & Saidouni, 2012) are two types of modal formalisms for time-critical systems. They are especially used to analyze parallel behavior of systems featuring actions with an elapsing non-atomic time duration. Complementing classical modeling approaches, for the specification of system models comprising spatial behavioral information, a process algebra-like formalism was introduced in (Caires & Cardelli, 2003), (Caires & Cardelli, 2004). Here, disjoint logical spaces are represented in terms of expressions by bracketing structures and carry or exchange concurrent process representations. For additional results on spatial interpretations see, e.g., (Hirschkoff, Lozes, & Sangiorgi, 2003). Many aspects of spatial logic are in general undecidable. A quantifier-free rational fragment of ambient logic (corresponding to regular language constraints), however, was shown to be decidable in (Dal Zilio, Lugiez, & Meyssonnier, 2004). Special modal logics for spatiotemporal reasoning go back to the seventies. The Region Connection Calculus (RCC) (Bennett, Cohn, Wolter, & Zakharyaschev, 2002) includes spatial predicates of separation (e.g., regions do not share points at all, points on the boundary of regions are shared, proper overlap of regions, or proper inclusion). Moreover, (Bennett, Cohn, Wolter, & Zakharyaschev, 2002) features an overview of the relation of these logics to various Kripke-style modal logics, reductions of RCC-style fragments to a minimal number of topological predicates, their relationship to interval-temporal logics and decidability. Other special logics for modeling cyber-physical systems are presented by (Bartocci, Bortolussi, Loreti, & Nenzi, 2017) and (Bouskela, Nguyen, & Jardin, 2017). In contrast, (Sezer & Atalay, 2011) use fuzzy logic to model control aspects of cyber-physical systems while (Gao, et al., 2013) specify their models using artificial neural networks.

The area of hybrid systems has seen the development of different tools for reasoning and verification. The tool SpaceEx (Frehse, et al., 2011) allows the modeling of continuous hybrid systems based on hybrid automata. It can be used for computing overapproximations of the space occupied by an object moving in time and space. Another tool making the analysis of spatial properties in hybrid systems possible, is PHAVer (Frehse G., 2008). Moreover, it is possible to model spatial behavior in more general purpose-oriented verification tools in Hybrid systems, e.g., KeYmaera of (Platzer & Quesel, 2008). This system was used to conduct formal verifications of train systems, see (Platzer & Quesel, 2009). Further approaches using model checking of spatial properties of cyber-physical systems comprise (Caires & Torres Vieira, 2012), (Cimatti, Griggio, Mover, & Tonetta, 2015), (Tiwari, 2015). (Koutsoukos, et al., 2018) developed a framework to model and simulate secure and resilient cyber-physical systems. This approach seems to be similar to ours but needs a higher degree of manual model transformation and code production.

Formal methods have also been widely used for safety property analysis in safety-critical systems. In (Slåtten, Herrmann, & Kraemer, 2013), we use an extension of Reactive Blocks to verify safety issues of software. In (Németh & Bartha, 2009), the authors use a CTL-subset for the verification of a safety procedure called primary-to-secondary leaking (PRISE) that is discussed by means of a model of a nuclear power plant.

CONCLUSION

We introduced a safety modeling and verification tool chain for the model-based engineering of controllers in distributed embedded systems that have to fulfill certain spatial behavioral properties. The models are created with Reactive Blocks while the real-time and probabilistic reliability verification is carried out with BeSpaceD in combination with UPPAAL or PRISM, respectively. In particular, we supplemented the existing transformation mechanism between Reactive Blocks and BeSpaceD (Han, Blech, Herrmann, & Schmidt, 2014) by a new one that is highly-automatic and more capable. Further, we created a library of reusable building blocks supporting the pattern matching used by this tool coupling. The building blocks of this library help also to create new Reactive Blocks models. In the adapted model of the example four of the overall twelve building blocks were copied from this library while further two were taken from another library of Reactive Blocks. Confirming our experience described in (Kraemer & Herrmann, 2009), the new model could be created in about a third of the time needed for the previous one for which the library did not exist yet. Except for the reason, that we needed to develop only six of the twelve blocks from scratch, we profited also from the interface layout of the blocks which provided a good guidance for the planning of the control and information flows in the model.

Besides extending the analysis tool of Reactive Blocks (Kraemer, Slåtten, & Herrmann, 2009) to carry out the property proofs discussed in Sect. 4, in the future, we plan to investigate additional specification mechanisms, i.e., spatial behavioral types following (Blech & Schmidt, 2013) for spatial verification aiming at storing, composing and reusing verification results. Moreover, we are interested in further optimizations and parallelization of the verification process using cloud and grid technology to speed up the analysis process of BeSpaceD and the model checkers. For instance, it should not be a problem to parallelize the BeSpaceD runs of the 5040 variants that we had to verify for the two worst-case scenarios. As an application domain for our work, we see the emerging field of Wireless Sensor Networks (WSNs), see (Han, Blech, Herrmann, & Schmidt, 2015). In particular, it seems highly interesting and practically relevant to find optimal correlations between spatial properties, communication channel bandwidth and signaling strength of the WSN transmitters and our approach might be helpful to solve this problem. Further, we already started to use our approach in Intelligent Transport Systems (ITS), another relevant research domain for using our approach, see (Hordvik, Øseth, Svendsen, Blech, & Herrmann, 2016), (Svae, Taherkordi, Herrmann, & Blech, 2017), (Puka, Herrmann, Levin, & Skjetne, 2018).

REFERENCES

Alur, R., & Dill, D. (1990). Automata for Modeling Real-Time Systems. *LNCS, 443*, 322–335.

Bartocci, E., Bortolussi, L., Loreti, M., & Nenzi, L. (2017). Monitoring Mobile and Spatially Distributed Cyber-Physical Systems. In *15th ACM-IEEE International Conference on Formal Methods and Models for System Design* (pp. 146-155). Vienna: ACM. 10.1145/3127041.3127050

Bengtsson, J., Larsson, F., Pettersson, P., Yi, W., Christensen, P., Jensen, J., ... Sorensen, T. (1996). UPPAAL: A Tool Suite for Validation and Verification of Real-Time Systems. *LNCS, 1066*, 232–243.

Bennett, B., Cohn, A., Wolter, F., & Zakharyaschev, M. (2002). Multi-Dimensional Modal Logic as a Framework for Spatio-Temporal Reasoning. *Applied Intelligence, 17*(3), 239–251. doi:10.1023/A:1020083231504

Blech, J., & Schmidt, H. (2013). Towards Modeling and Checking the Spatial and Interaction Behavior of Widely Distributed Systems. *Improving Systems and Software Engineering Conference (ISSEC).*

Blech, J. O., Fernando, L., Foster, K., Abilash, G., & Sudarsan, S. D. (2016). Spatio-Temporal Reasoning and Decision Support for Smart Energy Systems. In *IEEE 21st International Conference on Emerging Technologies and Factory Automation (ETFA)* (pp. 1-8). Berlin: IEEE Computer.

Bouskela, D., Nguyen, T., & Jardin, A. (2017). Toward a Rigorous Approach for Verifying Cyber-Physical Systems Against Requirements. *Canadian Journal of Electrical and Computer Engineering, 40*(2), 66–73.

Caires, L., & Cardelli, L. (2003). A Spatial Logic for Concurrency (Part I). *Information and Computation, 186*(2), 194–235. doi:10.1016/S0890-5401(03)00137-8

Caires, L., & Cardelli, L. (2004). A Spatial Logic for Concurrency (Part II). *Theoretical Computer Science, 322*(3), 517–565. doi:10.1016/j.tcs.2003.10.041

Caires, L., & Torres Vieira, H. (2012). SLMC: A Tool for Model Checking Concurrent Systems against Dynamical Spatial Logic Specifications. In *18th International Conference on Tools and Algorithms for the Construction and Analysis of Systems (TACAS)* (pp. 485-491). Tallinn: Springer-Verlag. 10.1007/978-3-642-28756-5_35

Chaochen, Z., Hoare, C., & Ravn, A. (1991). A Calculus of Durations. *Information Processing Letters, 40*(5), 269–276. doi:10.1016/0020-0190(91)90122-X

Cimatti, A., Griggio, A., Mover, S., & Tonetta, S. (2015). HyComp: An SMT-Based Model Checker for Hybrid Systems. In *21st International Conference on Tools and Algorithms for the Construction and Analysis of Systems (TACAS)* (pp. 52-67). London: Springer-Verlag. 10.1007/978-3-662-46681-0_4

Dal Zilio, S., Lugiez, D., & Meyssonnier, C. (2004). A Logic You Can Count On. In *Symposium on Principles of Programming languages*. ACM.

De Moura, L., & Bjørner, N. (2008). An Efficient SMT Solver. *LNCS, 4963*, 337–340.

Frehse, G. (2008, June). 2008). PHAVer: Algorithmic Verification of Hybrid Systems past HyTech. *International Journal of Software Tools for Technology Transfer, 10*(3), 263–279. doi:10.100710009-007-0062-x

Frehse, G., Le Guernic, C., Donzé, A., Cotton, S., Ray, R., Lebeltel, O., & Maler, O. (2011). *SpaceEx: Scalable Verification of Hybrid Systems. In Lecture Notes in Computer Science: Vol. 6806. Computer Aided Verification (CAV)* (pp. 379–395). Snowbird, UT: Springer-Verlag.

Gao, S., Dong, H., Chen, Y., Ning, B., Chen, G., & Yang, X. (2013). Approximation-Based Robust Adaptive Automatic Train Control: An Approach for Actuator Saturation. *IEEE Transactions on Intelligent Transportation Systems*, *14*(4), 1733–1742. doi:10.1109/TITS.2013.2266255

Guellati, S., Kitouni, I., & Saidouni, D. (2012). Verification of Durational Action Timed Automata using UPPAAL. *International Journal of Computers and Applications*, *56*(11), 33–41. doi:10.5120/8938-3077

Han, F., Blech, J. O., Herrmann, P., & Schmidt, H. (2014). Towards Verifying Safety Properties of Real-Time Probability Systems. *Electronic Proceedings in Theoretical Computer Science*, *147*, 1–15. doi:10.4204/EPTCS.147.1

Han, F., Blech, J. O., Herrmann, P., & Schmidt, H. (2015). Model-based Engineering and Analysis of Space-aware Systems Communicating via IEEE 802.11. In *IEEE 39th Annual Computer Software and Applications Conference* (pp. 638-646). Taichung, Taiwan: IEEE Computer.

Han, F., & Herrmann, P. (2012). Remedy of Mixed Initiative Conflicts in Model-based System Engineering. Electronic Communications of the EASST, 47.

Han, F., & Herrmann, P. (2013). Modeling Real-Time System Performance with Respect to Scheduling Analysis. In *Proceedings of the 6th IEEE International Conference on Ubi-Media Computing* (pp. 663-671). IEEE Computer. 10.1109/ICAwST.2013.6765522

Han, F., Herrmann, P., & Le, H. (2013). Modeling and Verifying Real-Time Properties of Reactive Systems. In *18th International Conference on Engineering of Complex Computer Systems (ICECCS)* (pp. 14-23). IEEE Computer. 10.1109/ICECCS.2013.13

Herrmann, P., Blech, J. O., Han, F., & Schmidt, H. (2016). A Model-based Toolchain to Verify Spatial Behavior of Cyber-Physical Systems. *International Journal of Web Services Research*, *13*(1), 40–52. doi:10.4018/IJWSR.2016010103

Herrmann, P., Svae, A., Svendsen, H. H., & Blech, J. O. (2016). Collaborative Model-based Development of a Remote Train Monitoring System. In *International Conference on Evaluation of Novel Approaches to Software Engineering (ENASE), special session on Collaborative Aspects of Formal Methods* (pp. 383-390). Rome: SciTePress. 10.5220/0005929403830390

Hirschkoff, D., Lozes, É., & Sangiorgi, D. (2003). Minimality Results for the Spatial Logics. *LNCS, 2914*.

Hordvik, S., Øseth, K., Svendsen, H. H., Blech, J. O., & Herrmann, P. (2016). Model-based Engineering and Spatiotemporal Analysis of Transport Systems. In L. Maciaszek & J. Filipe (Eds.), Evaluation of Novel Approaches to Software Engineering (pp. 44-65). Rome: Springer-Verlag. doi:10.1007/978-3-319-56390-9_3

International Electronical Commission. (2010). *International Standard IEC 61508-1 Functional Safety of Electrical/Electronic/Programmable Electronic Safety-related Systems – Part 1: General Requirements.* Retrieved from IEC Webstore: https://webstore.iec.ch/preview/info_iec61508-1%7Bed2.0%7Db.pdf

Koutsoukos, X., Karsai, G., Laszka, A., Neema, H., Potteiger, B., Volgyesi, P., ... Sztipanovits, J. (2018). SURE: A Modeling and Simulation Integration Platform for Evaluation of Secure and Resilient Cyber–Physical Systems. *Proceedings of the IEEE, 106*(1), 93–112. doi:10.1109/JPROC.2017.2731741

Kraemer, F., & Herrmann, P. (2007). Transforming Collaborative Service Specifications into Efficiently Executable State Machines. *Electronic Communications of the EASST, 7.*

Kraemer, F., & Herrmann, P. (2009). Automated Encapsulation of UML Activities for Incremental Development and Verification. *LNCS, 5795*, 571–585.

Kraemer, F., & Herrmann, P. (2010). Reactive Semantics for Distributed UML Activities. *LNCS, 6117*, 17-31.

Kraemer, F., Herrmann, P., & Bræk, R. (2006). Aligning UML 2.0 State Machines and Temporal Logic for the Efficient Execution of Services. *8th International Symposium on Distributed Objects and Applications (DOA06) (*pp. 1613-1632). Springer-Verlag. 10.1007/11914952_41

Kraemer, F., Slåtten, V., & Herrmann, P. (2009). Tool Support for the Rapid Composition, Analysis and Implementation of Reactive Services. *Journal of Systems and Software, 82*(12), 2068–2080. doi:10.1016/j.jss.2009.06.057

Kwiatkowska, M., Norman, G., & Parker, D. (2009). *Stochastic Games for Verification of Probabilistic Timed Automata.* Oxford, UK: Oxford University Computing Laboratory. doi:10.1007/978-3-642-04368-0_17

Kwiatkowska, M., Norman, G., & Parker, D. (2011). PRISM 4.0: Verification of Probabilistic Real-Time Systems. In *23rd International Conference on Computer Aided Verification (CAV)* (pp. 585-591). Snowbird, UT: Springer-Verlag. 10.1007/978-3-642-22110-1_47

Kwiatkowska, M., Norman, G., Segala, R., & Sproston, J. (2002). Automatic Verification of Real-time Systems with Discrete Probability Distributions. *Theoretical Computer Science, 286*(1), 101–150. doi:10.1016/S0304-3975(01)00046-9

Kwiatkowska, M., Norman, G., Sproston, J., & Wang, F. (2005). Symbolic Model Checking for Probabilistic Timed Automata. *Information and Computation, 205*(7), 1027–1077. doi:10.1016/j.ic.2007.01.004

Lamport, L. (2002). *Specifying Systems: The TLA+ Language and Tools for Hardware and Software Engineers*. Boston: Addison-Wesley.

Laroussinie, F., Markey, N., & Schnoebelen, P. (2004). Model Checking Timed Automata with One or Two Clocks. *LNCS, 3170*, 387–401.

Liu, H., Blech, J. O., Duckham, M., & Schmidt, H. (2017). Spatio-Temporal Aware Testing for Complex Systems. In *IEEE International Conference on Software Quality, Reliability and Security (Companion Volume)* (pp. 569-570). Prague: IEEE Computer.

Loiseaux, C., Graf, S., Sifakis, J., Bouajjani, A., Bensalem, S., & Probst, D. (1995). Property Preserving Abstractions for the Verification of Concurrent Systems. *Formal Methods in System Design, 6*(1), 1–35. doi:10.1007/BF01384313

Németh, E., & Bartha, T. (2009). Formal Verification of Safety Functions by Reinterpretation of Functional Block Based Specifications. *LNCS, 5596*, 199–214.

Platzer, A., & Quesel, J. (2008). KeYmaera: A Hybrid Theorem Prover for Hybrid Systems (System Description). *LNCS, 5195*, 171–178.

Platzer, A., & Quesel, J. D. (2009). *European Train Control System: A Case Study in Formal Verification. In Formal Methods and Software Engineering (ICFEM)* (pp. 246–265). Rio de Janeiro: Springer-Verlag.

Puka, E., Herrmann, P., Levin, T., & Skjetne, C. B. (2018). A Way to Measure and Analyze Cellular Network Connectivity on the Norwegian Road System. In *10th International Conference on Communication Systems & Networks (COMSNETS)* (pp. 595-600). Bengaluru: IEEE Computer. 10.1109/COMSNETS.2018.8328280

Sezer, S., & Atalay, A. E. (2011). Dynamic Modeling and Fuzzy Logic Control of Vibrations of a Railway Vehicle for Different Track Irregularities. *Simulation Modelling Practice and Theory, 19*(9), 1873–1894. doi:10.1016/j.simpat.2011.04.009

Slåtten, V., Herrmann, P., & Kraemer, F. (2013). Model-Driven Engineering of Reliable Fault-Tolerant Systems - A State-of-the-Art Survey. *Advances in Computers, 91*, 119–205. doi:10.1016/B978-0-12-408089-8.00004-5

Svae, A., Taherkordi, A., Herrmann, P., & Blech, J. O. (2017). Self-Adaptive Control in Cyber-Physical Systems: The Autonomous Train Experiment. In *32nd ACM SIGAPP Symposium On Applied Computing* (pp. 1436-1443). Marrakech, Morocco: ACM. 10.1145/3019612.3019651

Taherkordi, A., Herrmann, P., Blech, J. O., & Férnandez, Á. (2017). *Service Virtualization for Self-Adaptation in Mobile Cyber-Physical Systems. In Service-Oriented Computing - ICSOC 2016 Workshops* (pp. 56–68). Banff: Springer-Verlag.

Tiwari, A. (2015). Time-Aware Abstractions in HybridSal. In *27th International Conference on Computer Aided Verification (CAV)* (pp. 504-510). San Francisco: Springer-Verlag. 10.1007/978-3-319-21690-4_34

Tyagi, A. K. (2012). *MATLAB and Simulink for Engineers*. Oxford University Press.

ENDNOTES

[1]   Ignore for the moment the black and red real-time extensions in the markings.
[2]   We implemented a transformation to Z3 (De Moura & Bjørner, 2008).
[3]   We implemented a transformation to Sat4j: http://www.sat4j.org/.

Chapter 5
Minimum Database Determination and Preprocessing for Machine Learning

Angel Fernando Kuri-Morales
ITAM, Mexico

ABSTRACT

The exploitation of large databases implies the investment of expensive resources both in terms of the storage and processing time. The correct assessment of the data implies that pre-processing steps be taken before its analysis. The transformation of categorical data by adequately encoding every instance of categorical variables is needed. Encoding must be implemented that preserves the actual patterns while avoiding the introduction of non-existing ones. The authors discuss CESAMO, an algorithm which allows us to statistically identify the pattern preserving codes. The resulting database is more economical and may encompass mixed databases. Thus, they obtain an optimal transformed representation that is considerably more compact without impairing its informational content. For the equivalence of the original (FD) and reduced data set (RD), they apply an algorithm that relies on a multivariate regression algorithm (AA). Through the combined application of CESAMO and AA, the equivalent behavior of both FD and RD may be guaranteed with a high degree of statistical certainty.

DOI: 10.4018/978-1-5225-7268-8.ch005

INTRODUCTION

Nowadays, commercial enterprises are importantly oriented to continuously improving customer-business (CRM) relationship. With the increasing influence of CRM Systems, such companies dedicate more time and effort to maintain better customer-business relationships. The effort implied in getting to better know the customer involves the accumulation of very large data bases where the largest possible quantity of data regarding the customer is stored.

Data warehouses offer a way to access detailed information about the customer's history, business facts and other aspects of the customer's behavior. The databases constitute the information backbone for any well established company. However, from each step and every new attempted link of the company to its customers the need to store increasing volumes of data arises. Hence databases and data warehouses are always growing up in terms of number of registers and tables which will allow the company to improve the general vision of the customer.

Data warehouses are difficult to characterize when trying to analyze the customers from company's standpoint. This problem is generally approached through the use of data mining techniques (Palpanas, T., 2000; Silva, D. R., 2002; Han, J., Pei, J., & Kamber, M. 2011; Tan, P. N. 2006, Chaudhuri, S., & Dayal, U. (1997). To attempt direct clustering over a data base of several terabytes with millions of registers results in a costly and not always fruitful effort. There have been many attempts to solve this problem. For instance one may use parallel computation, optimization of clustering algorithms, alternative distributed and grid computing and so on. But still the more efficient methods are unwieldy when attacking the clustering problem for databases as considered above. In this work we present a methodology derived from the practical solution of an automated clustering process over large database from a real large sized (over 20 million customers) company. We emphasize the way we used statistical methods to reduce the search space of the problem as well as the treatment given to the customer's information stored in multiple tables of multiple databases.

Because of confidentiality issues the name of the company and the actual final results of the customer characterization are withheld.

CHAPTER OUTLINE

The outline of the chapter is as follows. First, we give an overview of the analysis of large databases; next we give an overview of the methodology we applied. We emphasize the problem of adequately pre-processing non-numerical attributes so that numerical algorithms are applicable, in general. We describe two possible methods to certify the equivalence of the original data set (the "Universe") which we denote with UD and the reduced (equivalent) data set which we denote with RD. Then we briefly discuss the case study treated with the proposed methodology. Finally, we offer our conclusions.

ANALYSIS OF LARGE DATABASES

To extract the best information of a database it is convenient to use a set of strategies or techniques which will allow us to analyze large volumes of data. These tools are generically known as data mining (DM) which targets on new, valuable, and nontrivial information in large volumes of data. It includes techniques such as clustering (which corresponds to non-supervised learning) and statistical analysis (which includes, for instance, sampling and multivariate analysis).

Clustering in Large Databases

Clustering is a popular data mining task which consist of processing a large volume of data to obtain groups where the elements of each group exhibit quantifiably (under some measure) small differences between them and, contrariwise, large dissimilarities between elements of different groups. Given its high importance as a data mining task, clustering has been the subject of multiple research efforts and has proven to be useful for many purposes (Jain, A. K., Murty, M. N., & Flynn, P. J., 1999; Steinbach, M., Karypis, G., & Kumar, V. 2000, August, Hartigan, J. A. 1975 Edgar, R. C. 2010).

Many techniques and algorithms for clustering have been developed, improved and applied (Berkhin, P., 2006; Kleinberg, J., Papadimitriou, C., & Raghavan, P., 1998; Guha, S., Rastogi, R., & Shim, K., 1998; Hartigan, J. A., & Hartigan, J. A. 1975; Jain, A. K., Murty, M. N., & Flynn, P. J. 1999). Some of them try to ease the process on a large database as in (Peter, W., Chiochetti, J., & Giardina, C., 2003; Ng, R. T., & Han, J., 1994; Freitas, A. A., & Lavington, S. H. 1997). On the other hand, the so-called "Divide and Merge" (Cheng, D., Kannan, R., Vempala, S., & Wang, G., 2006; DeWitt, D., & Gray, J. 1992) or "Snakes and Sandwiches" (Jagadish, H. V., Lakshmanan, L. V., & Srivastava, D., 1999) methods refer to clustering attending to the physical storage of the records comprising data warehouses. Another strategy to work with a large database is based upon the idea of working with statistical sampling optimization (Liu, H., & Motoda, H., 2012; Olken, F., & Rotem, D. 1995).

Sampling and Feature Selection

Sampling is a statistical method to select a certain number of elements from a population to be included in a sample. There exist two sampling types: probabilistic and nonprobabilistic. For each of these categories there exists a variety of sub methods. The probabilistic better known ones include: a) Random sampling, b) Systematic sampling and c) Stratified sampling. On the other hand the nonprobabilistic ones include methods such as convenience sampling, judgment sampling and quota sampling. There are many ways to select the elements from a data set and some of them are discussed in (Zhu, X., & Wu, X., 2006). This field of research, however, continues to be an open one (Brighton, H., & Mellish, C., 2002; Vu, K., Hua, K. A., Cheng, H., & Lang, S. D., 2006; Toivonen, H. 1996, September).

The use of sampling for data mining has received some criticism since there is always a possibility that such sampling may hamper a clustering algorithm's capability to find small clusters appearing in the original data. However, small clusters are not always significant; such is the case of costumer clusters. Since the main objective of the company is to find significant and, therefore, large customer clusters, a small cluster that may not be included in a sample is not significant for CRM.

Apart from the sampling theory needed to properly reduce the search space, we need to perform feature selection to achieve desirable smaller dimensionality. In this regard we point out that feature selection has been the main object of many researches (Zhang, D., Zhou, Z. H., & Chen, S., 2007; Fodor, I. K., 2002; Skalak, D. B. 1994, February), and these had resulted in a large number of methods and algorithms (Hair, J. F., 1999). One such method is "multivariate analysis". This is a scheme (as treated here) which allows us to synthesize a functional relation between a dependent and two or more independent variables. There are many techniques to perform a multivariate analysis. For instance: multivariate regression analysis, principal component analysis, variance and covariance analysis, canonical correlation analysis, etc. (Delmater, R., & Hancock, M., 2001; Johnson, R. A., & Wichern, D. W. 2014)). Here we focus on the explicit determination of a functional which minimizes the resulting approximation error while minimizing its standard error. This approach requires a general and efficient tool for model generation, as will be discussed in the sequel.

CASE STUDY

A data mining project was conducted for a very large multi-national company (one of the largest in the world) hereinafter referred to as the "Company". The Company has several databases with information about its different customers, including data about services contracted, services' billing (registered over a period of several years) and other pertinent characterization data. The Company offers a large variety of services to millions of users in several countries. Its databases are stored on several large tables. In our study we applied a specific data mining tool (which we will refer to as "the miner") which works directly on the database. We also developed a set of auxiliary programs intended to help in data pre-processing.

The actual customer information that was necessary for the clustering process was extracted from multiple databases in the Company. Prior to the data mining process, the Company's experts conducted an analysis of the different existent databases and selected the more important variables and associated data related to the project's purpose: to identify those customers amenable to become ad hoc clients for new products under development and others to be developed specifically from the results of the study. Due to the variety of platforms and databases, such process of selection and collection of relevant information took several months and several hundred man-hours.

The resulting database displayed a table structure that contains information about the characteristics of the customers, products or services contracted for the customer and monthly billing data over a one year period.

To test the working methodology the project team worked with a set of 12,000,000 customer's registers, consisting of a total of 118 variables per register.

Methodology

In order to ensure the reliability of the results, the following steps were taken:

1. Data analysis
2. Pre-processing
3. Programming language selection
4. Categorical variable encoding
5. Calculation of smallest equivalent sample
6. Seasonality analysis

In what follows we brieflys describe every step.

Data Analysis

In this step databases (DB) are filtered in order to eliminate deficiencies and/or limitations which may render them inconvenient for later analysis .

The DB is searched to detect:

1. Possible design and/or input errors.
2. Erroneous data types
3. Inadequate numerical type
4. Excessive numerical precision
5. Insufficient numerical precision
6. Variables with only one value
7. Variables with too many values
8. Outliers

Pre-Processing

In this phase, we subject the original data set to a series of possible transformations which greatly enhance the chances of a successful modeling of the phenomenon under analysis. The DB is processed to:

1. Identify and properly encode categorical variables. This step is important since most of the clustering algorithms operate on numerical data. On the other hand, many (if not most) of the databases include categorical data. Unless such data is properly encoded either (a) Valuable information may be lost and/or (b) Spurious patterns may be introduced and/or valid patterns may be obliterated. A more detailed discussion of this may be found in what follows.
2. Complete missing values. It is common to disregard unknown values. In many cases, such gaps in the data are filled-in with average values or moving averages. Another alternative is to obtain the natural spline for every variable and use it to interpolate missing values.
3. Stabilize potentially dangerous values which display linear dependence and may seriously hamper the models resulting from the data analysis.
4. Homogenize the data range of the data by scaling all the elements of its objects into the same value.
5. Eliminate temporal tendencies which tend to complicate and, in some extreme cases, mislead the clustering algorithms.

In every one of these steps it is, of course, necessary to store the values of the intervening parameters so as to be able recover the original data from the processed data. For example, the limit values of the scaled variables, the original and offset data from the tendency removal and so on.

Programming Language Selection

Originally we planned to use a general purpose algorithmic language. However, because the Company made extensive use of SAS® (Statistical Analysis System) which is an integrated software product which allows the efficient manipulation of DBs and includes a set of auxiliary utilities, it was selected as the main development tool. It does, however, have certain limitations as a programming tool which were circumvented by writing a set of special routines in a lower level language. The original DBs were originally stored in an Oracle® environment from which they were then migrated to SAS.

Right from the start the design of two basic utilities was considered: a) Calculation of the entropy in a subset of the original (called "U") DB to determine the minimum number of objects which preserved the information in U (called "M"). b) Testing of a large enough set of experimental probability distributions to determine the distribution equivalence between the pairs of variables in U and those in M.

Categorical Variable Encoding

Structured data bases may include both numerical and non-numerical attributes (categorical or CA). Databases which include CAs are called "mixed" databases (MD). Metric clustering algorithms are ineffectual when presented with MDs because, in such algorithms, the similarity between the objects is determined in accordance with some predefined metric. However, in the context of categorical databases no metric applies directly to the instances of a given category. For example, it makes no sense to try to determine (say from the attribute "color-of-the-eyes") whether the instance "green" is more like the instance "blue" than the instance "black" is to the instance "brown". Nevertheless, the information contained in the CAs of MDs is fundamental to understand and identify the patterns therein.

A vast majority of the clustering algorithms used in practice are restricted to working with numerical fields. Five classical ones, for example, are a) Average Linkage Clustering, b) Complete Linkage Clustering, c) Single Linkage Clustering, d) Within Groups Clustering, e) Ward's Method (Norusis, M. 2008). Alternative methods, based on computational intelligence, are f) K-Means, g) Fuzzy C-Means, h) Self-Organizing Maps, i) Fuzzy Learning Vector Quantization (Goebel, M., & Gruenwald, L. 1999). All of these methods have been designed to tackle the analysis of strictly numerical databases, i.e. those in which all the attributes are directly expressible as numbers.

In our DB, however, some of the fields were categorical (i.e. not expressible as by numbers). If any of the attributes is categorical none of the methods in the list is applicable. Clustering of categorical attributes is a difficult, yet important task:

many fields, from statistics to psychology deal with categorical data. Much of the published algorithms to cluster categorical data rely on the usage of a distance metric that captures the separation between two vectors of categorical attributes, such as the Jaccard coefficient (Sokal, R. R. 1985). An interesting alternative is explored in (Barbará, D., Li, Y., & Couto, J. 2002, November) where COOLCAT, a method which uses the notion of entropy to group records, is presented. It is based on information loss minimization. Another reason for the limited exploration of categorical clustering techniques is its inherent difficulty.

Encoding the instances of categorical variables with a number is, by no means, a new concept. MDs, however, offer a particular challenge when clustering is attempted because it is, in principle, impossible to impose a metric on CAs. There is no way in which numerical codes may be assigned to the CAs in general.

Pseudo-Binary Encoding

In what follows we denote the i instances of categorical variable c as ci; the number of categorical variables with c; the number of all attributes by n. A common choice is to replace every CA variable by a set of binary variables, each corresponding to the cis. The CAs in the MD are replaced by numerical ones where every categorical variable is replaced by a set of ci binary numerical codes. An MD will be replaced by an ND with $n-c+c \cdot ci$ variables. This is illustrated inTtable 1.

On the left three columns of Table 1 the original values are shown (the two leftmost are categorical; the rightmost is numerical). On the remaining 9 rightmost columns variable "buying" has been replaced by pseudo-binary variables f01_01, f01_02, f01_03 and f01_04. Each of these corresponds to the 4 different instances. Likewise, variable "maint(enance)" has been split into f02_01, f02_02, f02_03, f02_04. Finally, variable "doors" (which is outright numerical) has been retained "as is".

This approach avoids the problems associated to the naive strategy of assigning arbitrary numbers to the instances but suffers from the following limitations:

1. The number of attributes of ND will be larger than that of MD. In many cases this leads to unwieldy databases which are more difficult to store and handle.
2. The type of coding system selected implies an *a priori* choice since all pseudo-binary variables may be assigned any two values (typically "0" denotes "absence"; "1" denotes "presence"). This choice is subjective. Any two different values are possible. Nevertheless, the mathematical properties of ND will vary with the different choices, thus leading to clusters which depend on the way in which "presence" or "absence" is encoded.

Figure 1.

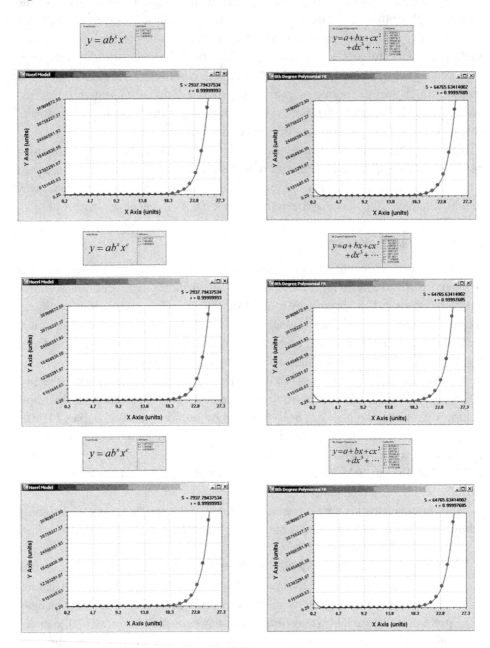

Table 1. Pseudo-binary encoding of categorical variables

buying	maint	doors	f01_01	f01_02	f01_03	f01_04	f02_01	f02_02	f02_03	f02_04	doors
vhigh	vhigh	2	0	0	0	1	0	0	0	1	2
vhigh	low	4	0	0	0	1	1	0	0	0	4
vhigh	low	2	0	0	0	1	1	0	0	0	2
high	vhigh	2	0	1	0	0	0	0	0	1	2
low	high	5	0	0	1	0	0	1	0	0	5
vhigh	high	2	0	0	0	1	0	0	0	1	2
vhigh	vhigh	2	0	0	0	1	0	0	0	1	2

3. Finally, with this sort of scheme the pseudo-binary variables do no longer reflect the essence of the idea conveyed by a category. A variable corresponding to the *i-th* instance of the category reflects the way a tuple is "affected" by belonging to the *i-th* categorical value, which is correct. But now the original issue "How does the behavior of the individuals change according to the category?" is replaced by "How does the behavior of the individuals change when the category's value is the *i-th*?" The two questions are not interchangeable.

Pattern Preserving Codes

A practical alternative is to encode the instances of the CAs numerically. To do this we must consider the fact that there is a limited subset of codes which will preserve the patterns in the MD. To identify such pattern-preserving codes (PPC) we appeal to a statistical methodology. It is possible to statistically identify a set of PPCs by selectively sampling a bounded number of codes (corresponding to the different instances of the CAs) and demanding the method to set the size of the sample dynamically. Two issues have to be considered for this method to be defined in practice: a) How to set the size of the sample and 2) How to define the adequateness of the codes.

A note is in order: the PPCs are NOT to be assumed as an instance applicable to DBs other than the original one. That is to say: a set of PPCs (say PPC1) obtained from a DB (say DB1) is not applicable to a different DB (say DB2) even if DB1 and DB2 are structurally identical. In other words, PPC1 ≠ PPC2 for the same DB when the tuples of such DB are different,

Consider a set of *n*-dimensional tuples (say *U*) whose cardinality is *m*. Assume there are *n* unknown functions of *n-1* variables each, which we denote with

$$f_k(v_1,...,v_{k-1},v_{k+1},...,v_n); k=1,...,n$$

Let us also assume that there is a method which allows us to approximate f_k (from the tuples) with F_k. Denote the resulting n functions of n-1 independent variables with F_i, thus

$$F_k \approx f(v_1,...,v_{k-1},v_{k+1},...,v_n); \; k=1,...,n \tag{1}$$

The difference between f_k and F_k will be denoted with ε_k such that, for attribute k and the m tuples in the database

$$\varepsilon_k = max \; [\; abs(f_{ki} - F_{ki})] \; ; \; i=1,...,m \tag{2}$$

Our contention is that the PPCs are the ones which minimize ε_k for all k. This is so because only those codes which retain the relationships between variable k and the remaining n-1 variables AND do this for ALL variables in the ensemble will preserve the whole set of relations (i.e. patterns) present in the data base, as in (3).

$$\varXi = min[\; max \; (\varepsilon_k \; ; \; k=1,...,n)] \tag{3}$$

Notice that this is a multi-objective optimization problem because complying with condition k in (2) for any given value of k may induce the non-compliance for a different possible k. Using the min-max expression of (3) equates to selecting a particular point in Pareto's front (Deb, K., Agrawal, S., Pratap, A., & Meyarivan, T. 2000, September). To achieve the purported goal we must have a tool which is capable of identifying the F_k's in (1) and the codes which attain the minimization of (3).

To this purpose w designed a new algorithm (called "CESAMO": Categorical Encoding by Statistical Applied Modeling) which relies on statistical and numerical considerations.

Here we denote the number of tuples in the DB by t and the number of categorical attributes by c; the number of numerical attributes by n; the i-th categorical variable by vi; the value obtained for variable i as a function of variable j by yi(j).

We will sample the codes yielding yi as a function of a sought for relationship. This relationship and the model of the population it implies will be selected so as to preserve the behavioral patterns embedded in the DB.

Two issues are of primordial importance in the proposed methodology:

1. How to define the function which will preserve the patterns.
2. How to determine the number of codes to sample.

Regarding (1), we use a mathematical model considering high order relations, as will be discussed below. Regarding (2), we know that, independently of the distribution of the yi's, the distribution of the means of the samples of yi (yi_{AVG}) will become Gaussian. Once the distribution of the yi_{AVG} becomes Gaussian, we will have achieved statistical stability, in the sense that further sampling of the yi's will not significantly modify the characterization of the population.

In essence, therefore, what we propose is to sample enough codes to guarantee the statistical stability of the values calculated from $yi \leftarrow f(vj)$. If f(vj) is adequately chosen the codes corresponding to the best approximation will be those inserted in MD. Furthermore, CESAMO relies on a double level sampling: only pairs of variables are considered and every pair is, in itself, sampling the multivariate space. This avoids the need to explicitly solve the multi-objective optimization underlying problem. The clustering problem may be, then, numerically tackled.

The CESAMO Algorithm

The general algorithm for CESAMO is as follows:

- Specify the mixed database MD.
- Specify the sample size (*ss*)
- MD is analyzed to determine n, t and $ci(i)$ for $i=1,...,c$.
- The numerical data are assumed to have been mapped into [0,1). Therefore, every ci will be, likewise, in
  - [0,1).

Box 1.

```
1. for i ← 1 to c
2. Do until the distribution of yi_AVG is Gaussian
3. Randomly select variable j (j ≠i)
 4. Assign random values to all instances of vi.
 5. yi_AVG ← 0
6. For k ←1 to ss
7. yi ← f(vj)
8. yi_AVG ← yi_AVG+yi
9. endfor
 10. yi_AVG = yi_AVG/ss
 11. enddo
 12. Select the codes corresponding to the best value of yi
13. endfor
```

Notice that vj may be, itself, categorical. In that cases every categorical instance of vj is replaced by random codes so that we may calculate $f(vj)$.

One of the key points of CESAMO is how to define the functional relation specified in step 7 (i.e. $yi \leftarrow f(vj)$). This selection defines the way in which our intent of preserving the patterns in the data is understood. In our experiments we set, in a first instance, $yi \leftarrow r(vj)$ where $r(vj)$ denotes Pearson correlation (Benesty, J., Chen, J., Huang, Y., & Cohen, I. 2009). In a second instance we set $yi \leftarrow P_{11}(x) \sim \beta_0 + \sum_{i=1}^{6} \beta_i x^{2i-1}$ as a universal polynomial approximation. In (Kuri-Morales, A., & Cartas-Ayala, A. 2014, May) it was shown that any continuous function may be approximately realized with a linear combination of monomials which has a constant plus terms of odd degree. In the case of $r(vj)$ we may preserve only linear relationships, whereas in the case of $P_{11}(x)$ the relationships are not limited *a priori*. The β_i of $P_{11}(x)$ were found with the so-called *Ascent Algorithm* (AA) (Cheney, E. W., 1966). The codes obtained from AA are called *functional* codes.

The Ascent Algorithm

The purpose of this algorithm is to express the behavior of a dependent variable (y) as a function of a set of n independent variables (v).

$$y = f(v_1, v_2, ..., v_n)$$
$$y = f(\mathbf{v}) \tag{4}$$

The approximant is defined to have the following form:

$$y = c_1 X_1 + c_2 X_2 + ... + c_m X_m \tag{5}$$

X_i denotes a combination of the independent variables. That is, $X_i = f_i(v)$. According to the way these combinations are defined one may obtain different approximants. The method assumes that there is a sample of size N such that for every set of the independent variables v there is a known value of the dependent variable f, as illustrated in figure 2; we call the i-th element of the sample its i-th object. By convention N stands for the number of objects in the sample and $M=m+1$ (m = number of desired terms of the approximant).

The goal of the Ascent Algorithm (AA) is to find the values of the coefficients in (5) such that the approximated values minimize the difference between the known values of the dependent variable f in the sample and those calculated from (5) for all the objects in the sample. We define the approximation error as

Figure 2. A data sample

v1	v2	v3	v4	v5	f
0.2786	0.2319	0.5074	0.9714	0.5584	0.4938
0.2429	0.4855	1.0000	0.8429	0.4416	0.8580
0.4929	0.9710	0.8676	1.0000	0.7411	0.9136
0.8429	1.0000	0.4485	0.9143	1.0000	0.8704
0.4357	0.9130	0.8309	0.6500	0.8579	0.7037

$\varepsilon_{MAX} = max\left(\varepsilon_1, ..., \varepsilon_m\right)$ where $\varepsilon_i = abs(f_i - y_i)$. Here f_i stands for the value of the dependent variable of object i and yi stands for the value which the approximant yields when the X_i are put into (5). The AA is based on a two-phase iterative methodology. First, a subset of the sample (of size M) is selected (this is called the inner set) and the best approximant (a set of coefficients) in the minimax sense is found. Second, the approximant is tested to see whether $y=f(X)$ satisfies the minimax norm for the remaining $N-M$ objects (this set of cardinality $N-M$ is called the outer set) of the sample. That is the yi are calculated for the external set. If the minimax condition is attained by all the objects the algorithm ends: the coefficients are those of the best possible approximant. If at least one of the objects in the outer set does not comply with the minimax condition then an object of the inner set is swapped with an object in the outer set and the process is repeated. In every step of the process there are two errors of interest:

The largest absolute approximation error of the internal set [denoted by $\varepsilon_\theta(t)$]
The largest absolute approximation error of the external set [denoted by $\varepsilon_\varphi(t)$]

$\varepsilon_\theta(t)$ is calculated during phase 1; $\varepsilon_\varphi(t)$ is calculated during phase 2. The convergence condition is that $\varepsilon_\theta(t) \geq \varepsilon_\varphi(t)$. It may be shown that $\varepsilon_\theta(t+1) > \varepsilon_\theta(t)$ monotonically and that $\varepsilon_\varphi(t+1) < \varepsilon_\varphi(t)$ non-monotonically. Therefore, they approach each other and the convergence condition is always reached.

This algorithm was chosen because, as opposed to other approximation algorithms (Moré, J. J., 1978; Powell, M. J., 1978), it does not necessitate the full data set to be in memory during the process. This characteristic makes it ideal when potentially large sets of data (as in this case) make it unwieldy or even downright impossible to guarantee the access to large amounts of data in the memory of the computer.

Experimental Example

We illustrate the method with a simple DB (MD1) illustrated in Figure 3.

Box 2.

The Ascent Algorithm
1. Input the data vectors (call them **D**).
2. Input the degrees of each of the variables of the approximating polynomial.
3. Map the original data vectors into the powers of the selected monomials (call them **P**).
4. Stabilize the vectors of **P** by randomly disturbing the original values as above (call the resulting data **S**).
5. Select a subset of size M from **S**. Call it **I**. Call the remaining vectors **E**.
BOOTSTRAP
6. Obtain the minimax signs (call the matrix incorporating the σ's **A**).
7. Obtain the inverse of **A** (call it **B**).
LOOP
8. Calculate the coefficients **C** = **f B**. The maximum internal ε_θ error is also calculated.
9. Calculate the maximum external error ε_φ from **C** and **E**. Call its index I_E
10. $\varepsilon_\theta \geq \varepsilon_\varphi$?
YES: Stop; the coefficients of **C** are those of the minimax polynomial for the **D** vectors.
11. Calculate the λ vector from $» = A^{I_E} B$
12. Calculate the **β** vector which maximizes $\sigma_{I_E} \dfrac{\lambda_j}{B_j}$. Call its index I_I.
13. Interchange vectors I_E and I_I.
14. Calculate the new inverse $\overline{\mathbf{B}}$. Make $\mathbf{B} \leftarrow \overline{\mathbf{B}}$.
15. Go to step 8.

Figure 3. Mixed data base 1 (MD1)

V001	V002	V003	V004	V005	V006	V007	V008	V009
0.260522524543	0.509411653392	0.700915045452	0.707703920124	PITTSBURG	0.943069973963	0.238061468236	0.138019787167	E
0.407041640749	0.637258876341	0.789221078153	0.556251922946	ZINNEON	0.708160858038	0.421635467433	0.007609086010	E
0.535205277140	0.731028964609	0.848474125909	0.429007103398	JONESVILLE	0.961372002944	0.044127392958	0.101728142478	F
0.126772292602	0.354737576201	0.577610777361	0.852891723761	ZINNEON	0.627321987848	0.334048866287	0.057648763948	E
0.469300405853	0.684411776614	0.819523265893	0.493880044410	MAYNE	0.896687346346	0.279710631585	0.103735589373	F
0.877291352488	0.936508870108	0.966276475038	0.108861371866	QUINCE	0.323149913797	0.719992235632	0.223451376457	D
0.592027568409	0.768962277686	0.871359035707	0.373968296977	MAYNE	0.942230907053	0.026164386062	0.083310044031	A
0.933211797131	0.965959479230	0.982056648825	0.058890803985	JONESVILLE	0.993506894522	0.168548211151	0.169576293996	D

It consists of 9 variables. Two of them V005 and V009 are categorical. The rest are numerical. V005 has 10 instances: PITTSBURG, ZINNEON, JONESVILLE, MAYNE, QUINCE, NEW YORK, ILLINOIS, FLORIANOPOLIS, VIENNA, BEIRUT; V009 has 6 instances: A, B, C, D, E, F.

Functional Approximation

We select an approximation function of 11th degree. Continuous data may be thusly approximated and its main components retained. The codes obtained from high degree approximation are shown in Figure 4.

Once the database has been populated by the numerical codes (that is, when every instance of every categorical variable is replaced by the numerical code) we may calculate Pearson´s correlation matrix as shown in Figure 5.

The variables display the expected of first order relations. That is, with 90% confidence, variables V001, V002 and V003 are equivalent. As, with the same confidence, are variables V006 and V007.

For the relations of order 3 codes (ie. exploring the third degree approximation) in a) Pearson's and b) Functional codes we find the next scenario (shown in Figure 6). Pearson's correlation misses third degree functional relations for variables V003 and V004. Likewise, (as shown in Figure 7), 7th degree relations are hidden from Pearson's encoding but not so for Functional encoding. Note that in the cases illustrated in Figures 6, 7 and 8 functional relations are restricted to those of degree

Figure 4. Categorical codes for 11th degree approximation

V005		V009	
Instance	Code	Instance	Code
ILLINOIS	0.43963343	A	0.88517244
BEIRUT	0.44122174	B	0.60492887
NEW YORK	0.26234098	C	0.40085276
JONESVILLE	0.51601808	D	0.6773322
FLORIANOPOLIS	0.42692392	E	0.92045191
MAYNE	0.63528312	F	0.51587932
PITTSBURG	0.8265257		
QUINCE	0.20145042		
VIENNA	0.64382076		
ZINNEON	0.60366524		

Figure 5. Pearson´s correlation matrix for 11th degree relation codes

	V001	V002	V003	V004	V005	V006	V007	V008	V009
V001	1.0000000000	0.9667892446	0.8983654887	-.9992139571	0.0592971389	-.0272705682	0.0340336531	-.0355132100	-.0075227681
V002	0.9667892446	1.0000000000	0.9784369164	-.9753008217	0.0582771788	-.0207185062	0.0298000972	-.0416465760	-.0116309639
V003	0.8983654887	0.9784369164	1.0000000000	-.9120617615	0.0589621759	-.0137345053	0.0243521074	-.0439454471	-.0093939537
V004	-.9992139571	-.9753008217	-.9120617615	1.0000000000	-.0586083162	0.0261284578	-.0333133847	0.0367530663	0.0089823674
V005	0.0592971389	0.0582771788	0.0589621759	-.0586083162	1.0000000000	0.0398152441	-.0263511824	-.0098329750	0.0358562580
V006	-.0272705682	-.0207185062	-.0137345053	0.0261284578	0.0398152441	1.0000000000	-.9692992222	-.6085091576	0.0430063404
V007	0.0340336531	0.0298000972	0.0243521074	-.0333133847	-.0263511824	-.9692992222	1.0000000000	0.5691163152	-.0493044161
V008	-.0355132100	-.0416465760	-.0439454471	0.0367530663	-.0098329750	-.6085091576	0.5691163152	1.0000000000	-.0483248681
V009	-.0075227681	-.0116309639	-.0093939537	0.0089823674	0.0358562580	0.0430063404	-.0493044161	-.0483248681	1.0000000000

Figure 6. First order dependencies

Significance %								
90								

Correlated Variables								
	V001	V002	V003	V004	V005	V006	V007	V008	V009
V001	X		X					
V002		X	X					
V003			X					
V004								
V005								
V006						X		
V007								
V008								
V009								

1, 3 and 7, respectively. That is, the codes were obtained by sampling approximation errors for polynomial expressions of degrees 1, 3 and 7 only, respectively.

However, when functional codes consider all combinations of the powers of the function (that is, approximations of up to degree 11 were calculated), we get the matrix illustrated in Figure 9. Notice that the values in Figure 9 all lie in the interval between 0 and 1. A "1" signals zero approximation error and "0" signifies maximum approximation error. Clearly we may not guarantee that the AA will yield perfect approximation. Nevertheless, to be consistent with the values obtained from

Figure 7. Relations of degree 3 for a) Pearson's codes and b) functional codes

	V001	V002	V003	V004	V005	V006	V007	V008	V009
V001		X	X	X	X	X	X	X	X
V002	X		X	X	X	X	X	X	X
V003									
V004									
V005									
V006									
V007									
V008									
V009									

	V001	V002	V003	V004	V005	V006	V007	V008	V009
V001		X	X	X	X	X	X	X	X
V002	X		X	X	X	X	X	X	X
V003				X					
V004									
V005									
V006									
V007									
V008									
V009									

Figure 8. Relations of degree 7 for a) Pearson´s codes and b) functional codes

	V001	V002	V003	V004	V005	V006	V007	V008	V009
V001									
V002									
V003									
V004									
V005									
V006									
V007									
V008									
V009									

	V001	V002	V003	V004	V005	V006	V007	V008	V009
V001		X	X	X	X	X	X	X	X
V002	X		X	X	X	X	X	X	X
V003				X					
V004									
V005									
V006									
V007									
V008									
V009									

Pearson´s correlation (where "1" denotes perfect direct linear relation) and, more importantly, to eliminate outliers, we proceeded as follows.

1. The mean ($avg(AE)$) and standard deviation ($std(AE)$) of the approximation errors (AE_i) were calculated.
2. We know (from Chebyshev´s inequality (Saw, J. G., Yang, M. C., & Mo, T. C., 1984) that no more than a certain fraction of values can be more than a certain distance from the mean. Specifically, at least $1 - 1/k^2$ of the distribution's values are within k standard deviations of the mean. Hence, for $k=\sqrt{5}$ (assuming a symmetrical distribution) more than 90% of the observed approximation errors will lbe larger than $avg(AE) - \sqrt{5}\ std(AE)$. Consequently we set the minimum value AE_{min} = avg(AE)-$\sqrt{5}\ std(AE)$. Likewise, we set AE_{max} = $avg(AE)$+ $\sqrt{5}$ $std(AE)$.
3. Scan all the approximation errors. If the error is smaller than AE_{min} underclip the value (the calculated error is replaced by AE_{min}); if the error is larger than AE_{max} overclip the value (the calculated error is replaced by AE_{max}). This step aims at eliminating outliers.
4. Map the clipped values into [0,1). AE_{0-1} =$(AE_i$-$AE_{min})/(AE_{max}$-$AE_{min})$.
5. AE_i = 1-AE_{0-1}. Values close to "1" mean approximation error is small (data is highly correlated).

It is the lack of simple relation of the variables remarked (with circles) which makes this case more interesting. For what we may see is that V001 and V009 have no detectable complex relations between them. That is the case for V003 and V009; V004 and V008 and so on. Notice also that this means that, for instance, V003 may not be expressed as a function of V009 but V009 may indeed be expressed as a function of V003. The preservation of these higher order relationships is what we mean by preserving the patterns in the data.

Figure 9. Matrix of relations for full power combinations

	V001	V002	V003	V004	V005	V006	V007	V008	V009
V001	1.0000000000	0.5351914557	0.5351914578	0.5351915232	0.5347595189	0.5351898425	0.5351871862	0.5351152174	0.2546840427
V002	0.5351805544	1.0000000000	0.5351862603	0.5351810995	0.5350538593	0.5351529387	0.5351530274	0.5317462920	0.5351522602
V003	0.5351037593	0.5351600780	1.0000000000	0.5351029048	0.5350206518	0.5350271954	0.5350221373	0.5098745497	0.4978701143
V004	0.5351915053	0.5351913809	0.5351910977	1.0000000000	0.5346712155	0.5351893965	0.5351573240	0.3457246016	0.0000000000
V005	0.5342934150	0.5342906928	0.5342924304	0.5342849135	1.0000000000	0.5342953904	0.5343094442	0.5342968509	0.5339350270
V006	0.5340588345	0.5340522215	0.5340606606	0.5340572362	0.5340503747	1.0000000000	0.5351446651	0.4881534669	0.5339557111
V007	0.5342328419	0.5342165796	0.5342032238	0.5342168610	0.5342194780	0.5348306875	1.0000000000	0.5151432500	0.5340178212
V008	0.5341517901	0.5342171171	0.5341199116	0.5340589879	0.5316718687	0.5351294259	0.5347265164	1.0000000000	0.5341438147
V009	0.5341523831	0.5341537751	0.5341471788	0.5341423750	0.5335682371	0.5341595085	0.5341553888	0.5341529202	1.0000000000

Figure 10. Independent variables

	V001	V002	V003	V004	V005	V006	V007	V008	V009
V001		X	X	X	X	X	X	X	◯
V002	X		X	X	X	X	X	X	X
V003	X	X		X	X	X	X	X	◯
V004	X	X	X		X	X	X	◯	◯
V005	X	X	X	X		X	X	X	X
V006	X	X	X	X	X		X	◯	X
V007	X	X	X	X	X	X		X	X
V008	X	X	X	X	X	X	X		X
V009	X	X	X	X	X	X	X	X	

Calculation of Smallest Equivalent Sample

To now reduce the search space we work with the original data to obtain a sample which is not merely a subspace but, rather, one that properly represents the original (full) set of data. We reduce the set both horizontally (reducing the number of tuples) and vertically (reducing the number of attributes) to obtain the "minable view". Simultaneous reduction - horizontal and vertical - yields the smallest representation of the original data set. Vertical reduction is possible from traditional statistical methods, while horizontal reduction, basically, consists of finding the best possible sample. The following subsections discuss how we performed both reductions.

Vertical Reduction

To perform vertical reduction, multivariate analysis is required. There exist many methods to reduce the original number of variables. Here we simply used Pearson's correlation coefficients. An exploration for correlated variables was performed over the original data. We calculated a correlation matrix for the 118 variables. We considered (after consulting with the experts) that those variables exhibiting a correlation factor equal or larger than 0.85 were redundant. Hence, from the original 118 variables only 73 remained as informationally interesting. In principle, out of a set of correlated variables only one is needed for clustering purposes. Which of these is to be retained is irrelevant; in fact, we wrote a program which simply performed a sequential binary search to select the (uncorrelated) variables to be retained.

$$H(X) = \sum_{i=1}^{m} \left(-p_i \log(p_i)\right)$$

$$H(X) \approx \sum_{i=1}^{m} \left(\sum_{j=1}^{n} \frac{'(S_i, v_j)}{n} \right) \log \left(\sum_{i=1}^{m} \frac{'(S_i, v_j)}{n} \right) \tag{6}$$

where X is the message, p_i is the probability of occurrence of symbol i. m is the number of symbols, n is the number of data elements, S_i is the i-th symbol value and v_j is the j-th data value and

$$'(s, v) = \begin{cases} 0 & if \quad v \neq s \\ 1 & if \quad v = s \end{cases} \tag{7}$$

We approximate the population's entropy by that of a properly selected sample to avoid accessing the full DB. The method consists of treating every attribute t to obtain a sample M_t, as follows. Initially M_t is empty. Then we proceed to extract randomly (uniform) selected elements of the population for attribute t iteratively and adding these elements to M_t. On each iteration i, the entropy is calculated and compared with the one of the previous iteration as follows

$$\Delta H(i)=H(i)-H(i-1) \tag{8}$$

As $\Delta H(i)$ becomes closer to a threshold parameter ε the entropy of M_t is asymptotically closer to the population's entropy as illustrated in Figure 11.

At this point the size $|M_t|$ has been determined. The value of ε is set by the user (we set $\varepsilon=0.0001$). This process is illustrated in Figure 12.

This process is performed on every attribute. Once the M_t's have been calculated then the overall sample size M is the largest one, thus ensuring the proper representativeness for all attributes.

Sample Validation

To further attest to the validity of any possible sample of size $|M|$, we must ensure that their entropies have the same or larger value than the one calculated before. Making use of the information available, a simple non parametric Monte Carlo test may be applied (Tu, D., 2006) to validate the entropy preservation on each variable.

It test should confirm the null hypothesis $H0: H(X) \leq Hc(X)$ where $H(X)$ is the value of the maximum entropy obtained from the sample size and $Hc(X)$ is the

Figure 11. Entropy dynamics on different sample sizes

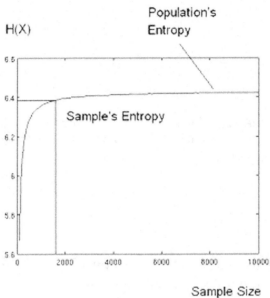

entropy of any sample of size IMI. The test consists of the generation of a set of samples of size IMI. If we set a confidence level of 95%, then at least 95% of the samples must be consistent with the null hypothesis, proving that the samples do comply. If the test is not passed then the sample size should be increased. In strict sense, to validate the preservation of the all patterns and relations, multivariate tests of high order should explored. Nevertheless, a mathematical model may be calculated to estimate the value of an arbitrary attribute as a function of another, also arbitrarily selected. We take advantage of SAS's ease in fitting data to mathematical models. We defined a set of 36 test models (a partial list is shown in Table 2). Every model can be evaluated on data from different samples. We calculate the approximation L_2 error for polynomial P, where $P(Xi)=Yi+e$. Where Xi, Yi are the values of the i-th value of the attributes and e is the L_2 approximation error on that data value. This error is defined as: $e = \sum \left(P(X_i) - Y_i\right)^2$. If the sample preserves all the couples' relations then the approximation error should be close on every sample. We calculate the ratio $r = e_{max}/e_{min}$. r must be close to 1 if the approximation errors are similar. A sample could be rejected if $r > 1+\gamma$ (where γ's value is determined by the user). This analysis should be applied to every couple to determine whether to accept or increase IMI.

Once M has been validated we are statistically certain that a clustering algorithm operated on it will yield similar results as if it were applied to the original database.

Figure 12. Incremental entropy calculation

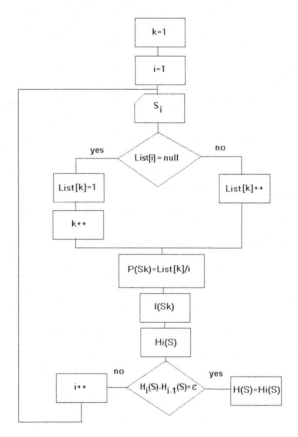

Several functions resulting from paired variables did yield similar regressive fits. For the entire set very similar remarks do apply. The self-regressive correlation coefficient in all cases is better than 0.93 indicating the very high quality of the fit. Hence, we rest assured that all samples display statistically significant equivalence. For different couples we obtain best fit with *different* models. For example, $[(ab+cx^d)/(b+x^d)]$ *(MMF)* for couple 1; $(a+bx+cx^2+dx^3+ex^4)$ (4th degree polynomial) for couple 2 and $[(a+bx)/(1+cx+dx^2)]$ (rational function) for couple 3. This fact reinforces our expectation that different variables distribute differently even though the samples behave equivalently. A hypothetical possibility which is ruled out from this behavior is that all variables were similarly distributed. If this were the case, then ALL models would behave similarly and no significant conclusion could be derived from our observations.

It may be argued, upon first analysis, that the high correlation coefficients contradict the fact that our variables derive from the elimination of such correlation.

Table 2. Evaluated regression models

Model	Equation
Linear	$y = a + bx$
Quadratic	$y = a + bx + cx^2$
nth Order Polynomial	$y = a + bx + cx^2 + dx^3 + ...$
Exponential	$y = ae^{bx}$
Modified Exponential	$y = ae^{b/x}$
Logarithm	$y = a + b \ln x$
Reciprocal Log	$y = \dfrac{1}{a + b \ln x}$
Vapor Pressure Model	$y = e^{a + b/x + c \ln x}$
Power	$y = ax^b$
Modified Power	$y = ab^x$
Shifted Power	$y = a(x - b)^c$
Geometric	$y = ax^{bx}$
Root	$y = ab^{1/x}$
Hoerl Model	$y = ab^x x^c$
Modified Hoerl Model	$y = ab^{1/x} x^c$
Hiperbolic	$y = a + \dfrac{b}{x}$
Heat Capacity	$y = a + bx + \dfrac{c}{x^2}$
Gaussian Model	$y = \dfrac{a + bx}{1 + cx + dx^2}$

Notice, however, that even if the variables with which we worked are not correlated this non-correlation is *linear* (from Pearson) whereas the models considered here are basically "non-linear", which resolves the apparent contradiction.

The probability of displaying results as discussed by chance alone is less than 10^{-12}. We also showed that, in every case, the said characterization was similar when required and dissimilar in other cases.

Automated Sample Validation

The validation method discussed above has the limitation of being dependent on a pool of possible models, such as the ones displayed in Table 2. If the variables under consideration do not conform themselves to the proposed models the comparative behavior between UD and RD will not be adequate.

The automated process consists of the following steps:

Step 1: Select two random samples of size C_X.

Step 2: Select n_θ (see below) couples of variables (To prove that, within each sample, the behavior of the selected variables is statistically equivalent).

Step 3: Find the best regressive function of the selected couples in both samples. If the functions exhibit different behaviors (see below) then make $C\_X \leftarrow C\_X + K$ (where K is an adequate increment size selected a priori) and go to step 1.

Step 4: Perform steps 2 and 3 as long as there are more variables to evaluate.

In step 3 we programmatically analyzed, in every case, polynomial models of degrees from 2 to 8. It is well known that any analytic function may be closely approximated by a polynomial expansion, as illustrated in Figure 2.

Pairs of variables (v_1, v_2) were randomly selected and polynomials $P_k(v_2)$ of degree k were found (one for each of the two samples) such that $v_1 = P_k(v_2)$ for $k=2,...,8$. Then the best fit for each of the two samples was compared, as shown in Figure 12. The headings "VAR1" and "VAR2" indicate which variables were selected; "BESTD1" and "BESTD2" indicate the degrees of the best approximation; "ABSDIF" indicates the absolute approximation difference and "PERCDIF" the percentage difference. If the percentage difference between the polynomials of sample 1 and sample 2 was larger than 5% the samples were rejected.

In principle we should compare all variable's couples. The number of possible pairings is given by $\sum_{i=1}^{n-1} i = n(n-1)/2$. However, this (in general) implies a very large number of comparisons, with the need of the corresponding calculation of a very large number of polynomials. Therefore, we randomly selected n_θ couples of variables, where we set the proportion of variables that we wish to satisfy the minimum error criterion (which we denote with π) and the reliability of the sample (which we denote with γ). Let $N_\theta \subset N$ be the number of couples which behave as expected and n_θ its cardinality. Then $n_\theta = \pi N$. The probability P_S that in a simple of size S all the elements are in N_θ is $P_S = \dfrac{(\pi N)!(N - S)!}{N!(\pi N - S)!}$ We, therefore,

specify that $\dfrac{n_\theta!(N - S)!}{N!(n_\theta - S)!} \leq 1 - \gamma$. Then, given π and γ we may solve for the value

of S and estimate the number of couples to test. For example, for *N=500*, *π = 0.95*, *γ=.95* (N_θ =475) we have that *S=55*. That is, where an exhaustive analysis would imply solving 500 functions, sampling the indicated couples we just have to analyze 55 to ensure, with a 95% reliability that 475 of those couples would satisfy our requirement: that the two samples be similar.

The probability of displaying the results shown in Figure 13 by chance alone is less than 10^{-12}. We must stress the fact that this analysis is only possible because we were able to numerically characterize each of the subsets. Furthermore, not only characterization was proven; we also showed that, in every case, the said characterization was similar when required and dissimilar in other cases.

Figure 13. Approximation of Hoerl's Model with a Polynomial of degree 8

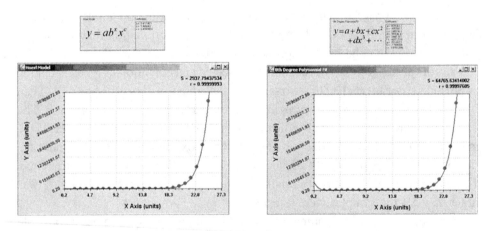

Approximation Algorithm

The algorithm which follows is based on the expression of the approximant as a linear combination of Chebyshev polynomials of the first kind (Mason, J. C., & Handscomb, D. C., 2002; Fox, L. P., 1968).

Two features of this algorithm are remarkable: (a) An approximant of degree $k+1$ may be calculated by adding a term to the approximant of degree k. That is, we do not need to re-calculate a polynomial for every successively higher degree approximation. Rather, given an approximant of degree k, we only need to calculate the new term of degree $k+1$ and add it to the yield the new approximant of degree $k+1$; and (b) The best approximation from the linear combination of Chebyshev polynomials attains the least square approximation (L_2 norm) to the data and simultaneously the best min-max (L_∞ norm) approximation. A detailed description follows.

Polynomial Approximation Algorithm

Step 1: Select the highest approximation degree d ($d=8$).

Step 2: Obtain the coefficients of the cubic natural spline. Discrete Chebyshev polynomial's orthogonality is only satisfied at the so-called orthogonality points. But the function $f(x)$ is unknown. Therefore it is approximated by a natural spline [$S(x)$] which is found in the interval [a,b]. $S(x_i) = f(x_i)$ and minimizes the curvature of the

Step 3: Order the data couples (x_i, y_i) in ascending order, keyed by x.

Step 4: Scale the n values of the x_i's into the [-1,+1] interval. This mapping is needed because Chebyshev polynomials are orthogonal in the interval [-1,+1].

Step 5: Find the number of intervals nn according to the smallest interval d_{min} from the sampled data.

$$d_{min}=\min\{d \mid x_i+1-x_i \text{ for } i=1,2,...,n-1$$

and

$$nn=\text{int}(x_{dif}/d_{min})$$

Step 6: Calculate the arguments a_i for the orthogonality points.

$$a_i = (2 \cdot ib - 1)\frac{\pi}{2nn} \text{ where } ib=nn-i+1 \text{ for } i=1,2,...,nn$$

Step 7: Calculate the orthogonality points $x_{bar}(i)$:

$x_{bar}(i) = \cos(a_i)$ for $i=1,2,...,nn$

Step 8: Interpolate from $S(x)$ the values of the dependent variable corresponding to the nn Chebyshev points.

$y_{bar}(i) \leftarrow S(x_{bar}(i))$ for $i=1,2,...,nn$

Step 9: Calculate the coefficients of the Chebyshev approximation

$T_k(x) = \cos(k \cos-1(x))$ for $k=0, 1, ..., n$

Step 10: Calculate the L_2 error for the approximating Chebyshev polynomials up to degree d. The degree of the best approximant is determined in this step.

Step 11: Calculate the coefficients of the polynomial expansion in the [-1,+1] interval.

Step 12: Calculate the coefficients of the polynomial expansion in the original interval [a,b].

In Figure 14 we illustrate the approximation for different sampled pairs of variables (denoted by VAR1 and VAR2) where *VAR1 = f(VAR2)*. We show the best degrees (i.e. those leading to the smallest fit errors) of the approximating polynomials (denoting BEST1 and BEST2), the absolute error between the VAR1 and *f(VAR2)* and the corresponding percentage difference (denoted by PERCDIF).

The advantage of this strategy over the one relying on predetermined models should be apparent. Here we are not limited by a finite reservoir of such models. Rather, the algorithm adapts itself to various data and will guarantee the determination of like behavior of the variable pairs whenever the size of the sample is adequately selected.

Seasonality

The last issue we had to consider had to do with seasonal tendencies of time-dependent variables. They add no information to the process but may induce a certain amount of numerical instability to the models. We Illustrate the fact in Figure 15 and Figure

Figure 14. Comparison of best polynomial approximations in two samples

VAR1	VAR2	BESTD1	BESTD2	ABSDIF	PERCDIF
10	3	7	8	0.0000445365	0.01%
16	10	3	7	0.0000196449	0.01%
24	16	4	6	0.0002663321	0.03%
2	1	8	3	0.0170915966	0.44%
20	16	4	8	0.0002044512	1.83%
7	20	7	4	0.0003220067	1.93%
19	1	8	6	0.0007318391	2.03%
10	15	8	8	0.0001581633	2.10%
5	1	8	8	0.0005979911	2.15%
13	3	5	2	0.0000306959	2.19%
4	10	8	2	0.0008559179	2.28%
24	11	8	7	0.0321750508	2.30%
19	5	8	8	0.0000132690	2.43%
5	27	5	8	0.0000291109	2.60%
10	8	7	5	0.0000142587	2.66%
1	5	6	6	0.0000155038	2.67%
27	7	8	4	0.0498684561	2.76%
15	10	6	6	0.0008779180	2.77%
21	7	8	8	0.0005055243	2.78%
23	3	8	6	0.0000228125	2.80%
19	13	8	6	0.0008211535	2.88%
25	21	8	5	0.2377070904	3.00%
20	17	5	8	0.0002921991	3.03%
4	26	8	7	0.0277383297	3.15%

16. Data before and after removing seasonal tendencies is shown. We calculated a moving average of 12 weeks, as illustrated in Figure 15.

The moving average values were directly subtracted from the original data. The graph corresponding to the resulting trend-free data is shown in Figure 16.

CLUSTERING PHASE

Once the search space is reduced the clustering phase is reached. We want the number of clusters to be determined automatically (without applying any aprioristic rules). Hence, the "best" number (N) of clusters is derived from information theoretical arguments. The theoretical N is to be validated empirically from the expert analysis of the characteristics of such clusters.

Figure 15. Original data displaying seasonal tendencies

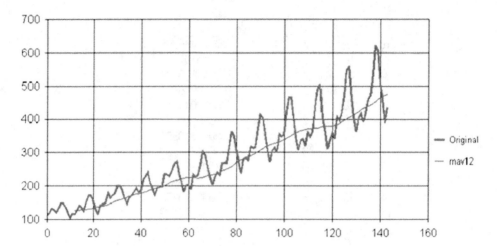

In order to comply with our assumptions we follow the next steps: a) Consecutively obtain the clusters (via a Fuzzy C Means (FCM) algorithm) assuming *n* clusters for *n=2, 3, ..., k*; where "*k*" represents the largest acceptable number of clusters. Determine the "optimal" number of clusters according to "elbow" criterion (Bezdek, J. C., 1974).

The reduced minable view was processed. FCM was used on the processed data and the elbow criterion was applied It is important to stress the fact that the use of fuzzy logic allows us to determine the content of information (the entropy) in every

Figure 16. Data with tendencies removed

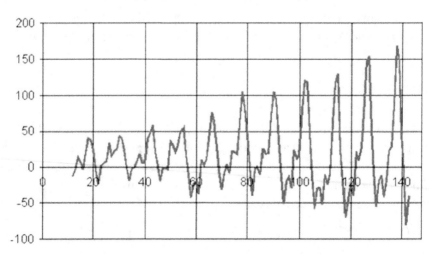

one of the N clusters into which the data set is divided. Other clustering algorithms based on crisp logic do not provide such alternative. Since the elements of a fuzzy cluster belong to all clusters it is possible to establish an analogy between the membership degree of an element in the set and the probability of its appearance. In this sense, the "entropy" is calculated as the expected value of the membership for a given cluster. Therefore we are able to calculate the partition's entropy PE (see below). Intuitively, as the number of clusters is increased the value of PE increases since the structure within a cluster is disrupted. In the limit, where there is a cluster for every member in the set, PE is maximal. On the other hand, we are always able to calculate the partition coefficient: a measure of how compact a set is. In this case, such measure of compactness decreases with N. The elbow criterion stipulates that the "best" N corresponds to the point where the corresponding tendencies of PE to increase and PC to decrease simultaneously change. That is, when the curvature of the graph of tendencies changes we are faced with an optimal number of clusters. Table 3 displays part of the numeric data values of PC and PE. These coefficients were calculated with formulas 9 and 10.

$$PC = \sum_{k=1}^{K} \sum_{i=1}^{c} \frac{(\mu_{ik})^2}{K} \tag{9}$$

$$PE = -\frac{1}{K} \sum_{k=1}^{K} \sum_{i=1}^{c} \mu_{ik} \ln(\mu_{ik}) \tag{10}$$

In Figure 17 the elbow behavior is illustrated.

DATA ANALYSIS

Once the number of clusters has been decided, we used Kohonen's Self-Organizing Maps (SOM) to find the definitive centers of the clusters. Hence, we defined a SOM

Table 3. Numerical data for elbow criterion

Clusters	2	3	4	5	6	7	8
Partition	0.879	0.770	0.642	0.560	0.498	0.489	0.413
Entropy	0.204	0.436	0.639	0.812	0.982	1.036	1.220

Figure 17. Elbow criterion for partition and entropy coefficients

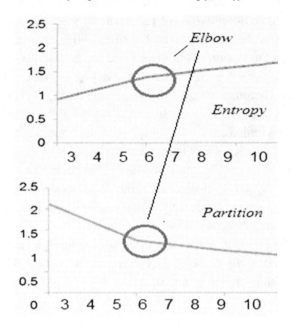

consisting of 6 neurons whose coordinates in the problem's space correspond to the centers of each of the 6 clusters.

The last phase of our analysis implied the use of SAS miner and the theoretically determined best number of clusters, as shown in Figure 18. The pie chart shows the percentage of elements grouped in each cluster. The cluster information. From it we infer that the number of clusters associated with de DB is 6. Intuitive conclusions for the Company can be extracted from the graph and reports supplied by the tool. We should now prove that clustering resulting from the reduced search space reflects a correct clustering view of the population.

Validation

The clustering effort reported here was undertaken simultaneously by independent groups in at least five different countries where the Company has ongoing operations.

The different proposed methodologies were subject to worldwide practical tests for over eight months and, when the results were assessed, the conclusions derived from M were the more accurate and economical of all the alternatives. As a result, the strategy reported herein was adopted as a standard for different regions of the Company's operations.

Figure 18. Pie Chart of the clustering result

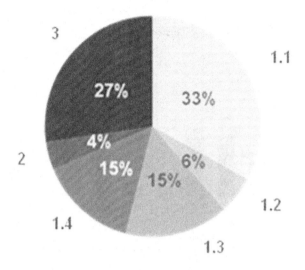

Intuitive Interpretation of the Results

One of the most difficult tasks when performing a kind of statistical clustering as the one reported here, is to achieve ease of understanding so that the clusters convey some intuitive sense to the end user. In this regard, we conducted a principal component's analysis and determined the eigenvectors. From these we extracted a set of simple rules which, although not exactly precise, allow us to establish a more intuitive view for each of the clusters. These are illustrated in Figure 19.

Finally, several statistics were obtained to characterize the clusters. For which consider the data en Figure 20.

Figure 19. A set of simple rules for the clusters

SEGMENT	INCOME	AVERAGE	MORT.	NOM.	CC	HIPO	TOK
1.1	500-3,500	<1,500	125-300	NO	NO	--	<3,500
	3,500-10,000	<10,000	NO	NO	NO	--	<10,500
1.2	5,000-13,000	<45,000	250-650	6-48	3,800-19,000		
		<4,500	300-600	5-27.5	NO		<17,000
1.3	<500	<1,000	250-650	2-20	NO		<100
1.4	11,000-20,000	<110,00	150-750	2.5-27.5	5,000-22,000	<5,000	<30,000
2	14,000-53,000	<320,000	336-1,000	34-97	15,000-89,000	<20,000	<190,000
	10,000-45,000	<105,000	190-700	10-80	<13,000	<500	<65,000
3	<500	--	125-800	5-50	<25,000	<1,500	

Figure 20. Socio-demographic characterization of Cluster 1.4

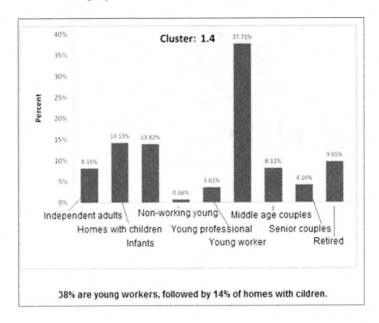

CONCLUSION

We have discussed a method which allows us to determine the number of clusters and their characteristics without appealing to expert knowledge of the information present in the data base under consideration. We have shown that it is, in general, possible to find a representative, usually much smaller, data set with which to work in more efficient (i.e. faster, easier to maintain) way instead of working with the original, usually much larger database. This is achieved without detriment of the statistical conclusions derived from the smaller DB. That is to say, we have shown how to replace a large data base with a smaller but statistically equivalent one. We have discussed the steps to determine the compact data base. We have argued that adequate pre-processing is imperative for the aforementioned procedure to be effective. Since the algorithms involved are of numerical nature it is imperative that even categorical data be numerically expressed. We pointed out that the naïve practice of replacing the instances of a categorical variable with arbitrarily selected numbers is to be avoided since its may induce non-existent behavioral tendencies or, contrariwise, it may mask existing ones. We mentioned two possible ways to replace the instances of the categorical variables: a) By introducing pseudo-binary variables (one for every instance of every variable) of b) By statistically determining numerical codes which preserve higher order relations between the categorical variables of the DB. From the compact data base we have successfully trained a

Fuzzy C-Means set of plausible clusters and measured the information behavior of the different alternatives from which we found the number of clusters to be 6. We have trained a SOM and determined the centers of the 6 clusters. From these we have conducted the interpretation of every cluster from a non-algorithmic more intuitive point of view.

The methodology is currently at use in the Company worldwide.

ACKNOWLEDGMENT

We wish to acknowledge the continued support and enthusiasm for our work from the Asociación Mexicana de Cultura, A.C.

REFERENCES

Amidan, B. G., Ferryman, T. A., & Cooley, S. K. (2005, March). Data outlier detection using the Chebyshev theorem. In Aerospace Conference, 2005 IEEE (pp. 3814-3819). IEEE. doi:10.1109/AERO.2005.1559688

Barbará, D., Li, Y., & Couto, J. (2002, November). COOLCAT: an entropy-based algorithm for categorical clustering. In Proceedings of the eleventh international conference on Information and knowledge management (pp. 582-589). ACM. doi:10.1145/584792.584888

Benesty, J., Chen, J., Huang, Y., & Cohen, I. (2009). Pearson correlation coefficient. In *Noise reduction in speech processing* (pp. 1–4). Springer Berlin Heidelberg.

Berkhin, P. (2006). A survey of clustering data mining techniques. In *Grouping multidimensional data* (pp. 25–71). Springer Berlin Heidelberg. doi:10.1007/3-540-28349-8_2

Bezdek, J. C. (1974). Cluster Validity with Fuzzy Sets. *Journal of Cybernetics*, (3): 58–72.

Brighton, H., & Mellish, C. (2002). Advances in instance selection for instance-based learning algorithms. *Data Mining and Knowledge Discovery*, 6(2), 153–172. doi:10.1023/A:1014043630878

Chaudhuri, S., & Dayal, U. (1997). An overview of data warehousing and OLAP technology. *SIGMOD Record*, 26(1), 65–74. doi:10.1145/248603.248616

Cheney, E. W. (1966). *Introduction to approximation theory*. Academic Press.

Cheng, D., Kannan, R., Vempala, S., & Wang, G. (2006). A divide-and-merge methodology for clustering. *ACM Transactions on Database Systems*, *31*(4), 1499–1525. doi:10.1145/1189769.1189779

Cybenko, G. (1989). Approximation by superpositions of a sigmoidal function. *Mathematics of Control, Signals, and Systems*, *2*(4), 303–314. doi:10.1007/BF02551274

Deb, K., Agrawal, S., Pratap, A., & Meyarivan, T. (2000, September). A fast elitist non-dominated sorting genetic algorithm for multi-objective optimization: NSGA-II. In *International Conference on Parallel Problem Solving From Nature* (pp. 849-858). Springer. 10.1007/3-540-45356-3_83

Delmater, R., & Hancock, M. (2001). *Data mining explained: a manager's guide to customer-centric business intelligence*. Digital Press.

Derakhshan, R., Orlowska, M. E., & Li, X. (2007, March). RFID data management: Challenges and opportunities. In *RFID, 2007. IEEE International Conference on* (pp. 175-182). IEEE.

DeWitt, D., & Gray, J. (1992). Parallel database systems: The future of high performance database systems. *Communications of the ACM*, *35*(6), 85–98. doi:10.1145/129888.129894

Edgar, R. C. (2010). Search and clustering orders of magnitude faster than BLAST. *Bioinformatics (Oxford, England)*, *26*(19), 2460–2461. doi:10.1093/bioinformatics/btq461 PMID:20709691

Fodor, I. K. (2002). A survey of dimension reduction techniques. U. S. Department of Energy, Lawrence Livermore National Laboratory.

Fox, L., & Parker, I. B. (1968). *Chebyshev polynomials in numerical analysis* (Vol. 29). London: Oxford university press.

Freitas, A. A., & Lavington, S. H. (1997). *Mining very large databases with parallel processing* (Vol. 9). Springer Science & Business Media.

Goebel, M., & Gruenwald, L. (1999). A survey of data mining and knowledge discovery software tools. *ACM SIGKDD Explorations Newsletter, 1*(1), 20-33.

Guha, S., Rastogi, R., & Shim, K. (1998, June). CURE: An efficient clustering algorithm for large databases. *SIGMOD Record, 27*(2), 73–84. doi:10.1145/276305.276312

Hair, J. F., Anderson, R. E., Tatham, R. L., & Black, W. C. (1999). *Análisis Multivariante* (5th ed.). Madrid: Pearson Prentice Hall.

Han, J., Pei, J., & Kamber, M. (2011). *Data mining: Concepts and techniques*. Elsevier.

Hartigan, J. A. (1975). *Clustering algorithms*. Academic Press.

Hartigan, J. A., & Hartigan, J. A. (1975). *Clustering algorithms* (Vol. 209). New York: Wiley.

Jagadish, H. V., Lakshmanan, L. V., & Srivastava, D. (1999, June). Snakes and sandwiches: Optimal clustering strategies for a data warehouse. *SIGMOD Record*, *28*(2), 37–48. doi:10.1145/304181.304186

Jain, A. K., Murty, M. N., & Flynn, P. J. (1999). Data clustering: A review. *ACM Computing Surveys*, *31*(3), 264–323. doi:10.1145/331499.331504

Jain, K., Murty, M. N., & Flynn, P. J. (1999). Data Clustering: A Review. *ACM Computing Surveys*, *31*(3), 264–323. doi:10.1145/331499.331504

Johnson, R. A., & Wichern, D. W. (2014). *Applied multivariate statistical analysis* (Vol. 4). Prentice-Hall.

Kleinberg, J., Papadimitriou, C., & Raghavan, P. (1998, May). Segmentation problems. In *Proceedings of the thirtieth annual ACM symposium on Theory of computing* (pp. 473-482). ACM. 10.1145/276698.276860

Kuri-Morales, A., & Cartas-Ayala, A. (2014, May). Polynomial multivariate approximation with genetic algorithms. In *Canadian Conference on Artificial Intelligence* (pp. 307-312). Springer.

Liu, H., & Motoda, H. (2002). On issues of instance selection. *Data Mining and Knowledge Discovery*, *6*(2), 115–130. doi:10.1023/A:1014056429969

Mason, J. C., & Handscomb, D. C. (2002). *Chebyshev polynomials*. CRC Press. doi:10.1201/9781420036114

McAfee, A., Brynjolfsson, E., Davenport, T. H., Patil, D. J., & Barton, D. (2012). Big data: The management revolution. *Harvard Business Review*, *90*(10), 60–68. PMID:23074865

Moré, J. J. (1978). The Levenberg-Marquardt algorithm: implementation and theory. In *Numerical analysis* (pp. 105–116). Berlin: Springer. doi:10.1007/BFb0067700

Norusis, M. (2008). *SPSS 16.0 advanced statistical procedures companion*. Prentice Hall Press.

Olken, F., & Rotem, D. (1995). Random sampling from databases: A survey. *Statistics and Computing*, *5*(1), 25–42. doi:10.1007/BF00140664

Palpanas, T. (2000). Knowledge discovery in data warehouses. *SIGMOD Record*, *29*(3), 88–100. doi:10.1145/362084.362142

Peter, W., Chiochetti, J., & Giardina, C. (2003, August). New unsupervised clustering algorithm for large datasets. In *Proceedings of the ninth ACM SIGKDD international conference on Knowledge discovery and data mining* (pp. 643-648). ACM. 10.1145/956750.956833

Powell, M. J. (1978). A fast algorithm for nonlinearly constrained optimization calculations. In *Numerical analysis* (pp. 144–157). Berlin: Springer. doi:10.1007/BFb0067703

Raymond, T. N., & Han, J. W. (1994). Efficient and effective clustering methods for spatial data mining. *Proc. of the 20th International Conference on Very Large Data Bases.*

Rudolph, G. (1994). Convergence analysis of canonical genetic algorithms. *IEEE Transactions on Neural Networks*, *5*(1), 96–101. doi:10.1109/72.265964 PMID:18267783

Saw, J. G., Yang, M. C., & Mo, T. C. (1984). Chebyshev inequality with estimated mean and variance. *The American Statistician*, *38*(2), 130–132.

Silva, D. R. (2002). MTP: Using Data Warehouse And Data Mining Resources For Ongoing Assessment Of Distance Learning. *Proceedings of IEEE Intl. Conf. on Advanced Learning Technologies (ICALT).*

Skalak, D. B. (1994, February). Prototype and feature selection by sampling and random mutation hill climbing algorithms. *Proceedings of the eleventh international conference on machine learning*, 293-301. 10.1016/B978-1-55860-335-6.50043-X

Slagle, J. R., Chang, C. L., & Heller, S. (1975). A Clustering and data-reorganization algorithm. *IEEE Trans. on Systems, Man and Cybernetics.*

Sokal, R. R. (1985). The principles of numerical taxonomy: twenty-five years later. *Computer-Assisted Bacterial Systematics, 15*, 1.

Steinbach, M., Karypis, G., & Kumar, V. (2000, August). A comparison of document clustering techniques. In *KDD workshop on text mining* (Vol. 400, No. 1, pp. 525-526). Academic Press.

Tan, P. N. (2006). *Introduction to data mining*. Pearson Education India.

Toivonen, H. (1996, September). *Sampling large databases for association rules* (Vol. 96). VLDB.

Tu, D. (2006). Nonparametric Monte Carlo Tests and Their Applications. *Biometrics*, *62*(3), 950–951. doi:10.1111/j.1541-0420.2006.00588_14.x

Vu, K., Hua, K. A., Cheng, H., & Lang, S. D. (2006, June). A non-linear dimensionality-reduction technique for fast similarity search in large databases. In *Proceedings of the 2006 ACM SIGMOD international conference on Management of data* (pp. 527-538). ACM. 10.1145/1142473.1142532

Zhang, D., Zhou, Z. H., & Chen, S. (2007, April). *Semi-Supervised Dimensionality Reduction*. SDM.

Zhu, X., & Wu, X. (2006, August). Scalable representative instance selection and ranking. In *Pattern Recognition, 2006. ICPR 2006. 18th International Conference* (*Vol. 3*, pp. 352-355). IEEE.

Chapter 6
Improving Recommendation Accuracy and Diversity via Multiple Social Factors and Social Circles

Yong Feng
Chongqing University, China

Zhuo Chen
Chongqing University, China

Heng Li
Chongqing University, China

Baohua Qiang
Guilin University of Electronic Technology, China

ABSTRACT

Recommender systems have been widely employed to suggest personalized online information to simplify users' information discovery process. With the popularity of online social networks, analysis and mining of social factors and social circles have been utilized to support more effective recommendations, but have not been fully investigated. In this chapter, the authors propose a novel recommendation model with the consideration of more comprehensive social factors and topics. To further enhance recommendation accuracy, four social factors are simultaneously injected into the recommendation model based on probabilistic matrix factorization. Meanwhile, the authors explore several new methods to measure these social factors. Moreover, they infer explicit and implicit social circles to enhance the performance of recommendation diversity. Finally, the authors conduct a series of experiments on publicly available data. Experimental results show the proposed model achieves significantly improved performance over the existing models in which social information have not been fully considered.

DOI: 10.4018/978-1-5225-7268-8.ch006

INTRODUCTION

With the development of Web 2.0 technologies and the popularity of online social networks, Web/Internet has become a huge platform for information sharing. That more and more people like to share daily experiences in social networks leads to the explosive growth of data on the WWW. When users are able to define their information requirements precisely, search engine is a powerful tool to help them to select online information, e.g., Google, Yahoo, etc. However, in many cases, users have difficulty in precisely describing what information they want, the keyword-based search engine is not efficient to fully meet the need of user information discovery. Under the background of this, personalized recommender system, a more intelligent tool, is needed to offer users new ways to engage with the topics, events, and items that matter to them.

Recommender systems can be divided into several different types based on data source. Content-based RS work by learning the item content for the ranking problem. Recent content-based approaches rank candidate items based on how well they match the topic interest of the user as their preference (Balabanović & Shoham, 1997; Phelan, McCarthy, & Smyth, 2009; Stefanidis, Pitoura, & Vassiliadis, 2011). The accuracy of recommendations depends on the completeness and comprehensiveness of item content. Collaborative Filtering methods make recommendations by exploring user-item interaction information to find correlations between users or items (Koren, 2010; Liu, Chen, Xiong, Ding, & Chen, 2012; Peng, Zeng, Zhao, & Wang, 2010; Sarwar, Karypis, Konstan, & Riedl, 2001), but these methods are unable to make full use of user profiles and item content.

Now, social network has become an integral part of our daily lives. The massive social data contributed by social network users contains rich social knowledge. Researchers have proposed several social trust based RS to improve recommendation accuracy in recent years (Chen, Zeng, Zheng, & Chen, 2013; Jamali & Ester, 2010; Ma, King, & Lyu, 2009; Ma, Zhou, Liu, Lyu, & King, 2011). In fact, a user may trust different friends in different categories. With the notion of this, social circle based RS have recently been investigated (Feng & Qian, 2013; Yang, Steck, & Liu, 2012). Yang, Steck, and Liu (2012) introduced the concept of "inferred trust circle" for recommendation in social networks, taking interpersonal trust influence into account. They focused on inferring category-specific social trust circles. Yang, Liang, and Zhao (2017) developed a set of matrix-factorization (MF) and nearest-neighbor (NN)-based recommender systems (RSs) that explore user social network and group affiliation information for social voting recommendation. However, some of the social network users prefer choosing products closely related to their individual preference, rarely considering interpersonal influence. Feng and Qian (2013) proposed a recommendation model to cater users' individualities, especially for experienced users. Moreover, their approach not only takes individual preference into account, but also combines interpersonal trust influence and interpersonal interest similarity.

However, there are some general weaknesses in existing social circle based RS. On the one hand, interpersonal closeness degree, an important factor of social contextual based on the sociology studies, has not been considered in existing social circle based approaches, which leads to a limitation of recommendation accuracy. On the other hand, for each user, social circle based RS only offer recommendations in a subset of categories that he has rated in the past, which results in a lack of prediction diversity. For example, user focuses on Books category for a long time although he has no rating in this category, and hopes to get some recommendations. Unfortunately, the existing social circle based methods are unable to make rating predictions for in the non-rated Books category. Thus, further research is needed to overcome these weaknesses.

In this paper, to approach these issues in a practical way, we focus on exploring social information in social networks. The main contributions of this paper are summarized as follows: (i) We propose a personalized recommendation model, called PTIC (PTIC is short for four social factors), employing matrix factorization techniques. In particular, four social factors, individual preference, interpersonal trust influence, interpersonal interest similarity and interpersonal closeness degree, are simultaneously injected into our recommendation model to enhance recommendation accuracy. (ii) We propose a set of methods to measure these social factors based on user rating activities and social network data. (iii) Moreover, we infer explicit and implicit trust circles, interest circles and closeness circles to improve the performance of recommendation diversity and enhance the intrinsic link between social network users. Note that all of these inferred circles are collectively called social circles in this paper. (iv) On the basis of theoretical work, we conduct a series of experiments on publicly available data. Experimental results show that our approach achieves more effective recommendations than the existing models in which social information have not been fully considered.

The rest of this paper is organized as follows. The next section introduces social factors and some related works. In section 3, we first introduce social circle inference, and then put forward several new methods to measure social factors. Finally, we propose our recommendation model for recommendation in social networks. Section 4 describes our experimental work and discussion of experimental results. We give some concluding reviews and directions for future research in the final section.

RELATED WORK

In this section, we introduce four social factors related to social networks and briefly review some relevant works to this paper.

Social Factors

In this paper, social factors consist of individual preference and social contextual factors. Individual preference is an important social factor for recommendation in social networks. The analysis of individual preference can help RS to better embody user's personality especially for experienced users who make decisions with little consideration of interpersonal relationship (Jiang, et al., 2012; Qian & Feng, 2014). In addition, social contextual factors have fundamentally changed the user decision journey. User decisions and behaviors are increasingly driven by the opinions, tastes and preferences of an exponentially large pool of friends and influencers in social networks. Social contextual factors contain three components: interpersonal trust influence, interpersonal interest similarity and interpersonal closeness degree. Interpersonal trust influence means that user's preference is to some extent influenced by his trusted friends. Interpersonal interest similarity denotes personal interest might be similar to his friends'. Recently, to better support users' social behaviors, some online social networks proposed the concept of "closeness degree". For example, Qzone (qzone.qq.com), a Twitter style website in China, launched a function that users can scan the list of their close friends sorted by interpersonal closeness degree. Most intuitive notions of a strong interpersonal tie should be satisfied by high closeness degree. Besides the experiential assumption, sociological studies have already shown the well-known fact that the contacts of two individuals who are closely acquainted tend to be more overlapping than those of two arbitrarily selected individuals (Granovetter, 1983; Rapoport & Horvath, 1961). Berscheid and Walster (1985) suggested that the closer the tie connecting two individuals, the more similar they are, in various ways. Intuitively, user's taste is more easily affected by his close friends. They often choose products recommended by their close friends. That motivates us to incorporate the factor of interpersonal closeness degree into our recommendation model for more accurate recommendations. Similar to interpersonal trust influence and interest similarity, user latent feature should be similar to the weighted average of latent features of his friends based on interpersonal closeness degree.

PRM Model

The PRM model is proposed by Feng and Qian (2013), and is found to achieve higher recommendation accuracy than BaseMF (Salakhutdinov & Mnih, 2007), CircleCon3 (Yang et al., 2012) and ContextMF (Jiang, et al., 2012). Thus, we use it as a baseline model in our experimental comparison study. This model incorporates three social factors, involving individual preference, interpersonal trust influence and interpersonal interest similarity. The actual rating data expressed by users is given in a matrix $R \in \mathbb{R}^{u_0 \times i_0}$, where u_0 is the number of users and i_0 is the number of items in all categories. $R_{u,i}$ that represents the actual rating of user u on item i is an integer in range [1, 5]. Regarding category c, $S_{u,v}^{c*}$ represents the trust value that u assigned to v. $W_{u,v}^{c*}$ denotes the interest similarity between u and v. $Q_{u,i}^{c*}$ denotes the relevance of user u's preference to the topic of item i. For each item category c, the objective function is as follows:

$$
\mathcal{L}^c \left(R^c, U^c, P^c, S^{c*}, W^{c*}, Q^{c*} \right)
$$
$$
= \frac{1}{2} \sum_{(u,i)obs} \left(R_{u,i}^c - \hat{R}_{u,i}^c \right)^2 + \frac{\lambda}{2} \left(\left\| P^c \right\|_F^2 + \left\| U^c \right\|_F^2 \right)
$$
$$
+ \frac{\beta}{2} \sum_{all\ u} \left[(U_u^c - \sum_v S_{u,v}^{c*} U_v^c)(U_u^c - \sum_v S_{u,v}^{c*} U_v^c)^T \right]
$$
$$
+ \frac{\gamma}{2} \sum_{all\ u} \left[(U_u^c - \sum_v W_{u,v}^{c*} U_v^c)(U_u^c - \sum_v W_{u,v}^{c*} U_v^c)^T \right]
$$
$$
+ \frac{\eta}{2} \sum_{(u,i)obs} \left| H_u^{c*} \right| \left(Q_{u,i}^{c*} - U_u^c P_i^{cT} \right)^2
$$

where row vectors U_u^c and P_i^c denote the latent user and item feature vectors respectively. Social factors are enforced by the last three terms in the objective function. The factor of interpersonal trust influence is enforced by the second term, which says that user latent feature U_u should be similar to the average of his friends' latent feature based on the weight of $S_{u,v}^{c*}$ in c. The idea of interpersonal interest similarity is enforced by the third term, which says that user latent feature should be similar to the average of his friends' latent feature with the weight of $W_{u,v}^{c*}$. The factor of individual preference is enforced by the last term, which says that user latent feature should connect with item latent feature. A local minimum of the objective function can be found by the gradient descent approach. As long as the

U_u^c and P_i^c have been learned, the predicted rating value of user u on a non-rated item i can be computed based on the following equation:

$$\hat{R}_{u,i}^c = r_m^c + U_u^c P_i^{cT}$$

where r_m^c is the average value of observed training ratings in category c.

RECOMMENDATION MODEL

In this section, we first introduce social circle inference, and then put forward several new methods to measure social factors. Finally, we propose our recommendation model, employing matrix factorization techniques.

Social Circle Inference

Given a user u and a specific category c, the inference of social circle concerns two cases, one is that u has ratings in category c, the other is that u has no rating in category c but is potentially interested in this category.

Explicit Social Circle Inference

In the first case, we use the same inference rules proposed by Yang et al. (2012) to construct social circles for users who have ratings in the current category. In particular, for category c, all the users v who meet the following conditions are in u's social circle C_u^c, i.e., $v \in C_u^c$:

- $SN_{u,v} = 1$ in the original social network, and
- $N_u^c > 0$ and $N_v^c > 0$ in the rating data,

where $SN_{u,v} = 1$ denotes u directly trust v in the original social network $SN \in \mathbb{R}^{u_0 \times u_0}$, N_u^c is the number of ratings explicitly assigned by u in category c. This kind of inferred social circle is referred to as explicit social circle.

Implicit Social Circle Inference

A situation that user u may focus on products belonging to category c for a long time although he has no rating in this category is likely to occur in real life. That is to say, u is potentially interested in category c. In fact, user u might issue a trust statement to v just because v has rating experience in c category. As a user, u hopes to get some recommendations about category c from his friends. In this case, we try to infer implicit social circle for u in the non-rated category c. Concretely, a user v is in the implicit social circle of u concerning category c, i.e., $v \in C_u^c$, if and only if the following conditions are met:

- $SN_{u,v} = 1$ in the original social network, and
- $N_u^c = 0$ and $N_v^c > 0$ in the rating data.

Note that the explicit and implicit social circles are collectively called social circles in this paper. To sum up, given a user u, we can infer his social circles in the subset of categories in which he has ratings or his trusted friends has ratings. Figure 1 shows the schematic diagram of the process of social circle inference. In this way, we can recommend not only the explicitly rated categories but also the implicitly interested categories to users.

Measurement of Individual Preference

Feng and Qian (2013) proposed an approach to measure user individual preference based on item category distribution vector, but ignore historical user rating values. However, the rating value that u assigned to item i reflects how much u favors i. Thus, combining item category distribution with user rating data, we can learn user's preference more accurately. Regarding category c, user rating data can be obtained from the rating matrix R^c. We normalize each row of the matrix R^c as follows:

$$R_{u,i}^{c*} = \frac{R_{u,i}^c}{\sum_{i \in H_u^c} R_{u,i}^c}$$

where H_u^c is the set of items that user u has rated in category c. Just like Feng and Qian (2013), since an item belongs to different categories, we use category distribution vector D_i to denote the topic of item i:

$$D_i = \left[I_{c_1}, I_{c_2}, \ldots, I_{c_n} \right]$$

Figure 1. Illustration of social circle inference. a): a sample original social network graph, each user is labeled with the categories in which he has ratings; b) and c): explicit social circles of user u regarding categories c_1 and c_2 respectively; d): implicit social circle of regarding category c_3

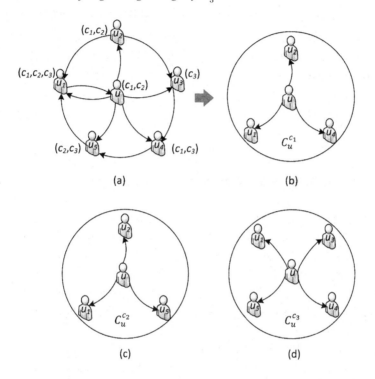

where I_{c_n} is the indicator that is equal to 1 if item i belongs to category c_n, and equal to 0 otherwise, and n is the number of categories, for Yelp $n = 8$. We utilize preference distribution vector D_u to denote u's individual preference. If u has ratings in category c, his individual preference should be similar to the weighted average of the item category distribution vectors. More formally, we provide the following expression to measure u's individual preference in the rated category c:

$$D_u^c = \sum_{i \in H_u^c} R_{u,i}^{c*} D_i$$

If u has never assigned ratings to items in category c, as an approximation to his individual preference, we use the average of individual preference of his friends who belong to his implicit social circle regarding category c. Thus,

$$D_u^c = \frac{1}{|C_u^c|} \sum_{v \in C_u^c} D_v^c$$

where $|C_u^c|$ represents the number of users within the implicit social circle C_u^c.

In practice, the relevance of user u's individual preference to the topic of item i can be regarded as the latent real rating value of user u on item i (Feng & Qian, 2013), and is denoted by $Q_{u,i}$.

$$Q_{u,i} = \text{Cosin}\left(D_u, D_i\right)$$

Measurement of Interpersonal Trust Influence

It should be noted that there is no general agreement on the standard definition of trust. Lifen (2008) defined trust as "the level of belief established between two entities in relation to a certain context". In this paper, a social trust relationship from user u to user v represents that u expresses an affirmative recognition to the reliability of v in a specific category. The trust value assignment should be proportional to user expertise level which reflects user's authority of ratings in a specific category.

We use a variant of PageRank algorithm (Brin & Page, 1998) to assign a numerical weighting to each user in a specific category, with the purpose of measuring his expertise level. The variant is called ExpertRank. The numerical weight assigned to any given user u is referred to as the ExpertRank of u. We denote the ExpertRank of u in category c by ER_u^c. The ER transferred from a given user to the targets of his outbound trust links upon the next iteration is divided equally among all outbound trust links. More formally, the equation is as follows:

$$ER_u^c = \left(1 - d\right) N_u^c + d \sum_v \frac{ER_v^c}{L_v}$$

where v are users who trust u regarding category c. L_v is the number of outbound trust links. The damping factor d denotes what the proportion of a user's ER is transferred. Here, we set it to be $d = 0.85$. ER of each user is initialized with the number of ratings that he assigned in category c. And each user's ER is derived in large part from the ExpertRanks of others. Thus, a user who is trusted by many users with high ER and few outbound trust links receives a high ER himself. Note that the calculation of ER is done in each category separately. We denote the trust values between users by $S_{u,v}^{c}$.

$$S_{u,v}^{c} = \begin{cases} ER_{v}^{c}, & if \ v \in C_{u}^{c} \\ 0, & otherwise \end{cases}$$

Finally, we normalize each row of the trust matrix S^{c} as follows:

$$S_{u,v}^{c*} = \frac{S_{u,v}^{c}}{\sum_{v \in C_{u}^{c}} S_{u,v}^{c}}$$

Measurement of Interpersonal Interest Similarity

Regarding category c, the interest similarity between u and v is denoted by $W_{u,v}^{c}$. Specifically, we employ the method proposed by Feng and Qian (2013) to compute the interpersonal interest similarity:

$$W_{u,v}^{c} = \mathrm{Cosin}\left(D_{u}^{c}, D_{v}^{c}\right)$$

We then normalize each row of the interest similarity matrix W^{c} as follows:

$$W_{u,v}^{c*} = \frac{W_{u,v}^{c}}{\sum_{v \in C_{u}^{c}} W_{u,v}^{c}}$$

Measurement of Interpersonal Closeness Degree

On the one hand, according to the social media report published by Nielsen (2012), most of the people decide to connect on online social networks just because of the friends they know in real life. On the other hand, consider, now, any two arbitrarily selected individuals in the offline social network, call them A and B, and the set, S=C, D, E..., of all persons with ties to either or both of them. From sociological views, Granovetter (1983), a celebrated sociologist, argued that the closer the tie between A and B, the larger proportion of individuals in S to whom they will both be tied. Those to whom one is closest are likely to have the greatest overlap in their friendship circles. Thus, as an approximation to interpersonal closeness degree, in this paper, we use the number of common friends between users. In other words, the more common friends between two individuals, the higher closeness degree they have. More formally, the user-user closeness degree $F_{u,v}^c$ is given by the following expression:

$$F_{u,v}^c = \begin{cases} 1 + M_{u,v}^c, & if\ v \in C_u^c \\ 0, & otherwise \end{cases}$$

where $M_{u,v}^c$ denotes the number of common friends between u and v regarding category c. If they have no common friend, we set the initial closeness degree $F_{u,v}^c = 1$. Then each row of the F^c matrix is also normalized as follows:

$$F_{u,v}^{c*} = \frac{F_{u,v}^c}{\sum_{v \in C_u^c} F_{u,v}^c}$$

Model Training

In this paper, regarding each category c, we utilize low-rank matrix factorization technique to learn latent user and item feature matrices represented by $U^c \in \mathbb{R}^{u_0 \times k}$ and $P^c \in \mathbb{R}^{i_0 \times k}$ respectively. The dimension of the latent space is represented by k. Let row vectors U_u^c and P_i^c denote k-dimensional latent user and item feature vectors. For each category c, we define training objective function as follows:

$$\mathcal{L}\left(R^c, U^c, P^c, S^{c*}, W^{c*}, F^{c*}, Q^{c*}\right)$$

$$= \frac{1}{2} \sum_{(u,i)obs} \left(R_{u,i}^c - \hat{R}_{u,i}^c\right)^2 + \frac{\lambda}{2} \left(\left\|P^c\right\|_F^2 + \left\|U^c\right\|_F^2\right)$$

$$+ \frac{\beta}{2} \sum_{all\ u} \left[(U_u^c - \sum_{v \in C_u^c} S_{u,v}^{c*} U_v^c)(U_u^c - \sum_{v \in C_u^c} S_{u,v}^{c*} U_v^c)^T\right]$$

$$+ \frac{\gamma}{2} \sum_{all\ u} \left[(U_u^c - \sum_{v \in C_u^c} W_{u,v}^{c*} U_v^c)(U_u^c - \sum_{v \in C_u^c} W_{u,v}^{c*} U_v^c)^T\right]$$

$$+ \frac{\mu}{2} \sum_{all\ u} \left[(U_u^c - \sum_{v \in C_u^c} F_{u,v}^{c*} U_v^c)(U_u^c - \sum_{v \in C_u^c} F_{u,v}^{c*} U_v^c)^T\right]$$

$$+ \frac{\eta}{2} \sum_{(u,i)obs} \left|H_u^{c*}\right| \left(Q_{u,i}^{c*} - U_u^c P_i^{cT}\right)^2$$

where $\left|H_u^{c*}\right|$ is the normalized number of items in set H_u^c. Generally speaking, the greater the number of rated items, the more likely u depends on his individual preference to make choices. If u has ratings in category c, then C_u^c is explicit social circle, otherwise C_u^c is implicit social circle. $R_{u,i}^c$ is the actual rating of user u on item i. The predicted rating $\hat{R}_{u,i}^c$ can be captured according to equation (2). That user's latent feature vector should be similar to the weighted average of his trusted friends' latent feature vectors based on interpersonal trust influence is enforced by the second term. Moreover, the third term denotes that user latent feature should be similar to the weighted average of his friends' based on interpersonal interest similarity. The fourth term denotes that user latent feature should be similar to the weighted average of his close friends' based on interpersonal closeness degree. And the last term denotes the factor of individual preference. We minimize the objective function by performing gradient descent on U_u^c and P_i^c:

$$\frac{\partial \mathcal{L}}{\partial U_u^c} = \sum_{i:i\in c} I_{u,i}^{R^c} \left(r_m^c + U_u^c P_i^{cT} - R_{u,i}^c \right) P_i^c + \lambda U_u^c$$
$$+ \beta(U_u^c - \sum_{v\in C_u^c} S_{u,v}^{c*} U_v^c) - \beta \sum_{v:u\in C_v^c} S_{v,u}^{c*} (U_v^c - \sum_{w\in C_v^c} S_{v,w}^{c*} U_w^c)$$
$$+ \gamma(U_u^c - \sum_{v\in C_u^c} W_{u,v}^{c*} U_v^c) - \gamma \sum_{v:u\in C_v^c} W_{v,u}^{c*} (U_v^c - \sum_{w\in C_v^c} W_{v,w}^{c*} U_w^c)$$
$$+ \mu(U_u^c - \sum_{v\in C_u^c} F_{u,v}^{c*} U_v^c) - \mu \sum_{v:u\in C_v^c} F_{v,u}^{c*} (U_v^c - \sum_{w\in C_v^c} F_{v,w}^{c*} U_w^c)$$
$$+ \eta \sum_{i:i\in H_u^c} I_{u,i}^{R^c} \left| H_u^{c*} \right| \left(U_u^c P_i^{cT} - Q_{u,i}^{c*} \right) P_i^c$$

where $i \in c$ denotes item i belongs to the category c.

$$\frac{\partial \mathcal{L}}{\partial P_i^c} = \sum_{all\ u} I_{u,i}^{R^c} \left(r_m^c + U_u^c P_i^{cT} - R_{u,i}^c \right) U_u^c + \lambda P_i^c$$
$$+ \eta \sum_{all\ u} I_{u,i}^{R^c} \left| H_u^{c*} \right| \left(U_u^c P_i^{cT} - Q_{u,i}^{c*} \right) U_u^c$$

where $I_{u,i}^{R^c}$ is the indicator function that is equal to 1 if u has rated i in category c, and equal to 0 otherwise. We initialize values of U^c and P^c by sampling from the normal distribution with zero mean. In each iteration, U^c and P^c are updated based on latent variables from the previous iteration to decrease the value of objective function. Once U^c and P^c are learned, we can predict rating values according to equation (2). Figure 2 shows the framework of recommendation model.

EXPERIMENT

In this section, we perform a series of experiments on Yelp dataset and compare the experimental results with several existing recommendation approaches.

Dataset

In this paper, we use the version of Yelp dataset (smiles.xjtu.edu.cn) published by Feng and Qian (2013). This dataset consists of 10555 real users and their social relationships with their friends. These users assigned ratings to a total of 1,783,922 different items from 22 big categories. The shared Yelp data contains eight item categories chosen from the 22 categories based on the popularity distribution,

Figure 2. The framework of PTIC recommendation model

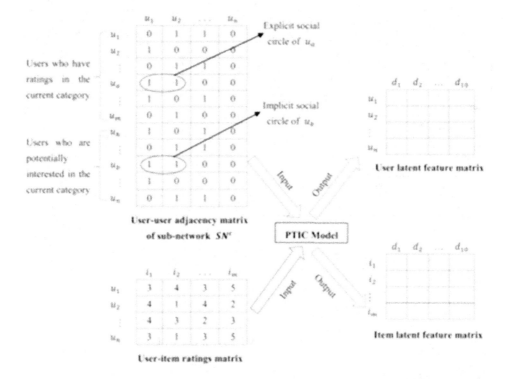

involving three most popular categories (Restaurants, Night Life and Shopping), three common categories (Active Life, Beauty and Spas, Hotels and Travel) and two less rating but interesting categories (Home Services, Pets). The total number of ratings in the eight categories is 300,847. The distribution of users, items and ratings in the eight categories is shown in Table 1. Moreover, the total number of issued trust statements in the eight categories is 1,432,110. The average number of user's common friends in each category is presented in Table 1 column Common Friends.

Performance Measures

In each category of Yelp dataset, we use 80% of data as the training set and the remaining 20% as the test set. We use Mean Absolute Error (MAE) as the evaluation metric in our experiments, because it is the most popular accuracy measures in the literature of recommender systems (Feng & Qian, 2013; Jiang, et al., 2012; Salakhutdinov & Mnih, 2007; Yang et al., 2012). MAE is defined as

Table 1. Yelp Data: Statistics of the eight categories

Category	User Count	Item Count	Rating Count	avg. rating	Trust Statements	Common Friends
Active Life	5237	7495	24395	4.021	372568	37.381
Beauty and Spas	5466	8495	21345	3.936	323411	35.764
Home Services	2500	3213	5180	3.707	124287	30.919
Hotel & Travel	4712	5883	21658	3.824	330786	37.239
Night Life	4000	21337	99878	3.594	110405	18.028
Pets	1624	1672	3093	3.975	53441	21.661
Restaurants	2000	32725	91946	3.677	24757	8.345
Shopping	3000	16154	33352	3.819	92455	18.981

$$MAE = \frac{\sum_{(u,i)\in\Re_{test}}\left|R_{u,i} - \hat{R}_{u,i}\right|}{\left|\Re_{test}\right|}$$

where $\Re_{test}$ is the set of all user-item pairs (u,i) in the test data.

Evaluation

To evaluate the performance of our methods, we compare the recommendation results of our method with the following methods on Yelp datasets:

- **BaseMF:** This method is the baseline matrix factorization approach proposed by Salakhutdinov and Mnih (2007), which does not take the social network information into account.
- **CircleCon3:** This method is proposed by Yang et al. (2012). It introduces the concept of "inferred circles of friends" and takes the social factor of interpersonal trust influence into account.
- **ContextMF:** This is the model proposed by Jiang, et al. (2012), which utilizes individual preference and interpersonal trust influence.
- **PRM:** This method is proposed by Feng and Qian (2013), which combines three social factors: individual preference, interpersonal interest similarity and interpersonal trust influence. It embodies the significance of user's individuality, especially for experienced users.

In our experiment, for the convenience of comparison, we set the dimension of the latent space to be $k = 10$, the regularization constant to be $\lambda = 0.1$ and the trade-off parameters to be $\beta = \gamma = \mu = \eta = 30$. Since we use the same dataset as PRM model, the experimental data exhibited in Feng and Qian (2013) is cited in this paper for the experimental comparison.

Recommendation Accuracy Evaluation

In detail, regarding PTIC model and each category of Yelp dataset, we utilize explicit social circles and actual ratings in the current category as input to train for the latent features of items and all users who have ratings in the current category. The performance of the five approaches are compared in Table 2 regarding MAE. From Table 2, we can see distinctly that the proposed PTIC model achieves the lowest MAE values overall. The percentage numbers in each cell are the relative improvements of PTIC over the various baseline models. The results demonstrate the benefit of the incorporation of interpersonal closeness degree in social network recommendation.

Table 2. MAE comparison for each category of Yelp

Category	BaseMF	CircleCon3	ContextMF	PRM	PTIC
Active Life	2.182 63.84%	1.409 44.00%	1.036 23.84%	1.018 22.50%	0.789
Beauty and Spas	2.481 61.58%	1.530 39.28%	1.202 22.72%	1.125 17.42%	0.929
Home Services	2.570 54.63%	1.642 28.99%	1.340 12.99%	1.348 13.50%	1.166
Hotels & Travel	2.208 59.56%	1.441 38.02%	1.103 19.04%	1.057 15.52%	0.893
Night Life	1.647 47.84%	1.155 25.63%	1.025 16.20%	0.914 6.01%	0.859
Pets	2.778 62.57%	1.694 38.61%	1.317 21.03%	1.266 17.85%	1.040
Restaurants	1.385 40.65%	1.056 22.16%	0.991 17.05%	0.876 6.16%	0.822
Shopping	1.900 52.79%	1.318 31.94%	1.085 17.33%	1.028 12.74%	0.897

Recommendation Diversity Evaluation

For a given user, on the one hand, consider the category set that the user has purchased or rated in the past. We utilize explicit social circles as input of PTIC to train for latent users and items features in the current category set. Once these latent features are learned, this model can predict rating for the user on items belonging to the rated category set. In this case, the performance of the proposed PTIC is shown in Table 2. On the other hand, consider the category set that the user has not rated but is potentially interested in, the latent users and items features in this category set can be learned when PTIC model is trained with explicit and implicit social circles. And this model can use these latent features to make rating predictions for the given user on items belonging to the non-rated but potentially interested category set. Thus, compared with other social circle based models, the proposed PTIC model can provide rating predictions for a given user not only in the rated categories but also in the potentially interested categories.

As to demonstrate the effectiveness of our approach for rating prediction in the non-rated categories, regarding each category of Yelp dataset, we extract 20% of users who actually have ratings in the current category as test users, and assume they have not rated items in this category. The actual ratings assigned by test users in the current category are not utilized to learn user and item latent features. We use implicit social circles of test users as input to train for the latent users features, and predict ratings for test users in these hypothetically non-rated categories. Through experiments, the recommendation errors between predicted ratings and actual ratings are presented in Table 3. We can see from Table 3 that the approach achieves low recommendation errors. In conclusion, our approach can offer recommendations from a set of categories that user explicitly and implicitly likes, and achieve low recommendation error in the non-rated categories. This demonstrates from two sides the proposed approach for recommendation diversity is quite effective.

For test users, when actual ratings of test users are utilized to learn user and item latent features, the recommendation errors in each category are shown in Table 4. Comparing PTIC in Table 3 and Table 4, we can see that the actual rating data combined with multiple social factors achieves more accurate predictions in all categories. This is because actual rating data provides us more information to learn user's preference.

Table 3. PTIC: MAE in each category for recommendation diversity

Category	Active Life	Beauty and Spas	Home Services	Hotels & Travel	Night Life	Pets	Restaurants	Shopping
MAE	0.908	0.997	1.115	0.930	0.873	1.094	0.846	0.951

Table 4. PTIC: MAE in each category using actual ratings assigned by test users

Category	Active Life	Beauty and Spas	Home Services	Hotels & Travel	Night Life	Pets	Restaurants	Shopping
MAE	0.785	0.827	1.053	0.854	0.839	1.053	0.824	0.922

DISCUSSION

In order to find the impact of interpersonal closeness degree on the recommendation accuracy, we divide the users of Active Life into seven groups according to average number of user's common friends. The distribution of users in the seven groups is presented in Table 5, where "0-9" means the average number of user's common friends is less than 9, and "60-" means the average number of user's common friends is more than 60. Based on the detailed statistic presented in Table 5, we can see that a number of users fall into the group of "0-9". The MAE histograms are illustrated in Figure 3, where the black dotted line represents the trend of MAE. As is suggested in this figure, with the increase in the average number of user's common friends, the values of MAE reveal a general trend of decrease. In addition, the proposed PTIC model provides the best prediction accuracy for users whose average number of common friends is more than 60. The results further demonstrate that the factor of interpersonal closeness degree plays an important role in user decision journey.

Table 5. The distribution of users according to the average number of user's common friends in Active Life of Yelp

Common Friend_num	0-9	10-19	20-29	30-39	40-49	50-59	60-
User_num	2489	1254	628	418	249	137	152

Figure 3. Impact of the average number of user's common friends on the MAE performance

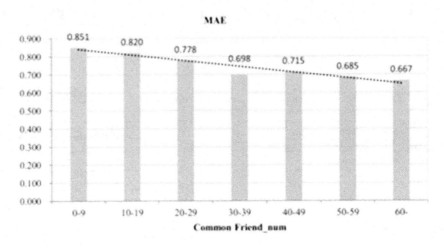

CONCLUSION

In this paper, we propose a novel PTIC model to improve recommendation accuracy and diversity. Four social factors, individual preference, interpersonal trust influence, interpersonal interest similarity and interpersonal closeness degree, are simultaneously injected into our recommendation model. We present several methods to measure these social factors. In particular, the usage of interpersonal closeness degree enables the proposed model to provide recommendations more accurately. Moreover, explicit and implicit social circles are both inferred to approach the issue of recommendation diversity. Through a series of experiments on the real life social rating data, we demonstrate that the proposed PTIC model achieves significantly reduced recommendation error over existing models in which social information have not been fully considered, and improves the performance of recommendation diversity. In the future, we will take the explicit interactions (such as comment, retweet…) between social network users into consideration to further enhance the recommendation performance.

ACKNOWLEDGMENT

The authors acknowledge the financial support of the National Nature Science Foundation of China (No. 61762025), Frontier and Application Foundation Research Program of CQ CSTC (No. cstc2017jcyjAX0340), The National Key Research and Development Program of China (No. 2017YFB1402400), Guangxi Key Laboratory of Trusted Software (No.kx201701), Guangxi Cooperative Innovation Center of Cloud Computing and Big Data (No.YD16E01), and Key Industries Common Key Technologies Innovation Projects of CQ CSTC (No. cstc2017zdcy-zdyxx0047), and Chongqing Postdoctoral Science Foundation (No. Xm2017125). The author is grateful to the anonymous referee for a careful checking of the details and for helpful comments that improved this paper.

REFERENCES

Balabanović, M., & Shoham, Y. (1997). Fab: Content-based, collaborative recommendation. *Communications of the ACM, 40*(3), 66–72. doi:10.1145/245108.245124

Berscheid, E., & Walster, E. H. (1985). Interpersonal attraction. Handbook of Social Psychology, 2, 413-484.

Brin, S., & Page, L. (1998). The anatomy of a large-scale hypertextual Web search engine. *Computer Networks and ISDN Systems, 30*(1), 107–117. doi:10.1016/S0169-7552(98)00110-X

Chen, C., Zeng, J., Zheng, X., & Chen, D. (2013). Recommender System Based on Social Trust Relationships. In *e-Business Engineering (ICEBE), 2013 IEEE 10th International Conference on* (pp. 32-37). IEEE.

Feng, H., & Qian, X. (2013). Recommendation via user's personality and social contextual. In *Proceedings of the 22nd ACM international conference on Conference on information & knowledge management* (pp. 1521-1524). ACM. 10.1145/2505515.2507834

Granovetter, M. (1983). The Strength of Weak Ties: A Network Theory Revisited. *Sociological Theory, 1*(1), 201–233. doi:10.2307/202051

Jamali, M., & Ester, M. (2010). A matrix factorization technique with trust propagation for recommendation in social networks. In *Proceedings of the fourth ACM conference on Recommender systems* (pp. 135-142). ACM. 10.1145/1864708.1864736

Jiang, M., Cui, P., Liu, R., Yang, Q., Wang, F., Zhu, W., & Yang, S. (2012). Social contextual recommendation. In *Proceedings of the 21st ACM international conference on Information and knowledge management* (pp. 45-54). ACM.

Koren, Y. (2010). Collaborative filtering with temporal dynamics. *Communications of the ACM, 53*(4), 89–97. doi:10.1145/1721654.1721677

Lifen, L. (2008). Trust Derivation and Transitivity in a Recommendation Trust Model. In *Computer Science and Software Engineering, 2008 International Conference on* (vol. 3, pp. 770-773). IEEE.

Liu, Q., Chen, E., Xiong, H., Ding, C., & Chen, J. (2012). Enhancing Collaborative Filtering by User Interest Expansion via Personalized Ranking. *IEEE Transactions on, 42*(1), 218–233. PMID:21880572

Ma, H., King, I., & Lyu, M. R. (2009). Learning to recommend with social trust ensemble. In *Proceedings of the 32nd international ACM SIGIR conference on Research and development in information retrieval* (pp. 203-210). ACM. 10.1145/1571941.1571978

Ma, H., Zhou, D., Liu, C., Lyu, M. R., & King, I. (2011). Recommender systems with social regularization. In *Proceedings of the fourth ACM international conference on Web search and data mining* (pp. 287-296). ACM. 10.1145/1935826.1935877

Nielsen. (2012). *State of the media - The social media report 2012*. Retrieved from http://www.nielsen.com/us/en/insights/reports/2012/state-of-the-media-the-social-media-report-2012.html

Peng, J., Zeng, D. D., Zhao, H., & Wang, F. (2010). Collaborative filtering in social tagging systems based on joint item-tag recommendations. In *Proceedings of the 19th ACM international conference on Information and knowledge management* (pp. 809-818). ACM. 10.1145/1871437.1871541

Phelan, O., McCarthy, K., & Smyth, B. (2009). Using twitter to recommend real-time topical news. In *Proceedings of the third ACM conference on Recommender systems* (pp. 385-388). ACM. 10.1145/1639714.1639794

Rapoport, A., & Horvath, W. J. (1961). A study of a large sociogram. *Behavioral Science, 6*(4), 279–291. doi:10.1002/bs.3830060402 PMID:14490358

Salakhutdinov, R., & Mnih, A. (2007). Probabilistic matrix factorization. *Advances in Neural Information Processing Systems*, 1257–1264.

Sarwar, B., Karypis, G., Konstan, J., & Riedl, J. (2001). Item-based collaborative filtering recommendation algorithms. *Proceedings of the 10th international conference on World Wide Web*, 285-295.

Stefanidis, K., Pitoura, E., & Vassiliadis, P. (2011). Managing contextual preferences. *Information Systems*, *36*(8), 1158–1180. doi:10.1016/j.is.2011.06.004

Yang, X., Liang, C., Zhao, M., Wang, H., Ding, H., Liu, Y., ... Zhang, J. (2017). Collaborative filtering-based recommendation of online social voting. *IEEE Transactions on Computational Social Systems*, *4*(1), 1–13. doi:10.1109/TCSS.2017.2665122

Yang, X., Steck, H., & Liu, Y. (2012). Circle-based recommendation in online social networks. In *Proceedings of the 18th ACM SIGKDD international conference on Knowledge discovery and data mining* (pp. 1267-1275). ACM.

ADDITIONAL READING

Boutet, A., Frey, D., Guerraoui, R., Jégou, A., & Kermarrec, A. M. (2016). Privacy-preserving distributed collaborative filtering. *Computing*, *98*(8), 827–846. doi:10.100700607-015-0451-z

Capdevila, J., Arias, M., & Arratia, A. (2016). Geosrs: A hybrid social recommender system for geolocated data. *Information Systems*, *57*, 111–128. doi:10.1016/j. is.2015.10.003

Klašnja-Milićević, A., Ivanović, M., Vesin, B., & Budimac, Z. (2017). Enhancing e-learning systems with personalized recommendation based on collaborative tagging techniques. *Applied Intelligence*, (1): 1–17.

Lee, W. P., & Ma, C. Y. (2016). Enhancing collaborative recommendation performance by combining user preference and trust-distrust propagation in social networks. *Knowledge-Based Systems*, *106*, 125–134. doi:10.1016/j.knosys.2016.05.037

Liu, X., Xie, R., Lin, C., & Cao, L. (2016). Question microblog identification and answer recommendation. *Multimedia Systems*, *22*(4), 487–496. doi:10.100700530-014-0411-z

Pan, W., & Ming, Z. (2017). Collaborative recommendation with multiclass preference context. *IEEE Intelligent Systems*, *32*(2), 45–51. doi:10.1109/MIS.2017.30

Pan, W., Xia, S., Liu, Z., Peng, X., & Ming, Z. (2016). Mixed factorization for collaborative recommendation with heterogeneous explicit feedbacks. *Information Sciences, 332*(C), 84-93. Bach, N. X., Hai, N. D., & Tu, M. P. (2016). Personalized recommendation of stories for commenting in forum-based social media ☆. *Information Sciences, 352–353*(C), 48–60.

Wu, C., Wang, J., Liu, J., & Liu, W. (2016). Recurrent neural network based recommendation for time heterogeneous feedback. *Knowledge-Based Systems, 109*(C), 90–103. doi:10.1016/j.knosys.2016.06.028

KEY TERMS AND DEFINITIONS

Interpersonal Trust: Interpersonal trust is a strong, deep, or close association or acquaintance between two or more people that may range in duration from brief to enduring.

Matrix Factorization: Matrix factorization is a factorization of a matrix into a product of matrices.

Recommendation Accuracy: The accuracy of recommendation system.

Recommendation Diversity: Provide items belonging to the non-rated but potentially interested category set.

Recommendation System: A recommendation system is a subclass of information filtering system that seeks to predict the "rating" or "preference" a user would give to an item.

Social Circle: A social circle has been defined as two or more people who interact with one another, share similar characteristics, and collectively have a sense of unity.

Social Network: A social network is a social structure made up of a set of social actors (such as individuals or organizations), sets of dyadic ties, and other social interactions between actors.

Chapter 7
Verification of Service-Based Declarative Business Processes:
A Satisfiability Solving-Based Formal Approach

Ehtesham Zahoor
National University of Computer and Emerging Sciences, Pakistan

Kashif Munir
National University of Computer and Emerging Sciences, Pakistan

Olivier Perrin
University of Lorraine, France

Claude Godart
University of Lorraine, France

ABSTRACT

Traditional business process specification approaches such as BPMN are procedural, as they require specifying exact and complete process flow. In contrast, a declarative process is specified by a set of constraints that mark the boundary of any solution to the process. In this chapter, the authors propose a bounded model-checking-based approach for the verification of declarative processes using satisfiability solving (SAT). The proposed approach does not require exponential space and is very efficient. It uses the highly expressive event calculus (EC) as the modeling formalism, with a sound and complete EC to SAT encoding process. The verification process can include both the functional and non-functional aspects. The authors have also proposed a filtering criterion to filter the clauses of interest from the large set of unsatisfiable clauses for complex processes. The authors have discussed the implementation details and performance evaluation results to justify the practicality of the proposed approach.

DOI: 10.4018/978-1-5225-7268-8.ch007

INTRODUCTION

A business process is a collection of related activities to accomplish a specific organizational goal. A business process can help an organization by improving agility, productivity, consistency, and can bring other important benefits such as repeatability or understanding. The methods used to manage business processes within an organization are collectively termed as Business Process Management (BPM). BPM involves methods to discover, model, analyze, improve, and automate business processes. First, the process designer needs to model the business process. The objective of business process modeling is to provide high-level specification independent from its implementation that should be easily understandable by the process modeler who creates the process, the developers responsible for implementing the process, and the business managers who monitor and manage the process. Then, the business process needs to be verified to identify any anomalies and conflicts (such as deadlocks) in the process specification before execution. Furthermore, the business process should be monitored while in execution to cater for unforeseen errors or for business process compliance monitoring (Gong, Knuplesch, Feng, & Jiang, 2017). In case of any monitored run-time conflicts, some recovery mechanisms should be provided (Babin, Ameur, & Pantel, 2017).

Web services are in the mainstream of information technology, paving way for inter and across organizational application integration. They can be defined as the software systems designed to support interoperable machine-to-machine interaction over a network. Web services allow heterogeneous systems based on heterogeneous platforms to not only communicate but to expose their operations to the rest of the world using Web services. In addition, the Web services can also be used to implement reusable application-components, such as currency conversion, weather reports etc. Web services are autonomous and they only present an interface that allows other systems to use the operations provided by them and internal implementation of these operations is hidden to the outside world. Web services can also be used to implement a Service Oriented Architecture (SOA), which is defined to be a flexible set of design principles for system development relying on the use of services. The vision associated with the SOA is to separate functions into services and compose them to support the development of distributed applications. As the Web services are autonomous, independent of platforms and programming languages, and are accessible over Internet, they can make functional building blocks of SOA. Business processes and SOA can converge as a business process can be executed using execution languages based on Web Services. Alternatively, from the services perspective, fine-grained services can be orchestrated into more coarse-grained value added processes. In this context, the business process can be considered as a Web services composition process and the terms will be uses interchangeably in this chapter.

BPM involves methods to discover, model (Du & Song, 2016), analyze (Zahoor, Munir, Perrin, & Godart, 2013), improve and automate business processes. In order to model business processes, they can be visualized as a flow chart of related activities and in this context, they are often modeled and specified using Business Process Model and Notation (BPMN). The BPMN specification provides a rich set of elements organized in Flow objects, Connecting objects, Swim lanes and Artifacts categories, and the specification also provides a partial mapping between the elements and the constructs of the execution language. However, BPMN requires specifying the exact and complete flow of the process.

A process model is termed as procedural when it contains explicit and complete information about the flow of the process. It only implicitly keeps track of why these design choices have been made and if they are indeed part of the requirements or merely assumed for specifying the process flow (Goedertier, 2008). In contrast, a declarative process model only requires specifying a set of constraints that mark the boundary of any solution to the composition process and any solution that respects these constraints is considered as a valid solution. Traditional approaches for modeling the business processes rely on a workflow-based approach where the process is modeled using approaches such as BPMN. While these approaches are intuitive and make it easier to model the processes, they are procedural in nature and they over-constrain the composition process, making it rigid and difficult to handle dynamically changing situations. In contrast, some declarative approaches have been proposed in the literature (Zahoor, Perrin, & Godart, 2010, July; van der Aalst & Pesic, 2006) that require the specification of constraints and are dynamic and flexible in nature. The graph-based composition modeling approaches are mostly procedural and although these graph-based approaches tend to be simpler and intuitive for the process modeler for the composition design, they over-constrain the process assuming the design choices that may not be present in the requirements but only added to specify the process flow. A typical example of such an approach is Business Process Modeling Notation (BPMN) and even if there is no dependency between the activities the process modeler is required to specify the process flow (possibly only using the sequence construct) that will result in over-constraining the process. The need for a declarative process is even more evident when business processes meet Internet of Things (IoT) and a business process within an IoT context should be modeled as a declarative process (Montali & Plebani, 2017).

An important feature of procedural approaches is that they provide well-known methods for verifying soundness of the process, and to define strict semantics associated to the processes. Specifying the exact and complete sequence of activities to be performed for the process, as required by the traditional procedural approaches, does make it possible to use proposed automata or Petri nets based approaches for design-time verification of composition process, as the state-space is already known and relatively small. In contrast, the state-space of a declarative process can be significantly large, as the process is only partially defined and as all the transitions have not been explicitly defined. This makes it difficult to use traditional approaches for the verification of declarative processes. In this chapter, the authors propose an approach for the verification of declarative composition processes using satisfiability solving. The proposed approach allows for identification of conflicts, hard constraints and inconsistencies in process specification and also allows resolving the identified conflicts. Specifically, the contribution of the authors include:

- A bounded model checking approach: For a declarative process, the state space can be significantly large, as all the transitions are not explicitly defined. The authors propose a SAT based bounded model checking approach, which does not require exponential space and is very efficient as the state space is searched in an arbitrary order.
- Event-Calculus (EC) based approach: The proposed approach relies on using EC as the modeling formalism with a sound and complete EC to SAT encoding process (Mueller, 2004). It also provides implementation support *(DECReasoner)* to directly convert the EC based models to SAT problem and to invoke a SAT-solver.
- An integrated approach: The traditional verification approaches require to map and transform the composition process to some formal logic and are mostly proposed as a separate layer to the composition model. Such a transformation can be complex, error-prone, possibly incomplete and on the expense of loss of semantics. The authors propose an integrated approach as they use the same modeling language and the same SAT encoding for finding the solution and for verifying properties of the composition process.
- Expressive approach: The use of EC as the modeling formalism allows for a highly expressive approach for both the specification of composition model and for the specification of verification properties. Verification properties can be specified for checking the connectivity, computability and behavioral correctness of the composition process. They can be based on both the functional and non-functional aspects. Furthermore, the properties can also be based on data or based on temporal and security aspects.
- Filtering approach to reduce the unsatisfiable-core: The set of unsatisfiable clauses returned by the SAT solver (unsatisfiable-core) can be significantly large for complex processes and large sets of verification properties. The authors propose a filtering criterion that can help to identify the clauses of interest. It is based on a set of patterns for process specification and uses

information about the structure of conflict clauses. The proposed filtering approach is generic and can be applied to any problem specified using EC.

- Implementation support: The authors have modified the *DECReasoner* code to allow for both the identification and filtering of unsatisfiable-core. They also present the detailed performance evaluation results justifying the gains of the proposed filtering approach.

RELATED WORK

The need to verify the correctness of the hardware and software systems has always been there. As a result, a number of approaches have been proposed in different domains. One particular family of approaches relies on the use of formal verification, which can be defined as the act of proving or disproving the correctness of a system with respect to formal specification, using formal methods of mathematics. The proposed approaches can be broadly categorized into automata, Petri nets and process-algebra based approaches as discussed in (Morimoto, 2008).

Automata Based Approaches

Automata are base model of formal specifications for systems (Hopcroft, Motwani, & Ullman, 2001). An automaton consists of a set of states and transition rules specify how to move from one state to another. It can be regarded as a graph where nodes represent the states, the arcs between the nodes represent the transition from one state to another and labels on the arcs represent what actions cause the transition. Numerous approaches have been proposed to verify the Web services composition process using the automata based approaches. In general, automata based approaches require to first convert the composition process model (specified using WS-BPEL, WS-CDL) to automata. Then, the proposed approaches require converting the automata to XML formats to be used with model-checkers such as SPIN and UPPAAL.

In (Fu, Bultan, & Su, 2004, May), the authors have extended the guarded automata model to allow the use of local XML variables and developed a tool, which translates WS-BPEL web services to extended guarded automata model. These guarded automata can then be translated into Promela (Process or Protocol Meta Language) for the SPIN model checker (Holzmann, 2004) to verify the properties (specified using Linear Time Temporal Logic) of composite web services specified in WS-BPEL and that communicate through asynchronous XML messages. In (Guermouche & Godart, 2009, July), the authors propose a formal framework for analyzing the compatibility of a choreography in which the Web services support asynchronous timed communications. Timed properties are modeled as the standard clocks of standard timed automata and the authors propose a set of required abstractions that allow to use the UPPAAL model checker to handle the timed asynchronous services.

In (Diaz, Pardo, Cambronero, Valero, & Cuartero, 2005), the authors discuss how to translate Web services with time restrictions (described by WS-BPEL/WSCDL) into a timed automata orchestration and then subsequently verify them by using the UPPAAL model checker. The authors present an extensive Travel Reservation System case study for discussing the translation and verification process using timed-automata. Furthermore, in (Dong, Liu, Sun, & Zhang, 2006), the authors use the composition process specified using an approach called Orc, which has precise semantics and is proposed to support a structured way of orchestrating services. The authors define the Timed Automata semantics for the Orc language and discuss how the Orc models are translated into timed-automata that can be verified using the UPPAAL model. In (Bentahar, Yahyaoui, Kova, & Maamar, 2013) authors have modeled the composition process using automata theory and used NuSMV model checker to verify properties such as absences of deadlocks and others.

Petri Net Based Approaches

Petri net is a framework to model concurrent systems. It has an easily understandable graphical notation. As the traditional graph-based composition process modeling approaches can include arbitrariness and lack strictness allowing for different interpretation of same process models (or multiple models for the same process requirements), numerous modeling approaches have their origin in Petri net theory (or on different variants of Petri nets to provide extra expressibility and functionality) including High Level Petri nets (Ellis & Nutt, 1993), Low Level Petri nets (Wikarski, 1996), and Colored Petri nets (Merz, Moldt, Müller, & Lamersdorf, 1995), a detailed discussion can be found in (Janssens, Verelst, & Weyn, 2000). In addition, different approaches investigate the use of Petri net for the composition process verification and, in general, the focus is how to translate business process diagrams into Petri net. Once the translation has been done, a variety of Petri net based tools can be used for process verification. However, as discussed in (Morimoto, 2008), various BPMN components such as gateways, event triggers, loop activities etc. are difficult to translate into Petri net.

The proposed Petri net based approaches include (Dijkman, Dumas, & Ouyang, 2008) in which the authors show how to correspond BPMN constructs into labeled Petri net by providing a mapping from a subset of BPMN elements to Petri nets. The authors have also implemented the proposed framework. However, the proposed mapping does not fully deal with some of BPMN constructs such as parallel multi-instance activities and OR-join gateways, and this scenario highlights the limitations of Petri nets. In (Narayanan & McIlraith, 2002), the authors define the semantics of relation WS-BPEL and OWL-S in terms of situation calculus and they formalize business processes in Petri net, and have developed a tool to describe and automatically verify composition of business processes. In (Hamadi & Benatallah, 2003), the authors have proposed a Petri net-based algebra for composing Web services. The authors have provided a direct mapping from each composition operator to a Petri net construction and have claimed that any service composition expressed using the algebra constructs can be translated into a Petri net representation that also allows for the process verification.

In (Yi & Kochut, 2004), authors have proposed a Petri net-based design and verification framework that allows for visualization and verification of the existing WS-BPEL processes and also provides support for creating the new WS-BPEL processes. The framework enables the use of verification techniques at the design time and the generated WS-BPEL specification skeleton is thus a verified process model. In (Zhang, Chang, Chung, & Kim, 2004), the authors introduce a Petri net based architectural description language called WS-Net, which is executable and incorporates the semantics of Colored Petri net and also supports the verification and monitoring of web services. WS-Net describes each Web services component in interface, interconnection, and interoperation layers. The approach requires manually transferring the WSDL specifications into the WS-Net specifications, which is not trivial according to the authors. Furthermore, in (Hinz, Schmidt, & Stahl, 2005), the authors propose formal Petri net semantics for WS-BPEL processes, which covers both standard behavior of WS-BPEL as well as the exceptional behavior such as faults, events and compensation, exception handling and compensations. In addition, the authors have implemented the proposed approach as a parser that can automatically convert WS-BPEL specification into the input language of the Petri net model-checking tool LoLA to analyze the composition process. In (Kheldoun, Barkaoui, & Ioualalen, 2017), the authors have proposed formal semantics of BPMN (including constructs such as cancellations, multiple instantiation of sub-processes, and exception handling) using recursive ECATNets. They have used the Maude LTL model checker to verify the resulting BPMN models. In (Xiu, Zhao, & Yang, 2017), the authors have proposed a Petri net based model with a hierarchical structure for the correctness verification of Web services based business processes.

Process Algebras Based Approaches

The process algebras are another family of approaches (including CSP, CCS, ACP, ambient calculus, fusion calculus, PEPA, and LOTOS) for formally modeling the concurrent systems. They provide support for both specifying the high-level description of interactions, communications, and synchronizations between processes and algebraic laws that allow specified process descriptions to be analyzed. They also provide support for bi-simulation analysis (formal reasoning about equivalences between processes), which can be helpful to verify whether a service can substitute another service or the redundancy of a service (Bordeaux, Salaün, Berardi, & Mecella, 2005). The process-algebraic based approaches for Web services composition include (Salaün, Bordeaux, & Schaerf, 2006), in which the authors discuss the application of process algebras to compose and verify business processes. The authors have shown an example in which they use CCS to specify and compose business processes and the use of Concurrency Workbench2 to verify the composition process. In (Ferrara, 2004), the authors have proposed correspondence between WS-BPEL and LOTOS (including compensations and exception handling). The verification of temporal properties is done with the CADP model checker.

Other Approaches

In (Boubaker, Klai, Schmitz, Graiet, & Gaaloul, 2017), the authors have proposed a model based on Symbolic Observation Graph (SOG) for identifying deadlock-free configuration decisions for variation points within configurable process models. In (Corradini et al., 2017), the authors have proposed BProVe, a verification framework for BPMN models based on an operational semantics and implemented using MAUDE. In (Wu, Lin, Wang, & Chen, 2016), the authors have advocated the need for dynamic business process model and both presented an algorithm and verification approach based on the Kripke structure and CTL based verification properties. An approach to model and verify composition processes based on model transformation is proposed in (Zhu, Huang, & Zhou, 2017). An approach for automatic service composition and its verification using model checking is proposed in (Huynh, Bui, & Quan, 2016). The model checking process is aided by heuristic-guided searching and logic-based clustering to make the process efficient. In (Khaled & Miller, 2017), the authors have proposed a formal model (Chor-calculus) for the design and verification of WS-CDL Choreographies using π-calculus model checkers.

Synthesis

In general, the traditional approaches for the composition process verification, as discussed in this section, require mapping the composition process (mostly defined using procedural approaches such as WS-BPEL) to some formal logic (such as Petri nets, automata or process logic) and then using verification tools such as model checkers to verify the composition process. This transformation-based approach has two major limitations. Firstly, the proposed verification approaches are based on traditional procedural approaches and, as discussed earlier, they over-constrain the composition process, making it rigid and difficult to handle dynamically changing situations. They have less expressiveness, flexibility, adaptability, and dynamism as compared to the declarative ones. Secondly, the limited expressiveness of traditional approaches makes it difficult to verify the non-functional properties (such as temporal, security requirements, or more importantly their combinations) associated with the composition process. It is difficult to specify the non-functional properties using the traditional approaches such as WS-BPEL and a number of approaches have been proposed as an extension to WS-BPEL for specifying non-functional aspects and then it is not trivial to add formal semantics to them for their verification.

Specifying the exact and complete sequence of activities to be performed for the composition process, as required by the traditional procedural approaches, however does make it possible to use proposed automata or Petri nets based approaches for design-time verification of composition process. However, with the declarative approaches, the process may only be partially defined and thus this makes it difficult to use traditional approaches for the process verification, as the state-space for a declarative process can be very large. Furthermore, the design-time verification should be coupled with execution-time monitoring and complexity of these approaches make them difficult to use for verifying the functional and non-functional constraints associated with the process while handling the process change or recovery.

Motivating Example

In order to highlight the contributions of proposed approach, the authors have chosen a motivating example from the logistics domain. The choice of the logistics domain stems from multiple interesting features of such processes. These processes involve many partners and intermediaries, from goods producers to shippers, considering also customs services. All these partners are using various heterogeneous systems, and processes should deal with interoperability issues. Then, these processes are highly dynamic processes, considering for instance delays, due to bad weather conditions or due to problems on flights/trucks. Finally, there are constraints that can be related to temporal issues, temperature-controlled freight, duties, taxes, and transportation for international shipments, regulations compliance of countries, or restricted trading parties. As such, verifying such processes can be difficult, particularly when these processes are modeled using a declarative framework.

The authors consider a composition process to handle the shipment and delivery of customer goods. The authors have based the composition process on the UPS delivery process and the Web services provided by the UPS Developer Kit, which allows an end-user to use services such as address validation, pickup scheduling etc. The authors consider a case study from the end-user's perspective who wants to send some goods from France to USA using UPS. Once the package is ready to be shipped, the user can use the Web services provided by UPS to handle package preprocessing such as to check address validity (*ValidateAddWS*), to calculate cost of different delivery options provided by UPS (*CalcCostWS*), to calculate the time required during the transit (*CalcTimeWS*), to locate the nearby UPS deposit center (*LocateStoreWS*), or to schedule a pickup (*SchPickupWS*), cost estimates for duties, taxes, (*CalcTaxWS*) or to add other services.

Once the package has been handed over to UPS (either by pickup or deposit, modeled as an activity *DepositOrCollect*), it is moved to a central sorting facility either by truck (modeled as an activity *CentralSortByTruck*) or by air (*CentralSortByAir*), and the employees there scan the labels (activity *ScanLabels*) to determine where the packages need to go. Regarding the case study, as the package is for an international shipment, it is then sorted to be sent to destination by air and while the package is being is in air (activity *InAirTransit*), the customs handling is electronically done (activity *DeclareCustoms*). Once the package arrives at USA, it is moved to some central sorting facility (activity *CentralSortUS*) and then to some regional shipping facility either by truck (*ShippingFacilityByTruck*) or by air (*ShippingFacilityByAir*) to be eventually delivered to the receiver (*DeliverPackage*). Regarding temporal constraints, consider that the activity *CentralSortByTruck* may take 5 hours while the activity *CentralSortByAir* can take 2 hours. The activity *ScanLabels* can take around one hour time in air-transit and eventually reaching the central sort at destination can take 20 hours, depending on the flights schedule. Once the package arrives at the central sorting facility at destination (*CentralSortUS*), it may take 5 hours to scan and transfer the package to regional shipping facility by truck (*ShippingFacilityByTruck*) or may take 3 hours to transfer by air (*ShippingFacilityByAir*). Finally, the eventual delivery (*DeliverPackage*) can take up to 10 hours.

This scenario is difficult to design with traditional approaches because instead of specifying the exact and complete sequence of activities that need to be executed in a pre-defined order, the solution depends on a set of constraints that are coming from different systems and that are difficult to solve manually as shown in Figure 1.

The verification of such a (possibly) partially defined declarative process is even more challenging as the state space to explore can be very large given the fact the all the transitions have not been defined. Figure 2 shows some of the possible solutions to a fragment of the declarative process and it shows that it is difficult to have a complete transition system for declarative process. Furthermore, introducing time and temporal aspects make the situation even more challenging.

Figure 1. Declarative process specification

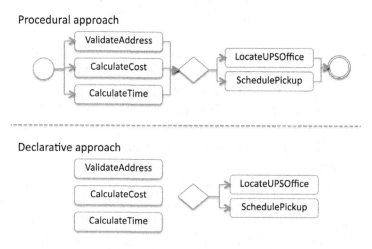

Figure 2. Possible executions for a declarative process

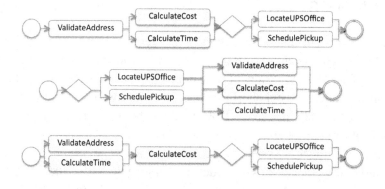

BACKGROUND

In this section, the authors provide a brief overview about the core concepts needed to understand the proposed approach including the Business Process Modeling Notation (BPMN), model checking, and the Event Calculus (EC).

Business Process Modeling Notation (BPMN)

Business Process Modeling Notation (BPMN) provides a graphical notation for specifying business processes using a flowcharting technique. BPMN aims to serve as a standard notation that is understandable by all business stakeholders. Process modeling using BPMN is simple and intuitive and it has a small set of graphical elements that are categorized into following categories:

- **Flow Objects:** Including Events (that specify something that happens), Activities (that specify the kind of work which must be done), and Gateways (that represent forking and merging of paths).
- **Connecting Objects:** Including Sequence Flow (which shows in which order the activities will be performed), Message Flow (that represent what messages flow), and Association (which is used to associate an Artifact to flow objects).
- **Swimlanes:** Including Pool (which represents participants in a process) and Lanes (that are used to organize and categorize activities within a pool according to function or role).
- **Artifacts:** Including Data Object (representing input/output data of an activity), Group (to group different activities), and Annotations.

Model Checking

Model checking is a technique for automatically verifying correctness of finite-state systems. It refers to the algorithms for exhaustively and automatically checking the state space of a transition system to determine if a given model of the system meets a given specification. Model checking tools have improved a lot in last decade and are being commercially marketed. However, one major challenge has always been the state explosion problem, which refers to the exponential growth of states with increase in the number of system components.

The initial implementations of model checking, in the early 1980s, used explicit representations of state transition graphs and used graph traversal techniques to explore them. However, the state explosion problem limited such techniques to be widely used. To cater for scalability and associated state space explosion problem of model checking approaches, symbolic model checking approach was introduced around 1990. In the symbolic model checking, a breadth first search of the state space is affected through the use of BDDs (Binary Decision Diagrams). The BDD based symbolic model checkers allow for an order of magnitude increase in the size of systems that could be checked but still the state space explosion has been a critical challenge. In addition, BDDs often become too large and they require variable orderings to be uniform along paths. In order to have smaller BDDs, it is important to select right variable ordering, which is a time-consuming process and requires manual intervention.

In bounded model checking, a Boolean formula is constructed that is satisfiable if and only if the underlying state transition system can realize a finite sequence of state transitions that reaches certain states of interest. If such a path segment cannot be found at a given length, K, the process can be repeated with the larger values of K. There are several advantages of bounded model checking over BDDs. First, the SAT tools do not require exponential space while BDDs often do as they usually operate in breadth first search consuming more memory. Thus, bounded model checking allows checking large designs in an efficient manner since the state space is searched in an arbitrary order. Another significant advantage is that bounded model checking requires little by-hand manipulation from the user. In contrast, in case of BDDs, it is important to select right variable ordering to have smaller BDDs, which requires manual intervention.

Event Calculus (EC)

The proposed approach is based on EC (Kowalski & Sergot, 1989). EC is a logic programming formalism for representing events and their effects and can infer "what is true when" given "what happens when" and "what actions do" as shown in Figure 3. The "what is true when" part both represents the state of the world called initial situation and the objective or goal. The "what actions do" part states the effects of the actions. The "what happens when" part is a narrative of events. A detailed presentation can be found in (Zahoor et al., 2010, July).

The EC comprises the following elements: A is the set of events (or actions), F is the set of fluents (fluents are reified), T is the set of time points, and X is a set of objects related to the particular context. In EC, events are the core concept that triggers changes to the world. A fluent is anything whose value is subject to change over time. EC uses predicates to specify actions and their effects. Basic EC predicates that are used for modeling the proposed framework are:

Initiates(e, f, t) fluent f holds after timepoint t if event e happens at t.
Terminates(e, f, t) fluent f does not hold after timepoint t if event e happens at t.
Happens(e, t) is true iff event e happens at timepoint t.
HoldsAt(f, t) is true iff fluent f holds at timepoint t.

Figure 3. EC components

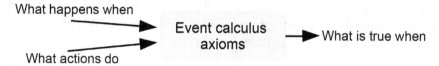

The choice of EC is motivated by several reasons. For the bounded model checking approach, it is first required to encode the sequential behavior of a transition system over a finite interval as a propositional formula. The encoded formula is then given to a propositional decision procedure, satisfiability (SAT) solver. The proposed approach relies on using EC as the modeling formalism with a sound and complete EC to SAT encoding process (Mueller, 2004). It also provides implementation support *(DECReasoner)* to directly convert the EC based models to SAT problem and to invoke a SAT-solver. Furthermore, EC is highly expressive and integrates an explicit time structure independent of any sequence of events (possibly concurrent). Then, given the composition design specified in the EC, a reasoner can be used to instantiate the composition design. EC is very interesting as the same logical representation can be used for verification at both design time (static analysis) and runtime (dynamic analysis and monitoring).

The EC models are presented using the discrete EC language (Mueller, 2010). The authors only present the simplified models that represent the core aspects, intentionally leaving out the supporting axioms. All the variables (such as service, time, etc.) are universally quantified. In case of existential quantification, it is represented with variable name within curly brackets, {*variablename*}. For spacing issues, some abbreviations are used.

Declarative Process Specification Using DISC Framework

The proposed verification approach is based on a declarative event-oriented framework, DISC - Declarative Integrated Self-healing web services Composition (Zahoor et al., 2010, July), which serves as a unified framework to bridge the gap between the process design, verification, and monitoring. The DISC framework is declarative and is based on EC.

In order to have an efficient, generic and extensible approach for composition process design and verification, the authors have structured the DISC framework on a pattern-based approach. Thus, all the EC models for specifying different components, control and data flow between them, and for modeling temporal and security aspects are organized into independent patterns. These patterns can be included to the EC based process specification. This pattern-based approach assists the proposed filtering criterion to identify the clauses of interest. For the DISC framework, the various components that constitute the composition design can be broadly divided into activity and service categories. Activity is a general term for any work being performed. The services include either the Web services instances already known or abstract Web services (called nodes) that need to be instantiated (discovered) based on some specified constraints.

Activities

Each activity can have an activity life cycle as it changes states from being started till its completion. In order to model the activities using EC, events can be defined that represent the actions required to start and finish the activities and EC fluents to represent the activity state. The EC based model for representing activities is shown in Table 1. A detailed discussion about modeling *activities* without intermediate states, *activities* that may require restart - possibly within loop body and *activity* model for dynamic task delegation can be found in (Zahoor E., 2011).

In the EC model shown in Table 1, an EC sort named *activity* is defined and instances of the sort will represent the actual *activities*. Then, *events* that represent the actions to change activity state and *fluents* that represent the activity state are defined. An activity state can either be *Started* or *Finished* and the events that are responsible for state change are the *Start* and *End* events respectively. Further, the *Initiates* axioms are defined that specify that if the *Start* event happens at some time, the fluent *Started* holds *true* after that time point and thus the *Initiates* axioms represent the state change. Further, as a result of *End* event, the activity state changes to *Finished* (represented by the second *Initiates* axiom). A *Terminates* axiom is also defined, which specifies that as a result of *End* event, the activity state is no longer *Started* (and thus the fluent *Started*, does not hold). Further, some axioms to control the invocation of specified events are defined such as the *End* event should only *happen* once the activity has already been *started*, and the fluent *Started* holds. Similarly, other axioms specify that once the activity has *Started* (or *Finished*) the *Start* (and *End*) events should not *happen*. Finally, the last two axioms specify that the initial condition for the fluents that they do not hold at time point 0.

An EC based *activity* usage model with two instances (*ActivityA* and *ActivityB*) of sort *activity* is shown in Table 2. The model first imports the EC core files (root.e and ec.e) and then imports the *activitywithstate.e* file containing the EC

Table 1. Activities model (with states)

```
sort activity
fluent Started(activity), Finished(activity)
event Start(activity), End(activity)
Initiates(Start(activity), Started(activity),time).
Initiates(End(activity), Finished(activity),time).
Terminates(End(activity), Started(activity),time).
Happens(End(activity), time) → HoldsAt(Started(activity), time).
HoldsAt(Started(activity), time) → !Happens(Start(activity), time).
HoldsAt(Finished(activity), time) → !Happens(End(activity), time).
HoldsAt(Finished(activity), time) → !Happens(Start(activity), time).
!HoldsAt(Started(activity), 0).
!HoldsAt(Finished(activity), 0).
```

model for activities modeling shown in Table 1. Then, the model defines instances of sort *activity* that represent the activities and also the goal for the process that is to have the activities *Finished* (and thus requiring the fluent *Finished* to hold) at time-point 2. Finally, the model specifies the range for time/offset and any options for the *DECReasoner*, in this case requiring not showing predicates (*showpred off*).

Invoking the EC reasoner, *DECReasoner*, for the EC model as shown in Table 2, gives the solution shown in Table 3. The solution returned by the reasoner shows that if the *Start* events happen (representing that the activities are thus being started) at time-point 0, the fluents *Started* hold at time-point 1 as indicated by the + sign shown next to them at time-point 1 (representing that the activities state has been changed to *Started*). Further, once the activities have been started the *End* events happen at time-point 1 to have the fluent *Finished* hold at time-point 2, that was the specified process goal. Notice that the *End* events also make the fluent *Started* does not hold as indicated by the − sign shown next to them at time-point 2, representing the activity state is no longer *Started*.

Web Services

The DISC framework also allows modeling the Web services and different Web services models have been proposed including Web services with different synchronization modes (synchronous / pull-push based asynchronous), Web services that require re-invocation, possibly within loop body, and Web services to be discovered based on constraints, called Nodes. The event-calculus model for the synchronous Web services is shown in Table 4.

Table 2. Activities definition using activitywithstate.e

```
;including helper files
load foundations/Root.e
load foundations/EC.e
load includes/activitywithstate.e
;creating instances representing activities
activity ActivityA, ActivityB
;initial conditions for the fluents
!HoldsAt(Finished(activity), 0).
;composition goal
HoldsAt(Finished (activity), 2).
range time 0 2
range offset 1 1
option showpred off
```

Table 3. Solution returned by the DECReasoner

```
Discrete Event Calculus Reasoner 1.0
loading foundations/Root.e
loading foundations/EC.e
loading includes/activitywithstate.e
32 variables and 78 clauses
relsat solver
1 model
—
model 1:
0
Happens(Start (ActivityA), 0). Happens(Start (ActivityB), 0).
1
+Started (ActivityA). +Started (ActivityB).
Happens(End (ActivityA), 1).
Happens(End (ActivityB), 1).
2
-Started (ActivityA). -Started (ActivityB).
+Finished (ActivityA).
+Finished (ActivityB)
```

Table 4. Web services (synchronous invocation)

```
sort synchserv
fluent RespRecvd_synchserv(synchserv)
event Invoke(synchserv)
Initiates(Invoke(synchserv), RespRecvd_synchserv(synchserv),time).
HoldsAt(RespRecvd_synchserv(synchserv), time) → !Happens(Invoke (synchserv),time).
!HoldsAt(RespRecvd_synchserv(synchserv),0).
```

Control/Data Flow Specification

DISC framework provides EC based patterns for specifying different control/data flow constructs, such as *Dependency*, *Split* construct with different *split-schemes (parallel/alternative/exclusive)*, *Join* construct with different join modes *(all/exactly-one/at-least-one/subset)*, *Conditions* and conditional invocation of components, *Iterations and Request/Response data* associated with and *Message flow* between components. As an example, the dependency construct, shown in Table 5, specifies the control and/or data flow dependency between different components.

In order to use the pattern for dependency specification shown in Table 5, one first needs to choose between two different patterns for dependency specification. The first pattern is for dependency specification without explicitly defining the delay between the components. As a result the dependent component is started/ invoked after some time (which is not explicitly specified) after the completion of other component. Then the second pattern for dependency specification is for

Table 5. The dependency construct

```
;Dependency specification without explicitly defining the delay
Happens(DEPENDENT_EVENT, time) → HoldsAt(SOURCE_FLUENT, time).
;Dependency specification with explicitly defining the delay (delay value 1 means immediately
after) Happens(SOURCE_EVENT, time) → Happens(DEPENDENT_EVENT, time+DELAY).
Happens(DEPENDENT_EVENT, time) → Happens(SOURCE_EVENT, time-DELAY).
```

explicitly specifying the delay with a delay value of 1 signifying immediately after. Furthermore, one needs to update the source and target events/fluents in the patterns above. For the first pattern the *DEPENDENT_EVENT* should be substituted by the start/invocation event for the dependent component while the *SOURCE_FLUENT* should be substituted by the fluent representing the completion/response reception of the component on which other is dependent. For the second dependency pattern, *SOURCE_EVENT* specifies the completion/invocation end event for the component on which other is dependent, while the *DELAY* specifies the invocation delay of dependent component after the completion of other component.

The *Split* construct requires the parallel start/invocation of multiple components (termed as split target) after the completion of a component (called split source). The split construct can take three forms; the *AND-Split* requires the parallel start/invocation of all components, the *OR-Split* requires the parallel start/invocation of at-least-one of the components while the *XOR-Split* requires the parallel start/invocation of exactly-one of the components specified in the split target. Further, the *Join* construct handles the control aggregation after the parallel invocation of components using the split construct and requires the components (to which control was splitted) to complete before the start/invoke of the component after the join construct. Different aggregation schemes can be used that can be used requiring *all/exactly-one/at-least-one/subset* of components to complete. Detailed EC models and their usage requirements can be found in (Zahoor E., 2011).

Modeling Non-Functional Aspects

The use of EC as formalism also allows modeling different non-functional (temporal and security) aspects. Different patterns include Response time, Restart/Refresh, Invocation time frame/delay, Allen's interval algebra and security concerns such as authorization policies. Allen's Interval Algebra is a calculus for temporal reasoning that was introduced by James F. Allen in 1983. The calculus defines possible relations between time intervals and provides a composition table that can be used as a basis for reasoning about temporal descriptions of events. The base relations for the Allen's interval algebra can be modeled using EC as shown in Table 6.

Table 6. EC patterns for Allen's interval algebra

COMP_A after COMP_B
Happens(EVENT_B, time) → Happens(EVENT_A, time+DELAY).
Happens(EVENT_A, time) → Happens(EVENT_B, time-DELAY).
COMP_A meets COMP_B
Happens(EVENT_B, time) → Happens(EVENT_A, time).
Happens(EVENT_A, time) → Happens(EVENT_B, time).
COMP_A overlaps COMP_B
Happens(EVENT_B, time) → Happens(EVENT_A, time-OVERLAP_DELAY).
Happens(EVENT_A, time) → Happens(EVENT_B, time+OVERLAP_DELAY).
COMP_A starts COMP_B
Happens(EVENT_A, time) → Happens(EVENT_B, time).
COMP_A ends COMP_B
Happens(EVENT_A, time) → Happens(EVENT_B, time).
COMP_A during(starts after and finishes before) COMP_B
Happens(EVENT_B_START, time) → Happens(EVENT_A_START, time+START_DELAY).
Happens(EVENT_A_START, time) → Happens(EVENT_B_START, time+START_DELAY).
Happens(EVENT_B_END, time) → Happens(EVENT_A_END, time-END_DELAY). Happens(EVENT_A_END, time) → Happens(EVENT_B_END, time+END_DELAY).

For the *after/meets/overlaps* relations, *EVENT_A* is the start event of component *COMP_A* and *EVENT_B* is the end event of the component *COMP_B*. For the *after* relation the *DELAY* specifies the delay time between the start of the components and for the meets relation there is no *DELAY*, as *COMP_A* starts at the same time as *COMP_B* finishes. Further, in case of the overlaps relation, the delay is called the *OVERLAP_DELAY*, which specifies the time in which both components are in concurrent execution.

For the *starts (ends)* relation, *EVENT_A* is the *start (end)* event of component *COMP_A* and *EVENT_B* is the *start (end)* event of the component *COMP_B*. For *during* and *equals* relations, *EVENT_A_START* and *EVENT_A_END* are the start/end events of the component *COMP_A* while *EVENT_B_START* and *EVENT_B_END* are start/end events of the component *COMP_B*. For the *during* relation, the *START_DELAY* specifies after how much time the *COMP_A* should start after starting *COMP_B* and *END_DELAY* specifies before how much time is should finish before *COMP_B* finishes. The equals relation uses the same axioms as for the *during* relation, without specifying the delay (or having delay equals 0).

The choice of Event-Calculus as the modeling formalism also allows handling the security requirements. In (Gaaloul, Proper, Zahoor, Charoy, & Godart, 2011) and (Gaaloul, Zahoor, Charoy, & Godart, 2010) authors have used EC to reason about delegation events to specify delegation policies dynamically. In (Bouchami, Perrin, & Zahoor, 2015) authors address the problem of the authorization's delegation in federated collaborative environments like Enterprise Social Networks. In (Zahoor, Perrin, & Bouchami, 2014) authors have proposed a formal Cloud-based authorization framework. They have considered trust to be a dynamic attribute to facilitate authorization decisions and have proposed models to handle different qualitative, quantitative and periodicity based temporal constraints. In (Zahoor, Asma, & Perrin, 2017) authors have proposed a formal Attribute Based Access Control (ABAC) model, which is based on Event-Calculus and is able to model and verify Amazon Web Services (AWS) Identity and Access Management (IAM) policies.

BPMN and Event-Calculus

The DISC framework can be extended to model core BPMN elements using EC. The objective is twofold; on one hand, this allows to provide formal-logic semantics to the BPMN elements, while on the other hand, the resulting design is highly expressive, flexible, and allows for reasoning about the BPMN elements to identify conflicts. An overview of the mapping BPMN core elements in event-calculus is shown in Table 7. In general, different BPMN elements can be regarded as event-calculus sorts (which are types) and a particular BPMN entity of some element type can be regarded as the instance of corresponding EC sort. Furthermore, sub-sorts in the EC can be used to model hierarchy among BPMN elements. In order to model properties of and relationships between different elements, EC predicates can then be used to reason about them.

BPMN *events* can be regarded as the instances of basic EC sort *event* and each *event* has a *trigger* and *impact*. Their *trigger* can be defined as axioms that define the necessary conditions for the *events* to happen and their *impact* can be defined by the effect on fluents and/or the triggering of other events. Events can have parameters and can have multiple (combination of) impacts and triggers. All the events can have impact(s) and trigger(s) and in order to mark the entry and exit point of the process, events named Start and End, can be used. However, in contrast to BPMN

Table 7. Modeling BPMN constructs using EC

Element	Event-calculus model
Event Activity Gateway Sequence/ Message flow Association Pool/Lane/Group Data object/ Mess-age/Text	*Instances of basic EC sort event, their trigger can be defined as axioms and their impact can be defined by effect on fluents.* *Can be mapped directly to Activities model discussed earlier. BPMN gateway constructs can be mapped to the Split/Join constructs.* *Sequence flow corresponds to the dependency construct (discussed earlier) with some difference as discuss below. Message flow can be mapped to the message flow construct discussed in (Zahoor E., 2011).* *An EC predicate, for instance HasAssociation(parameters), can be used to define associations for different elements.* *EC sorts for pool, lane, and group, and predicates (as similar to the association) can be used to specify which activity belongs to which pool/lane/group.* *Can be mapped to the request/response data elements modeling (Zahoor E., 2011).*

notation, the End event can also have impact(s), for instance changing the process status fluent, *ProcessTerminated( )*.

Activities as proposed in BPMN notation, can be mapped directly to the *activities* models discussed earlier. Regarding the control/data flow BPMN constructs modeling using event-calculus, the *sequence* (message) flow BPMN element can be mapped as specifying the (data) *dependency* between different components with one major difference; in BPMN notation, a *sequence* flow is used to show the order in which the activities will be performed in a process which may or may not be based on *dependency*. As a result, the process gets over-constrained and becomes highly procedural. In contrast, the EC based approach allows specifying the *dependency* between components if and only if there exists the dependency. One important advantage of the EC based approach is that it allows defining events-based dependency and thus dependency can be specified between any two events. This in-turn makes it possible to specify dependency not only on the successful completion of a component but also on the partial state of a component. Some examples include the dependency on an activity being started, in execution or on a service being invoked (and not yet completed) or on the data, such as data reception, expiry or the reception of some particular data values.

For the BPMN *gateways*, the XOR Split (Zahoor E., 2011) is an *Exclusive gateway*, the OR split is *Inclusive* gateway while the *AND-Split* is the *Parallel* gateway. The event based split is different from the BPMN event-based gateway in a way that the split decision is based on the occurrence or absence of the events, while the BPMN event-based gateway can be converted to a *data based* split gateway. The association BPMN construct is used to associate information and artifacts with the data elements. In EC this can be modeled by defining a predicate called *HasAssociation(artifact, activity)* to define associations for different artifacts, that can be instances of a defined sort named *artifact*. Then, for the *Pool/Lane/Group*, sorts called pool, lane, group, and EC predicates (similar to the association) to specify which activity belongs to which pool/lane/group can be used. For the *Data object/Message/Text*, corresponding EC sorts *object/message/text* and the predicate *HasDataObject(activity, object)* can be used.

VERIFICATION PROPERTIES

The proposed approach for process verification allows for both model checking the verification properties and for identifying and resolving the conflicts in the process specification (a result of process verification). In this section the authors focus on the verification properties.

Categories

The proliferation of approaches that have been proposed to verify the composition process has lead to the verification properties that are dependent on some specific case study. Some seminal work on categorizing the verification properties and defining correctness of the composition process can be found in (Roglinger, 2009). The proposed approach considers the verification properties for checking the connectivity, computability, and behavioral correctness of the composition process.

As the composition process is possibly partially defined, a basic (but critical) verification objective is to verify that a solution exists, and that this solution respects all the associated functional and non-functional constraints associated with the process. In other words, it must be ensured that the fragments of possibly partially defined process can be connected in a way that the orchestration exists and is compatible with the constraints associated with the composition process. The connectivity and computability verification properties make indeed a necessary condition for defining the correctness of the process. A connected process may represent a solution but the connectivity itself cannot be considered as a sufficient condition. The verification properties must be augmented to also include the behavioral properties, such as the liveness and safety properties. A safety property stipulates that nothing bad will happen, ever, during the execution of a system. A very important type of safety property is an invariant, which is defined to be a property that must hold in all reachable states. A liveness property stipulates that something good will happen, eventually, during the execution of a system. Connectivity and computability can ensure the safety properties for the solutions returned as the process is connected and solution is returned only if safety claims hold. On the other hand, the liveness properties can ensure that the alternatives to the solutions returned (if needed to cater for process change during execution) can still hold the safety claims, or identify which claims are violated.

Structure

For the proposed approach, the verification properties are not external properties associated to the process; they are part of the process and can be added to the process specification. In general, they can either be based on occurrence (or absence) of some specific event, as represented by EC events, or they can be based on satisfaction (or dissatisfaction) of some property, as represented by EC fluents. Table 8 presents the general form of verifications properties.

This way of modeling the verification properties results in a highly expressive specification approach as the process specification includes any process state (represented by fluents) and any action as represented by events.

Table 8. Verification properties: General form

```
;General form
(!)Happens(SomeEvent( ), SomeTimePoint).
(!)HoldsAt(SomeFluent( ), SomeTimePoint).
```

Table 9. Verification properties: Web services example

```
Happens(Invoke(SomeServiceB),time) → HoldsAt(ResponseReceived (SomeServiceA), time).
HoldsAt(ResponseReceived(SomeService), SomeSpecificTimePoint).
;Invariant property
!Happens(InvalidateResponse(service), time).
```

Some verification properties for any Web services added to the composition process are presented in Table 9. The first axiom specifies a dependency constraint between two Web services requiring *ServiceB* to be only invoked once the response from *ServiceA* has been received. The second axiom specifies a temporal constraint that the result after the invocation of a Web service should be available at some particular time-point. The last axiom specifies an Invariant that the data from some services should never be invalid.

Some axioms related to activities (a general terms for any work done) are shown in the Table 10. The first two axioms can be used to either specify if two activities should always be executed in parallel *(Happens)* or in sequence *(!Happens)*. One important advantage of the proposed approach is that it allows defining events-based axioms and thus verification properties can be specified between any two events. This, in-turn, makes it possible to specify dependency not only on the successful completion of a component but also on the partial state of a component. Examples include defining the dependency on an activity being started, as modeled in the last axiom.

In general, the verification properties can be based on functional aspects (such as verifying the invocation order of Web services), non-functional (such as temporal and security aspects), data based properties (such as verifying data availability and

Table 10. Verification properties: Activities example

```
Happens(Start(ActivityA),time) → (!) Happens(Start(ActivityB),time).
Happens(Start(ActivityB),time) → (!) Happens(Start(ActivityA),time).
;dependency on intermediate state of an activity
Happens(Start(ActivityB),time) → HoldsAt(Started(ActivityA), time).
```

validity). One major advantage of this approach is that the use of the same formalism (EC) allows combining all these aspects. As an example, consider the verification property to check data validity or access control within specific time frame during dynamic task delegation.

PROCESS VERIFICATION USING SATISFIABILITY SOLVING

The proposed approach for composition process verification is based on bounded model checking and this requires first encoding the sequential behavior of a transition system over a finite interval as a propositional formula as shown in the last section. The encoded formula is then given to a propositional decision procedure, a SAT solver. In this section, the authors first provide a brief overview about the proposed approach and then discuss and categorize the conflicts identified as a result of process verification. Then, the proposed approach to filter the set of unsatisfiable clauses is presented.

Overview

For the proposed approach, the verification properties are added to the process specification (in terms of EC axioms) and then the *DECReasoner* is invoked for finding a solution to the composition process. The *DECReasoner* then encodes the EC based process specification into a satisfiability problem and invokes the SAT solver which either returns solution(s) to the composition problem or a set of unsatisfiable clauses that represent some conflicts or hard-constraints in the process specification. This results in an extensible approach as the same encoding can be analyzed by different off-the-shelf SAT solvers.

For the motivating example, invoking the SAT solver for the composition process (specified using EC) returns a set of solutions satisfying the connectivity (and safety properties regarding control flow such as mutual exclusion), including the one shown in Table 11:

The solution returned by the reasoner shows which events happen at which time-points and their effect on the fluents as indicated by the +/− sign shown with the fluents. The fragment above shows that there exists a solution (and thus the connectivity property is satisfied) but one may also want to investigate if the other possible solutions are feasible. The activities *CentralSortByTruck* and *CentralSortByAir*, representing the transfer of package to central sorting facility, are mutually exclusive and have different temporal constraints. The solution above suggests to use Air-service for transfer to shipping facility *(Happens(Start(Shippin*

Table 11. Solution returned by the reasoner for the motivating example

```
0 Happens(Invoke(CalcCostWS/LocateStoreWS/SchPickupWS), 0).
1 +ResponseReceived(CalcCostWS). +ResponseReceived(LocateStoreWS)...
...
11 Happens(Start(DepositOrCol lect), 11).
12 +Started(DepositOrCol lect). Happens(End(DepositOrCollect), 12).
13 -Started(DepositOrCollect). +Finished(DepositOrCollect).
 Happens(Start(CentralSortByTruck), 13).
14 +Started(CentralSortByTruck).
18 Happens(End(CentralSortByTruck), 18).
19 -Started(CentralSortByTruck). +Finished(CentralSortByTruck).
 Happens(Start(ScanLabels), 19).
20 +Started(ScanLabels). Happens(End(ScanLabels), 20).
21 -Started(ScanLabels). +Finished(ScanLabels).
22 Happens(Start(InAirTransit), 22).
23 +Started(InAirTransit).
...
33 Happens(Start(DeclareCustoms), 33).
34 +Started(DeclareCustoms). Happens(End(DeclareCustoms), 34).
35 -Started(DeclareCustoms).+Finished(DeclareCustoms).
42 Happens(End(InAirTransit), 42).
43 -Started(InAirTransit). +Finished(InAirTransit).
 Happens(Start(CentralSortUS), 43).
44 +Started(CentralSortUS). Happens(End(CentralSortUS), 44).
45 -Started(CentralSortUS). +Finished(CentralSortUS).
 Happens(Invoke(TrackWS), 45). Happens(Start(ShippingFacilityByAir), 45).
46 +ResponseReceived(TrackWS). +Started(ShippingFacilityByAir).
48 Happens(End(ShippingFacilityByAir), 48).
49 -Started(ShippingFacilityByAir). +Finished(ShippingFacilityByAir).
 Happens(Start(DeliverPackage), 49).
50 +Started(DeliverPackage).
...
59 Happens(End(DeliverPackage), 59).
```

gFacilityByAir), 45).) and to use the truck facility for transfer to central sort *(Hap pens(Start(CentralSortByTruck),13))*.

However, as such a decision can change while the process is in execution (due to bad weather conditions for instance), one would like to see if alternative solution exists (by using truck facility to shipping facility). This can be achieved by adding a liveness property to the process specification, as shown in Table 12.

Table 12. Liveness property for the Motivating Example

```
{time} Happens(Start(Shipping FacilityByTruck), time)
```

Invoking the SAT solver again returns an updated model in which it suggests now to use *Airservice* to transfer to the *Central sort*. In this context, adding another liveness property for *CentralSortByAir* results in a conflict, as it is not possible to use both *Air-facilities.*

Conflicts

Violations of verification properties, hard constraints or incorrect process specification lead to conflicts that need to be identified and resolved. These conflicts can be broadly categorized into the syntactic and semantic categories. The syntactic conflicts result due to erroneous process specification and to erroneous syntactic rules for process specification using Discrete EC Language, which can be identified using *DECReasoner*. Semantic conflicts result from the process specification including deadlocks, hard and conflicting constraints. The specified composition goal (to hold at specified time-point) may not be possible to achieve if the dependency between two components cannot be respected within the specified time frame. The conflicts can be based on local temporal constraints or occur due to the temporal constraints specified between different components by the composition process. Furthermore, the conflicts can be based on security constraints associated with the composition process such as the Separation of Duties (SoD) constraint requiring prohibition to invoke of a service if another service had been executed, possibly combined with temporal conditions (e.g., the ban lasts only two hours), access control aspects such as the permission/prohibition to invoke a service given a role.

Filtering the Unsatisfiable-Core

The EC to SAT encoding can be very large especially with the increase in time-points/free variables in axioms and with the complexity of the composition process. As a result, the set of un-satisfiable clauses (termed as unsatisfiable core) can be very large. The authors thus propose to filter the unsatisfiable core but this requires brief introduction to the EC to SAT encoding process.

The encoding process is detailed in (Mueller, 2010). It works by first applying syntactic transformations to all the input formulas containing the predicate symbols such as Initiates, Terminates, Releases, or Trajectory to reduce resulting SAT problem size and the transformed formulas are added to the conjunction of problem formulas. Then, conjunction of any problem formulas not modified by syntactic transformations is also added and the Happens predicates are completed in the conjunction of problem formulas. In order to enforce the common sense law of inertia, explanation closure frame axioms from Initiates, Terminates, and Releases axioms are added to the conjunction of problem formulas. Then, the conjunction of problem formulas is transformed into a propositional calculus formula. Finally, the ground atoms are mapped to the variables of the satisfiability problem.

In order to filter the unsatisfiable core, the authors propose to only consider the encoded clauses added for formula axioms (that specify the control/data flow, temporal, security or other constraints for the particular problem). This allows to ignore the encoded clauses added for the frame and completion axioms, encoding of Initiates/Terminates symbols, initial conditions for fluents, the composition goal and the initial conditions for Releases axioms. The use of pattern-based approach, further allows ignoring the encoding of generic axioms needed to model the services and activities. In order to demonstrate the process verification in case of a conflict in process specification and corresponding filtering of the unsatisfiable-core, consider a simple example considering only two activities *ScanLabels* and *SortPackage*. These activities need to be executed to have *SortPackage* finished at time-point 1 (the composition process goal). However, a conflicting axiom is intentionally added to have the activity *SortPackage* dependent on activity *ScanLabels*, as shown in Table 13.

Invoking the SAT-solver for the process verification gives a set of unsatisfiable clauses, as shown in Table 14. The unsatisfiable core returned by the reasoner contains 7 clauses for a very simple composition process and with the increase in problem complexity and size; the unsatisfiable core can be very large. However, the proposed filtering on the unsatisfiable core can be very effective for reducing the size.

The unsatisfiable-core returned by the reasoner contains 7 unsatisfied clauses. The clauses 4 6 14 -5 0 and 16 -6 0 are the frame axioms so they can be ignored. Then the axioms -16 0, -14 0 and -13 0 are the initial conditions for the fluents and initial conditions for the ReleasedAt. Further, the axiom 5 0 is the composition goal and the only clause left is 13 -4 0: (HoldsAt(Finished(ScanLabels), 0) | !Happens(Start(SortPackage), 0)). This clause is transformed form of the dependency axiom in the process specification requiring SortPackage to be started if the ScanLabels has finished. This clause is causing the conflict because respecting the dependency; it is not possible to achieve the composition goal.

Table 13. Process specification with a conflict

load includes/activitywithoutstate.e *activitywithoutstate ScanLabels, SortPackage* *Happens(Start(SortPackage), time) → HoldsAt (Finished (ScanLabels), time).* *HoldsAt(Finished(SortPackage), 1).* *range time 0 2*

Table 14. Unsatisfiable clauses for process specification with a conflict

---

7 unsatisfied clauses:
-16 0: (!ReleasedAt(Finished(SortPackage), 0)).
-14 0: (!HoldsAt(Finished(SortPackage), 0)).
-13 0: (!HoldsAt(Finished(ScanLabels), 0)).
4 6 14 -5 0: (Happens (Start(SortPackage), 0) | ReleasedAt (Finished(SortPackage),
1) | HoldsAt (Finished(SortPackage), 0) | !HoldsAt (Finished(SortPackage), 1)).
5 0: HoldsAt (Finished(SortPackage), 1).
16 -6 0: (ReleasedAt (Finished(SortPackage), 0) | !ReleasedAt (Finished(SortPackage), 1)).
13 -4 0: (HoldsAt (Finished(ScanLabels), 0) | !Happens (Start(SortPackage), 0)).

The unsatisfiable core for the simple example contained only 7 conflict clauses and they were filtered to have only one clause. The conflict clause is in fact based on the proposed patterns for specifying the dependency amongst components. The use of the pattern-based approach thus further allows to concentrate only on specific kind of clauses, once the unsatisfiable core has been filtered. In general, the unsatisfiable-core can be significantly large to be manually analyzed. In order to automate the filtering process, the authors have modified the *DECReasoner* EC to SAT encoding process to log the type of clause being encoded (either a frame/completion axiom or the input formula) and the corresponding encoding. This allows to later parse the log file in order to filter out frame/completion axioms and initial conditions for the fluents. The extension of the original DISC framework with a pattern-based approach further allows filtering out the encoding for generic models for specifying different aspects. The overall approach works as follows:

1. Modified *DECReasoner* encodes the problem into a SAT problem and also creates a detailed log about the encoding process.
2. The modified reasoner then invokes zchaff/zverify df solver (if no solution is found by relsat solver). The output is a set of unsatisfiable clauses.
3. A Java application then parses the log file and the unsatisfiable-core returned by the SAT solver to filter and identify clauses of interest.
4. The resulting output is not only significantly smaller but also the clauses correspond to the patterns for specifying different aspects that can help in identifying the source of conflicts.

As another example of the proposed filtering approach, a deadlock can be introduced within the composition process specification of the motivating example, as shown in Table 15.

Table 15. Motivating example specification with a deadlock

Happens(Start(DeliverPackage), time) → HoldsAt(Finished (ShipFacByTruck), time) I HoldsAt(Finished (ShipFacByAir), time). *;adding deadlock by introducing cyclic dependency Happens(Start(ShipFacByTruck),time)→HoldsAt(Finished(DeliverPackage),time). Happens(Start(ShipFacByAir),time)→HoldsAt(Finished(DeliverPackage),time).*

The *zchaff/zverify df* SAT solver returns a set of 682 unsatisfied clauses which are indeed difficult to manually analyze. This increase in unsatisfied clauses stems from the fact that the deadlock was added to the motivating example and there are 15763 encoded clauses for the motivating example. Then, encoding log and unsatisfiable-core are provided as input to the Java application, which first considers only the encoding for problem axioms (and filtering others). Then, for these clauses, the application checks if indeed they belong to the unsatisfiable-core. This results in a set of 283 unsatisfiable clauses (from 2075 filtered clauses considering only problem axioms), which may still seem large enough. However, the large size is primarily due to a small set of clauses grounded to different time-points. There are 278 clauses involving the *ShipFacByTruck*, *ShipFacByAir* and *DeliverPackage* that correspond to the (conflicting) dependency axioms and their temporal constraints. This in-turn indicates the problem source.

As another example, consider a composition process being setup to semi-automate the disaster plan for the Australian National Herbarium (ANH) Canberra, as discussed in (Zahoor, 2011). It involves a composition process for the recovery of the items for priority salvage and treatment at ANH. The composition process is large, complex, highly dynamic and has different functional and non functional constraints and it makes it an interesting case study to apply the proposed process verification approach.

A deadlock in the process specification can be introduced as shown in Table 16. Invoking the SAT-solver for the process verification gives a set of unsatisfiable clauses as shown below. Analyzing the unsatisfiable core, one can identify that the last two axioms are the transformed clauses for the newly added axiom causing the deadlock.

Table 16. ANH Process specification with a deadlock

;check if it is a false alarm only if CRR is available *Happens(EvalCondTrue(FalseAlarmCheckByCRR), time) & Happens(EvalCondFalse(FalseAlarmCheckByCRR), time) →HoldsAt(CondTrue(IsCRRAvailable),time).* *;the conflicting axiom deadlock* *Happens(EvalCondTrue(IsCRRAvailable), time) & Happens(EvalCondFalse (IsCRRAvailable), time) →HoldsAt(CondTrue(FalseAlarmCheckByCRR),time).*

Table 17. Unsatisfiable clauses for process specification with a deadlock

5 unsatisfied clauses:
-11125 0: (!HoldsAt(CondTrue(FalseAlarmCheckByCRR), 0)).
4215 0: Happens(Start activityWS(Start), 0).
5118 8118 -4215 0: (Happens(EvalCondTrue(IsCRRAvailable), 0) & Happens (EvalCondFalse (IsCRRAvailable), 0) & !Happens(StartactivityWS(Start), 0)).
11125 -5118 0: (HoldsAt(CondTrue(FalseAlarmCheckByCRR), 0) &
!Happens (EvalCondTrue(IsCRRAvailable), 0)).
11125 -8118 0: (HoldsAt(CondTrue(FalseAlarmCheckByCRR), 0) & !Happens(EvalCondFalse (IsCRRAvailable), 0)).

IMPLEMENTATION DETAILS

The EC models for the proposed framework are specified using the discrete EC language (Mueller, 2010) and all the models mentioned earlier can be directly used for reasoning purposes. In order to abstract the EC models from the process-designer and automate the composition process specification and verification, the authors have implemented a Java-based application, called ECWS, which provides a user friendly interface for specifying the composition design and allows to generate EC models for the specification and automatically invokes the *DECReasoner* to reason about the generated EC models.

Enhancements to the DECReasoner

As discussed earlier, in order to use the *DECReasoner* domain description (specified using Discrete EC Reasoner language) that includes an axiomatization describing domains of interest, observations of world properties at various times, and a narrative of known event occurrences is placed in a file. The *DECReasoner* is then invoked for the domain description and it first transforms the domain description into a satisfiability (SAT) problem. It then invokes a SAT solver (*relsat*), which produces zero or more solutions and the resulting solutions are decoded and displayed to the user.

However, if relsat solver produces no models (as a result of some conflict in the process specification), the *DECReasoner* then invokes the *walksat* solver first with the *-target* parameter having value 1 and then (if previous run fails) with *-target* parameter having 2. If the *walksat* run fails again, the *DECReasoner* gives up without providing any solution. If the invocation of *walksat* solver does return a set of unsatisfiable clauses it is suggested that one or two unsatisfied clauses may be helpful for debugging while three or more unsatisfied clauses tend to be less useful (Mueller, 2010). Furthermore, it is suggested that as the walksat is stochastic, it is possible to get a different set of unsatisfiable clauses on different runs and by looking at different sets of unsatisfiable clauses would be helpful in debugging the process model.

This approach may be somewhat helpful for simpler models, however, it is not possible to use this as a verification approach as neither *walksat* is always able to identify unsatisfiable core, nor the size of unsatisfiable core is small enough to be manually observed. As a result, the authors have modified the *DECReasoner* code to have *zchaff/zverify df* as the solver to be used for the process verification. *Zchaff* is an implementation of the Chaff algorithm and won the Best Complete Solver in both industrial and handmade benchmark categories for SAT 2002 Competition. The output from *zchaff* can also be used by *zverify df* tool to get a set of unsatisfiable clauses that can be used for the process verification. The modified verification approach thus first invokes the *zchaff* solver instead of *walksat* and the output from the *zchaff* is passed to *zverify df* for identifying a set of unsatisfiable clauses. These unsatisfiable clauses can then be filtered. The authors have also modified the encoding process to log that which clauses represent the frame axioms (and others) and this information can help to automate the filtering process.

Performance Evaluation Results

The performance evaluation tests are conducted on a MacBook Pro Core 2 Duo 2.53 Ghz and 4GB RAM. The *DECreasoner* version 1.0 and the SAT reasoner, *relsat-2.0* are used for reasoning in order to test the performance evaluation of *zchaff* solver for the process verification and to highlight the effectiveness of the proposed unsatisfiable-core filtering approach.

Regarding the performance evaluation results, different test-cases are used to measure both the efficiency of the SAT solvers and the effectiveness of the proposed filtering approach. The performance evaluation results for the time taken by the *relsat* and *zchaff/zverify* df solvers are shown in Figure 4. The Y-axis shows the time taken by the SAT solvers (in seconds) for either identifying the unsatisfiable-core to resolve a deadlock or to find an updated solution as a result of adding a liveness property to the motivating example. The X-axis shows the problem size in terms of time-points (increase in time-point increases SAT encoding and the results are consistent with increasing number of services and activities). As evident from the performance evaluation results, the SAT solvers are very efficient and even with large problems, time taken to find the solution/unsatisfiable-core remains low. The second test case aims to identify the effectiveness of proposed filtering approach to reduce the number of clauses in the unsatisfiable-core. The performance evaluation results are shown in Figure 5, Y-axis shows the number of clauses for the motivating example while the X-axis shows the problem size in terms of time-points. From the results, it can be observed that the increase in problem size results in the increase

Figure 4. Performance evaluation for the SAT solvers

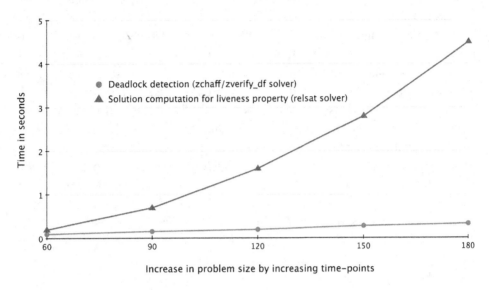

in the number of encoded clauses justifying claim for the large state space of the declarative process. However, the set of clauses corresponding to problem axioms is relatively small justifying proposed approach to filter out frame-axioms and other clauses. Furthermore, using the filtered set of clauses and the unsatisfiable-core returned by the solver, one can have a relatively small set of filtered unsatisfiable-core and the distinct clauses (only separated by grounded time points) remain constant.

Figure 5. Effectiveness of proposed filtering approach

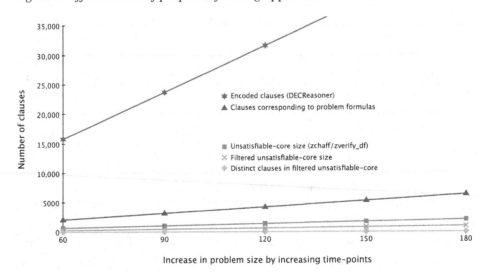

CONCLUSION

In this chapter, the authors have proposed a complete and consistent bounded model-checking based approach for the verification of declarative Web services composition processes using satisfiability solving (SAT). The need for the bounded model-checking approach stems from the nature of declarative processes as they are defined by only specifying the constraints that mark the boundary of the solution to the composition process. As a result, their state space can be significantly large, as all the transitions are not explicitly defined. The authors propose a SAT based bounded model checking approach, which does not require exponential space and is very efficient as the state space is searched in an arbitrary order. The proposed approach relies on using EC as the modeling formalism with a sound and complete EC to SAT encoding process. The use of EC as the modeling formalism allows for a highly expressive approach for both the specification of composition model and for the specification of verification properties. Verification properties can be specified for checking the connectivity, computability, and behavioral correctness of the composition process. They can be based on both the functional and non-functional aspects. Furthermore, the properties can also be based on data or based on temporal and security aspects.

The set of unsatisfiable clauses returned by the SAT solver (unsatisfiable-core) can be significantly large for complex processes and large sets of verification properties. To handle this problem, the authors have proposed a filtering criterion that can help to identify the clauses of interest. It is based on a set of patterns for process specification and uses information about the structure of conflict clauses. The proposed filtering approach is generic and can be applied to any problem specified using EC. The authors have modified the *DECReasoner* code to allow for both the identification and filtering of unsatisfiable-core. They have also presented the detailed performance evaluation results justifying the need and contributions of the proposed approach.

REFERENCES

Babin, G., Ameur, Y. A., & Pantel, M. (2017). Web service compensation at runtime: Formal modeling and verification using the event-b refinement and proof based formal method. *IEEE Transactions on Services Computing, 10*(1), 107–120. doi:10.1109/TSC.2016.2594782

Bentahar, J., Yahyaoui, H., Kova, M., & Maamar, Z. (2013). Symbolic model checking composite web services using operational and control behaviors. *Expert Systems with Applications*, *40*(2), 508–522. doi:10.1016/j.eswa.2012.07.069

Bordeaux, L., Salaün, G., Berardi, D., & Mecella, M. (2005). When are two web services compatible? In. Lecture Notes in Computer Science: Vol. 3324. *Technologies for E-Services* (pp. 15–28). Berlin: Springer. doi:10.1007/978-3-540-31811-8_2

Boubaker, S., Klai, K., Schmitz, K., Graiet, M., & Gaaloul, W. (2017). Deadlock-freeness verification of business process configuration using SOG. In Service-oriented computing, ICSOC 2017 (vol. 10601, pp. 96-112). Springer. doi:10.1007/978-3-319-69035-3_7

Bouchami, A., Perrin, O., & Zahoor, E. (2015). Trust-based formal delegation framework for enterprise social networks. In *2015 IEEE trustcom/bigdatase/ispa* (pp. 127–134). IEEE. doi:10.1109/Trustcom.2015.366

Corradini, F., Fornari, F., Polini, A., Re, B., Tiezzi, F., & Vandin, A. (2017). Bprove: a formal verification framework for business process models. In *Proceedings of the 32nd IEEE/ACM international conference on automated software engineering, ASE 2017* (pp. 217–228). IEEE/ACM. 10.1109/ASE.2017.8115635

Diaz, G., Pardo, J. J., Cambronero, M. E., Valero, V., & Cuartero, F. (2005). Automatic translation of ws-cdl choreographies to timed automata. In. Lecture Notes in Computer Science: Vol. 3670. *Formal Techniques for Computer Systems and Business Processes* (pp. 230–242). Berlin: Springer. doi:10.1007/11549970_17

Dijkman, R. M., Dumas, M., & Ouyang, C. (2008). Semantics and analysis of business process models in BPMN. *Information and Software Technology*, *50*(12), 1–14. doi:10.1016/j.infsof.2008.02.006

Dong, J. S., Liu, Y., Sun, J., & Zhang, X. (2006). Verification of computation orchestration via timed automata. In *Formal Methods and Software Engineering* (Vol. 4260, pp. 226–245). Berlin: Springer. doi:10.1007/11901433_13

Du, X., & Song, W. W. (2013). Conceptual graph: An approach to improve quality of business services modeling. In *Web Information Systems Engineering*, *8182*, 239–251.

Ellis, C. A., & Nutt, G. J. (1993). Modeling and enactment of workflow systems. In *Application and Theory of Petri Nets 1993* (Vol. 691, pp. 1–16). Springer Berlin Heidelberg. doi:10.1007/3-540-56863-8_36

Ferrara, A. (2004). Web services: a process algebra approach. In *Proceedings of the 2nd international conference on Service oriented computing* (pp. 242-251). ACM.

Fu, X., Bultan, T., & Su, J. (2004). Analysis of interacting BPEL web services. In *Proceedings of the 13th international conference on World Wide Web* (pp. 621-630). ACM.

Gaaloul, K., Proper, H. A., Zahoor, E., Charoy, F., & Godart, C. (2011). A logical framework for reasoning about delegation poli- cies in workflow management systems. *IJICS, 4*(4), 365–388. doi:10.1504/IJICS.2011.044825

Gaaloul, K., Zahoor, E., Charoy, F., & Godart, C. (2010). Dynamic authorisation policies for event-based task delegation. In *Advanced information systems engineering, 22nd international conference* (pp. 135–149). doi: 1210.1007/978-3- 642-13094-6

Goedertier, S. (2008). Declarative techniques for modeling and mining business processes. KU.

Gong, P., Knuplesch, D., Feng, Z., & Jiang, J. (2017). bpCMon: A rule-based monitoring framework for business processes compliance. *International Journal of Web Services Research, 14*(2), 81–103. doi:10.4018/IJWSR.2017040105

Guermouche, N., & Godart, C. (2009). Timed model checking based approach for web services analysis. In *Web Services, 2009. ICWS 2009. IEEE International Conference on* (pp. 213-221). IEEE. 10.1109/ICWS.2009.42

Hamadi, R., & Benatallah, B. (2003). A Petri net-based model for web service composition. In *Proceedings of the 14th Australasian database conference* (vol. 17, pp. 191-200). ACM.

Hinz, S., Schmidt, K., & Stahl, C. (2005). Transforming BPEL to Petri nets. In *Business Process Management* (Vol. 3649, pp. 220–235). Berlin: Springer. doi:10.1007/11538394_15

Holzmann, G. (2003). *SPIN Model Checker The: Primer and Reference Manual.* Addison-Wesley.

Hopcroft, J. E., Motwani, R., & Ullman, J. D. (2001). Introduction to Automata Theory, Languages, and Computation. *ACM SIGACT News, 32*(1), 60–65. doi:10.1145/568438.568455

Huynh, K. T., Bui, T. H., & Quan, T. T. (2016). WSCOVER: A tool for automatic composition and verification of web services using heuristic-guided model checking and logic-based clustering. In *Multi-disciplinary Trends in Artificial Intelligence* (Vol. 10053, pp. 50–62). Berlin: Springer. doi:10.1007/978-3-319-49397-8_5

Janssens, G. K., Verelst, J., & Weyn, B. (2000). Techniques for modelling workflows and their support of reuse. In *Business Process Management* (Vol. 1806, pp. 1–15). Berlin: Springer. doi:10.1007/3-540-45594-9_1

Khaled, A., & Miller, J. (2017). Using π-calculus for formal modeling and verification of WS-CDL choreographies. *IEEE Transactions on Services Computing*, *10*(2), 316–327. doi:10.1109/TSC.2015.2449850

Kheldoun, A., Barkaoui, K., & Ioualalen, M. (2017). Formal verification of complex business processes based on high-level petri nets. *Information Sciences*, *385-386*, 39–54. doi:10.1016/j.ins.2016.12.044

Kowalski, R., & Sergot, M. (1989). A logic-based calculus of events. In *Foundations of knowledge base management* (pp. 23–55). Berlin: Springer. doi:10.1007/978-3-642-83397-7_2

Merz, M., Moldt, D., Müller, K., & Lamersdorf, W. (1995). *Workflow modelling and execution with coloured Petri nets in COSM*. University of Hamburg.

Montali, M., & Plebani, P. (2017). Iot-based compliance checking of multi-party business processes modeled with commitments. In *Service-oriented and cloud computing* (Vol. 10465, pp. 179–195). Springer. doi:10.1007/978-3-319-67262-5_14

Morimoto, S. (2008). A survey of formal verification for business process modeling. In *Computational Science–ICCS 2008* (Vol. 5102, pp. 514–522). Berlin: Springer. doi:10.1007/978-3-540-69387-1_58

Mueller, E. T. (2004). Event calculus reasoning through satisfiability. *Journal of Logic and Computation*, *14*(5), 703–730. doi:10.1093/logcom/14.5.703

Mueller, E. T. (2010). *Commonsense reasoning*. Morgan Kaufmann.

Narayanan, S., & McIlraith, S. A. (2002). Simulation, verification and automated composition of web services. In *Proceedings of the 11th international conference on World Wide Web* (pp. 77-88). ACM. 10.1145/511446.511457

Röglinger, D. W. I. M. (2009). Verification of web service compositions: An operationalization of correctness and a requirements framework for service-oriented modeling techniques. *Business & Information Systems Engineering*, *1*(6), 429–437. doi:10.100712599-009-0074-z

Salaün, G., Bordeaux, L., & Schaerf, M. (2006). Describing and reasoning on web services using process algebra. *International Journal of Business Process Integration and Management*, *1*(2), 116–128. doi:10.1504/IJBPIM.2006.010025

Van Der Aalst, W. M., & Pesic, M. (2006). DecSerFlow: Towards a truly declarative service flow language. In *Web Services and Formal Methods* (Vol. 4184, pp. 1–23). Berlin: Springer. doi:10.1007/11841197_1

Wikarski, D. (1996). *An introduction to modular process nets*. ICSI.

Wu, B., Lin, R., Wang, P., & Chen, J. (2016). Dynamic business process generation and verification. In IEEE international conference on services computing, SCC 2016 (pp. 836– 839). IEEE. doi:10.1109/SCC.2016.118

Xiu, P., Zhao, W., & Yang, J. (2017). Correctness verification for service-based business processes. In IEEE international conference on web services, ICWS 2017 (pp. 752–759). IEEE. doi:10.1109/ICWS.2017.90

Yi, X., & Kochut, K. J. (2004). A cp-nets-based design and verification framework for web services composition. In *Web Services, 2004. Proceedings. IEEE International Conference on* (pp. 756-760). IEEE.

Zahoor, E. (2011). *Gouvernance de service: aspects sécurité et données* (Doctoral dissertation). Université Nancy II.

Zahoor, E., Asma, Z., & Perrin, O. (2017). A formal approach for the verifi- cation of AWS IAM access control policies. In *Service-oriented and cloud computing - 6th IFIP WG 2.14 European conference* (pp. 59–74). Academic Press. doi:510.1007/978-3- 319-67262-5

Zahoor, E., Munir, K., Perrin, O., & Godart, C. (2013). A bounded model checking approach for the verification of web services composition. *International Journal of Web Services Research*, *10*(4), 62–81. doi:10.4018/ijwsr.2013100103

Zahoor, E., Perrin, O., & Bouchami, A. (2014). CATT: A cloud based authorization framework with trust and temporal aspects. In *10th IEEE international conference on collaborative computing: Net- working, applications and worksharing, collaboratecom 2014* (pp. 285–294). Academic Press. 10.4108/icst.collaboratecom.2014.257312

Zahoor, E., Perrin, O., & Godart, C. (2010). Disc: A declarative framework for self-healing web services composition. In *Web Services (ICWS), 2010 IEEE International Conference on* (pp. 25-33). IEEE. 10.1109/ICWS.2010.70

Zahoor, E., Perrin, O., & Godart, C. (2010). Disc-set: Handling temporal and security aspects in the web services composition. In *Web Services (ECOWS), 2010 IEEE 8th European Conference on* (pp. 51-58). IEEE.

Zahoor, E., Perrin, O., & Godart, C. (2012). Web services composition verification using satisfiability solving. In *IEEE International conference on web services* (pp. 242–249). IEEE. 10.1109/ICWS.2012.75

Zhang, J., Chang, C. K., Chung, J. Y., & Kim, S. W. (2004). WS-Net: A Petri-net based specification model for Web services. In *Web Services, 2004. Proceedings. IEEE International Conference on* (pp. 420-427). IEEE. 10.1109/ICWS.2004.1314766

Zhu, Y., Huang, Z., & Zhou, H. (2017). Modeling and verification of web services composition based on model transformation. *Journal of Software: Practice and Experience*, *47*(5), 709–730.

KEY TERMS AND DEFINITIONS

Business Process: A collection of related activities to accomplish a specific organizational goal. A business process can help an organization by improving agility, productivity, consistency, and understandability of processes.

Business Process Management (BPM): Set of methods to discover, model, analyze, improve and automate business processes. Process model involves high-level specification and can be visualized as a flow chart. The process needs to be analyzed (verified) to identify inconsistencies such as deadlocks.

Declarative Process Model: A flexible process specification approach which requires only specifying a set of constraints that mark the boundary of any solution to the process. Any solution that respects these constraints is considered as a valid solution.

DECReasoner: A tool to reason about EC models. It encodes the EC based process specification into a satisfiability problem and then invokes the SAT solver which either returns solution(s) or a set of unsatisfiable clauses.

Event-Calculus (EC): A logic programming formalism for representing events and their effects. In EC, events are the core concept that triggers changes. A fluent is anything whose value is subject to change over time. EC uses predicates to specify actions and their effects.

Model Checking: A technique for automatically verifying correctness of finite-state systems. It refers to the algorithms for exhaustively and automatically checking the state space of a transition system to determine if a given model of the system meets a given specification.

Service-Oriented Architecture (SOA): A flexible set of design principles for system development relying on the use of services. The vision associated with the SOA is to separate functions into services and compose them to support the development of distributed applications. Web services can be functional building blocks of SOA.

Web Services: The software systems designed to support interoperable machine-to-machine interaction over a network. They allow heterogeneous systems to communicate and to expose their operations. They can also be used to implement reusable application-components, such as currency conversion, weather reports, and others.

Chapter 8
Context and End-User Privacy Policies in Web Service-Based Applications

Georgia Kapitsaki
University of Cyprus, Cyprus

ABSTRACT

Privacy protection plays a vital role in pervasive and web environments, where users contact applications and services that may require access to their sensitive data. The current legislation, such as the recent European General Data Protection Regulation, is putting more emphasis on user protection and on placing users in the center of privacy choices. SOAP (simple object access protocol)-based and RESTful services may require access to sensitive data for their proper functioning, but users should be able to express their preferences on what should and should not be accessed. In this chapter, the above issues are discussed and a solution is presented for reconciling user preferences expressed in privacy policies and the service data needs tailored to SOAP-based services. A use example is provided and the main open issues providing directions for future research are discussed.

DOI: 10.4018/978-1-5225-7268-8.ch008

INTRODUCTION

Sensitive data may be used in different applications and it is important to make sure that they cannot uniquely identify a person, as this may pose a danger for her private sphere. Sensors in mobile devices can be accessed both by native application code and by cross-platform applications that use features of HTML5, e.g. geolocation, battery status, network information, device motion and orientation. Other sensitive data may be returned when invoking web services that contain information of this nature (e.g. location, weather services).

At the same time web services are considered as building blocks of larger applications and are used in different environments, from mobile and pervasive computing to cloud and web applications leading to web-service based applications (Georgantas, 2018). Many such applications require user data in order to function properly or offer a personalized used experience. Some services provide even context-aware capabilities, when the user environment or context is considered in order to adapt the service to user needs. Therefore, utilizing user data is in many cases desirable, in order to make appropriate adaptations of services and applications to user surroundings. Examples of such context elements can be found in the user location, current or past activities, health and weather conditions. There are different solutions that allow context acquisition by using the aforementioned HTML5 APIs, accessing device sensors with platform-specific code or using different kinds of services (Lee et al., 2015).

Importance to privacy has also been given by legislation. The Health Insurance Portability and Accountability Act (HIPAA) (Boyce, 2017), the Act on the Protection of Personal Information (APPI) (Adams, 2009) and the recent European General Data Protection Regulation (GDPR) (Voss, 2017) put a lot of emphasis on user privacy and on placing user in the center of the decision process of how her personal data will be handled (Kolter, 2010). There recent advances call for mechanisms and technologies that enable web services and service-based applications to be privacy-aware considering user's view, by reducing the risk of contravening legislation, forming part of Privacy Enhancing Technologies (PETs).

In the framework of this chapter, privacy is viewed as "the ability of individual's control over the use and dissemination of sensitive information", where the term sensitive is subjective. Many web services are stateless in the sense that they do not store the state of the session with the user. A request is made and a response is sent back. Nevertheless, there is no guarantee that information present in user requests is not stored for future use, statistical or marketing purposes.

Having as motivation the above, in this chapter the user view is targeted. It is described how user preferences can be captured and considered in the invocation of web services, especially for the case, when these web services request access to context information in order to function properly. They may be able to retrieve this information from different sources, but in many cases other web services can also be utilized. Specifically, the work presented formulates end-user preferences in context-aware web service-based applications and these preferences are subsequently combined with adaptation during web service invocation. Nevertheless, the service provider side is also important and mechanisms that reconcile the views of the two sides, i.e. user and provider, are also required.

The user preferences and the web service invocation mechanism can be found in previous publications (Kapitsaki, 2013a; Kapitsaki, 2013b). This chapter outlines the content of the user privacy preferences providing extensions to the original content captured in Consumer Privacy Language version 2.0 (CPL-2.0). It also provides the structure of the management architecture for SOAP (Simple Object Access Protocol)-based services extending a previous message interception approach (Kapitsaki et al. 2008). How other types of environments (i.e. RESTful services) can be considered for message interception and adaptation is also discussed. Finally, it builds on recent advances in the field discussing open research directions offering thus, a current view of privacy protection for web service-based applications that require user context.

The rest of the text is structured as follows. The next section presents background information focusing on related works on web service descriptions, privacy policies and web service privacy protection mechanisms. The section that comes next is dedicated to how user preferences can be expressed with semantics focusing on the end-user side, whereas afterwards it is presented how SOAP-based web services can consider user preferences when requesting context information. A demonstration of an example use case and a presentation of open issues follow. The final section concludes the text.

BACKGROUND

Web Service Descriptions

Web services can be described in different ways to expose the service functionality. The interface of SOAP-based web services is most usually described in the Web Services Description Language (WSDL), an XML (eXtensible Markup Language)-based interface definition language (Chinnici et al., 2004). There have been however, attempts to give more expressiveness to web services by adding semantic annotations. Semantic Annotations for WSDL (SAWSDL) enables to annotate the syntactic WSDL descriptions with pointers to semantic concepts, e.g. in RDFS or OWL (Kopecký et al., 2007). As such, it introduces a set of extensions for WSDL using the XML notation. RESTful services refer to resources and do not offer formal service descriptions, but SA-REST (Semantic annotation of web resources) suggests to enrich API descriptions in HTML or XHTML (Gomadam et al., 2010). This way different kinds of metadata can be added, expressed e.g. in ontologies, taxonomies or tag clouds.

Linked USDL (Unified Service Description Language) and its predecessor USDL were developed for describing business and software services using computer-readable and computer-understandable specifications in order to be available through the Internet (Cardoso et al., 2010}. It is a master data schema constructed using semantic, web technologies and linked data principles. Linked USDL is consisted by a number of modules, where each one targets a specific service aspect and adopts a Linked Data based semantic model to describe and share information (Bizer et al., 2009). The main usage of Linked USDL is to describe typical business and software services. The basic module of Linked USDL is Core and covers the concepts that are related with service descriptions, service offering descriptions, business entities that are involved in the service delivery chain and interaction points that allow users to benefit from the purchased services. Price and Agreement are the other two established modules, where Price is used to describe adequately the price structures in the business, while Agreement gathers functional and non-functional information that is related with the provided service quality (García et al., 2015). Linked USDL outlines also modules for Security and Privacy. The latter can be used to describe how the service provider is using user data and how they are distributed (Kapitsaki et al., 2018).

Context can also be added as a parameter in service descriptions, in order to explain how the service uses it (Kapitsaki, 2012). A detailed overview of service description approaches that automate specific activities can be found in a respective survey (Fanjiang et al., 2017).

Privacy Policies

Privacy policies can be defined either for the service provider or for the consumer side. On the web, the Platform for Privacy Preferences (P3P) and its user-side complement offer a computer-readable language for handling privacy policies (Cranor et al., 2002). APPEL (A P3P Preference Exchange Language) is used for expressing privacy preferences in websites addressing the needs of websites and users (Cranor, 2002). Those approaches were targeting websites and have received critique (e.g. it is hard to express simple preferences in APPEL). XPref replaces the body of APPEL rules with XPath expressions (Agrawal et al., 2005).

Enterprise Privacy Authorization Language (EPAL) and eXtensible Access Control Markup Language (XACML) are widespread languages for generic-purpose privacy policies specification (Ashley et al., 2003; Parducci et al., 2013). EPAL assumes that information access policies always depend on the purpose for which the access is requested. XACML is designed to capture Attribute-Based Access Control (ABAC) policies but is covering also Role-based access control (RBAC). Yet both lack formal, rigorous semantics and are not totally platform-independent. The PRIME project has created PPL (Primelife Policy Language) as an extension to XACML with data handling and credential capabilities to help users control their information by specifying usage control restrictions (Ardagna et al., 2009).

The above works have more applicability on the web and can be adapted for use also with web services. However, other works focus on the specifics of web services. Rezgui et al. (2002) distinguish between user privacy, data privacy and service privacy. User privacy has the concept of user privacy profile that is typically defined for the user or a group of individuals. In the work of Allison et al. (2012)., privacy policy is defined in XML with each privacy rule consisting of: 1) collector that refers to the one collecting the data (usually the service provider), 2) what that refers to the information to be collected, 3) purpose related to the goal of the service and the operational reasons for data access. It is stated that this work also covers context situations by having rules that include elements that allow for specific input, such as purpose, goal and collector, and allowing multiple rules per policy. The elements proposed were extracted from the analysis of the Fair Information Practices (FIP) of the Organisation for Economic Cooperation and Development (OECD).

In (Xu et al. 2006), in order to integrate privacy in web services consumers express their requirements in the form of policies, while providers specify their use of consumer data using models. User privacy policies capture what types of consumer data they are willing to share with which types of service providers. Consumers can also specify which providers (e.g. Hertz) they trust or not.

Privacy from the provider's perspective is addressed by Hamadi et al. (2007). A formal technique that can be used by service providers to describe the use and storage of personal data is proposed. The end-user view is linked with a requester profile that consists of a set of privacy attributes, such as identity of user, age, purchase history, membership to a certain group. The authors specify which elements should be present in the service provider policy. More information for earlier works on privacy policies can be found in an existing publication (Kumaraguru et al., 2007).

Privacy Protection in Web Services

Some of the approaches that help in defining user policies offer also architectures for their management. For instance, in (Rezgui et al., 2002), the privacy credentials of a user are appended to the requests a user sends to a web service. User privacy profiles are handled by the Privacy Profiles Manager (PPM). PPM is a translation of the consent-based privacy model of individual citizens. An approach for mobile environment is presented by Del Alamo et al. (2011). Similarly to the approach described here, the authors introduce a broker between the user and the service provider, the Mobile Information Service Broker. Privacy is handled through a Privacy Controller that provides privacy and identity dashboards for the user through its web user interface. Users can define policies in natural language. However, this work does not go into details on the description of privacy policies and their construction.

Some approaches target negotiation between the requester and the provider concerning the use of user data. The DARPA agent markup language for services (DAML-S) Service Profile is used to express consumer preferences in (Tumer et al. 2005). Users utilize a domain specific service ontology based on DAML-S using three levels for data disclosure, i.e. Free, Limited, NotGiven, whereas web services express their requirements in DAML-S Service Profile input parameter. A two-step negotiation process is subsequently used to match the requirements of the parties.

A Privacy Protection Framework for Service-Oriented Architecture (PPFSOA) is described by Allison et al. (2012). Policies are defined as aforementioned in XML and from this description a service contract is created using the comparison of the privacy policy of the consumer and the policy of the provider. Another work focuses on services on the cloud introducing the Privacy Negotiation Language (PNL) based on description logic and a policy negotiation algorithm using also pre-negotiation (Ke et al., 2013).

USER PRIVACY POLICIES

Consumer Privacy Language (CPL) profile contains user privacy policies expressed in a simplified way for end-users, so that they can be considered by the services during web service invocation. The initial version of CPL has been presented in the existing publication (Kapitsaki, 2013a). The updated version, i.e. CPL-2.0, with its main elements is shown in the UML class diagram of Figure 1. In relevance to the initial version the following aspects have been added along with other minor changes: 1) support for more flexible context-dependent rules (conditions and other information can be added to restrict the block rules, whereas this was feasible only for allow rules in the first version of CPL), 2) use of system type as condition for user rules, so that users can define specific information for the device they are using, 3) consideration of additional condition types captured in the generic *OtherType* class, 4) indication of whether the user wants her data to be distributed and shared with third-party providers.

Figure 1. Elements of consumer privacy language version 2.0

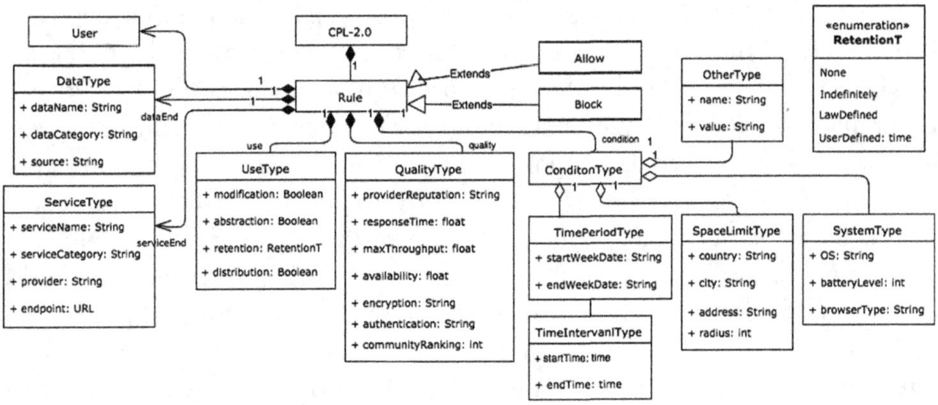

Each user (*User* class) may define a set of rules (*Rule* class) in the form of *Block* or *Allow* elements, to specify respectively that she wants to forbid or allow the access to specific data. If the consumer specifies only allow (or block) elements, then all other context information is considered blocked (or allowed), whereas when both are specified, the remaining data is also considered blocked.

Data end (*DataType* class) refers to the data linked with the current allow or block instance and comprises of a *data category*, a *data name* and a *source* of the data (if available). Data ends may refer to any context information or resource to which access is requested. If only the data category is defined, the respective rule applies to all data belonging to this category. Different categories can be considered for characterizing the data. In the first version of CPL, a specific taxonomy has been employed adopting some elements from the work of Chen and Kotz (2000), dividing context to the following two main categories:

- **Personal Context:** Personal information, employment status, education level, contacts, personal preferences and payment information.
- **Surrounding Context:** Activities, location, environment and time, communication and computing.

The new version of CPL-2.0 supports linking to an external taxonomy. An example can be found in the work of Wiese et al. (2017), where personal data range from low-level data like sensor data to very high level data that describe information about individuals that they might not even know about themselves:

- Low-level streams (e.g. accelerometer, microphone)
- Events human-readable (e.g. purchases, application usage)
- Personal inference (e.g. stressed)
- Holistic understanding (e.g. depression)

The first two categories are more suitable for linking with CPL-2.0, as services may rarely require as input complex inferences about the user. External taxonomies may be even more elaborated provided in the form of an ontology. Ontology-based context models can be found in SOUPA (Standard Ontology for Ubiquitous and Pervasive Applications) (Chen et al., 2004), context-aware computing ontology (CACOnt) (Xu et al., 2013) and ECOPPA (Extensible Context Ontology for Persuasive Physical-Activity Applications) (El Saddik, 2018). In the examples in this text, the original taxonomy with personal and surrounding context is used, since it covers basic data about the user and her context.

Service end (*ServiceType* class) provides details on the service requesting the data end and permits specifying one or more of the following: s*ervice category*, n*ame*, p*rovider* and *endpoint*, where the service is available. Service end information is optional. In case it is missing, user rules apply to all services the user may interact with. Similarly, the user may define only partial information for the service end (e.g. provider name only).

Use Type class contains more information about how user data will be provided to the service, at which level and how they will be stored. The user can this way specify how she wishes her data is being handled by the service. Specifically, the following information is included:

- **Modification:** Expresses whether data modification may be performed by the service, e.g. aggregating data for statistical purposes.
- **Abstraction:** Shows whether an abstracted representation of the data end should be used instead of its original value. Abstraction provides the possibility of expressing data at different levels of granularity. This is used in many cases in location services in the form of obfuscation, where location data become more obscure (e.g. providing a location in the proximity to the user), but do not reveal her real location (Yang et al., 2015). Some services may function properly, even when the exact location of the user is not known, e.g. weather services, whereas others may require the exact coordinates to be able to assist the user, e.g. navigation services. Moreover, a service that needs to know whether the requester is an adult should not have access to the age of the user. In this case, age can be abstracted to a value above or below 18.

- **Retention:** The user may specify for how long her data should be retained. In essence, web services are stateless but the provider may maintain or even store user data for other purposes, e.g. marketing. The available choices are: no retention (data is used only in one interaction with the service), law defined (the service provider should comply with the respective regulations), user defined (the user specifies a specific retention duration) and indefinitely (information can be maintained for all future interactions).

- **Distribution:** The service the user is interacting with is considered the first-party. The user may specify here whether her data may be distributed to third-party providers the service is interacting with (e.g. a social network, if the user used her credentials on the social network to log in to the web-service based application).

Quality Type class is related with the trust level of the user to the services. Quality of service (QoS) contains different elements, such as availability, security properties, response time and throughput (Menascé, 2002). For the elements contained, a subset from the Web Services Quality Model by OASIS has been adopted (Eunju et al., 2011). Service provider reputation, response time, maximum throughput, availability, encryption and authentication. We added an additional element corresponding to community ranking as given by the users of the service representing the quality, as perceived by the end-users. Retention and trust are also elements of a previous work on privacy policies (Allison et al., 2012).

Context is an important parameter for specifying the access rules, even though existing data types refer to user context. The most widely used definition for context states that context is "*any information that can be used to characterize the situation of an entity*" (Abowd et al. 1999). In the framework of this work, context is "*any information relevant to an entity and its surroundings that can assist in adapting a service or application*". Context status in CPL-2.0 (*ConditionType* class) may refer to location (e.g. allow access, when the user is at specific locations), but also to specific times of the day the user wants to have context-aware service provision (e.g. users may allow access to specific data only during work hours, but not at any other time at their free time or when they are on vacations). For the above, a condition is expressed either as a time period restriction (e.g. specified by a start and end time or/and start and end day), a space limit restriction (corresponding to location restriction) or both. For instance, for a user wishing to allow access to a specific data end when she is at her hometown (e.g. Zagreb). The parameters of the device used by the user is also a contextual parameter, containing information on the operating system, the browser type and the battery level, so that for instance, access may be denied to a service, when the battery level is low and the resources required by the service are high. *OtherType* element has been added to provide space for additional contextual parameters that may be considered (e.g. device motion). Any kind of data can be considered here and for this purpose the user may specify a *name* and a *value* for the data. Apart from the above, in CPL users can specify their preference for specific services or providers they might trust.

The initial notation used for the representation of CPL was XML. CPL-2.0 has evolved to JSON (JavaScript Object Notation) that has gained more popularity lately. Since XACML is also intended to be provided in JSON notation, future work that will consider both service provider and user privacy policies will follow a similar notation.

An example of the new notation in JSON is depicted in Figure 2. The data taxonomy follows the structure of the data of the first version of CPL (Kapitsaki, 2013a). The user has defined three allow and two block rules. She allows access to her *Geolocation*, in specific days of the week (Monday to Friday) and times (9:00-18:00) for a specific city location (Nicosia, Cyprus) with the additional condition that the battery level of the device she is using is above the threshold of 30%. Access to user *Environment* and specific elements of *PersonalInfo* (*Name* and *Age*) is also allowed. The data retention is as defined by law, whereas no abstraction will be applied. At the same time, the user blocks access to her personal preferences and contacts for all service interactions. This example (along with other examples) is available in the relevant repository of CPL on GitHub (GitHub CPL, 2018).

SERVICE ENFORCEMENT MECHANISM

Adaptation Approach

In this section the approach used for the adaptation of the web-service based application to the user preferences defined in CPL-2.0 is described. In regard to web services, two kind of web services can be encountered: services that offer basic functionality (e.g. hotel room reservation services) and services that provide context data (e.g. user location). The first category is referred to as Business Web Services (BWSs), whereas the second as Context Web Services (CWSs). BWSs can be used in conjunction with CWSs in order to obtain the context data they require. BWSs depend on context in different ways: one or more input parameters may need to be adapted to context (parameter injection), the service operation to be invoked may be selected among the available web service operations based on context data (operation selection) or the contents of the response may be either filtered or ordered based on contextual conditions (response manipulation). More

Figure 2. Example of allow and block rules in CPL-2.0

```
{
  "cpl:privacyPreferences": {
    "user":"janedoe",
    "cpl:allow": [
      {
        "cpl:dataEnd": { "dataCategory": "Geolocation" },
        "cpl:condition": {
          "cpl:timePeriod": {
            "cpl:startWeekDay": "Monday",
            "cpl:endWeekDay": "Friday",
            "cpl:time": {
                "cpl:startTime": "09:00:00",
                "cpl:endTime": "18:00:00"
            }
          },
          "cpl:spaceLimit": {
              "cpl:country": "Cyprus",
              "cpl:city": "Nicosia"
          },
          "cpl:system": {
              "cpl:batteryLevel": 30,
          }
        }
      },
      {
        "cpl:dataEnd": { "dataCategory": "Environment" },
        "cpl:use": {
            "cpl:retention": "LawDefined",
            "cpl:abstraction": "None"
        }
      },
      {
        "cpl:dataEnd": {
          "dataCategory": "PersonalInfo", "dataName": "Name" },
        "cpl:dataEnd": {
          "dataCategory": "PersonalInfo", "dataName": "Age" },
        "cpl:use": {
            "cpl:retention": "LawDefined",
            "cpl:abstraction": "None"
        }
      }
    ],
    "cpl:block": [
      {
        "cpl:dataEnd": { "dataCategory": "PersonalPreferences" }
      },
      {
        "cpl:dataEnd": { "dataCategory": "Contacts" }
      }
    ]
  }
}
```

information on these definitions can be found in previous publications (Kapitsaki et al., 2008). They are relevant to adaptation to context and not to privacy policies that are described here. In order to retrieve user data different kinds of sources can be used by the BWSs apart from the most common case of CWSs: RESTful services, HTML5 APIs, platform-specific code that accesses device data. These data sources may be exposed as services, so that they can be easily invoked from the original BWS for context adaptation purposes.

The architecture of the service adaptation approach that considers user privacy preferences and may use different sources of context is depicted in Figure 3. For the case of SOAP-based services, SOAP messages are intercepted and appropriately adapted to context (request and response messages). Specifically, SOAP-based services are invoked by the end-user but the process is handled by the adapter that performs the appropriate actions. Specifically, from the steps shown in Figure 3, incoming (*request*) or outgoing (*response*) SOAP messages are intercepted by a handler (*Message Interception* phase). Message are adapted to the current contextual conditions (*Message Adaptation* phase) through a number of plugins. The appropriate plugins are loaded on runtime (*Plugin Loading* phase). Message adaptation is performed either on request or response messages on the following basis: request messages can be adapted for parameter injection or operation selection, whereas response messages can be adapted through response manipulation. Adaptation combinations for the same request or response message are also feasible. Context adaptation is performed by the plugins through the invocation of additional services.

The user privacy preferences provision is available as an independent module and has not been integrated in the main handler. Each handler can be integrated in each service provider, whereas the privacy module can be provided as an external service, so that it remains provider-independent. An alternative is to consider the privacy module at the web service-based application. In this case, any adaptation may be performed before the actual invocation of the BWS. Due to the existing legislation (e.g. GDPR), it is important to examine whether the data accessed by the web service are specified by the service provider in its respective privacy policies. This aspect of legislation is also considered in the proposed architecture to verify that when user privacy preferences are used, the relevant legislation is also enforced.

Taking into consideration the above, the following actions are performed by the *Rule Enforcement* phase:

- It is examined whether the data requested by the service are in alignment with the legislation and with the privacy policies published by the specific provider.

- If the service request complies with the above, a comparison between the instance of the CPL-2.0 of the end-user and the context information needed for the service execution is performed.
- Code segments in the context plugins are activated or deactivated. If the code is activated, the services that provide actual access to user context data are invoked. Otherwise, no action is performed and the data is not accessed by the service.

One of the main aims of the proposed architecture is to leave the BWS description and implementation intact. However, in the current state of work web services that do not contain in their descriptions any information on the context data they require for their functionality are taken into account, i.e. the service description is captured in WSDL. The inclusion of context dependencies in existing semantic service descriptions has been addressed in existing works and may constitute future research direction for the evolution of the adaptation mechanism (Kapitsaki, 2012; Pokraev et al., 2003), whereas additional service description approaches will be considered. Although CPL has been integrated in the privacy-aware mechanism described here, a different privacy language may also be injected since the end-user privacy preference exposer mechanism is a separate entity.

Implementation

The privacy enforcement mechanism builds on a message adaptation architecture for context-aware web services implemented in the Apache Axis2 framework (Perera et al., 2006). Axis2 provides the possibility of implementing additional modules and such a module implementation has been used for the message adaptation process.

Figure 3. Adapting service messages to privacy policies

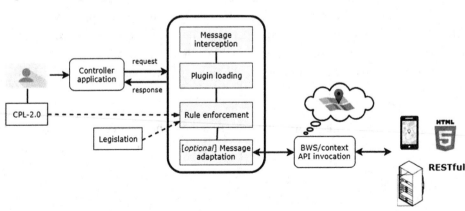

Similar principles can be found in other web service frameworks (e.g., interceptors in Apache CXF). The privacy module has been implemented through an Axis2 web service that has access to consumer preferences and is invoked each time access to context data is requested by a context plugin. In the framework of this work, the adaptation approach can be applied to SOAP-based services, whereas in the case of RESTful services a different approach needs to be followed. Tools, such as the Interceptor extension of Postman (Postman), can intercept HTTP traffic and perform this way appropriate actions. The rationale and the steps of the mechanism remain the same.

USE CASE DEMONSTRATION

For demonstration purposes an example use case is utilized. *BookShopWebApp* is a web application, where users can view available books after getting a personalized welcoming message and can view whether the book they select is available in a bookstore nearby. Different BWSs compose this context-aware application.

1. **WelcomingService:** Returns a welcome message to the user.
2. **BooklistService:** Returns available books with information on the book title, publication year and book price in Euros.
3. **BookstoreService:** Provides information on bookstores in close proximity to the end-user (bookstore name and address).

In order to be able to adapt its functionality to the user context, the application requires access to a set of context data. Context data come from different context sources. Some of the data is available from a user profile and for this purpose an initial user registration is necessary. Preferences on book genres, payment methods and other data, such as preferred language, are inserted upon profile creation. The user profile contains personal user information implemented with key-value pairs. Taking into consideration the above, the following services are used as sources for context data:

1. **ProfileService:** Exposes the user profile providing the value of the data for a given key provided as input.
2. **IPstack (IPstack):** Provides information about the current user location.
3. **WeatherForecastService (Weather Forecast Service):** Provides weather reports for a given city (World Weather Online (World Weather Online) is also utilized for cities not supported by the weather forecast service).

BookShopWebApp raises some privacy issues for context data: user location is needed to provide location-based data, along with personal information for the requester. Specifically, each service requires the following type of data about the user:

1. **WelcomingService:** 1) User name, 2) nationality (used for adapting the language of the application based on user's native language), and 3) temperature (used for showing to the user information about the weather that is in essence requiring access also to user's location).
2. **BooklistService:** 1) User age (to filter out books not appropriate for younger ages), and 2) user preferences on book types, so that these book types are only displayed to the user screen.
3. **BookstoreService:** User location (used for returning only bookstores that are in close proximity to the user).

The use of the proposed privacy enforcement mechanism will be demonstrated for the case of the book shop application making the application privacy-aware. On the one hand, *BookShopWebApp* will take into account context-aware aspects, and on the other hand, it will apply users' privacy preferences in the application execution.

An example of the application for a specific user is depicted in Figure 4. The user considered has defined two allow rules in CPL, where she denotes that she allows access to her geolocation, her first name (part of user's personal information context stored in her profile) and any information relevant to her environment (Environment context category). On the other hand, she has blocked access to her age for any service she might interact with. The data, the user has allowed access to, are marked in the Figure with the plus (+) sign, whereas minus (-) is used for data that cannot be used by the service according to the user. Since the user has blocked access to information about her age, this is not considered in the invocation of the *BooklistService,* i.e. all available books are retrieved regardless of the age of the requester. Since access to user location is allowed, only bookstores in Nicosia (Cyprus) are returned. However, the name of the requester and the outside temperature are shown as part of the welcome message of the application, since the user has allowed access to both.

More details on a more enriched use case and scenarios of its use are available in the existing publication, where an extended evaluation of the enforcement approach is also available (Kapitsaki, 2013a). A mobile device was used for measuring the effect of using the interception mechanism on CPU usage and of incoming and outgoing network traffic usage comparing native Android applications to web applications, such as the use case demonstrated. No large deviations were observed. Execution time was also measured and in this case it was observed that execution time reaches high levels, when the adaptation mechanism is enforced in comparison to the case

Figure 4. Example of adapted application for the BookShopWebApp

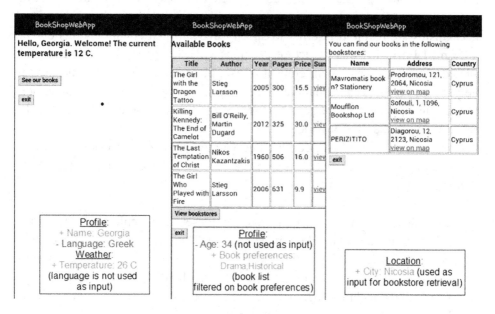

without adaptation. Nevertheless, execution time depends also on the availability and the response time of the services employed for context data acquisition. The response time remains less than 0.8 seconds per web service, which is an acceptable limit according to studies on application response times (Nielsen, 1993). It is argued however, that further work needs to be performed toward this direction.

FUTURE RESEARCH DIRECTIONS

This work has showed a main approach, but this approach can be further enhanced considering recent advances and open research areas for privacy protection on the web and web-service based applications. The study of the combination with XACML features has been indicated in the text. The consideration of services that indicate in their descriptions which kind of context data they use is also a useful future addition, along with the use of semantic web services (Kapitsaki, 2012). According to Naessens et al. (2009), important challenges on "Disclosure of Information" lie not only on the disclosure of one's own personal data but also on the disclosure of personal data by another party to another party. This is considered in CPL-2.0 via the introduction of the element that allows the user to specify whether distribution of her data to third-party providers is allowed. Nevertheless, more elaborated mechanisms are required in order to specify under which conditions this can be performed. Enriching web service descriptions will also assist toward this direction, since it will also allow the enrichment of user preferences with elements, such as the purpose of use of personal data (e.g. data forwarding to an external service, data calculations) that can be accompanied by a negotiation procedure between the end-user and the service provider.

Current advances in Service Oriented Computing and in privacy legislation have opened some issues that should form part of future research works in privacy protection for web services:

1. **Compliance to Legislation:** Mechanisms for service compliance to legislation need to be put into place. Automated tools that assist in GDPR compliance have begun to emerge. For instance, the PIA software aims to help data controllers build and demonstrate compliance to the GDPR (PIA). However, it does not focus on the technical perspective. Tools dedicated to services and service-based applications need to be developed.

2. **Effect of Microservices Architecture:** Many organizations, such as Netflix and eBay, are adopting the microservices architecture separating their systems as loosely coupled services (Balalaie, 2016). Addressing context-awareness and privacy issues in such environments is a challenge, as each microservice may contain specific mechanisms to enforce security and privacy, whereas others may not. It needs to be addressed how user preferences can be enforced in such environments, when the enforcement should apply across various and often heterogeneous microservices.

3. **Web Service Availability and Openness:** A large number of web services is available online, but not all may necessarily be active. A previous work found that the success rate of finding a real or functional service implementation is set to 63% (Al-Masri, 2008). The issues discussed in this chapter require the availability of web services in order to provide functional applications. Although this is not a research direction, it is an open issue that needs to be handled. In many cases, providers are using SOAP-based web services internally without offering access to external users. This is not the case for RESTful services that are more easily accessible, e.g. from ProgrammableWeb and similar API directories.

CONCLUSION

In this chapter, the enforcement of privacy preferences in the provision of web service-based context-aware application as specified by end-users has been addressed. Use privacy preferences or privacy policies are formulated using Consumer Privacy Language version 2.0, whereas the architecture of the enforcement mechanism has been outlined for different kinds of services and sources of information. Special emphasis has been given to the case of SOAP-based services and how SOAP request and response messages are adapted considering user policies. The relevant implementation has used SOAP-based services. The language and the respective mechanism have been demonstrated via an example web application. Some open research issues remain in the area od privacy protection for web services and they have been presented in this work.

REFERENCES

Abowd, G. D., Dey, A. K., Brown, P. J., Davies, N., Smith, M., & Steggles, P. (1999, September). Towards a better understanding of context and context-awareness. In *International Symposium on Handheld and Ubiquitous Computing* (pp. 304-307). Springer. 10.1007/3-540-48157-5_29

Adams, A. A., Murata, K., & Orito, Y. (2009). The Japanese sense of information privacy. *AI & Society*, *24*(4), 327–341. doi:10.100700146-009-0228-z

Agrawal, R., Kiernan, J., Srikant, R., & Xu, Y. (2005). XPref: A preference language for P3P. *Computer Networks*, *48*(5), 809–827. doi:10.1016/j.comnet.2005.01.004

Al-Masri, E., & Mahmoud, Q. H. (2008, April). Investigating web services on the world wide web. In *Proceedings of the 17th international conference on World Wide Web* (pp. 795-804). ACM. 10.1145/1367497.1367605

Allison, D. S., & Capretz, M. A., El Yamany, H. F., & Wang, S. (2012). Privacy protection framework with defined policies for service-oriented architecture. *Journal of Software Engineering and Applications*, *5*(3), 200. doi:10.4236/jsea.2012.53026

Ardagna, C., Bussard, L., De Capitani Di Vimercati, S., Neven, G., Pedrini, E., Paraboschi, S., . . . Verdicchio, M. (2009). Primelife policy language. In *W3C Workshop on Access Control Application Scenarios*. W3C.

Ashley, P., Hada, S., Karjoth, G., Powers, C., & Schunter, M. (2003). *Enterprise privacy authorization language (EPAL)*. IBM Research.

Balalaie, A., Heydarnoori, A., & Jamshidi, P. (2016). Microservices architecture enables devops: Migration to a cloud-native architecture. *IEEE Software, 33*(3), 42–52. doi:10.1109/MS.2016.64

Bizer, C., Heath, T., & Berners-Lee, T. (2009). Linked data-the story so far. *International Journal on Semantic Web and Information Systems, 5*(3), 1–22. doi:10.4018/jswis.2009081901

Boyce, B. (2017). Emerging Technology and the Health Insurance Portability and Accountability Act. *Journal of the Academy of Nutrition and Dietetics, 117*(4), 517–518. doi:10.1016/j.jand.2016.05.013 PMID:27436531

Cardoso, J., Barros, A., May, N., & Kylau, U. (2010, July). Towards a unified service description language for the internet of services: Requirements and first developments. In *Services Computing (SCC), 2010 IEEE International Conference on* (pp. 602-609). IEEE.

Chen, G., & Kotz, D. (2000). *A survey of context-aware mobile computing research* (Vol. 1, No. 2.1, pp. 2-1). Technical Report TR2000-381, Dept. of Computer Science, Dartmouth College.

Chen, H., Perich, F., Finin, T., & Joshi, A. (2004, August). Soupa: Standard ontology for ubiquitous and pervasive applications. In *Mobile and Ubiquitous Systems: Networking and Services, 2004. MOBIQUITOUS 2004. The First Annual International Conference on* (pp. 258-267). IEEE.

Chinnici, R., Gudgin, M., Moreau, J. J., Schlimmer, J., & Weerawarana, S. (2004). Web services description language (WSDL) version 2.0 part 1: Core language. *W3C working draft, 26*.

Cranor, L., Langheinrich, M., & Marchiori, M. (2002). Preference Exchange Language. Academic Press.

Cranor, L., Langheinrich, M., Marchiori, M., Presler-Marshall, M., & Reagle, J. (2002). *The Platform for Privacy Preferences 1.0 (P3P1.0) Specification*. Retrieved from https://www.w3.org/TR/P3P/

Del Álamo, J. M., Fernández, A. M., Trapero, R., Yelmo, J. C., & Monjas, M. A. (2011). A privacy-considerate framework for identity management in mobile services. *Mobile Networks and Applications, 16*(4), 446–459. doi:10.100711036-011-0325-3

El Saddik, A. (2018, January). ECOPPA: Extensible Context Ontology for Persuasive Physical-Activity Applications. In *Proceedings of the International Conference on Information Technology & Systems (ICITS 2018)* (Vol. 721, p. 309). Springer. 10.1007/978-3-319-73450-7_30

Eunju, K., Yongkon, L., Yeongho, K., Hyungkeun, P., Jongwoo, K., Byoungsun, M., . . . Guil, K. (2011). *Web Services Quality Factors Version 1.0*. Retrieved from http://docs.oasis-open.org/wsqm/WS-Quality-Factors/v1.0/cs01/WS-Quality-Factors-v1.0-cs01.html

Fanjiang, Y. Y., Syu, Y., Ma, S. P., & Kuo, J. Y. (2017). An overview and classification of service description approaches in automated service composition research. *IEEE Transactions on Services Computing*, *10*(2), 176–189. doi:10.1109/TSC.2015.2461538

García, J. M., Pedrinaci, C., Resinas, M., Cardoso, J., Fernández, P., & Ruiz-Cortés, A. (2015, June). Linked USDL agreement: effectively sharing semantic service level agreements on the web. In *Web Services (ICWS), 2015 IEEE International Conference on* (pp. 137-144). IEEE. 10.1109/ICWS.2015.28

Georgantas, N. (2018). *Service Oriented Computing in Mobile Environments: Abstractions and Mechanisms for Interoperability and Composition* (Doctoral dissertation). Sorbonne Université.

GitHub CPL (Consumer Privacy Language repository). (2018). Retrieved from https://github.com/CS-UCY-SEIT-lab/CPL

Gomadam, K., Ranabahu, A., & Sheth, A. (2010). *SA-REST: Semantic Annotation of Web Resources*. Retrieved from https://www.w3.org/Submission/SA-REST

Hamadi, R., Paik, H. Y., & Benatallah, B. (2007, June). Conceptual modeling of privacy-aware web service protocols. In *International Conference on Advanced Information Systems Engineering* (pp. 233-248). Springer. 10.1007/978-3-540-72988-4_17

IPstack. (n.d.). Retrieved from https://ipstack.com

Kapitsaki, G. M. (2012). *Enhancing Web Service Descriptions with Context Functions*. WEBIST.

Kapitsaki, G. M. (2013a). Consumer Privacy Enforcement in Context-Aware Web Services. *International Journal of Web Services Research*, *10*(3), 24–41. doi:10.4018/ijwsr.2013070102

Kapitsaki, G. M. (2013b). Reflecting user privacy preferences in context-aware web services. In *Web Services (ICWS), 2013 IEEE 20th International Conference on* (pp. 123-130). IEEE. 10.1109/ICWS.2013.26

Kapitsaki, G. M., Ioannou, J., Cardoso, J., & Pedrinaci, C. (2018). Linked USDL Privacy: Describing Privacy Policies for Services In Web Services, 2018. ICWS 2018. IEEE International Conference on (pp. 50-57). IEEE.

Kapitsaki, G. M., Kateros, D. A., & Venieris, I. S. (2008, September). Architecture for provision of context-aware web applications based on web services. In *Personal, Indoor and Mobile Radio Communications, 2008. PIMRC 2008. IEEE 19th International Symposium on* (pp. 1-5). IEEE. 10.1109/PIMRC.2008.4699629

Ke, C., Huang, Z., & Tang, M. (2013). Supporting negotiation mechanism privacy authority method in cloud computing. *Knowledge-Based Systems*, *51*, 48–59. doi:10.1016/j.knosys.2013.07.001

Kolter, J. P. (2010). *User-centric Privacy: A Usable and Provider-independent Privacy Infrastructure* (Vol. 41). BoD–Books on Demand.

Kopecký, J., Vitvar, T., Bournez, C., & Farrell, J. (2007). Sawsdl: Semantic annotations for wsdl and xml schema. *IEEE Internet Computing*, *11*(6), 60–67. doi:10.1109/MIC.2007.134

Kumaraguru, P., Cranor, L., Lobo, J., & Calo, S. (2007, July). A survey of privacy policy languages. In *Workshop on Usable IT Security Management (USM 07): Proceedings of the 3rd Symposium on Usable Privacy and Security*. ACM.

Lee, J. Y., & Kim, S. D. (2015, June). IoT Contexts Acquisition with High Accuracy and Efficiency. In *Services (SERVICES), 2015 IEEE World Congress on* (pp. 9-16). IEEE. 10.1109/SERVICES.2015.10

Menascé, D. A. (2002). QoS issues in web services. *IEEE Internet Computing*, *6*(6), 72–75. doi:10.1109/MIC.2002.1067740

Naessens, V., Sandikkaya, M. T., Lapon, J., Verslype, K., Verhaeghe, P., Nigusse, G., & De Decker, B. (2009). Privacy policies, tools and mechanisms of the future. In iNetSec 2009–Open Research Problems in Network Security (pp. 125-138). Springer. doi:10.1007/978-3-642-05437-2_12

Nielsen, J. (1994). *Usability engineering*. Elsevier.

Parducci, B., Lockhart, H., & Rissanen, E. (2013). Extensible access control markup language (XACML) version 3.0. *OASIS Standard*, 1-154.

Perera, S., Herath, C., Ekanayake, J., Chinthaka, E., Ranabahu, A., Jayasinghe, D., . . . Daniels, G. (2006, September). Axis2, middleware for next generation web services. In *Web Services, 2006. ICWS'06. International Conference on* (pp. 833-840). IEEE. PIA. Retrieved from https://www.cnil.fr/en/open-source-pia-software-helps-carry-out-data-protection-impact-assesment

Pokraev, S., Zhang, L. J., Koolwaaij, J., & Wibbels, M. (2003). *Extending UDDI with context-aware features based on semantic service descriptions.* Postman. Retrieved from https://www.getpostman.com/

Rezgui, A., Ouzzani, M., Bouguettaya, A., & Medjahed, B. (2002, November). Preserving privacy in web services. In *Proceedings of the 4th international workshop on Web information and data management* (pp. 56-62). ACM.

Tumer, A., Dogac, A., & Toroslu, I. H. (2005). A semantic-based user privacy protection framework for web services. In *Intelligent Techniques for Web Personalization* (pp. 289–305). Berlin: Springer. doi:10.1007/11577935_16

Voss, W. G. (2017). European union data privacy law reform: General data protection regulation, privacy shield, and the right to delisting. *Weather Forecast Service*. Retrieved from http://www.pathfinder-xml.com/development/WSDL/WeatherForecastService.wsdl

Wiese, J., Das, S., Hong, J. I., & Zimmerman, J. (2017). Evolving the ecosystem of personal behavioral data. *Human-Computer Interaction*, *32*(5-6), 447–510. doi:10.1080/07370024.2017.1295857

World Weather Online. (n.d.). Retrieved from http://www.worldweatheronline.com

Xu, N., Zhang, W. S., Yang, H. D., Zhang, X. G., & Xing, X. (2013). CACOnt: A ontology-based model for context modeling and reasoning. *Applied Mechanics and Materials*, *347*, 2304–2310. doi:10.4028/www.scientific.net/AMM.347-350.2304

Xu, W., Venkatakrishnan, V. N., Sekar, R., & Ramakrishnan, I. V. (2006, September). A framework for building privacy-conscious composite web services. In *Web Services, 2006. ICWS'06. International Conference on* (pp. 655-662). IEEE. 10.1109/ICWS.2006.4

Yang, J., Zhu, Z., Seiter, J., & Tröster, G. (2015, November). Informative yet unrevealing: Semantic obfuscation for location based services. In *Proceedings of the 2nd Workshop on Privacy in Geographic Information Collection and Analysis* (p. 4). ACM. 10.1145/2830834.2830838

Chapter 9
Pattern–Based Cloud Migration:
Take Blockchain as a Service as an Example

Zhitao Wan
Ge Lian Corporation, China

ABSTRACT

To migrate on-premises business systems to the cloud environment faces challenges: the complexity, diversity of the legacy systems, cloud, and cloud migration services. Consequently, the cloud migration faces two major problems. The first one is how to select cloud services for the legacy systems, and the second one is how to move the corresponding workload from legacy systems to cloud. This chapter presents a total cloud migration solution including cloud service selection and optimization, cloud migration pattern generation, and cloud migration pattern enforcement. It takes the pattern as the core, and unifies the cloud migration request, the cloud migration service pattern, and the cloud migration service composition. A cloud migration example of blockchain system shows that the proposed approach improves the cloud service selection, cloud migration service composition generation efficiency, migration process parallelization, and enables long transaction support by means of pattern reuse.

DOI: 10.4018/978-1-5225-7268-8.ch009

INTRODUCTION

With the skyrocketing of the cloud computing deployment, the demands of cloud migration increase dramatically. To migrate the on-premises business systems to the cloud environment faces challenges (Linthicum, 2017). Firstly, the complexity of business systems and the diversity of operating environment lead to complex initial states of the cloud migration. Secondly, the diversity of the cloud computing environment causes the complexity of the target environments. Thirdly, the diversity of cloud migration services worsens the cloud migration. Besides, the cloud migration is also subject to the constraints of time, cost and other non-technical factors. The cloud migration plan generation faces two major problems. The first one is how to plan the target cloud environment and cloud service selection of the legacy systems. The current cloud migration approaches usually adopt experts' recommendation basing on the users' prefers and constraints (Al-Masri & Mahmoud, 2007a, 2007b). The automation mechanisms are usually unavailable. The second one is how to perform the cloud migration, i.e., how to move the corresponding workload from legacy systems to the cloud services. Manual migration is expensive, time consuming and error prone. Recently dedicated cloud migration services emerge in the market for fine granular cloud migration (Huang, Gao, Zhang, & Xiao, 2017).

However, migrating existing on-premises enterprise applications to cloud is still a costly, labor-intensive, and error-prone activity due to the complexity of the applications, the constraints of the clouds, and the limitations of existing migration techniques provided by migration service vendors. It fails to handle complex legacy system migration. Approaches have been proposed to find out the most cost effective solution by composing multiple migration services from different vendors together to complete specific migration task (Fan, Wang, & Chang, 2011; Frey & Hasselbring, 2010). They are sandbox approaches and these only provide one-off solutions by calculating without verified precedent. These approaches adopt exhaustive searching based algorithm with pruning to improve the efficiency. In these sandbox approaches, the metric for migration service selection and composition is usually simple, e.g., only the total cost. In fact, the reliability, privacy and other nonfunctional constraints should be considered as well. Besides, there are other nontechnical factors that will impact the selection. For example, a customer may prefer services from specific vendors. More critically, a case by case solution discovery approach has not explicitly process logic for tracing, benchmarking, debugging and optimization.

Fortunately, pattern has been proven as an appealing approach to accelerate the service composition and alleviate the defects (Ejarque, Micsik, & Badia, 2015; Tilsner, Fiech, Zhan, & Specht, 2011). It can also be applied to the cloud migration service composition to solve the mentioned challenges (Emna, Jmaiel, Dupuy, & Tazi, 2012). Pattern is basing on the fact that an idea has been proven useful in one practical context and will probably be useful in others (Yan, Dijkman, & Grefen, 2010). Even though, every system has its own set of prerequisites, hidden costs, one-off requirements and special case exceptions, the best practices could tell us how to cope with these issues. More specifically, service patterns are defined over services and present the typical ways of composing services to achieve certain goals. The pattern in this chapter refers service composition pattern dedicates to the service composition for the cloud migration. Service composition patterns facilitate the service composition and accelerate the response to the market. This is exactly why the patterns are appealing as a medium to convey solutions.

A complete on-premises application/system migration to cloud generally involves two major phases: the target cloud selection and the migration process. The target cloud service selection and optimization is to find out proper cloud services. The requirements for each node can be described as cloud service parameters. This chapter presents a clustering based approach to select corresponding cloud services, and also introduces a cloud layer based node merging and splitting approach. Thus solving the problem that it is difficult to quickly and automatically select cloud services for complex system migration out of a large number of cloud services. This chapter also presents a cloud migration service composition approach, which adopts pattern based approach by classifying and analyzing of service composition approaches. It can be abstracted as graph generation problem and further the problem of service composition pattern generation is abstracted as graph similarity calculation, which simplifies the pattern generation. In this way, it solves the problem that the cloud migration service composition pattern cannot be effectively generated in the rapid evolution environment that lacks precedence. Besides, this chapter also presents cloud migration service pattern enforcement approach, which improves the service composition generation efficiency, parallel execution efficiency and enables long transaction support by means of pattern reuse and bipartite graph analysis. It solves the problem that it is difficult to quickly form a cloud migration service composition from a large number of cloud migration services. Compared with the existing cloud migration approaches the proposed approach is faster, and more robust and can be used for other dynamic service composition scenarios.

BACKGROUND

Cloud migration can be considered as a process of transforming application from an initial state in the source environment, usually hosted by on-premises servers, to a target state accepted by the cloud. With the development of cloud computing technology, more and more cloud services are available. The diversity of cloud services has led to the complexity of cloud service selection. Cloud services are selected out of various cloud services to form a cloud service matching scheme. Currently, cloud migration has characteristics such as large scale of demand, multiple constraints, and candidate service competition. Regarding the scale of the migration, report shows that around 26% of the respondents have a production environment with a scale of more than 1,000 migration needs involving Web services, development environments, databases, mail systems, business applications, file services and etc. A wide variety of applications such as analytics, customer relationship systems, enterprise resource planning systems, e-commerce and online tools. Meanwhile, the legacy systems to be migrated are designed for traditional hardware and software platforms. Their deployment plans are constrained by the software and hardware. When perform the cloud migration, it should also consider the adjustment and optimization of the workload to fit the gap to cloud.

A cloud migration process can be modeled by a hierarchy of components with configuration attributes and corresponding interdependencies. Existing pattern generation approaches can be classified into two families: deduction and induction. The former is usually based on business process knowledge. The latter discovers patterns by abstracting execution instances. The top-down approaches can be classified as deductive approach. In the top-down approach domain experts review business processes to discover patterns (Pfitzmann & Joukov, 2011). The bottom-up approaches can be classified as induction approach. It mines the business processes from the execution logs of applications and then abstract the processes as service composition pattern (Tang & Zou, 2010). The demand of the migration to cloud drives the emerging of related services for migration. The migration to cloud has its own characteristics: the application to be migrated and the target platform are known, the services for migration is also enumerable. But how to process the complex application migration is not clear. Consequently, there is no clear business processes available and the deductive approaches are not applicable under this circumstance. Comparing with other business processes, the migration to cloud is relatively new and few best practices available. Lack of migration practices prevents the application execution logs acquirement and bottom-up approaches fail to work as well.

In the cloud migration pattern generation context, a cloud migration solution can be modeled as a graph and the pattern generation can be modeled as discovering common graph out of candidate graphs using graph matching. Basing on the formal definition of solution graph this chapter formalizes the similarity between nodes and edges of two different solution graphs to find out the pattern graph (Wan, Meng, Xu, & Wang, 2014). Classical graph matching approaches can be classified in two categories:

1. **Exact Graph Matching:** It is used to find isomorphic mapping between the nodes (vertices) of two graphs that have the same number of nodes and corresponding edges. In the context of cloud migration pattern generation, the drawback is that a given cloud migration solution may be implemented in various forms that different from a pattern. It is insufficient for cloud migration pattern generation.
2. **Inexact Graph Matching:** It aims at finding the best matching between both graphs when an isomorphic mapping between two graphs cannot be found. There are three sub categories:
    a. Edit distance based approach, which calculates the number of modifications that one graph has to undertake to reach an isomorphic mapping to another graph. But, the inaccurate mapping result get by addition and deletion operation of edit may be inaccurate. However, the fatal drawback is the operations may incur not reasonable relative higher similarity score for migration process by removing few critical steps.
    b. Feature extraction based approach, which aggregate statistics to calculate similarity score. The idea is that similar graphs probably share certain properties, such as degree distribution, diameter, and eigenvalues. Usually extracting these features and applying a similarity measure can be used to calculate the similarity between the graphs. However, it is possible to get not intuitive results. For instance, it is possible to get high similarity between two graphs that have very different node scale, which is not always reasonable.
    c. Iteration based approach, which exchange node similarity scores recursively and the iteration ends when convergence is achieved. The principle is that two similar nodes have similar neighbor nodes. Belief propagation approach proposes algorithm using iterative message passing. However, the assumption is that one somehow knows which the possible correspondences between two graphs are.

Consequently, the exact graph matching and the current inexact graph matching fail to work in cloud migration pattern generation. This chapter presents a graph matching that calculates similarity score by mapping compatible nodes and edges to avoid the drawback of mentioned inexact graph matching approaches. The main improvements include: Keeping critical steps aligned with the similarity score calculating to avoid not realistic results. Keeping the graph sizes as a major factor for similarity score calculating to avoid not intuitive results. Performing similarity calculating without any assumption or knowledge on the graphs.

The main contributions of this chapter is summarized as follows:

1. **Target Cloud Service Selection and Optimization:** This chapter presents a requirement specification of legacy system based cloud selection approach. The legacy system to be migrated is divided into nodes by the requirement specification. The requirements for each node can be described as cloud service parameters. Thus, this chapter presents a clustering based approach to select corresponding cloud service, a cloud layer based node merging and splitting approach for workload redistribution. Thus solving the problem that it is difficult to quickly and automatically select cloud services required for complex system migration out of a large number of cloud services.

2. **Cloud Migration Pattern Generation:** This chapter presents the cloud migration service composition, which adopts pattern based dynamic approach. According to the characteristics of cloud migration, it can be abstracted as graph generation problem and further the problem of service composition pattern generation is abstracted as graph similarity calculation, which simplifies the pattern generation. This chapter presents a graph similarity calculation algorithm for fast pattern generation. In this way, it solves the generation problem that the cloud migration service composition pattern cannot be effectively generated in the environment of lack of execution precedence and rapid evolution of cloud migration service.

3. **Cloud Migration Pattern Enforcement:** This chapter presents a constraints oriented cloud migration plan generation and execution approach, which takes the pattern as the core, and unifies the cloud migration request, the cloud migration service pattern and the cloud migration service composition. It improves the service composition generation efficiency, parallel execution efficiency and enables long transaction support by means of pattern reuse. It can accurately and quickly adapt to the customer's specific application environment, and further improve the quality of cloud migration. It solves the problem that it is difficult to quickly form a cloud migration service composition from a large number of cloud migration services. Comparing with the existing cloud migration approaches the proposed approach is faster, and more robust. The approach is open and evolution, and can be used for other dynamic service composition scenarios.

CLOUD SERVICE SELECTION AND OPTIMIZATION

Cloud Service Metrics

A cloud service includes functional and non-functional requirements (Zhang, Lei, & Qin, 2018). The metrics for cloud services begin with basic functional requirements. NIST defines the SLA (Service Level Agreement) as a legal document for the contractual rules between cloud users and cloud providers. The SLA is a technical performance commitment made by the cloud vendor, how the dispute is discovered and handled, and documentation of the solution. For example, response time can be specified in the SLA, while other technical measures such as hops and bandwidth can be used to dynamically adjust the resources to meet the response time SLA. The ISO uses the SMI (Service Measurement Index) to give definitions of SLA attributes including meterability, agility, service assurance, cost, performance, security and privacy, and availability. Cost based metering is a major component of SLA or SMI. Some examples of usage based metrics are: number of users, instance minutes, storage resource capacity, CPU minutes, and RAM size. The cost indicator is based on the cost per unit, for example: fee/(instance#×time). SLA indicators need to be properly classified to clarify the consequences of non-compliant SLAs. The various constraints of both functional and non-functional on cloud services can be abstracted into the following two types:

1. **Enumeration Type:** There is an enumerable attribute set, a constraint is the same as the enumeration value of the corresponding attribute of the cloud service, then satisfiability is T, otherwise is F. For example, the operating system types supported by cloud services can be represented as enumeration type.
2. **Interval Type:** There is a satisfiable upper bound and/or lower bound. Satisfaction may have a difference, i.e., there may be satisfaction above the constraint requirement, or it may be below the satisfaction of the constraint requirement. For a global constraint decomposed into multiple local constraints, there is an acceptable possibility to satisfy the global constraint by satisfying the compromise of the constraint, but it is necessary to balance the multiple related nodes. For example, the price range of a cloud service under a certain pricing rule.

Cloud Service Selection Approaches

The same or similar cloud services by different vendors continue to emerge. Test results of services are used to predict the performance and cost of the applications deployed on them. These results show that the performance and costs of cloud services vary widely (Moreno, Garraghan, Townend, & Xu, 2013). The approaches of cloud service selection can be fitted into the following three categories:

1. **Instructive Selection:** The focuses of the cloud migration problem should be on two aspects: one is the component of the software product, i.e., it is considered to be mapped to a different cloud service; the other is the use of metering and billing. The choice of cloud deployment model and cloud service model are two key issues in cloud migration scenario.

2. **Multiple Attributes Selection:** Cloud services vary widely in performance and cost. In addition, multiple attributes of cloud services must be considered when making cloud service selection decisions. In the case of multiple standards, compromises must be made because in most real-world situations, a cloud service is difficult to outperform other cloud services in all aspects, but some cloud services may be better in some aspects. Hybrid cloud service selection be performed on two levels: a hybrid cloud service layer and a hybrid cloud resource layer. The hybrid cloud service selection and optimization problem can be decomposed into a two-level sequence of Lagrangian relaxation and gradient optimization problems. Balance can be reached and the benefits of hybrid cloud users can be maximized locally.

3. **Proxy and Aggregation Based Selection:** Intermediary service proxy model allows each intermediary service agent to manage a type of cloud services. An adaptive learning mechanism consisting of incentive and forgetting capabilities to dynamically perform optimized cloud service selection and return integrated solutions to users. Cloud service list is used when the client sends a cloud service request to the cloud service agent, the cloud service agent requests the cloud service discovery to obtain the current cloud service list and the related cloud service availability. Cloud service availability may include many aspects, with weights and thresholds determining the choice of cloud services. The weighted approach is used to calculate revenue and cost and to balance the benefits and costs in a weighted way. Supporting cloud service selection by aggregating feedback information from cloud users and objective performance analysis from trusted third parties. Cloud service filtering and user reviews are two basic approaches. The former uses a feature based filtering function for cloud service matching; the latter provides user feedback collection and experience based rating approaches, which are personalized by

allowing users to specify important factors (e.g., compatible operating systems, control interfaces, features, costs). Third-party auditing provides a trustworthy view of the performance, reliability, and consistency of cloud services. The portal as an agent for cloud services and provided comparison tools between different cloud service providers to help cloud users identify and locate cloud providers that meet their needs, and perform cloud service selection through quick search. However, the single cloud service ordering and search approaches lack the flexibility of choice, and the comparison of cloud services cannot fully reflect the differences in application scenarios.

Clustering Based Cloud Service Selection

Cloud migration decisions include the selection of cloud migration objects and target cloud services, considerations for migration implementation, and changes to management after migration. The choice of the cloud migration objects and the applicable target cloud service is the core issue, i.e., selecting the objects to be migrated and selecting the cloud services that can provide the corresponding operating environment.

The cloud migration objects are determined by the system to be migrated, and the functional and non-functional requirements of the cloud migration objects on the operating environment determine the choice of the target cloud service. The actual deployment of the original system and the corresponding requirements documents and delivery documents serve as the basis for analysis of the cloud migration objects. The requirements for cloud migration can generally be established basing on the operating environment requirements of the system to be migrated and its proper adjustments. The migration of the system to be migrated can be described from the structure of the deployment document, and the corresponding cloud can be further characterized by constraints and optimization objectives. In the scenario of large-scale cloud migration, it is also necessary to consider the interdependence and restriction of large-scale demands formed by the aggregation of different migration requirements.

This section proposes a description approach of the cloud migration object environment requirements and target cloud service attributes in cloud migration scenario. A target cloud service selection approach basing on clustering and partial order relationships is proposed. The requirements should define the constraints on the software and hardware environment. These constraints should be resolved and satisfied when the original system is deployed. The choice of cloud services is based on the environment requirements of the migration target.

This section proposes a candidate cloud service clustering approach, which takes the cloud migration object environment requirement as a dummy service, i.e., only the cloud service attributes described but does not have the actual service function;

put the dummy service into the candidate cloud service set, and later dumb services are clustered as the initial core.

Cloud Service Optimization: Merging and Splitting

Cloud computing provides different levels of cloud services through three service models. Cloud migration objects can use different cloud service models. In general, if the underlying migration is performed, the above layers are generally implicitly included. For example, if virtual machine level migration is performed, a virtual machine created by a physical machine includes the operating system and the runtime environments and applications of the above layers. For simplicity of discussion, the content to be migrated is divided into application/system layer, middleware/runtime/ database layer, and operating system layer, which represent cloud migration objects corresponding to three cloud service models that can be migrated to the same cloud environment (Wan, Duan, & Wang, 2017).

Consider the corresponding relationship between the three levels of cloud services and the legacy system. According to the level containing relationships the cloud migration is divided into seven categories:

1. Operating system and above layers to IaaS.
2. Operating system and middleware/runtime environment/database layers to IaaS.
3. Operating system and application/system layers to IaaS.
4. Operating system layer to IaaS.
5. Middleware/runtime environment/database and application/system layers to PaaS.
6. Middleware/runtime environment/database layer to PaaS.
7. Application/operating system layers to SaaS.

Through the analysis of the migration system and cloud service matching scheme, the principles of merging and splitting are summarized as follows:

1. **Distance Principle:** Bandwidth and delay are the key indicators for evaluating the distance between nodes. If there is a high-bandwidth or low-latency constraint between the split nodes, it is not recommended to split them. Or it is still recommended to deploy in the same geographical space to meet relevant requirements when splitting occurs.
2. **Platform Principle:** Objects to be migrated are basing on the same platform or platform-independent can be merged, but configuration conflicts should be avoided.

3. **Dynamic Expansion Principle:** Application entities with high scalability requirements are generally split with those do not have high expansion capability requirements.
4. **Resource Conflict Principle:** There should be no conflict between hardware and software resources in the merged system.
5. **Isolation Principle:** Different security level requirements should not be combined, different user operation permissions or nodes used by a specific user group should not be merged.
6. **Cost Principle:** Considering the cloud service capacity, the number of instances, and the cost of management, independent cloud migration objects whose resource consumption is stable at lower levels and should consider appropriate merging.
7. **Professional Service Priority Principle:** GPU, FPGA and other hardware can be provided through a dedicated cloud service.

PATTERN BASED CLOUD MIGRATION MODELING

Pattern Generation Problem

Cloud migration can be considered as a process of transforming application from an initial state in the source environment, usually hosted in on-premises servers, to a target state accepted by the cloud. A solution can be modeled by a hierarchy of components with valued configuration attributes and corresponding interdependencies. This chapter formalizes the individual cloud migration service composition solution as a solution graph and then the pattern generation problem as abstracting similar solution graphs into a cloud migration pattern. Therefore, the solution graph similarity calculation algorithm is the core of the proposed cloud migration pattern generation approach (Wan, Wang, Duan, Meng, & Xu, 2015). This section presents the outline of the graph matching approach includes the underlying theory and the cloud migration pattern generation problem modeling, which described as the formal definitions of related concepts.

Pattern Modeling

The following definitions embody the basic concepts discussed. They are also the formal modeling and specification of the problem and the guide for algorithm implementation.

$G = (N, E)$ is a directed acyclic graph which denotes a cloud migration service composition solution.

$N = (n_1, n_2, ..., n_i)$ is a set of nodes, i.e., a repetitive set of services which are selected to collaboratively accomplish the migration task, $i \in \{1, m\}$. For each $n_i \in N \{n_i.a_j, j \in \{1,k\}\}$ is a parameter set of the node or service n_i.

$E = \{(n_i, n_j, P_{i,j}) | i,j \in \{1,m\}\}$ is a set edges, i.e., directed links (e.g., from n_i to n_j) representing their precedent order in migration, and context information, $P_{i,j}$ is called global context which contains necessary information about vendor interactions during migration regarding each link. $P_{i,j} = (Type, Value)$, The $Type \in \{I/O, dependency, conditional\}$ is the context of the link and the $Value$ is intermediate state according to the $Type$.

Let $G_1 = (N_1, E_1)$ and $G_2 = (N_2, E_2)$ be two graphs and $n_1 \in N_1$ and $n_2 \in N_2$ be two nodes. The similarity of n_1 and n_2 is:

$$S_N(n_1, n_2) = \begin{cases} 1, & n_1 = n_2 \\ \dfrac{2 \times mCount(n_1, n_2)}{aCount(n_1) + aCount(n_2)}, & Grp(n_1, n_2) \\ 0, & other \end{cases}$$

$Grp(n_i, n_j)$ is a function that holds iff n_i can substitute n_j or vice versa. mCount(n_1, n_2) is a function to calculate the number of identical parameter between n_1 and n_2. $aCount(n_1)$ is a function to count the parameter number of n_1. Obviously, the node similarity score is in [0, 1]. All the following similarity score are designed to distribute in the same range.

Let $G_1 = (N_1, E_1)$ and $G_2 = (N_2, E_2)$ be two graphs and $(n_{i1}, n_{j1}, P_{i1,j1}) \in E_1$ and $(n_{i2}, n_{j2}, P_{i2,j2}) \in E_2$ be two edges. The similarity of $(n_{i1}, n_{j1}, P_{i1,j1})$ and $(n_{i2}, n_{j2}, P_{i2,j2})$ is:

$$S_E\left((n_{i1}, n_{j1}, P_{i1,j1}), (n_{i2}, n_{j2}, P_{i2,j2})\right) = \begin{cases} 1, & \begin{pmatrix} n_{i1} = n_{i2}, \\ n_{j1} = n_{j2} \end{pmatrix} \\ Sim(P_{i1,j1}, P_{i2,j2}) & Other \end{cases}$$

$Sim(P_{i1,j1}, P_{i2,j2})$ is the function to calculate the similarity between two edges (contexts).

Let $G_1 = (N_1, E_1)$ and $G_2 = (N_2, E_2)$ be two graphs and $M_i: N_1 \rightarrow N_2$ be a full ($|N_1| = |N_2|$) or partial ($|N_1| \neq |N_2|$) injective mapping that maps nodes in G_1 to nodes in

G_2. M_i is noted a set of node pairs. $(n_1, n_2) \in M_i$ iff $n_1 \in N_1$, $n_2 \in N_2$ and n_1 is mapped to n_2. The similarity of G_1 and G_2 under M_i is $S_{GM}(G_1, G_2, M_i)$

$|N_1|$ is the node count of G_1 and $|N_1|/|N_2|$ is the edge count of G_1 attached to the nodes present in the pairs of M_i. α, β ($\alpha + \beta = 1$) are the weight of node and edge similarity. Let M denotes the set of all possible M_i. The similarity of G_1 and G_2 is:

$$S_G\left(G_1, G_2\right) = \underset{M_i \in M}{Max}\left(S_{GM}\left(G_1, G_2, M_i\right)\right)$$

To find out patterns in the solutions can be formalized as classify the solution into subsets by graph similarity scores of solutions. A solution graph with most similar solutions is a pattern graph.

Let $C_G = \{G_1, \ldots, G_n\}$ be the set of all acceptable cloud migration solution graphs on a service set. Let C_c be a subset of C_G and exist $G_i \in C_c$, for all $G_j \in C_c$ satisfy:

$$S_G\left(G_i, G_j\right) > Threshold \quad (0 \leq Threshold \leq 1)$$

C_c is a subset under the similarity factor of *Threshold*. Graph G_i is the pattern graph of C_c when G_i satisfies:

$$\underset{G_i \in C_c}{Max}\left(\sum_{G_j \in C_c} S_G\left(G_i, G_j\right)\right)$$

The pattern graph number depends on the given C_G and also relates to the parameters α, β and *Threshold*. For each C_c only one pattern graph with the maximum similarity score is selected. It also embodies a service composition pattern of a class of similar solutions.

Given a solution graph set C_G, and a service set S_s, which includes all service nodes in the graph set. *SIM* is graphs and their corresponding subset under the given similarity factor *Threshold* sorted by the subset size in descent order.

PATTERN GENERATION PROCESS

Pattern generation process includes following steps: *solution collection, service similarity measurement, graph similarity calculation* and *pattern identification*. Generally, the proposed approach accepts solution graphs and output the pattern graph(s).

1. **Solution Collection:** Cloud migration solutions are the foundation of pattern generation. This step should enclose all related solutions as the input of this approach. The solutions are represented as graphs. Square matrix is used to depict solution graphs. Rows and columns represent services and entries represent service interactions. An extra array is used for a graph to represent the nodes (services) and their parameters. The matrix entries represent the context types.

2. **Service Similarity Measurement:** A cloud migration solution is based on a series of migration services. All migration services included in the solution set compose the service set. These services perform identical or similar functions can be classified into a group. In a given context the services in same group can be or partly be substituted by each other. i.e., the services can be roughly predefined as groups based on the service functionality. The service parameters are defined to measure the similarity of the services in the same group. The similar services in two graphs usually indicate the meaningful candidate node mapping. Beside the service parameters, in the cloud migration there are three types of context, or service interaction, in the service composition: I/O, dependency and conditional. The I/O denotes the intermediate state of the component set passed between two services. The dependency denotes the dependency between two services and conditional denotes no information need to be conveyed.

3. **Graph Similarity Calculation:** The similarity of two graphs is defined in previous section. And, the graph similarity can be split into node (service) similarity and edge (context) similarity. Because a node may connect to many other nodes, node mapping of two graphs as the base of graph similarity calculation and then the affiliated edges. To find out the maximum similarity the complexity of plain exhaustive approach is $n!$. Considering the node and edge similarities are approximation, a proper approximate algorithm is also acceptable. Greedy algorithm can get local optimal result usually with very high computation efficiency. This chapter presents a greedy algorithm to calculate the graph similarity scores by mapping two graphs. This chapter presents an improved the greedy algorithm by exhaustively shuffling the start node and iterating the greedy algorithm to seek higher score. i.e., the first round running of the greedy algorithm gets a local optimal solution. The rest rounds attempt to change the mapping for higher similarity score to find out optimal result.

4. **Pattern Identification:** All the similarity scores are stored in a square matrix. Each row and column denotes a graph. An entry in the corresponding row and column is their similarity score. For each graph G_i, choose the similar graphs with similarity score higher than *Threshold* and sum up the similarity scores. Then put all similar graphs in a set labeled as G_i. Further, sort all sets by the

similar graph count and similarity score. Finally, select all mutual exclusive sets by removing the sets contain few graphs. The label graph of each set is a pattern graph.

PATTERN ENFORCEMENT

The cloud migration service composition pattern is a reusable abstraction that satisfies the requirements of the cloud migration domain. The purpose is to simplify the process of cloud migration service composition (Jamshidi, Pahl, & Mendonça, 2017; Li, Cheng, Zhang, & Leung, 2016). No matter how the service composition pattern is generated, the pattern based service composition generation process is an instantiation process from the service composition pattern to the specific service composition. However, this process is related to the characteristics of the pattern itself. In the process of generating service compositions, services are selected and configured according to specific requirements. In general, the service composition can be divided into two categories: static composition and dynamic composition. The static service composition completes the binding of the service before the service composition is executed to meet the user's functional and non-functional requirements; the dynamic service composition is in the process of running to select and call the required service. Service composition will be called as a service process to meet the needs of users raised. These approaches are proven to be NP-hard problem. The service composition optimization problem has always been one of the research focuses in the field of service computing. In fact, both static service composition and dynamic service composition have advantages and disadvantages. The services in static service composition are determined before execution, and the execution efficiency is high, but if the service in the composition is abnormal, the composition service may fail. The dynamic service composition selects the required service at runtime, and has more flexibility in the dynamic selection of services, but the execution efficiency is relatively low. Combining the advantages of the two is of great significance to improve service composition. The pattern based cloud migration service composition starts from the pattern for service selection and execution. It enables the supporting of the composition of static and dynamic service selection.

Long Transaction

The long transaction support of the cloud migration service composition firstly depends on the transaction attributes that make up the service composition. If a service has transaction support, there is no relevant interventions or few relevant interventions needed during the execution of the service composition. If a certain service does not support transaction related attributes, it is necessary to consider extra process to ensure the related services could be processed when failure occurs to ensure the transactionality of the entire cloud migration service composition. When a constituent service fails, by restarting the failed service or by calling another service with the same function to continue execution (noted as r). The transactional defects caused by the restart feature can be handled in two directions: the first is that the service execution fails beyond the restart limit and the replacement service is used. When the replacement service can be executed successfully, the entire service composition continues. Both service restart and service replacement are called forward recovery. When the replacement service fails to execute, it needs to perform compensation (noted as c). In fact, some services can only be restart after compensation (noted as rc). Any modification of the cloud migration object or the target cloud service should be recovered. Consider the success rate of service y_i performed is P_{yi}. The failure of service execution is handled at the transaction level. The probability of a successful retry operation after all n restarts of k services is:

$$\prod_{i=1}^{k}\left(1-\left(1-P_{yi}\right)^{n}\right)$$

Consider the case where $k=1$, $Py_i=0.5$, and $n=10$. The final success rate is about 0.999, i.e., even a service has a success rate of only 50%, and the probability of successful execution after 10 restarts is 0.999. Restart mechanism improves service reliability at the expense of response time. At the same time, during the execution of the cloud migration service composition, the cloud migration service composition ensures transactionality. When some of the constituent services fail to execute, it is necessary to perform related recovery operations on the entire transactional composite service.

Parallelization Migration Execution

During the execution of service composition for cloud migration, there may be problems with resource competition and access conflicts. However, the cloud migration service composition has a long execution time. How to ensure parallel execution of services on the basis of transaction support can greatly shorten the execution time to improve migration efficiency. In the face of increasingly stringent cloud migration requirements, especially the requirement for migration time, the parallelization of cloud migration is a problem that needs to be solved. The cloud migration service composition can be divided according to the cloud migration object, and the cloud migration service composition is structurally decomposed to find independent execution branches of the cloud migration service composition.

IMPLEMENTATION AND EVALUATION

In this section, a blockchain system depicted in Figure 1 is used to validate the similarity model and algorithm (Joshi, 2017). Synthetic solution graphs driven benchmarking is performed basing on a proof-of-concept prototype. For a cloud migration task the artifacts can be abstracted as application profile, cloud profile, service profile and user requirement profile. These profiles can be used to classify current migration tasks and future requests. The nodes of solution graphs denote the migration services and the edges denote the interactions. Simulated solution graphs by constructing matrixes with random discovered artificial services and interactions are used for performance benchmarking.

Cloud Service Selection and Optimization

According to the discussion in previous section, the generation of a cloud service matching scheme based on the needs of the system to be migrated and the candidate cloud service set can be divided into two steps. The first step uses the candidate cloud service clustering approach to put the cloud migration object environment requirement as a dummy service node into the cloud service set, and uses the dummy service as the initial core to generate the candidate cloud service clusters. The second step is to establish a partial order relationship of each cloud service subset, perform cloud service selection according to local demand and global demand decomposition, generate corresponding cloud service matching scheme, and implement the system to be migrated according to the migration entity represented by the dummy service. The experiment uses the service attributes of the QWS data set to evaluate the effectiveness of the algorithms for clustering and partial ordering. All the service sets are listed in Table 1.

Clustering

From the QWS dataset, each of the 10 types of services is randomly selected. The attributes of the selected cloud services are used as the requirements of the migration target environment. These dummy services that represent requirements are the initial core of the cluster. Cloud services that are mismatched with all dummy services will not be further clustered. The pseudo-code of improved k-means algorithm is as following.

Figure 1. An on-premises blockchain network consisting of four members leveraging channels to be migrated to cloud

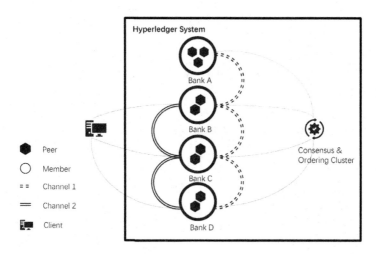

Table 1. A subset of QWS data set to verify the clustering approach

Service Set	Response Time			Availability			Throughput		
	Avg (ms)	Max (ms)	Min (ms)	Avg (%)	Max (%)	Min (%)	Avg (t/s)	Max (t/s)	Min (t/s)
11	41.27	46	37	71.77	72	71	16.4	21.3	13.2
13(1)	105.1	328.67	47.27	21.69	61	17	5.93	20.3	3.7
13(2)	318.05	1177.5	108	93.6	99	87	9.44	30	2.5
14	225.46	563	117.67	75.57	98	26	2.68	5.8	1.5
17(1)	320	344	293	92.35	100	85	24.38	28	20.4
17(2)	496.51	2909.47	41	89.05	100	61	15.88	43.1	1.3
25	133.59	305.37	57.42	81.04	92	61	8.69	13.3	6.4
28	564.43	3356.5	91.5	68.03	98	16	4.7	17.2	1
43	158.2	505	111.67	92.72	100	85	7.83	11.3	6.1
102	315.42	1567.09	220.96	84.94	92	71	3.5	11.1	0.2

```
INPUT:
    Service set: Y=y₁,y₂,…,yₘ
    Nodes set S=s₁,s₂,…,sₙ
OUTPUT:
 Cluster set: {Y₁,Y₂,…Yₖ}
BEGIN
```

```
REPEAT
Unique the Node set as k initial cluster core mᵢ(1≤i≤k)
Yᵢ=mᵢ (1≤i≤k)
FOR each node yⱼ∈ S∪Y
 Calculate distance to all mᵢ(1≤i≤k)
Yᵢ=Yᵢ∪yⱼ iff min(d(mᵢ, yⱼ))∧d(mᵢ, yⱼ)<∞
ENDFOR
   FOR each Yᵢ (1≤i≤k)
Calculate the average yₐᵥ₉=sum(yⱼ∈Yᵢ)/|Yᵢ|
update mᵢ iff yₐᵥ₉<mᵢ
   Calculate E
ENDFOR
UNTIL min(E)
RETURN Y₁,Y₂,…,Yₖ
END
```

The calculation of the cluster distance vector uses Euclidean distance. The response time, availability, and throughput rate are normalized separately. Interval attributes have directionality, response time is generally the lower the better, and availability with a percentage measurement is the higher the better, and throughput is generally the higher the better. When optimizing the service selection, the direction is determined according to the optimization principle within the corresponding interval. In addition, there are correlations between some attributes. For example, the throughput is generally positively correlated with the price, and the attributes such as time delay and capacity are negatively correlated with the price.

The examine clustering of cloud services in nine dimensions, the enumerated attributes of the function description and three dimensions of Response Time, Availability, and Throughput are selected and the normalized Euclidean distances are used. There are 2507 services of the QWS dataset are clustered. A service is randomly selected from a subset of services with a number of services greater than 10 as a clustering core for clustering. The experiment was repeated 10 times and the clustering results were consistent. To perform cluster analysis, the clustering result is finally obtained. The results are presented in Figure 2. From the results shown in the figure, it can be concluded that the clustering approach used by the algorithm in composition with the Euclidean distance of the enumeration class and the Euclidean distance of the interval type attribute is effective.

Figure 2. Result of QWS subset generated by k-means clustering

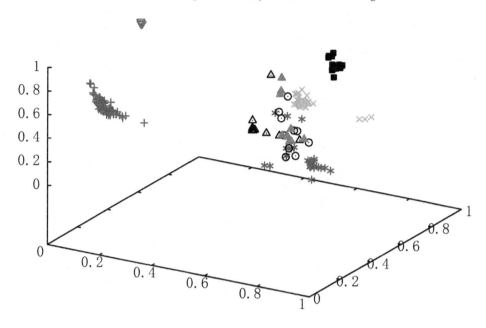

Partial Order Establishment

Following the clustering result, Figure 3 shows the partial order constructed by three key attributes of the service, latency, availability, and throughput. Among them, services 1, 3, 14, and 16 constitute the Pareto optimal solution set of this functional service. The arrow connected nodes in the figure represent the services represented by the nodes of the service Pareto dominant arc heads. Figure 4 shows a partially ordered graph generated by adding a dummy service 17 (339ms delay, 95% availability, throughput 23.7t/s). The dummy service represents a specific requirement. From the figure, it can be concluded that services 10 and 1 are determined services that meet the requirements. Following the service selection of the connection path in the figure, it can be determined that when the value of some of the attributes of the service after replacement is changed, the other attribute values are not inferior to the original service. Reduce the workload of service comparison and constraint checking, improve the reliability of service selection, and improve service replacement efficiency. Compared with the uncertainty obtained by the global optimal solution of the multi-parameter optimization algorithm in the existing service composition, the approach of service selection using the partially ordered graph generated by this algorithm is more robust.

```
INPUT:
 Y/R={[y₁]}U{[y₂]}U…U{[yₖ]}
OUTPUT:
 Partial Order Tree T_p
BEGIN
 Sort y₁,y₂,…yₖ
 Initial empty Treap T_p
 FOR all y_i
   Assign random key to y_i
   FOR all y_ij (1≤j≤d)
 IF y_ij does not exist in Tp
   THEN
 Insert into Tp
   Rotate Tp
   ENDIF
 ENDFOR
      ENDFOR
     RETURN Tp
END
```

Cloud Migration Pattern Generation

Metrics and Benchmarking

The pattern generation approach in this chapter intends to discover the reusable service compositions based on the assumption that there exist recurring similar service compositions. This approach is to identify the most typical solutions that can be reused as patterns. Consequently, the metrics to measure the pattern are

Figure 3. Partial order example

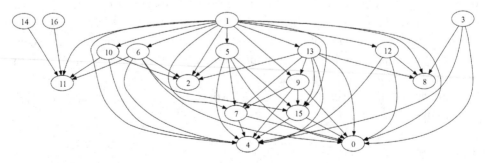

Figure 4. Partial order example with dummy service

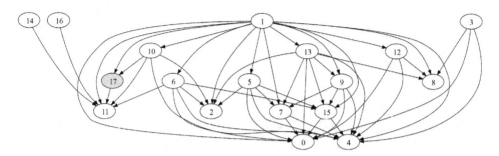

coverage, *cohesion* and *quantity*. The *coverage* ensures that the pattern graphs selected can cover most solution graphs. The *cohesion* indicates that all the solution graphs related to a graph pattern has low similarity score to any other graph pattern. It requires the distance between graph patterns should be considered. The *quantity* ensures that the graph pattern number is reasonable for future application and the necessary adjustment in a new application scenario. In this approach, the *Threshold* of similarity score, the weight of the node similarity and weight of the edge similarity are parameters which can be adjusted in the pattern graph discovery.

There are two facets, performance and functionality, in benchmarking of the algorithm implementation. The performance benchmarking collects the execution time of the algorithm on different graph node scales. The functionality benchmarking is applicable for several scenarios. This chapter focuses on the following two scenarios: One is to find out patterns cover all solution graphs. The other is to find a pattern out of a solution set of a given problem. The purpose is to investigate a pattern that most alternative service compositions similar to. It provides a pattern for the most flexible on service selection. It is solo pattern generation. In this scenario the solution graphs are expected to occur again and again. To extract the patterns that can cover all solution graphs with proper quantity. It is full coverage pattern generation. This chapter benchmarks these two scenarios respectively.

```
INPUT:
 Solution Graph Set C_G={G_1,…,G_n}
 Service Set SS={n_1,…,n_s}
  Similarity Threshold Threshold
OUTPUT:
 Pattern Graph Array SIM
BEGIN
 FOR each graph pair G_x,G_y∈ C_G
 IF (|N_x|≠|N_y|)
```

```
THEN
Extend graph with dummy node and let |N_x|=|N_y|
ENDIF
Map N_x to N_y in init node order as M_0
Calculate S_GM(G_x,G_y,M_0)
DO
FOR each n_i ∈ N_x
FOR each n_j ∈ N_y and (n_i,n_k)∈ M_1 and (n_1,n_j)∈ M_1 and Grp(n_i,n_j)
IF S_N (n_i, n_j) > S_N (n_1, n_k) and (n_i, n_j) ∉ M_0
THEN
Copy M_0 to M_1, Remove (n_i,n_k)∈ M_1, (n_1,n_j)∈M_1,
Add (n_i,n_j), (n_1, n_k) to M_1 in random R
IF  S_GM(G_x,G_y,M_1)>S_GM(G_x,G_y,M_0)
THEN
Let M_1  be M_0
ENDIF
ENDIF
ENDFOR
ENDFOR
Put S_GM(G_x,G_y,M_0) in similarity score matrix Score
WHILE iteration time < |N_x| and shuffle start node n_i
    ENDFOR
    FOR each G_i ∈ C_G
Count subset size and store in array SIM with corresponding
subset
ENDFOR
Sort SIM by subset size under Threshold in descent order
RETURN SIM
END
```

Full Coverage Pattern Generation

The full coverage patterns are derived from the output of applying the algorithm on a solution set. Figure 5 shows the number of pattern graphs with different *Threshold*. The lower *Threshold* needs fewer graphs to cover all similar cases. The line with 5 nodes has fewest graph number. But for the graph set with more nodes, the full coverage patterns are not easy to be identified from 100 solutions with higher similarity *Threshold*.

Figure 5. Full coverage pattern graph numbers

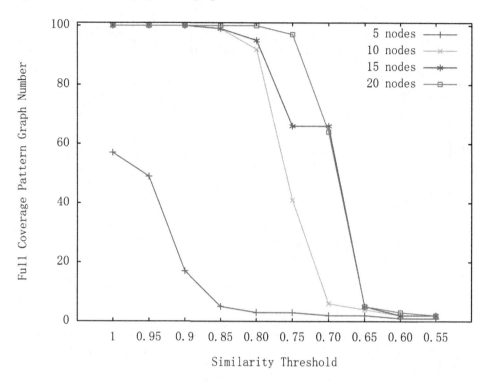

Solo Pattern Generation

In this approach the *Threshold* of similarity score and the weight of the node similarity α and weight of edge similarity β can be adjusted for intend results. From this test results, it can be find out that the edge similarity has very minor difference from the node similarity. Because the type of service interaction depends on the service type in the cloud migration context set $\alpha = 0.8,\ \beta = 0.2$. Synthetic solutions by random generating matrix with a service set of 32 services for 5 service solutions and a service set of 64 services for 10, 15 and 20 service solutions are prepared. For each solution set with 5, 10, 15 and 20 services, 100 random synthetic solutions are generated. Changing the similarity solution *Threshold* to discover solution pattern from each solution set. Figure 6 shows the similar graph numbers of solo pattern of 5 nodes. The lines show more isomorphic solutions appear while the fewer nodes included. It also infers that the probability of recurrence increases when more instances occur and pattern graph will be reused.

Figure 6. Full coverage pattern graph number and solo pattern (5 nodes)

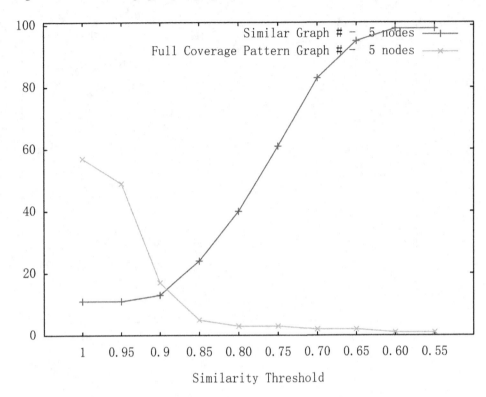

Quantitative Analysis of Pattern Graph Selection

As shown in Figure 6, solo pattern generation results with different *Threshold* cover different solution graph number. The number is a nature the selection criterion. For the full coverage pattern generation, the *Threshold* choosing is hard to balance the pattern number and cohesion of the groups. This chapter presents a composition of similar graph number and full coverage pattern number and set the cross point as the *Threshold*. In Figure 6 the *Threshold* = *0.9* is the closest point to the cross point with similar graph number 13 of solo pattern and full coverage pattern graph number of 17. When *Threshold* = *0.95* the latter increases to 49, around 3 times, but the former only decreases to 11, around 0.15 times. It is similar to *Threshold* = *0.85*. The *Threshold* = *0.9* is a good balance point observed that the production of similar graph number and coverage pattern graph number is minimum. There are similar balance points near the cross points for more nodes. Two conclusions can be deduced from the figures. One is the positive correlation between acceptable full coverage pattern graph number and the complexity of service composition solutions. The other is the negative correlation between the reasonable *Threshold* and complexity of service composition solutions.

Pattern Enforcement

After receiving the input pattern and related constraints from the pattern generation, the service selection performs scheme verification, service restart and replacement schemes that generate long transaction support according to the pattern, and constructs the maximum migration path association to support the parallelization of cloud migration service composition. In addition to the functions provided by the pattern, other factors such as cost, response time, delay, throughput, availability, and reliability are the basis for selection. The relevant parameters of a cloud migration service composition can be calculated. In the process of cloud migration, different paths from the cloud migration object to the cloud service may be relatively independent.

Long Transaction

Long transaction is basing on the service composition pattern. Pattern based cloud migration can replace services with alternative services. When the current cloud migration service cannot be performed normally, the service is restarted firstly. When the restarting fails, the alternative service is introduced to continue the work, so as to enter the successful submission state. Forward recovery is the core of transactionality guarantee as the following pseudo-code. It is used to generate service migration and replacement services when generating an exception in the cloud migration service. Once the cloud migration service completes normally, the service does not need to continue to retry or start the replacement service.

```
INPUT:
 Failed Service n_f with success probability P_nf
 Service Composition G_i
OUTPUT:
 Forward Recovery Sequence S_FR
BEGIN
P_FR = NULL
T = Ceiling -3log_(1-Pnf) 10
IF G_i.t ∈ {r,rc}
THEN
 IF n_f.t = r
  THEN
 S_FR ← Run n_f T Times
```

```
ELSE
IF n_{f.t} = rc
  THEN
S_{FR} ← Compensate n_f, Run n_f T times
ELSE
RETURN S_{FR}
  ENDIF
RETURN S_{FR}
END
```

Parallelization Migration Execution

Follow the steps in the proposed approach to discover the possible cloud migration pattern. The cloud migration service composition can be divided according to the cloud migration object, and the cloud migration service composition is structurally decomposed to find independent implementation of the cloud migration service execution branches. There are no common nodes or edges in these branches. Correspondingly, the sequence of migration operations completed by these four branches can be performed in parallel. The subgraph node set can be generated by the following pseudo-code. The execution process is depicted in Figure 7.

```
INPUT:
 Expand Bigraph G=<X,Y>
 Cloud Migration Solution Graph G'=<N',E'>
OUTPUT:
 Subgraph Node Set N
BEGIN
Construct migration path graph G_p
FOR each node X_i∈X
 Insert X_i into N as a set{X_i}
 FOR each S_j∈N' in the migration path of X_i
 Insert S_j into set{X_i}
 ENDFOR
 FOR each node Y_i∈Y is the terminal node of the migration path
of X_i
  Insert Y_i into set{X_i}
 ENDFOR
ENDFOR
FOR each node S_i∈ N'
```

```
 Merge the sets contain S_i
ENDFOR
FOR each node Y_i ∈ Y
 Merge the sets contain Y_i in N
ENDFOR        ·
RETURN N
END
```

FUTURE RESEARCH DIRECTIONS

This chapter focuses on the issue of the pattern based cloud migration, discovers the deficiencies of existing approaches, and carries out some targeted explorations and attempts. Basing on the study of this chapter, the following aspects of cloud migration are possible future research directions:

1. Further enhance the adaptability of the cloud migration service composition pattern, and efficiently update the pattern when the cloud migration service changes. This chapter proposes an approach to generate cloud migration service composition pattern. At the same time, the cloud migration service is dynamically

Figure 7. A blockchain network consisting of four members to be migrated to cloud by cloud migration service composition contains different services

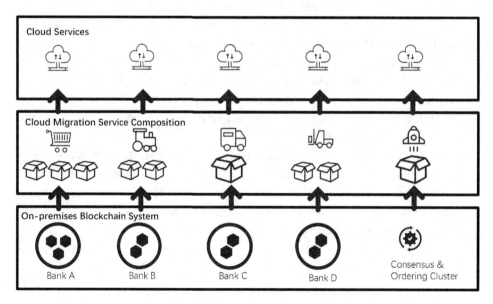

changing, and the update speed is relatively fast. This is an important reason why this chapter does not use an abstract service but a specific service instance to represent a pattern. The generation of cloud migration service composition patterns relies on cloud migration services. How to efficiently update cloud migration service composition patterns based on changes in cloud migration services is a question worthy of study.

2.   Further enhance scalability and strengthen collaboration with other cloud migration approaches. The pattern based cloud migration approach proposed in this chapter provides a targeted solution to the emerging issues of cloud migration that lacks sufficient domain knowledge and precedent. The core of the pattern is reuse, and the composition of cloud migration services and patterns derived from other migration practices should also be incorporated as part of the pattern collection. The judgment and inference approaches for these patterns should be further established. At the same time, the pattern may also contain sub-patterns that are more deterministic and applicable. The generation and application of these sub-patterns are also worthy of in-depth research.

3.   Further expand the application of cloud migration service composition pattern after the completion of cloud migration. Cloud migration in this chapter does not cover the post cloud migration phase. In fact, after the cloud migration to the target cloud service is completed, some testing, optimization, and reconfiguration work is needed. Further study of the use of patterns to provide automated testing, optimization and reconfiguration approaches, make the program's generation, use, and evaluation can be further unified.

4.   Further strengthen the fault-tolerance mechanism of the cloud migration plan. Execution errors in a dynamic cloud migration environment is difficult to avoid. During the execution of the service composition, it detects and predicts real-time deviations based on the composition of service progress and actual service quality information. Evaluate the overall impact of cloud migration on the basis of errors. The assessment of impacts can be made in two ways: first, the possible impact on the overall goal, and second, the impact on the local associated cloud services.

5.   Further study of the security mechanism. The cloud migration service provides open, standard interfaces. In order to ensure the security of services, in addition to the security mechanisms provided by service providers, in-depth research on the relevant security technologies of service compositions ensures the security in the process of cloud migration.

CONCLUSION

The process of pattern based cloud migration can be divided into two steps: The first step starts from the system to be migrated, select cloud services, and generate corresponding cloud service matching scheme. According to the requirements of the cloud migration object environments in the system to be migrated, the corresponding cloud services are selected to replace the legacy environments of the objects to be migrated. Basing on the requirements, design and delivery documents of the system to be migrated, corresponding functional entity partitions and corresponding structures are obtained. The candidate cloud services are clustered accordingly. The construction approach of service partial order relationship and the Pareto dominant service selection approach are introduced. According to the requirements of the system to be migrated, the cloud services within the cluster are selected and a cloud service matching scheme is generated to improve the selection efficiency of a large number of candidate cloud services, and provide a new approach to solve the cloud service selection problem. The second step is to realize the automation of cloud migration of complex systems by compositing cloud migration services out of a large number of professional cloud migration services. Basing on the analysis of the existing cloud migration service composition approach, a graph similarity based service composition pattern generation approach and a pattern based service composition generation approach are proposed to improve the service composition generation and execution efficiency. The pattern based approach supports the long transaction, parallelism during the cloud migration service composition execution. Analysis and verification of a blockchain system cloud migration show that the approach proposed in this chapter has a significant increase in efficiency compared with the existing approaches. It also has better tailorability, traceability, scalability, and lower dependence on domain experts.

REFERENCES

Al-Masri, E., & Mahmoud, Q. H. (2007a). Discovering the best web service. In C. L. Williamson, M. E. Zurko, P. F. Patel-Schneider, & P. J. Shenoy (Eds.), In *Proceedings of the International Conference on World Wide Web* (pp. 1257–1258). ACM.

Al-Masri, E., & Mahmoud, Q. H. (2007b). QoS-based Discovery and Ranking of Web Services. In *Proceedings of the 16th International Conference on Computer Communications and Networks* (pp. 529–534). IEEE. 10.1109/ICCCN.2007.4317873

Ejarque, J., Micsik, A., & Badia, R. M. (2015). Towards Automatic Application Migration to Clouds. In *Proceedings of the IEEE International Conference on Cloud Computing* (pp. 25–32). IEEE.

Emna, F., Jmaiel, M., Dupuy, C. S. C., & Tazi, S. (2012). A flexible approach for service composition using service patterns. In *Proceedings of the 27th Annual ACM Symposium on Applied Computing* (pp. 1976–1983). ACM. 10.1145/2245276.2232102

Fan, C.-T., Wang, W.-J., & Chang, Y.-S. (2011). Agent-Based Service Migration Framework in Hybrid Cloud. In *Proceedings of the IEEE International Conference on High Performance Computing and Communications* (pp. 887–892). IEEE. 10.1109/HPCC.2011.127

Frey, S., & Hasselbring, W. (2010). Model-based migration of legacy software systems to scalable and resource-efficient cloud-based applications: The cloudmig approach. In *Proceedings of the International Conference on Cloud Computing, GRIDs, and Virtualization* (pp. 155–158). IARIA.

Huang, K., Gao, X., Zhang, F., & Xiao, J. (2017). Customer Oriented Migration Service. In *Proceedings of the IEEE 10th International Conference on Cloud Computing* (pp. 692–695). IEEE.

Jamshidi, P., Pahl, C., & Mendonça, N. C. (2017). Pattern-based multi-cloud architecture migration. *Software, Practice & Experience*, 47(9), 1159–1184. doi:10.1002pe.2442

Joshi, D. (n.d.). *IBM, Amazon & Microsoft are offering their blockchain technology as a service*. Retrieved from http://www.businessinsider.com/ibm-azure-aws-blockchain-service-2017-10

Li, W., Cheng, Y., Zhang, P., & Leung, H. (2016). An Automatic Recovery Mechanism for Cloud Service Composition. *International Journal of Web Services Research*, 13(1), 23–39. doi:10.4018/IJWSR.2016010102

Linthicum, D. S. (2017). Cloud-Native Applications and Cloud Migration: The Good, the Bad, and the Points Between. *IEEE Cloud Computing*, 4(5), 12–14. doi:10.1109/MCC.2017.4250932

Moreno, I. S., Garraghan, P., Townend, P., & Xu, J. (2013). An Approach for Characterizing Workloads in Google Cloud to Derive Realistic Resource Utilization Models. In *Proceedings of the IEEE International Symposium on Service Oriented System Engineering* (pp. 49–60). IEEE. 10.1109/SOSE.2013.24

Pfitzmann, B., & Joukov, N. (2011). Migration to Multi-image Cloud Templates. In *Proceedings of IEEE International Conference on Services Computing* (pp. 80–87). IEEE.

Tang, R., & Zou, Y. (2010). An Approach for Mining Web Service Composition Patterns from Execution Logs (short). In *Proceedings of the IEEE International Conference on Web Services*, (pp. 678–679). IEEE.

Tilsner, M., Fiech, A., Zhan, G., & Specht, T. (2011). Patterns for service composition. In *Proceedings of the Fourth International C* Conference on Computer Science and Software Engineering*, (pp. 133–137). ACM.

Wan, Z., Duan, L., & Wang, P. (2017). Cloud Migration: Layer Partition and Integration. In *Proceedings of the IEEE International Conference on Edge Computing* (pp. 150–157). IEEE.

Wan, Z., Meng, F. J., Xu, J. M., & Wang, P. (2014). Service Composition Pattern Generation for Cloud Migration: A Graph Similarity Analysis Approach. In *Proceedings of the 2014 IEEE International Conference on Web Services* (pp. 321–328). IEEE. 10.1109/ICWS.2014.54

Wan, Z., Wang, P., Duan, L., Meng, F. J., & Xu, J. M. (2015). Graph Similarity based Cloud Migration Service Composition Pattern Discovery. *International Journal of Web Services Research*, *12*(2), 26–46. doi:10.4018/IJWSR.2015040102

Yan, Z., Dijkman, R., & Grefen, P. (2010). Fast business process similarity search with feature-based similarity estimation. *On the Move to Meaningful Internet Systems OTM*, *2010*, 60–77.

Zhang, Y., Lei, T., & Qin, Z. (2018). A Service Recommendation Algorithm Based on Modeling of Dynamic and Diverse Demands. *International Journal of Web Services Research*, *15*(1), 47–70. doi:10.4018/IJWSR.2018010103

ADDITIONAL READING

Becker, S., Brataas, G., & Lehrig, S. (Eds.). (2017). *Engineering Scalable, Elastic, and Cost-Efficient Cloud Computing Applications - The CloudScale Method.* Springer. doi:10.1007/978-3-319-54286-7

Cecowski, M., Becker, S., & Lehrig, S. (2017). Cloud Computing Applications. In S. Becker, G. Brataas, & S. Lehrig (Eds.), *Engineering Scalable, Elastic, and Cost-Efficient Cloud Computing Applications - The CloudScale Method* (pp. 47–60). Springer. doi:10.1007/978-3-319-54286-7_3

Ghumman, W. A. (2017). *Automation of The SLA Life Cycle in Cloud Computing.* Germany: Dresden University of Technology.

Holloway, M. (2017). *Service Level Management in Cloud Computing - Pareto-Efficient Negotiations, Reliable Monitoring, and Robust Monitor Placement.* Springer Vieweg.

Mohr, F. (2016). *Automated Software and Service Composition - A Survey and Evaluating Review.* Springer. doi:10.1007/978-3-319-34168-2

Paik, H.-Y., Lemos, A. L., Barukh, M. C., Benatallah, B., & Natarajan, A. (2017). *Web Service Implementation and Composition Techniques.* Springer. doi:10.1007/978-3-319-55542-3

Petrie, C. J. (2016). *Web Service Composition.* Springer. doi:10.1007/978-3-319-32833-1

Pino, L. (2015). *Security aware service composition.* City University London.

Reichle, D.-E. (2015). *Managing Quality Properties of Web Service Compositions.* University of Kassel.

Ziegler, W. (2017). *A Framework for managing Quality of Service in Cloud Computing through Service Level Agreements.* Germany: University of Göttingen.

KEY TERMS AND DEFINITIONS

Blockchain: A continuously growing list of records, called blocks, which are linked and secured using cryptography. Each block typically contains a cryptographic hash of the previous block, a timestamp, and transaction data.

Cloud Migration: The process of partially or completely deploying an organization's digital assets, services, IT resources, or applications from on-premises to the cloud.

Dummy Service: A pseudo service only has service attributes described but hasn't actual service function.

Euclidean Distance: The ordinary straight-line distance between two points in Euclidean space.

Forward Recovery: Redo the efforts, usually as services, of the previously failed transaction.

Hyperledger: An umbrella project of open source blockchains and related tools, started in December 2015 by the Linux Foundation, to support the collaborative development of blockchain based distributed ledgers.

Lagrangian Relaxation: A relaxation method which approximates a difficult problem of constrained optimization by a simpler problem. A solution to the relaxed problem is an approximate solution to the original problem, and provides useful information.

Pareto Optimal: Describing a situation in which the profit of one party cannot be increased without reducing the profit of another.

Compilation of References

Abdullah, A., & Li, X. (2016). An efficient similarity-based model for web service recommendation. *Services Transactions on Services Computing*, *4*(3), 15–28. doi:10.29268tsc.2016.4.3.2

Abowd, G. D., Dey, A. K., Brown, P. J., Davies, N., Smith, M., & Steggles, P. (1999, September). Towards a better understanding of context and context-awareness. In *International Symposium on Handheld and Ubiquitous Computing* (pp. 304-307). Springer. 10.1007/3-540-48157-5_29

Adams, A. A., Murata, K., & Orito, Y. (2009). The Japanese sense of information privacy. *AI & Society*, *24*(4), 327–341. doi:10.100700146-009-0228-z

Adel, A., Omar, N., & Al-Shabi, A. (2014). A comparative study of combined feature selection methods for Arabic text classification. *Journal of Computational Science*, *10*(11), 2232–2239. doi:10.3844/jcssp.2014.2232.2239

Agrawal, R., Kiernan, J., Srikant, R., & Xu, Y. (2005). XPref: A preference language for P3P. *Computer Networks*, *48*(5), 809–827. doi:10.1016/j.comnet.2005.01.004

Allison, D. S., & Capretz, M. A., El Yamany, H. F., & Wang, S. (2012). Privacy protection framework with defined policies for service-oriented architecture. *Journal of Software Engineering and Applications*, *5*(3), 200. doi:10.4236/jsea.2012.53026

Al-Masri, E., & Mahmoud, Q. H. (2007a). Discovering the best web service. In C. L. Williamson, M. E. Zurko, P. F. Patel-Schneider, & P. J. Shenoy (Eds.), In *Proceedings of the International Conference on World Wide Web* (pp. 1257–1258). ACM.

Al-Masri, E., & Mahmoud, Q. H. (2007b). QoS-based Discovery and Ranking of Web Services. In *Proceedings of the 16th International Conference on Computer Communications and Networks* (pp. 529–534). IEEE. 10.1109/ICCCN.2007.4317873

Al-Masri, E., & Mahmoud, Q. H. (2008, April). Investigating web services on the world wide web. In *Proceedings of the 17th international conference on World Wide Web* (pp. 795-804). ACM. 10.1145/1367497.1367605

Alur, R., & Dill, D. (1990). Automata for Modeling Real-Time Systems. *LNCS*, *443*, 322–335.

Amidan, B. G., Ferryman, T. A., & Cooley, S. K. (2005, March). Data outlier detection using the Chebyshev theorem. In Aerospace Conference, 2005 IEEE (pp. 3814-3819). IEEE. doi:10.1109/AERO.2005.1559688

Amin, A. (2018). *Evaluating the quality of integrated software systems based on service-oriented architecture* (Doctoral dissertation). Sudan University of Science & Technology.

Ardagna, C., Bussard, L., De Capitani Di Vimercati, S., Neven, G., Pedrini, E., Paraboschi, S., . . . Verdicchio, M. (2009). Primelife policy language. In *W3C Workshop on Access Control Application Scenarios*. W3C.

Ashley, P., Hada, S., Karjoth, G., Powers, C., & Schunter, M. (2003). *Enterprise privacy authorization language (EPAL)*. IBM Research.

Babin, G., Ameur, Y. A., & Pantel, M. (2017). Web service compensation at runtime: Formal modeling and verification using the event-b refinement and proof based formal method. *IEEE Transactions on Services Computing*, *10*(1), 107–120. doi:10.1109/TSC.2016.2594782

Balabanović, M., & Shoham, Y. (1997). Fab: Content-based, collaborative recommendation. *Communications of the ACM*, *40*(3), 66–72. doi:10.1145/245108.245124

Balalaie, A., Heydarnoori, A., & Jamshidi, P. (2016). Microservices architecture enables devops: Migration to a cloud-native architecture. *IEEE Software*, *33*(3), 42–52. doi:10.1109/MS.2016.64

Barbará, D., Li, Y., & Couto, J. (2002, November). COOLCAT: an entropy-based algorithm for categorical clustering. In Proceedings of the eleventh international conference on Information and knowledge management (pp. 582-589). ACM. doi:10.1145/584792.584888

Bartalos, P., & Bielikova, M. (2011). Automatic dynamic web service composition: A survey and problem formalization. *Computer Information*, *30*(4), 793–827.

Bartocci, E., Bortolussi, L., Loreti, M., & Nenzi, L. (2017). Monitoring Mobile and Spatially Distributed Cyber-Physical Systems. In *15th ACM-IEEE International Conference on Formal Methods and Models for System Design* (pp. 146-155). Vienna: ACM. 10.1145/3127041.3127050

Bartsch, M. A., & Wakefield, G. H. (2004). Singing voice identification using spectral envelope estimation. *IEEE Transactions on Speech and Audio Processing*, *12*(2), 100–109. doi:10.1109/TSA.2003.822637

Benesty, J., Chen, J., Huang, Y., & Cohen, I. (2009). Pearson correlation coefficient. In *Noise reduction in speech processing* (pp. 1–4). Springer Berlin Heidelberg.

Bengtsson, J., Larsson, F., Pettersson, P., Yi, W., Christensen, P., Jensen, J., ... Sorensen, T. (1996). UPPAAL: A Tool Suite for Validation and Verification of Real-Time Systems. *LNCS*, *1066*, 232–243.

Beniwal, S., & Arora, J. (2012). Classification and feature selection techniques in data mining. *Int J Eng Res Technol*, *1*(6), 2278–2284.

Bennett, B., Cohn, A., Wolter, F., & Zakharyaschev, M. (2002). Multi-Dimensional Modal Logic as a Framework for Spatio-Temporal Reasoning. *Applied Intelligence*, *17*(3), 239–251. doi:10.1023/A:1020083231504

Bentahar, J., Yahyaoui, H., Kova, M., & Maamar, Z. (2013). Symbolic model checking composite web services using operational and control behaviors. *Expert Systems with Applications*, *40*(2), 508–522. doi:10.1016/j.eswa.2012.07.069

Berenzweig, A., Ellis, D. P. W., & Lawrence, S. (2002). Using voice segments to improve artist classification of music. *Proc. Int. Conf. Virtual, Synthetic, and Entertainment Audio*.

Berkhin, P. (2006). A survey of clustering data mining techniques. In *Grouping multidimensional data* (pp. 25–71). Springer Berlin Heidelberg. doi:10.1007/3-540-28349-8_2

Berscheid, E., & Walster, E. H. (1985). Interpersonal attraction. Handbook of Social Psychology, 2, 413-484.

Bezdek, J. C. (1974). Cluster Validity with Fuzzy Sets. *Journal of Cybernetics*, (3): 58–72.

Bizer, C., Heath, T., & Berners-Lee, T. (2009). Linked data-the story so far. *International Journal on Semantic Web and Information Systems*, *5*(3), 1–22. doi:10.4018/jswis.2009081901

Blech, J. O., Fernando, L., Foster, K., Abilash, G., & Sudarsan, S. D. (2016). Spatio-Temporal Reasoning and Decision Support for Smart Energy Systems. In *IEEE 21st International Conference on Emerging Technologies and Factory Automation (ETFA)* (pp. 1-8). Berlin: IEEE Computer.

Blech, J., & Schmidt, H. (2013). Towards Modeling and Checking the Spatial and Interaction Behavior of Widely Distributed Systems. *Improving Systems and Software Engineering Conference (ISSEC)*.

Boakye, K., Trueba-Hornero, B., Vinyals, O., & Friedland, G. (2008). Overlapped speech detection for improved speaker diarization in multiparty meetings. *Proc. IEEE International Conference on Acoustics, Speech, and Signal Processing.* 10.1109/ICASSP.2008.4518619

Bollegala, D., Matsuo, Y., & Ishizuka, M. (2007). Measuring Semantic Similarity between Words using Web Search Engines. *Proceeding of the 16th International World Wide Web Conference*, 757-766.

Bordbar, B., Howells, G., Evans, M., & Staikopoulos, A. (2007). Model Transformation from OWL-S to BPEL Via SiTra. In D. Akehurst, R. Vogel, & R. Paige (Eds.), *Model Driven Architecture- Foundations and Applications* (Vol. 4530, pp. 43–58). Springer Berlin Heidelberg. doi:10.1007/978-3-540-72901-3_4

Bordeaux, L., Salaün, G., Berardi, D., & Mecella, M. (2005). When are two web services compatible? In. Lecture Notes in Computer Science: Vol. 3324. *Technologies for E-Services* (pp. 15–28). Berlin: Springer. doi:10.1007/978-3-540-31811-8_2

Boubaker, S., Klai, K., Schmitz, K., Graiet, M., & Gaaloul, W. (2017). Deadlock-freeness verification of business process configuration using SOG. In Service-oriented computing, ICSOC 2017 (vol. 10601, pp. 96-112). Springer. doi:10.1007/978-3-319-69035-3_7

Bouchami, A., Perrin, O., & Zahoor, E. (2015). Trust-based formal delegation framework for enterprise social networks. In *2015 IEEE trustcom/bigdatase/ispa* (pp. 127–134). IEEE. doi:10.1109/Trustcom.2015.366

Bouchiha, D., Malki, M., Djaa, D., Alghamdi, A., & Alnafjan, K. (2013). Semantic Annotation of Web Services: A Comparative Study. In R. Lee (Ed.), *Software Engineering, Artificial Intelligence, Networking and Parallel/Distributed Computing* (Vol. 492, pp. 87–100). Springer International Publishing. doi:10.1007/978-3-319-00738-0_7

Bouguettaya, A., Singh, M., Huhns, M., Sheng, Q. Z., Dong, H., Yu, Q., & Ouzzani, M. (2017). A service computing manifesto: The next 10 years. *Communications of the ACM, 60*(4), 64–72. doi:10.1145/2983528

Bouskela, D., Nguyen, T., & Jardin, A. (2017). Toward a Rigorous Approach for Verifying Cyber-Physical Systems Against Requirements. *Canadian Journal of Electrical and Computer Engineering, 40*(2), 66–73.

Boyce, B. (2017). Emerging Technology and the Health Insurance Portability and Accountability Act. *Journal of the Academy of Nutrition and Dietetics, 117*(4), 517–518. doi:10.1016/j.jand.2016.05.013 PMID:27436531

Brewka, G., Eiter, T., & Truszczyński, M. (2011). Answer set programming at a glance. *Communications of the ACM, 54*(12), 92–103. doi:10.1145/2043174.2043195

Brighton, H., & Mellish, C. (2002). Advances in instance selection for instance-based learning algorithms. *Data Mining and Knowledge Discovery, 6*(2), 153–172. doi:10.1023/A:1014043630878

Brin, S., & Page, L. (1998). The anatomy of a large-scale hypertextual Web search engine. *Computer Networks and ISDN Systems, 30*(1), 107–117. doi:10.1016/S0169-7552(98)00110-X

Caires, L., & Cardelli, L. (2003). A Spatial Logic for Concurrency (Part I). *Information and Computation, 186*(2), 194–235. doi:10.1016/S0890-5401(03)00137-8

Caires, L., & Cardelli, L. (2004). A Spatial Logic for Concurrency (Part II). *Theoretical Computer Science, 322*(3), 517–565. doi:10.1016/j.tcs.2003.10.041

Caires, L., & Torres Vieira, H. (2012). SLMC: A Tool for Model Checking Concurrent Systems against Dynamical Spatial Logic Specifications. In *18th International Conference on Tools and Algorithms for the Construction and Analysis of Systems (TACAS)* (pp. 485-491). Tallinn: Springer-Verlag. 10.1007/978-3-642-28756-5_35

Cardoso, J., Barros, A., May, N., & Kylau, U. (2010, July). Towards a unified service description language for the internet of services: Requirements and first developments. In *Services Computing (SCC), 2010 IEEE International Conference on* (pp. 602-609). IEEE.

Casati, F., Ilnicki, S., Jin, L., Krishnamoorthy, V., & Shan, M. C. (2000). Adaptive and dynamic service composition in eFlow. *Advanced Information Systems Engineering*, 13–31.

Casey, M., Veltkamp, R., Goto, M., Leman, M., Rhodes, C., & Slaney, M. (2008). Content-Based Music Information Retrieval: Current Directions and Future Challenges. *Proceedings of the IEEE*, *96*(4), 668–696. doi:10.1109/JPROC.2008.916370

Çetin, Ö., & Shriberg, E. (2006). Speaker overlaps and ASR errors in meetings: effects before, during, and after the overlap. *Proc. IEEE International Conference on Acoustics, Speech, and Signal Processing*. 10.1109/ICASSP.2006.1660031

Chaochen, Z., Hoare, C., & Ravn, A. (1991). A Calculus of Durations. *Information Processing Letters*, *40*(5), 269–276. doi:10.1016/0020-0190(91)90122-X

Chaudhuri, S., & Dayal, U. (1997). An overview of data warehousing and OLAP technology. *SIGMOD Record*, *26*(1), 65–74. doi:10.1145/248603.248616

Chen, C., Zeng, J., Zheng, X., & Chen, D. (2013). Recommender System Based on Social Trust Relationships. In *e-Business Engineering (ICEBE), 2013 IEEE 10th International Conference on* (pp. 32-37). IEEE.

Chen, G., & Kotz, D. (2000). *A survey of context-aware mobile computing research* (Vol. 1, No. 2.1, pp. 2-1). Technical Report TR2000-381, Dept. of Computer Science, Dartmouth College.

Chen, H., Perich, F., Finin, T., & Joshi, A. (2004, August). Soupa: Standard ontology for ubiquitous and pervasive applications. In *Mobile and Ubiquitous Systems: Networking and Services, 2004. MOBIQUITOUS 2004. The First Annual International Conference on* (pp. 258-267). IEEE.

Cheney, E. W. (1966). *Introduction to approximation theory*. Academic Press.

Cheng, D., Kannan, R., Vempala, S., & Wang, G. (2006). A divide-and-merge methodology for clustering. *ACM Transactions on Database Systems*, *31*(4), 1499–1525. doi:10.1145/1189769.1189779

Chen, L., Yang, G., Zhang, Y., & Chen, Z. (2010). Web services clustering using SOM based on kernel cosine similarity measure. *Proceeding of the 2nd International Conference on Information Science and Engineering*, 846–850. 10.1109/ICISE.2010.5689254

Chen, W., Paik, I., & Hung, P. C. K. (2014). Constructing a Global Social Service Network for Better Quality of Web Service Discovery. *IEEE Transactions on Services Computing*, *26*(5), 1466–1476.

Chinnici, R., Gudgin, M., Moreau, J. J., Schlimmer, J., & Weerawarana, S. (2004). Web services description language (WSDL) version 2.0 part 1: Core language. *W3C working draft, 26.*

Cimatti, A., Griggio, A., Mover, S., & Tonetta, S. (2015). HyComp: An SMT-Based Model Checker for Hybrid Systems. In *21st International Conference on Tools and Algorithms for the Construction and Analysis of Systems (TACAS)* (pp. 52-67). London: Springer-Verlag. 10.1007/978-3-662-46681-0_4

Corradini, F., Fornari, F., Polini, A., Re, B., Tiezzi, F., & Vandin, A. (2017). Bprove: a formal verification framework for business process models. In *Proceedings of the 32nd IEEE/ACM international conference on automated software engineering, ASE 2017* (pp. 217–228). IEEE/ACM. 10.1109/ASE.2017.8115635

Cranor, L., Langheinrich, M., & Marchiori, M. (2002). Preference Exchange Language. Academic Press.

Cranor, L., Langheinrich, M., Marchiori, M., Presler-Marshall, M., & Reagle, J. (2002). *The Platform for Privacy Preferences 1.0 (P3P1.0) Specification.* Retrieved from https://www.w3.org/TR/P3P/

Cybenko, G. (1989). Approximation by superpositions of a sigmoidal function. *Mathematics of Control, Signals, and Systems*, *2*(4), 303–314. doi:10.1007/BF02551274

Dal Zilio, S., Lugiez, D., & Meyssonnier, C. (2004). A Logic You Can Count On. In *Symposium on Principles of Programming languages.* ACM.

Dasgupta, S., Bhat, S., & Lee, Y. (2011). Taxonomic clustering and query matching for efficient service discovery. *Proceeding of the 9th IEEE International Conference on Web Services*, 363–370. 10.1109/ICWS.2011.112

Davis, S. B., & Mermelstein, P. (1980). Comparison of Parametric Representations for Monosyllabic Word Recognition in Continuously Spoken Sentences. *IEEE Transactions on Acoustics, Speech, and Signal Processing*, *28*(4), 357–366. doi:10.1109/TASSP.1980.1163420

De Moura, L., & Bjørner, N. (2008). An Efficient SMT Solver. *LNCS*, *4963*, 337–340.

Deb, K., Agrawal, S., Pratap, A., & Meyarivan, T. (2000, September). A fast elitist non-dominated sorting genetic algorithm for multi-objective optimization: NSGA-II. In *International Conference on Parallel Problem Solving From Nature* (pp. 849-858). Springer. 10.1007/3-540-45356-3_83

Del Álamo, J. M., Fernández, A. M., Trapero, R., Yelmo, J. C., & Monjas, M. A. (2011). A privacy-considerate framework for identity management in mobile services. *Mobile Networks and Applications*, *16*(4), 446–459. doi:10.100711036-011-0325-3

Delmater, R., & Hancock, M. (2001). *Data mining explained: a manager's guide to customer-centric business intelligence*. Digital Press.

Derakhshan, R., Orlowska, M. E., & Li, X. (2007, March). RFID data management: Challenges and opportunities. In *RFID, 2007. IEEE International Conference on* (pp. 175-182). IEEE.

DeWitt, D., & Gray, J. (1992). Parallel database systems: The future of high performance database systems. *Communications of the ACM*, *35*(6), 85–98. doi:10.1145/129888.129894

Diaz, G., Pardo, J. J., Cambronero, M. E., Valero, V., & Cuartero, F. (2005). Automatic translation of ws-cdl choreographies to timed automata. In. Lecture Notes in Computer Science: Vol. 3670. *Formal Techniques for Computer Systems and Business Processes* (pp. 230–242). Berlin: Springer. doi:10.1007/11549970_17

Dijkman, R. M., Dumas, M., & Ouyang, C. (2008). Semantics and analysis of business process models in BPMN. *Information and Software Technology*, *50*(12), 1–14. doi:10.1016/j.infsof.2008.02.006

Dong, J. S., Liu, Y., Sun, J., & Zhang, X. (2006). Verification of computation orchestration via timed automata. In *Formal Methods and Software Engineering* (Vol. 4260, pp. 226–245). Berlin: Springer. doi:10.1007/11901433_13

Dorn, J., Hrastnik, P., & Rainer, A. (2007). Web service discovery and composition for virtual enterprises. *International Journal of Web Services Research*, *4*(1), 23–39. doi:10.4018/jwsr.2007010102

Duan, Y. C., Duan, Q., Sun, X. B., Fu, G. H., Narendra, N. C., Zhou, N., ... Zhou, Z. (2016). Everything as a service (XaaS) on the cloud: Origins, current and future trends. *Services Transactions on Cloud Computing*, *4*(2), 32–45. doi:10.29268tcc.2016.0006

Dustdar, S., & Schreiner, W. (2005). A survey on web services composition. *International Journal of Web and Grid Services*, *1*(1), 1–30. doi:10.1504/IJWGS.2005.007545

Du, X., & Song, W. W. (2013). Conceptual graph: An approach to improve quality of business services modeling. In *Web Information Systems Engineering*, *8182*, 239–251.

Du, Y. Y., Zhang, Y. J., & Zhang, X. L. (2013). A semantic approach of service clustering and web service discovery. *Inf Technol J*, *12*(5), 967–974. doi:10.3923/itj.2013.967.974

Edgar, R. C. (2010). Search and clustering orders of magnitude faster than BLAST. *Bioinformatics (Oxford, England)*, *26*(19), 2460–2461. doi:10.1093/bioinformatics/btq461 PMID:20709691

Ejarque, J., Micsik, A., & Badia, R. M. (2015). Towards Automatic Application Migration to Clouds. In *Proceedings of the IEEE International Conference on Cloud Computing* (pp. 25–32). IEEE.

El Saddik, A. (2018, January). ECOPPA: Extensible Context Ontology for Persuasive Physical-Activity Applications. In *Proceedings of the International Conference on Information Technology & Systems (ICITS 2018)* (Vol. 721, p. 309). Springer. 10.1007/978-3-319-73450-7_30

Elgazzar, K., Hassan, A. E., & Martin, P. (2010). Clustering WSDL Documents to Bootstrap the Discovery of Web Services. *Proceeding of the 8th IEEE International Conference on Web Services*, 147-154. 10.1109/ICWS.2010.31

Ellis, C. A., & Nutt, G. J. (1993). Modeling and enactment of workflow systems. In *Application and Theory of Petri Nets 1993* (Vol. 691, pp. 1–16). Springer Berlin Heidelberg. doi:10.1007/3-540-56863-8_36

Emna, F., Jmaiel, M., Dupuy, C. S. C., & Tazi, S. (2012). A flexible approach for service composition using service patterns. In *Proceedings of the 27th Annual ACM Symposium on Applied Computing* (pp. 1976–1983). ACM. 10.1145/2245276.2232102

Endrei, M., Ang, J., Arsanjani, A., Chua, S., Comte, P., Krogdahl, P., Luo, M., Newling, T. (2004, April). Patterns: Service-Oriented Architecture and Web Services. *IBM Redbooks*.

Endrei, M., Ang, J., Arsanjani, A., Chua, S., Comte, P., Krogdahl, P., & Newling, T. (2004). *Patterns: service-oriented architecture and web services* (pp. 17–44). IBM Corporation, International Technical Support Organization.

Erdem, E., Gelfond, M., & Leone, N. (2016). Applications of Answer Set Programming. *AI Magazine*, *37*(3), 53. doi:10.1609/aimag.v37i3.2678

Eunju, K., Yongkon, L., Yeongho, K., Hyungkeun, P., Jongwoo, K., Byoungsun, M., . . . Guil, K. (2011). *Web Services Quality Factors Version 1.0*. Retrieved from http://docs.oasis-open.org/wsqm/WS-Quality-Factors/v1.0/cs01/WS-Quality-Factors-v1.0-cs01.html

Fan, C.-T., Wang, W.-J., & Chang, Y.-S. (2011). Agent-Based Service Migration Framework in Hybrid Cloud. In *Proceedings of the IEEE International Conference on High Performance Computing and Communications* (pp. 887–892). IEEE. 10.1109/HPCC.2011.127

Fanjiang, Y. Y., Syu, Y., Ma, S. P., & Kuo, J. Y. (2017). An overview and classification of service description approaches in automated service composition research. *IEEE Transactions on Services Computing*, *10*(2), 176–189. doi:10.1109/TSC.2015.2461538

Feng, H., & Qian, X. (2013). Recommendation via user's personality and social contextual. In *Proceedings of the 22nd ACM international conference on Conference on information & knowledge management* (pp. 1521-1524). ACM. 10.1145/2505515.2507834

Ferrara, A. (2004). Web services: a process algebra approach. In *Proceedings of the 2nd international conference on Service oriented computing* (pp. 242-251). ACM.

Fodor, I. K. (2002). A survey of dimension reduction techniques. U. S. Department of Energy, Lawrence Livermore National Laboratory.

Fox, L., & Parker, I. B. (1968). *Chebyshev polynomials in numerical analysis* (Vol. 29). London: Oxford university press.

Frehse, G. (2008, June). 2008). PHAVer: Algorithmic Verification of Hybrid Systems past HyTech. *International Journal of Software Tools for Technology Transfer*, *10*(3), 263–279. doi:10.100710009-007-0062-x

Frehse, G., Le Guernic, C., Donzé, A., Cotton, S., Ray, R., Lebeltel, O., & Maler, O. (2011). *SpaceEx: Scalable Verification of Hybrid Systems. In Lecture Notes in Computer Science: Vol. 6806. Computer Aided Verification (CAV)* (pp. 379–395). Snowbird, UT: Springer-Verlag.

Freitas, A. A., & Lavington, S. H. (1997). *Mining very large databases with parallel processing* (Vol. 9). Springer Science & Business Media.

Frey, S., & Hasselbring, W. (2010). Model-based migration of legacy software systems to scalable and resource-efficient cloud-based applications: The cloudmig approach. In *Proceedings of the International Conference on Cloud Computing, GRIDs, and Virtualization* (pp. 155–158). IARIA.

Fujihara, H., Goto, M., Kitahara, T., & Okuno, H. G. (2010). A modeling of singing voice robust to accompaniment sounds and its application to singer identification and vocal-timbre-similarity-based music information retrieval. *IEEE Transactions on Audio, Speech, and Language Processing*, *18*(3), 638–648. doi:10.1109/TASL.2010.2041386

Fujihara, H., Kitahara, T., Goto, M., Komatani, K., Ogata, T., & Okuno, H. G. (2005). Singer identification based on accompaniment sound reduction and reliable frame selection. *Proc. Int. Conf. Music Information Retrieval.*

Fu, X., Bultan, T., & Su, J. (2004). Analysis of interacting BPEL web services. In *Proceedings of the 13th international conference on World Wide Web* (pp. 621-630). ACM.

Gaaloul, K., Proper, H. A., Zahoor, E., Charoy, F., & Godart, C. (2011). A logical framework for reasoning about delegation poli- cies in workflow management systems. *IJICS, 4*(4), 365–388. doi:10.1504/IJICS.2011.044825

Gaaloul, K., Zahoor, E., Charoy, F., & Godart, C. (2010). Dynamic authorisation policies for event-based task delegation. In *Advanced information systems engineering, 22nd international conference* (pp. 135–149). doi: 1210.1007/978-3- 642-13094-6

Gales, M., & Young, S. (1996). Robust continuous speech recognition using parallel model combination. *IEEE Transactions on Speech and Audio Processing*, *4*(5), 352–359. doi:10.1109/89.536929

Gao, H., Wang, S., Sun, L., Nian, F., Liu, K., Gulliver, S., . . . Yu, C. (2014). Hierarchical clustering based web service discovery. Berlin: Springer.

Gao, S., Dong, H., Chen, Y., Ning, B., Chen, G., & Yang, X. (2013). Approximation-Based Robust Adaptive Automatic Train Control: An Approach for Actuator Saturation. *IEEE Transactions on Intelligent Transportation Systems*, *14*(4), 1733–1742. doi:10.1109/TITS.2013.2266255

García, J. M., Pedrinaci, C., Resinas, M., Cardoso, J., Fernández, P., & Ruiz-Cortés, A. (2015, June). Linked USDL agreement: effectively sharing semantic service level agreements on the web. In *Web Services (ICWS), 2015 IEEE International Conference on* (pp. 137-144). IEEE. 10.1109/ICWS.2015.28

Garriga, M., Mateos, C., Flores, A., Cechich, A., & Zunino, A. (2016). RESTful service composition at a glance: A survey. *Journal of Network and Computer Applications*, *60*, 32–53. doi:10.1016/j.jnca.2015.11.020

Gebser, M., Kaminski, R., Kaufmann, B., Ostrowski, M., Schaub, T., & Thiele, S. (2010). A user's guide to gringo, clasp, clingo, and iclingo. University of Potsdam, Tech. Rep.

Georgantas, N. (2018). *Service Oriented Computing in Mobile Environments: Abstractions and Mechanisms for Interoperability and Composition* (Doctoral dissertation). Sorbonne Université.

GitHub CPL (Consumer Privacy Language repository). (2018). Retrieved from https://github.com/CS-UCY-SEIT-lab/CPL

Goebel, M., & Gruenwald, L. (1999). A survey of data mining and knowledge discovery software tools. *ACM SIGKDD Explorations Newsletter*, *1*(1), 20-33.

Goedertier, S. (2008). Declarative techniques for modeling and mining business processes. KU.

Gomadam, K., Ranabahu, A., & Sheth, A. (2010). *SA-REST: Semantic Annotation of Web Resources*. Retrieved from https://www.w3.org/Submission/SA-REST

Gong, P., Knuplesch, D., Feng, Z., & Jiang, J. (2017). bpCMon: A rule-based monitoring framework for business processes compliance. *International Journal of Web Services Research*, *14*(2), 81–103. doi:10.4018/IJWSR.2017040105

Granovetter, M. (1983). The Strength of Weak Ties: A Network Theory Revisited. *Sociological Theory*, *1*(1), 201–233. doi:10.2307/202051

Guellati, S., Kitouni, I., & Saidouni, D. (2012). Verification of Durational Action Timed Automata using UPPAAL. *International Journal of Computers and Applications*, *56*(11), 33–41. doi:10.5120/8938-3077

Guermouche, N., & Godart, C. (2009). Timed model checking based approach for web services analysis. In *Web Services, 2009. ICWS 2009. IEEE International Conference on* (pp. 213-221). IEEE. 10.1109/ICWS.2009.42

Guha, S., Rastogi, R., & Shim, K. (1998, June). CURE: An efficient clustering algorithm for large databases. *SIGMOD Record*, *27*(2), 73–84. doi:10.1145/276305.276312

Hair, J. F., Anderson, R. E., Tatham, R. L., & Black, W. C. (1999). *Análisis Multivariante* (5th ed.). Madrid: Pearson Prentice Hall.

Hamadi, R., & Benatallah, B. (2003). A Petri net-based model for web service composition. In *Proceedings of the 14th Australasian database conference* (vol. 17, pp. 191-200). ACM.

Hamadi, R., Paik, H. Y., & Benatallah, B. (2007, June). Conceptual modeling of privacy-aware web service protocols. In *International Conference on Advanced Information Systems Engineering* (pp. 233-248). Springer. 10.1007/978-3-540-72988-4_17

Han, F., & Herrmann, P. (2012). Remedy of Mixed Initiative Conflicts in Model-based System Engineering. Electronic Communications of the EASST, 47.

Han, F., & Herrmann, P. (2013). Modeling Real-Time System Performance with Respect to Scheduling Analysis. In *Proceedings of the 6th IEEE International Conference on Ubi-Media Computing* (pp. 663-671). IEEE Computer. 10.1109/ICAwST.2013.6765522

Han, F., Blech, J. O., Herrmann, P., & Schmidt, H. (2015). Model-based Engineering and Analysis of Space-aware Systems Communicating via IEEE 802.11. In *IEEE 39th Annual Computer Software and Applications Conference* (pp. 638-646). Taichung, Taiwan: IEEE Computer.

Han, F., Herrmann, P., & Le, H. (2013). Modeling and Verifying Real-Time Properties of Reactive Systems. In *18th International Conference on Engineering of Complex Computer Systems (ICECCS)* (pp. 14-23). IEEE Computer. 10.1109/ICECCS.2013.13

Han, F., Blech, J. O., Herrmann, P., & Schmidt, H. (2014). Towards Verifying Safety Properties of Real-Time Probability Systems. *Electronic Proceedings in Theoretical Computer Science, 147*, 1–15. doi:10.4204/EPTCS.147.1

Han, J., Pei, J., & Kamber, M. (2011). *Data mining: Concepts and techniques.* Elsevier.

Hartigan, J. A. (1975). *Clustering algorithms*. Academic Press.

Hartigan, J. A., & Hartigan, J. A. (1975). *Clustering algorithms* (Vol. 209). New York: Wiley.

Herrmann, P., Blech, J. O., Han, F., & Schmidt, H. (2016). A Model-based Toolchain to Verify Spatial Behavior of Cyber-Physical Systems. *International Journal of Web Services Research*, *13*(1), 40–52. doi:10.4018/IJWSR.2016010103

Herrmann, P., Svae, A., Svendsen, H. H., & Blech, J. O. (2016). Collaborative Model-based Development of a Remote Train Monitoring System. In *International Conference on Evaluation of Novel Approaches to Software Engineering (ENASE), special session on Collaborative Aspects of Formal Methods* (pp. 383-390). Rome: SciTePress. 10.5220/0005929403830390

Hinz, S., Schmidt, K., & Stahl, C. (2005). Transforming BPEL to Petri nets. In *Business Process Management* (Vol. 3649, pp. 220–235). Berlin: Springer. doi:10.1007/11538394_15

Hippisley, A., Cheng, D., & Ahmad, K. (2005). The head-modifier principle and multilingual term extraction. *Natural Language Engineering*, *11*(2), 129–157. doi:10.1017/S1351324904003535

Hirschkoff, D., Lozes, É., & Sangiorgi, D. (2003). Minimality Results for the Spatial Logics. *LNCS, 2914.*

Holzmann, G. (2003). *SPIN Model Checker The: Primer and Reference Manual.* Addison-Wesley.

Hopcroft, J. E., Motwani, R., & Ullman, J. D. (2001). Introduction to Automata Theory, Languages, and Computation. *ACM SIGACT News*, *32*(1), 60–65. doi:10.1145/568438.568455

Hordvik, S., Øseth, K., Svendsen, H. H., Blech, J. O., & Herrmann, P. (2016). Model-based Engineering and Spatiotemporal Analysis of Transport Systems. In L. Maciaszek & J. Filipe (Eds.), Evaluation of Novel Approaches to Software Engineering (pp. 44-65). Rome: Springer-Verlag. doi:10.1007/978-3-319-56390-9_3

Huang, K., Gao, X., Zhang, F., & Xiao, J. (2017). Customer Oriented Migration Service. In *Proceedings of the IEEE 10th International Conference on Cloud Computing* (pp. 692–695). IEEE.

Hu, Y., & Liu, G. (2015). Separation of Singing Voice Using Nonnegative Matrix Partial Co-Factorization for Singer Identification, *IEEE/ACM Transactions on Audio. Speech, and Language Processing*, *23*(4), 643–653.

Huynh, K. T., Bui, T. H., & Quan, T. T. (2016). WSCOVER: A tool for automatic composition and verification of web services using heuristic-guided model checking and logic-based clustering. In *Multi-disciplinary Trends in Artificial Intelligence* (Vol. 10053, pp. 50–62). Berlin: Springer. doi:10.1007/978-3-319-49397-8_5

Huynh, K. T., Quan, T. T., & Bui, T. H. (2017). A quality-controlled logic-based clustering approach for web service composition and verification. *International Journal of Web Information Systems*, *13*(2), 173–198. doi:10.1108/IJWIS-12-2016-0068

International Electronical Commission. (2010). *International Standard IEC 61508-1 Functional Safety of Electrical/Electronic/Programmable Electronic Safety-related Systems – Part 1: General Requirements.* Retrieved from IEC Webstore: https://webstore.iec.ch/preview/info_iec61508-1%7Bed2.0%7Db.pdf

IPstack. (n.d.). Retrieved from https://ipstack.com

Jagadish, H. V., Lakshmanan, L. V., & Srivastava, D. (1999, June). Snakes and sandwiches: Optimal clustering strategies for a data warehouse. *SIGMOD Record*, *28*(2), 37–48. doi:10.1145/304181.304186

Jain, A. K., Murty, M. N., & Flynn, P. J. (1999). Data clustering: A review. *ACM Computing Surveys*, *31*(3), 264–323. doi:10.1145/331499.331504

Jamali, M., & Ester, M. (2010). A matrix factorization technique with trust propagation for recommendation in social networks. In *Proceedings of the fourth ACM conference on Recommender systems* (pp. 135-142). ACM. 10.1145/1864708.1864736

Jamshidi, P., Pahl, C., & Mendonça, N. C. (2017). Pattern-based multi-cloud architecture migration. *Software, Practice & Experience*, *47*(9), 1159–1184. doi:10.1002pe.2442

Janssens, G. K., Verelst, J., & Weyn, B. (2000). Techniques for modelling workflows and their support of reuse. In *Business Process Management* (Vol. 1806, pp. 1–15). Berlin: Springer. doi:10.1007/3-540-45594-9_1

Jiang, M., Cui, P., Liu, R., Yang, Q., Wang, F., Zhu, W., & Yang, S. (2012). Social contextual recommendation. In *Proceedings of the 21st ACM international conference on Information and knowledge management* (pp. 45-54). ACM.

Johnson, R. A., & Wichern, D. W. (2014). *Applied multivariate statistical analysis* (Vol. 4). Prentice-Hall.

Joshi, D. (n.d.). *IBM, Amazon & Microsoft are offering their blockchain technology as a service*. Retrieved from http://www.businessinsider.com/ibm-azure-aws-blockchain-service-2017-10

Jula, A., Sundararajan, E., & Othman, Z. (2014). Cloud computing service composition: A systematic literature review. *Expert Systems with Applications*, *41*(8), 3809–3824. doi:10.1016/j.eswa.2013.12.017

Kapitsaki, G. M. (2013b). Reflecting user privacy preferences in context-aware web services. In *Web Services (ICWS), 2013 IEEE 20th International Conference on* (pp. 123-130). IEEE. 10.1109/ICWS.2013.26

Kapitsaki, G. M., Ioannou, J., Cardoso, J., & Pedrinaci, C. (2018). Linked USDL Privacy: Describing Privacy Policies for Services In Web Services, 2018. ICWS 2018. IEEE International Conference on (pp. 50-57). IEEE.

Kapitsaki, G. M., Kateros, D. A., & Venieris, I. S. (2008, September). Architecture for provision of context-aware web applications based on web services. In *Personal, Indoor and Mobile Radio Communications, 2008. PIMRC 2008. IEEE 19th International Symposium on* (pp. 1-5). IEEE. 10.1109/PIMRC.2008.4699629

Kapitsaki, G. M. (2012). *Enhancing Web Service Descriptions with Context Functions*. WEBIST.

Kapitsaki, G. M. (2013a). Consumer Privacy Enforcement in Context-Aware Web Services. *International Journal of Web Services Research*, *10*(3), 24–41. doi:10.4018/ijwsr.2013070102

Karthiban, R. (2014). A QoS-Aware Web Service Selection Based on Clustering. *International Journal of Scientific and Research Publications*, *4*(2).

Ke, C., Huang, Z., & Tang, M. (2013). Supporting negotiation mechanism privacy authority method in cloud computing. *Knowledge-Based Systems*, *51*, 48–59. doi:10.1016/j.knosys.2013.07.001

Khaled, A., & Miller, J. (2017). Using π-calculus for formal modeling and verification of WS-CDL choreographies. *IEEE Transactions on Services Computing*, *10*(2), 316–327. doi:10.1109/TSC.2015.2449850

Kheldoun, A., Barkaoui, K., & Ioualalen, M. (2017). Formal verification of complex business processes based on high-level petri nets. *Information Sciences, 385-386*, 39–54. doi:10.1016/j.ins.2016.12.044

Kim, Y. E., & Whitman, B. (2002). Singer identification in popular music recordings using voice coding features. *Proc. Int. Conf. Music Information Retrieval.*

Kleinberg, J., Papadimitriou, C., & Raghavan, P. (1998, May). Segmentation problems. In *Proceedings of the thirtieth annual ACM symposium on Theory of computing* (pp. 473-482). ACM. 10.1145/276698.276860

Klusch, M., Fries, B., & Sycara, K. (2006). Automated semantic Web service discovery with OWLS-MX. *Proceeding of the 5th International Conference on Autonomous Agents and Multi-Agent Systems*, 915-922. 10.1145/1160633.1160796

Kolter, J. P. (2010). *User-centric Privacy: A Usable and Provider-independent Privacy Infrastructure* (Vol. 41). BoD–Books on Demand.

Kopecký, J., Vitvar, T., Bournez, C., & Farrell, J. (2007). Sawsdl: Semantic annotations for wsdl and xml schema. *IEEE Internet Computing, 11*(6), 60–67. doi:10.1109/MIC.2007.134

Koren, Y. (2010). Collaborative filtering with temporal dynamics. *Communications of the ACM, 53*(4), 89–97. doi:10.1145/1721654.1721677

Koutsoukos, X., Karsai, G., Laszka, A., Neema, H., Potteiger, B., Volgyesi, P., ... Sztipanovits, J. (2018). SURE: A Modeling and Simulation Integration Platform for Evaluation of Secure and Resilient Cyber–Physical Systems. *Proceedings of the IEEE, 106*(1), 93–112. doi:10.1109/JPROC.2017.2731741

Kowalski, R., & Sergot, M. (1989). A logic-based calculus of events. In *Foundations of knowledge base management* (pp. 23–55). Berlin: Springer. doi:10.1007/978-3-642-83397-7_2

Kraemer, F., & Herrmann, P. (2007). Transforming Collaborative Service Specifications into Efficiently Executable State Machines. *Electronic Communications of the EASST, 7.*

Kraemer, F., & Herrmann, P. (2010). Reactive Semantics for Distributed UML Activities. *LNCS, 6117*, 17-31.

Kraemer, F., & Herrmann, P. (2009). Automated Encapsulation of UML Activities for Incremental Development and Verification. *LNCS*, *5795*, 571–585.

Kraemer, F., Herrmann, P., & Bræk, R. (2006). Aligning UML 2.0 State Machines and Temporal Logic for the Efficient Execution of Services. *8th International Symposium on Distributed Objects and Applications (DOA06)* (pp. 1613-1632). Springer-Verlag. 10.1007/11914952_41

Kraemer, F., Slåtten, V., & Herrmann, P. (2009). Tool Support for the Rapid Composition, Analysis and Implementation of Reactive Services. *Journal of Systems and Software*, *82*(12), 2068–2080. doi:10.1016/j.jss.2009.06.057

Kumara, B. T. G. S., Paik, I., Chen, W., & Ryu, K. (2014). Web Service Clustering using a Hybrid Term-Similarity Measure with Ontology Learning. *International Journal of Web Services Research*, *11*(2), 24–45. doi:10.4018/ijwsr.2014040102

Kumaraguru, P., Cranor, L., Lobo, J., & Calo, S. (2007, July). A survey of privacy policy languages. In *Workshop on Usable IT Security Management (USM 07): Proceedings of the 3rd Symposium on Usable Privacy and Security*. ACM.

Kuri-Morales, A., & Cartas-Ayala, A. (2014, May). Polynomial multivariate approximation with genetic algorithms. In *Canadian Conference on Artificial Intelligence* (pp. 307-312). Springer.

Küster, U., König-Ries, B., Stern, M., & Klein, M. (2007). DIANE: an integrated approach to automated service discovery, matchmaking and composition. In *Proceedings of the 16th international conference on World Wide Web* (pp. 1033-1042). ACM. 10.1145/1242572.1242711

Kwiatkowska, M., Norman, G., & Parker, D. (2009). *Stochastic Games for Verification of Probabilistic Timed Automata*. Oxford, UK: Oxford University Computing Laboratory. doi:10.1007/978-3-642-04368-0_17

Kwiatkowska, M., Norman, G., & Parker, D. (2011). PRISM 4.0: Verification of Probabilistic Real-Time Systems. In *23rd International Conference on Computer Aided Verification (CAV)* (pp. 585-591). Snowbird, UT: Springer-Verlag. 10.1007/978-3-642-22110-1_47

Kwiatkowska, M., Norman, G., Segala, R., & Sproston, J. (2002). Automatic Verification of Real-time Systems with Discrete Probability Distributions. *Theoretical Computer Science*, *286*(1), 101–150. doi:10.1016/S0304-3975(01)00046-9

Kwiatkowska, M., Norman, G., Sproston, J., & Wang, F. (2005). Symbolic Model Checking for Probabilistic Timed Automata. *Information and Computation, 205*(7), 1027–1077. doi:10.1016/j.ic.2007.01.004

Lamport, L. (2002). *Specifying Systems: The TLA+ Language and Tools for Hardware and Software Engineers*. Boston: Addison-Wesley.

Laroussinie, F., Markey, N., & Schnoebelen, P. (2004). Model Checking Timed Automata with One or Two Clocks. *LNCS, 3170*, 387–401.

Le, D. N., Nguyen, V. Q., & Goh, A. (2009, September). Matching WSDL and OWL-S web services. In *Semantic Computing, 2009. ICSC'09. IEEE International Conference on* (pp. 197-202). IEEE. 10.1109/ICSC.2009.12

Lee, J. Y., & Kim, S. D. (2015, June). IoT Contexts Acquisition with High Accuracy and Efficiency. In *Services (SERVICES), 2015 IEEE World Congress on* (pp. 9-16). IEEE. 10.1109/SERVICES.2015.10

Li, H., Zhang, L., & Jiang, R. (2014). Study of manufacturing cloud service matching algorithm based on OWL-S. In *Control and Decision Conference (2014 CCDC), The 26th Chinese* (pp. 4155-4160). IEEE. 10.1109/CCDC.2014.6852909

Lifen, L. (2008). Trust Derivation and Transitivity in a Recommendation Trust Model. In *Computer Science and Software Engineering, 2008 International Conference on* (vol. 3, pp. 770-773). IEEE.

Lifschitz, V. (2002). Answer set programming and plan generation. *Artificial Intelligence, 138*(1), 39–54. doi:10.1016/S0004-3702(02)00186-8

Linthicum, D. S. (2017). Cloud-Native Applications and Cloud Migration: The Good, the Bad, and the Points Between. *IEEE Cloud Computing, 4*(5), 12–14. doi:10.1109/MCC.2017.4250932

Liu, H., Blech, J. O., Duckham, M., & Schmidt, H. (2017). Spatio-Temporal Aware Testing for Complex Systems. In *IEEE International Conference on Software Quality, Reliability and Security (Companion Volume)* (pp. 569-570). Prague: IEEE Computer.

Liu, C. C., & Huang, C. S. (2002). A singer identification technique for content-based classification of MP3 music objects. *Proc. Int. Conf. Information and Knowledge Management*. 10.1145/584792.584864

Liu, H., & Motoda, H. (2002). On issues of instance selection. *Data Mining and Knowledge Discovery*, 6(2), 115–130. doi:10.1023/A:1014056429969

Liu, J. X., Liu, F., Li, X. X., He, K. Q., Ma, Y. T., & Wang, J. (2015). Web Service Clustering Using Relational Database Approach. *International Journal of Software Engineering and Knowledge Engineering*, 25(8), 1365–1393. doi:10.1142/S021819401550028X

Liu, Q., Chen, E., Xiong, H., Ding, C., & Chen, J. (2012). Enhancing Collaborative Filtering by User Interest Expansion via Personalized Ranking. *IEEE Transactions on*, 42(1), 218–233. PMID:21880572

Liu, W., & Wong, W. (2009). Web service clustering using text mining techniques. *International Journal of Agent-oriented Software Engineering*, 3(1), 6–26. doi:10.1504/IJAOSE.2009.022944

Liu, Z., Wang, H., Xu, X., & Wang, Z. (2016). Web services optimal composition based on improved artificial bee colony algorithm with the knowledge of service domain features. *Services Transactions on Services Computing*, 4(1), 27–38. doi:10.29268tsc.2016.4.1.3

Li, W., Cheng, Y., Zhang, P., & Leung, H. (2016). An Automatic Recovery Mechanism for Cloud Service Composition. *International Journal of Web Services Research*, 13(1), 23–39. doi:10.4018/IJWSR.2016010102

Li, Y., & Wang, D. L. (2007). Separation of singing voice from music accompaniment for monaural recordings. *IEEE Transactions on Audio, Speech, and Language Processing*, 15(3), 1475–1487. doi:10.1109/TASL.2006.889789

Loiseaux, C., Graf, S., Sifakis, J., Bouajjani, A., Bensalem, S., & Probst, D. (1995). Property Preserving Abstractions for the Verification of Concurrent Systems. *Formal Methods in System Design*, 6(1), 1–35. doi:10.1007/BF01384313

Maddage, N. C., Xu, C., & Wang, Y. (2004). Singer identification based on vocal and instrumental models. *Proc. Int. Conf. Pattern Recognition*. 10.1109/ICPR.2004.1334225

Ma, H., King, I., & Lyu, M. R. (2009). Learning to recommend with social trust ensemble. In *Proceedings of the 32nd international ACM SIGIR conference on Research and development in information retrieval* (pp. 203-210). ACM. 10.1145/1571941.1571978

Ma, H., Zhou, D., Liu, C., Lyu, M. R., & King, I. (2011). Recommender systems with social regularization. In *Proceedings of the fourth ACM international conference on Web search and data mining* (pp. 287-296). ACM. 10.1145/1935826.1935877

Mason, J. C., & Handscomb, D. C. (2002). *Chebyshev polynomials*. CRC Press. doi:10.1201/9781420036114

McAfee, A., Brynjolfsson, E., Davenport, T. H., Patil, D. J., & Barton, D. (2012). Big data: The management revolution. *Harvard Business Review*, *90*(10), 60–68. PMID:23074865

Menascé, D. A. (2002). QoS issues in web services. *IEEE Internet Computing*, *6*(6), 72–75. doi:10.1109/MIC.2002.1067740

Merz, M., Moldt, D., Müller, K., & Lamersdorf, W. (1995). *Workflow modelling and execution with coloured Petri nets in COSM*. University of Hamburg.

Mesaros, A., & Astola, J. (2005). The mel-frequency cepstral coefficients in the context of singer identification. *Proc. Int. Conf. Music Information Retrieval*.

Mesaros, A., Virtanen, T., & Klapuri, A. (2007). Singer Identification in polyphonic music using vocal separation and pattern recognition methods. *Proc. Int. Conf. Music Information Retrieval*.

Montali, M., & Plebani, P. (2017). Iot-based compliance checking of multi-party business processes modeled with commitments. In *Service-oriented and cloud computing* (Vol. 10465, pp. 179–195). Springer. doi:10.1007/978-3-319-67262-5_14

Moré, J. J. (1978). The Levenberg-Marquardt algorithm: implementation and theory. In *Numerical analysis* (pp. 105–116). Berlin: Springer. doi:10.1007/BFb0067700

Moreno, I. S., Garraghan, P., Townend, P., & Xu, J. (2013). An Approach for Characterizing Workloads in Google Cloud to Derive Realistic Resource Utilization Models. In *Proceedings of the IEEE International Symposium on Service Oriented System Engineering* (pp. 49–60). IEEE. 10.1109/SOSE.2013.24

Morimoto, S. (2008). A survey of formal verification for business process modeling. In *Computational Science–ICCS 2008* (Vol. 5102, pp. 514–522). Berlin: Springer. doi:10.1007/978-3-540-69387-1_58

Mueller, E. T. (2004). Event calculus reasoning through satisfiability. *Journal of Logic and Computation*, *14*(5), 703–730. doi:10.1093/logcom/14.5.703

Mueller, E. T. (2010). *Commonsense reasoning*. Morgan Kaufmann.

Naessens, V., Sandikkaya, M. T., Lapon, J., Verslype, K., Verhaeghe, P., Nigusse, G., & De Decker, B. (2009). Privacy policies, tools and mechanisms of the future. In iNetSec 2009–Open Research Problems in Network Security (pp. 125-138). Springer. doi:10.1007/978-3-642-05437-2_12

Narayanan, S., & McIlraith, S. A. (2002). Simulation, verification and automated composition of web services. In *Proceedings of the 11th international conference on World Wide Web* (pp. 77-88). ACM. 10.1145/511446.511457

Nayak, R., & Lee, B. (2007). Web service discovery with additional semantics and clustering. *IEEE/WIC/ACM International Conference on Web Intelligence*, 555–558. 10.1109/WI.2007.82

Németh, E., & Bartha, T. (2009). Formal Verification of Safety Functions by Reinterpretation of Functional Block Based Specifications. *LNCS, 5596*, 199–214.

Nepal, S., Friedrich, C., Wise, C., Sinnott, R. O., Jaccard, J. J., & Chen, S. P. (2016). Key management service: Enabling secure sharing and deleting of documents on public clouds. *Services Transactions on Cloud Computing, 4*(2), 15–31. doi:10.29268tcc.2016.0005

Nielsen. (2012). *State of the media - The social media report 2012*. Retrieved from http://www.nielsen.com/us/en/insights/reports/2012/state-of-the-media-the-social-media-report-2012.html

Nielsen, J. (1994). *Usability engineering*. Elsevier.

Norusis, M. (2008). *SPSS 16.0 advanced statistical procedures companion*. Prentice Hall Press.

Nwe, T. L., & Li, H. (2008). On fusion of timbre-motivated features for singing voice detection and singer identification. Proc. IEEE Int. Conf. Acoustics, Speech, and Signal Processing. doi:10.1109/ICASSP.2008.4518087

Nwe, T. L., & Li, H. (2007). Exploring Vibrato-Motivated Acoustic Features for Singer Identification. *IEEE Transactions on Audio, Speech, and Language Processing, 15*(2), 519–530. doi:10.1109/TASL.2006.876756

Okuno, H. G., Nakatani, T., & Kawabata, T. (1999). Listening to two simultaneous speeches. *Speech Communication, 27*(3-4), 299–310. doi:10.1016/S0167-6393(98)00080-6

Olken, F., & Rotem, D. (1995). Random sampling from databases: A survey. *Statistics and Computing*, *5*(1), 25–42. doi:10.1007/BF00140664

Paik, I., Chen, W., & Huhns, M. (2014). A scalable architecture for automatic service composition. *Services Computing. IEEE Transactions on*, *7*(1), 82–95.

Paik, I., Chen, W., & Huhns, M. N. (2014). A scalable architecture for automatic service composition. *IEEE Transactions on Services Computing*, *7*(1), 82–95. doi:10.1109/TSC.2012.33

Palpanas, T. (2000). Knowledge discovery in data warehouses. *SIGMOD Record*, *29*(3), 88–100. doi:10.1145/362084.362142

Parducci, B., Lockhart, H., & Rissanen, E. (2013). Extensible access control markup language (XACML) version 3.0. *OASIS Standard*, 1-154.

Pauwels, P., Zhang, S., & Lee, Y. C. (2017). Semantic web technologies in AEC industry: A literature overview. *Automation in Construction*, *73*, 145–165. doi:10.1016/j.autcon.2016.10.003

Peng, J., Zeng, D. D., Zhao, H., & Wang, F. (2010). Collaborative filtering in social tagging systems based on joint item-tag recommendations. In *Proceedings of the 19th ACM international conference on Information and knowledge management* (pp. 809-818). ACM. 10.1145/1871437.1871541

Perera, S., Herath, C., Ekanayake, J., Chinthaka, E., Ranabahu, A., Jayasinghe, D., . . . Daniels, G. (2006, September). Axis2, middleware for next generation web services. In *Web Services, 2006. ICWS'06. International Conference on* (pp. 833-840). IEEE. PIA. Retrieved from https://www.cnil.fr/en/open-source-pia-software-helps-carry-out-data-protection-impact-assesment

Peter, W., Chiochetti, J., & Giardina, C. (2003, August). New unsupervised clustering algorithm for large datasets. In *Proceedings of the ninth ACM SIGKDD international conference on Knowledge discovery and data mining* (pp. 643-648). ACM. 10.1145/956750.956833

Pfitzmann, B., & Joukov, N. (2011). Migration to Multi-image Cloud Templates. In *Proceedings of IEEE International Conference on Services Computing* (pp. 80–87). IEEE.

Phelan, O., McCarthy, K., & Smyth, B. (2009). Using twitter to recommend real-time topical news. In *Proceedings of the third ACM conference on Recommender systems* (pp. 385-388). ACM. 10.1145/1639714.1639794

Platzer, A., & Quesel, J. (2008). KeYmaera: A Hybrid Theorem Prover for Hybrid Systems (System Description). *LNCS, 5195*, 171–178.

Platzer, A., & Quesel, J. D. (2009). *European Train Control System: A Case Study in Formal Verification. In Formal Methods and Software Engineering (ICFEM)* (pp. 246–265). Rio de Janeiro: Springer-Verlag.

Platzer, C., Rosenberg, F., & Dustdar, S. (2009). Web service clustering using multidimensional angles as proximity measures. *ACM Transactions on Internet Technology, 9*(3), 1–26. doi:10.1145/1552291.1552294

Pokraev, S., Zhang, L. J., Koolwaaij, J., & Wibbels, M. (2003). *Extending UDDI with context-aware features based on semantic service descriptions*. Postman. Retrieved from https://www.getpostman.com/

Powell, M. J. (1978). A fast algorithm for nonlinearly constrained optimization calculations. In *Numerical analysis* (pp. 144–157). Berlin: Springer. doi:10.1007/BFb0067703

Puka, E., Herrmann, P., Levin, T., & Skjetne, C. B. (2018). A Way to Measure and Analyze Cellular Network Connectivity on the Norwegian Road System. In *10th International Conference on Communication Systems & Networks (COMSNETS)* (pp. 595-600). Bengaluru: IEEE Computer. 10.1109/COMSNETS.2018.8328280

Qian, J., Huang, G., & Zhao, L. (2011). Semantic Web Service Composition: From OWL-S to Answer Set Programming. In *Computer Science for Environmental Engineering and EcoInformatics* (pp. 112–117). Springer Berlin Heidelberg. doi:10.1007/978-3-642-22691-5_20

Qu, X., Sun, H., Li, X., Liu, X., & Lin, W. (2009). WSSM: A WordNet-Based Web Services Similarity Mining Mechanism. *Proceeding of the Future Computing, Service Computation, Cognitive, Adaptive, Content, Patterns, 2009. COMPUTATIONWORLD '09. Computation World*, 339–345. 10.1109/ComputationWorld.2009.96

Rainer, A. (2005). *Web service composition using answer set programming. In 19. Workshop" Planen, Scheduling und Konfigurieren*. Koblenz: Entwerfen.

Rao, J., & Su, X. (2005). A survey of automated web service composition methods. In *Semantic Web Services and Web Process Composition* (pp. 43–54). Springer Berlin Heidelberg. doi:10.1007/978-3-540-30581-1_5

Rapoport, A., & Horvath, W. J. (1961). A study of a large sociogram. *Behavioral Science, 6*(4), 279–291. doi:10.1002/bs.3830060402 PMID:14490358

Raymond, T. N., & Han, J. W. (1994). Efficient and effective clustering methods for spatial data mining. *Proc. of the 20th International Conference on Very Large Data Bases.*

Reynolds, D., Quatieri, T., & Dunn, R. (2000). Speaker verification using adapted Gaussian mixture models. *Digital Signal Processing, 10*(1-3), 19–41. doi:10.1006/dspr.1999.0361

Reynolds, D., & Rose, R. (1995). Robust text-independent speaker identification using Gaussian mixture speaker models. *IEEE Transactions on Speech and Audio Processing, 3*(1), 72–83. doi:10.1109/89.365379

Rezgui, A., Ouzzani, M., Bouguettaya, A., & Medjahed, B. (2002, November). Preserving privacy in web services. In *Proceedings of the 4th international workshop on Web information and data management* (pp. 56-62). ACM.

Rodriguez-Mier, P., Pedrinaci, C., Lama, M., & Mucientes, M. (2016). An integrated semantic web service discovery and composition framework. *IEEE Transactions on Services Computing, 9*(4), 537–550. doi:10.1109/TSC.2015.2402679

Röglinger, D. W. I. M. (2009). Verification of web service compositions: An operationalization of correctness and a requirements framework for service-oriented modeling techniques. *Business & Information Systems Engineering, 1*(6), 429–437. doi:10.100712599-009-0074-z

Rudolph, G. (1994). Convergence analysis of canonical genetic algorithms. *IEEE Transactions on Neural Networks, 5*(1), 96–101. doi:10.1109/72.265964 PMID:18267783

Salakhutdinov, R., & Mnih, A. (2007). Probabilistic matrix factorization. *Advances in Neural Information Processing Systems*, 1257–1264.

Salaün, G., Bordeaux, L., & Schaerf, M. (2006). Describing and reasoning on web services using process algebra. *International Journal of Business Process Integration and Management, 1*(2), 116–128. doi:10.1504/IJBPIM.2006.010025

Sarwar, B., Karypis, G., Konstan, J., & Riedl, J. (2001). Item-based collaborative filtering recommendation algorithms. *Proceedings of the 10th international conference on World Wide Web*, 285-295.

Saw, J. G., Yang, M. C., & Mo, T. C. (1984). Chebyshev inequality with estimated mean and variance. *The American Statistician, 38*(2), 130–132.

Schedl, M., Gómez, E., & Urbano, J. (2014). Music Information Retrieval: Recent Developments and Applications. *Journal Foundations and Trends in Information Retrieval, 8*(2-3), 127–261. doi:10.1561/1500000042

Schuster, H., Georgakopoulos, D., Cichocki, A., & Baker, D. (2000). Modeling and composing service-based and reference process-based multi-enterprise processes. *Advanced Information Systems Engineering*, 247–263.

Sezer, S., & Atalay, A. E. (2011). Dynamic Modeling and Fuzzy Logic Control of Vibrations of a Railway Vehicle for Different Track Irregularities. *Simulation Modelling Practice and Theory, 19*(9), 1873–1894. doi:10.1016/j.simpat.2011.04.009

Sheng, Q. Z., Qiao, X., Vasilakos, A. V., Szabo, C., Bourne, S., & Xu, X. (2014). Web services composition: A decade's overview. *Information Sciences, 280*, 218–238. doi:10.1016/j.ins.2014.04.054

Shriberg, E., Stolcke, A., & Baron, D. (2001). Observations on overlap: findings and implications for automatic processing of multi-party conversation. *Proc. European Conference on Speech Communication and Technology.*

Silva, D. R. (2002). MTP: Using Data Warehouse And Data Mining Resources For Ongoing Assessment Of Distance Learning. *Proceedings of IEEE Intl. Conf. on Advanced Learning Technologies (ICALT).*

Singh, A., Juneja, D., & Malhotra, M. (2017). A novel agent based autonomous and service composition framework for cost optimization of resource provisioning in cloud computing. *Journal of King Saud University-Computer and Information Sciences, 29*(1), 19–28. doi:10.1016/j.jksuci.2015.09.001

Skalak, D. B. (1994, February). Prototype and feature selection by sampling and random mutation hill climbing algorithms. *Proceedings of the eleventh international conference on machine learning*, 293-301. 10.1016/B978-1-55860-335-6.50043-X

Skoutas, D., Sacharidis, D., Simitsis, A., & Sellis, T. (2010). Ranking and clustering web services using multicriteria dominance relationships. *IEEE Transactions on Services Computing, 3*(3), 163–177. doi:10.1109/TSC.2010.14

Slagle, J. R., Chang, C. L., & Heller, S. (1975). A Clustering and data-reorganization algorithm. *IEEE Trans. on Systems, Man and Cybernetics.*

Slåtten, V., Herrmann, P., & Kraemer, F. (2013). Model-Driven Engineering of Reliable Fault-Tolerant Systems - A State-of-the-Art Survey. *Advances in Computers, 91*, 119–205. doi:10.1016/B978-0-12-408089-8.00004-5

Sokal, R. R. (1985). The principles of numerical taxonomy: twenty-five years later. *Computer-Assisted Bacterial Systematics, 15*, 1.

Sousa, E., Lins, F., Tavares, E., & Maciel, P. (2016). A Modeling strategy for cloud infrastructure planning considering performance and cost requirements. *Services Transactions on Cloud Computing, 4*(1), 30–43. doi:10.29268tcc.2016.0003

Stefanidis, K., Pitoura, E., & Vassiliadis, P. (2011). Managing contextual preferences. *Information Systems, 36*(8), 1158–1180. doi:10.1016/j.is.2011.06.004

Steinbach, M., Karypis, G., & Kumar, V. (2000, August). A comparison of document clustering techniques. In KDD workshop on text mining (Vol. 400, No. 1, pp. 525-526). Academic Press.

Surianarayanan, C., & Ganapathy, G. (2016). An Approach to Computation of Similarity Inter-Cluster Distance and Selection of Threshold for Service Discovery using Clusters. *IEEE Transactions on Services Computing, 9*(4), 524–536. doi:10.1109/TSC.2015.2399301

Svae, A., Taherkordi, A., Herrmann, P., & Blech, J. O. (2017). Self-Adaptive Control in Cyber-Physical Systems: The Autonomous Train Experiment. In *32nd ACM SIGAPP Symposium On Applied Computing* (pp. 1436-1443). Marrakech, Morocco: ACM. 10.1145/3019612.3019651

Syu, Y., Ma, S. P., Kuo, J. Y., & FanJiang, Y. Y. (2012). A survey on automated service composition methods and related techniques. In *Services Computing (SCC), 2012 IEEE Ninth International Conference on* (pp. 290-297). IEEE.

Taherkordi, A., Herrmann, P., Blech, J. O., & Férnandez, Á. (2017). *Service Virtualization for Self-Adaptation in Mobile Cyber-Physical Systems. In Service-Oriented Computing - ICSOC 2016 Workshops* (pp. 56–68). Banff: Springer-Verlag.

Tang, R., & Zou, Y. (2010). An Approach for Mining Web Service Composition Patterns from Execution Logs (short). In *Proceedings of the IEEE International Conference on Web Services*, (pp. 678–679). IEEE.

Tan, P. N. (2006). *Introduction to data mining*. Pearson Education India.

Tilsner, M., Fiech, A., Zhan, G., & Specht, T. (2011). Patterns for service composition. In *Proceedings of the Fourth International C* Conference on Computer Science and Software Engineering*, (pp. 133–137). ACM.

Tiwari, A. (2015). Time-Aware Abstractions in HybridSal. In *27th International Conference on Computer Aided Verification (CAV)* (pp. 504-510). San Francisco: Springer-Verlag. 10.1007/978-3-319-21690-4_34

Toivonen, H. (1996, September). *Sampling large databases for association rules* (Vol. 96). VLDB.

Tsai, W. H., & Lin, H. P. (2011). Background Music Removal Based on Cepstrum Transformation for Popular Singer Identification. IEEE Trans. Audio, Speech, Lang. Process., 19(5), 1196-1205.

Tsai, W. H., Liao, S. J., & Lai, C. (2008). Automatic Identification of Simultaneous Singers in Duet Recordings. *Proc. Int. Conf. Music Information Retrieval.*

Tsai, W. H., & Ma, C. H. (2017). Automatic Identification of Simultaneous and Non-Simultaneous Singers for Music Data Indexing. *International Journal of Web Services Research, 14*(1), 29–43. doi:10.4018/IJWSR.2017010103

Tsai, W. H., Rodgers, D., & Wang, H. M. (2004). Blind clustering of popular music recordings based on singer voice characteristics. *Computer Music Journal, 28*(3), 68–78. doi:10.1162/0148926041790630

Tsai, W. H., & Wang, H. M. (2004). Automatic detection and tracking of target singer in multi-singer music recordings. *Proc. IEEE Conf. Acoustics, Speech, and Signal Processing (ICASSP).*

Tsai, W. H., & Wang, H. M. (2006). Automatic singer recognition of popular music recordings via estimation and modeling of solo vocal signals. *IEEE Transactions on Audio, Speech, and Language Processing, 14*(1), 333–341.

Tu, D. (2006). Nonparametric Monte Carlo Tests and Their Applications. *Biometrics, 62*(3), 950–951. doi:10.1111/j.1541-0420.2006.00588_14.x

Tumer, A., Dogac, A., & Toroslu, I. H. (2005). A semantic-based user privacy protection framework for web services. In *Intelligent Techniques for Web Personalization* (pp. 289–305). Berlin: Springer. doi:10.1007/11577935_16

Tyagi, A. K. (2012). *MATLAB and Simulink for Engineers.* Oxford University Press.

Van Der Aalst, W. M., & Pesic, M. (2006). DecSerFlow: Towards a truly declarative service flow language. In *Web Services and Formal Methods* (Vol. 4184, pp. 1–23). Berlin: Springer. doi:10.1007/11841197_1

Virtanen, T. (2007). Monaural sound source separation by non-negative matrix factorization with temporal continuity and sparseness criteria. *IEEE Transactions on Audio, Speech, and Language Processing, 15*(3), 1066–1074. doi:10.1109/TASL.2006.885253

Voss, W. G. (2017). European union data privacy law reform: General data protection regulation, privacy shield, and the right to delisting. *Weather Forecast Service*. Retrieved from http://www.pathfinder-xml.com/development/WSDL/WeatherForecastService.wsdl

Vu, K., Hua, K. A., Cheng, H., & Lang, S. D. (2006, June). A non-linear dimensionality-reduction technique for fast similarity search in large databases. In *Proceedings of the 2006 ACM SIGMOD international conference on Management of data* (pp. 527-538). ACM. 10.1145/1142473.1142532

Wagner, F., Ishikawa, F., & Honiden, S. (2011). QoS-aware Automatic Service Composition by Applying Functional Clustering. *Proceeding of the 9th IEEE International Conference on Web Services*, 89–96. 10.1109/ICWS.2011.32

Wan, Z., Duan, L., & Wang, P. (2017). Cloud Migration: Layer Partition and Integration. In *Proceedings of the IEEE International Conference on Edge Computing* (pp. 150–157). IEEE.

Wan, Z., Meng, F. J., Xu, J. M., & Wang, P. (2014). Service Composition Pattern Generation for Cloud Migration: A Graph Similarity Analysis Approach. In *Proceedings of the 2014 IEEE International Conference on Web Services* (pp. 321–328). IEEE. 10.1109/ICWS.2014.54

Wan, Z., Wang, P., Duan, L., Meng, F. J., & Xu, J. M. (2015). Graph Similarity based Cloud Migration Service Composition Pattern Discovery. *International Journal of Web Services Research, 12*(2), 26–46. doi:10.4018/IJWSR.2015040102

Wen, T., Sheng, G., Li, Y., & Guo, Q. (2011). Research on Web service discovery with semantics and clustering. *Proceeding of the 6th IEEE Joint International Information Technology and Artificial Intelligence Conference*, 62–67. 10.1109/ITAIC.2011.6030151

Wiese, J., Das, S., Hong, J. I., & Zimmerman, J. (2017). Evolving the ecosystem of personal behavioral data. *Human-Computer Interaction, 32*(5-6), 447–510. doi:10.1080/07370024.2017.1295857

Wikarski, D. (1996). *An introduction to modular process nets.* ICSI.

World Weather Online. (n.d.). Retrieved from http://www.worldweatheronline.com

Wu, B., Lin, R., Wang, P., & Chen, J. (2016). Dynamic business process generation and verification. In IEEE international conference on services computing, SCC 2016 (pp. 836– 839). IEEE. doi:10.1109/SCC.2016.118

Wu, J., Chen, L., Zheng, Z., Lyu, M. R., & Wu, Z. (2014). Clustering web services to facilitate service discovery. *Knowledge and Information Systems, 38*(1), 207–229. doi:10.100710115-013-0623-0

Xia, Y., Chen, P., Bao, L., Wang, M., & Yang, J. (2011). A QoS-Aware Web service selection algorithm based on clustering. *IEEE International Conference on Web Services,* 428-435. 10.1109/ICWS.2011.36

Xie, L., Chen, F., & Kou, J. (2011). Ontology-based semantic Web services clustering. *Proceeding of the 18th IEEE International Conference on Industrial Engineering and Engineering Management,* 2075–2079.

Xiu, P., Zhao, W., & Yang, J. (2017). Correctness verification for service-based business processes. In IEEE international conference on web services, ICWS 2017 (pp. 752–759). IEEE. doi:10.1109/ICWS.2017.90

Xu, W., Venkatakrishnan, V. N., Sekar, R., & Ramakrishnan, I. V. (2006, September). A framework for building privacy-conscious composite web services. In *Web Services, 2006. ICWS'06. International Conference on* (pp. 655-662). IEEE. 10.1109/ICWS.2006.4

Xu, N., Zhang, W. S., Yang, H. D., Zhang, X. G., & Xing, X. (2013). CACOnt: A ontology-based model for context modeling and reasoning. *Applied Mechanics and Materials, 347,* 2304–2310. doi:10.4028/www.scientific.net/AMM.347-350.2304

Yamamoto, K., Asano, F., Yamada, T., & Kitawaki, N. (2006). Detection of overlapping speech in meetings using support vector machines and support vector regression. *IEICE Trans. Fundamentals, 89*(8), 2158-2165.

Yang, J., Zhu, Z., Seiter, J., & Tröster, G. (2015, November). Informative yet unrevealing: Semantic obfuscation for location based services. In *Proceedings of the 2nd Workshop on Privacy in Geographic Information Collection and Analysis* (p. 4). ACM. 10.1145/2830834.2830838

Yang, X., Liang, C., Zhao, M., Wang, H., Ding, H., Liu, Y., ... Zhang, J. (2017). Collaborative filtering-based recommendation of online social voting. *IEEE Transactions on Computational Social Systems*, *4*(1), 1–13. doi:10.1109/TCSS.2017.2665122

Yang, X., Steck, H., & Liu, Y. (2012). Circle-based recommendation in online social networks. In *Proceedings of the 18th ACM SIGKDD international conference on Knowledge discovery and data mining* (pp. 1267-1275). ACM.

Yan, Z., Dijkman, R., & Grefen, P. (2010). Fast business process similarity search with feature-based similarity estimation. *On the Move to Meaningful Internet Systems OTM*, *2010*, 60–77.

Ye, Z., Mistry, S., Bouguettaya, A., & Dong, H. (2016). Long-term QoS-aware cloud service composition using multivariate time series analysis. *IEEE Transactions on Services Computing*, *9*(3), 382–393. doi:10.1109/TSC.2014.2373366

Yi, X., & Kochut, K. J. (2004). A cp-nets-based design and verification framework for web services composition. In *Web Services, 2004. Proceedings. IEEE International Conference on* (pp. 756-760). IEEE.

Yu, Q., Liu, X., Bouguettaya, A., & Medjahed, B. (2008). Deploying and managing Web services: issues, solutions, and directions. *The VLDB Journal—The International Journal on Very Large Data Bases*, *17*(3), 537-572.

Yue, K., Wang, X. L., & Zhou, A. Y. (2004). Underlying techniques for Web services: A survey. *Journal of Software*.

Zahoor, E. (2011). *Gouvernance de service: aspects sécurité et données* (Doctoral dissertation). Université Nancy II.

Zahoor, E., Asma, Z., & Perrin, O. (2017). A formal approach for the verifi- cation of AWS IAM access control policies. In *Service-oriented and cloud computing - 6th IFIP WG 2.14 European conference* (pp. 59–74). Academic Press. doi: 510.1007/978-3- 319-67262-5

Zahoor, E., Perrin, O., & Bouchami, A. (2014). CATT: A cloud based authorization framework with trust and temporal aspects. In *10th IEEE international conference on collaborative computing: Net- working, applications and worksharing, collaboratecom 2014* (pp. 285–294). Academic Press. 10.4108/icst.collaboratecom.2014.257312

Zahoor, E., Perrin, O., & Godart, C. (2010). Disc: A declarative framework for self-healing web services composition. In *Web Services (ICWS), 2010 IEEE International Conference on* (pp. 25-33). IEEE. 10.1109/ICWS.2010.70

Zahoor, E., Perrin, O., & Godart, C. (2010). Disc-set: Handling temporal and security aspects in the web services composition. In *Web Services (ECOWS), 2010 IEEE 8th European Conference on* (pp. 51-58). IEEE.

Zahoor, E., Perrin, O., & Godart, C. (2012). Web services composition verification using satisfiability solving. In *IEEE International conference on web services* (pp. 242–249). IEEE. 10.1109/ICWS.2012.75

Zahoor, E., Munir, K., Perrin, O., & Godart, C. (2013). A bounded model checking approach for the verification of web services composition. *International Journal of Web Services Research*, *10*(4), 62–81. doi:10.4018/ijwsr.2013100103

Zhang, J., Chang, C. K., Chung, J. Y., & Kim, S. W. (2004). WS-Net: A Petri-net based specification model for Web services. In *Web Services, 2004. Proceedings. IEEE International Conference on* (pp. 420-427). IEEE. 10.1109/ICWS.2004.1314766

Zhang, T. (2003). Automatic singer identification. Proc. IEEE Int. Conf. Multimedia Expo. doi:10.1109/ICME.2003.1220847

Zhang, D., Zhou, Z. H., & Chen, S. (2007, April). *Semi-Supervised Dimensionality Reduction*. SDM.

Zhang, L. J., & Chen, H. (2015). BDOA: Big data open architecture. *Services Transactions on Big Data*, *2*(4), 24–48. doi:10.29268tbd.2015.2.4.3

Zhang, L. J., & Li, C. (2017). Internet of things solutions. *Services Transactions on Internet of Things*, *1*(1), 1–22. doi:10.29268tiot.2017.1.1.1

Zhang, L. J., & Zeng, J. (2015). 5C, a new model of defining big data. *Services Transactions on Big Data*, *2*(4), 10–23. doi:10.29268tbd.2015.2.4.2

Zhang, X., Jing, L., Hu, X., Ng, M., & Zhou, X. (2007). A comparative study of ontology based term similarity measures on PubMed document clustering. *Proceeding of the 12th International Conference on Database Systems for Advanced Applications*, 115-126. 10.1007/978-3-540-71703-4_12

Zhang, Y., Lei, T., & Qin, Z. (2018). A Service Recommendation Algorithm Based on Modeling of Dynamic and Diverse Demands. *International Journal of Web Services Research*, *15*(1), 47–70. doi:10.4018/IJWSR.2018010103

Zheng, K., Xiong, H., Cui, Y., Chen, J., & Han, L. (2012). User clustering based web service discovery. *2012 Sixth International Conference on Internet Computing for Science and Engineering*, 276–279.

Zhou, Y., Liu, L., Pu, C., Bao, X., Lee, K., Palanisamy, B., ... Zhang, Q. (2015). Clustering Service Networks with Entity, Attribute, and Link Heterogeneity. *2015 IEEE International Conference on Web Services*, 257-264. 10.1109/ICWS.2015.43

Zhu, X., & Wu, X. (2006, August). Scalable representative instance selection and ranking. In *Pattern Recognition, 2006. ICPR 2006. 18th International Conference* (*Vol. 3*, pp. 352-355). IEEE.

Zhu, Y., Huang, Z., & Zhou, H. (2017). Modeling and verification of web services composition based on model transformation. *Journal of Software: Practice and Experience*, *47*(5), 709–730.

Related References

To continue our tradition of advancing information science and technology research, we have compiled a list of recommended IGI Global readings. These references will provide additional information and guidance to further enrich your knowledge and assist you with your own research and future publications.

Aasi, P., Rusu, L., & Vieru, D. (2017). The Role of Culture in IT Governance Five Focus Areas: A Literature Review. *International Journal of IT/Business Alignment and Governance, 8*(2), 42-61. doi:10.4018/IJITBAG.2017070103

Abdrabo, A. A. (2018). Egypt's Knowledge-Based Development: Opportunities, Challenges, and Future Possibilities. In A. Alraouf (Ed.), *Knowledge-Based Urban Development in the Middle East* (pp. 80–101). Hershey, PA: IGI Global. doi:10.4018/978-1-5225-3734-2.ch005

Abu Doush, I., & Alhami, I. (2018). Evaluating the Accessibility of Computer Laboratories, Libraries, and Websites in Jordanian Universities and Colleges. *International Journal of Information Systems and Social Change, 9*(2), 44–60. doi:10.4018/IJISSC.2018040104

Adeboye, A. (2016). Perceived Use and Acceptance of Cloud Enterprise Resource Planning (ERP) Implementation in the Manufacturing Industries. *International Journal of Strategic Information Technology and Applications, 7*(3), 24–40. doi:10.4018/IJSITA.2016070102

Adegbore, A. M., Quadri, M. O., & Oyewo, O. R. (2018). A Theoretical Approach to the Adoption of Electronic Resource Management Systems (ERMS) in Nigerian University Libraries. In A. Tella & T. Kwanya (Eds.), *Handbook of Research on Managing Intellectual Property in Digital Libraries* (pp. 292–311). Hershey, PA: IGI Global. doi:10.4018/978-1-5225-3093-0.ch015

Adhikari, M., & Roy, D. (2016). Green Computing. In G. Deka, G. Siddesh, K. Srinivasa, & L. Patnaik (Eds.), *Emerging Research Surrounding Power Consumption and Performance Issues in Utility Computing* (pp. 84–108). Hershey, PA: IGI Global. doi:10.4018/978-1-4666-8853-7.ch005

Afolabi, O. A. (2018). Myths and Challenges of Building an Effective Digital Library in Developing Nations: An African Perspective. In A. Tella & T. Kwanya (Eds.), *Handbook of Research on Managing Intellectual Property in Digital Libraries* (pp. 51–79). Hershey, PA: IGI Global. doi:10.4018/978-1-5225-3093-0.ch004

Agarwal, R., Singh, A., & Sen, S. (2016). Role of Molecular Docking in Computer-Aided Drug Design and Development. In S. Dastmalchi, M. Hamzeh-Mivehroud, & B. Sokouti (Eds.), *Applied Case Studies and Solutions in Molecular Docking-Based Drug Design* (pp. 1–28). Hershey, PA: IGI Global. doi:10.4018/978-1-5225-0362-0.ch001

Ali, O., & Soar, J. (2016). Technology Innovation Adoption Theories. In L. Al-Hakim, X. Wu, A. Koronios, & Y. Shou (Eds.), *Handbook of Research on Driving Competitive Advantage through Sustainable, Lean, and Disruptive Innovation* (pp. 1–38). Hershey, PA: IGI Global. doi:10.4018/978-1-5225-0135-0.ch001

Alsharo, M. (2017). Attitudes Towards Cloud Computing Adoption in Emerging Economies. *International Journal of Cloud Applications and Computing, 7*(3), 44–58. doi:10.4018/IJCAC.2017070102

Amer, T. S., & Johnson, T. L. (2016). Information Technology Progress Indicators: Temporal Expectancy, User Preference, and the Perception of Process Duration. *International Journal of Technology and Human Interaction, 12*(4), 1–14. doi:10.4018/IJTHI.2016100101

Amer, T. S., & Johnson, T. L. (2017). Information Technology Progress Indicators: Research Employing Psychological Frameworks. In A. Mesquita (Ed.), *Research Paradigms and Contemporary Perspectives on Human-Technology Interaction* (pp. 168–186). Hershey, PA: IGI Global. doi:10.4018/978-1-5225-1868-6.ch008

Anchugam, C. V., & Thangadurai, K. (2016). Introduction to Network Security. In D. G., M. Singh, & M. Jayanthi (Eds.), Network Security Attacks and Countermeasures (pp. 1-48). Hershey, PA: IGI Global. doi:10.4018/978-1-4666-8761-5.ch001

Anchugam, C. V., & Thangadurai, K. (2016). Classification of Network Attacks and Countermeasures of Different Attacks. In D. G., M. Singh, & M. Jayanthi (Eds.), Network Security Attacks and Countermeasures (pp. 115-156). Hershey, PA: IGI Global. doi:10.4018/978-1-4666-8761-5.ch004

Anohah, E. (2016). Pedagogy and Design of Online Learning Environment in Computer Science Education for High Schools. *International Journal of Online Pedagogy and Course Design*, 6(3), 39–51. doi:10.4018/IJOPCD.2016070104

Anohah, E. (2017). Paradigm and Architecture of Computing Augmented Learning Management System for Computer Science Education. *International Journal of Online Pedagogy and Course Design*, 7(2), 60–70. doi:10.4018/IJOPCD.2017040105

Anohah, E., & Suhonen, J. (2017). Trends of Mobile Learning in Computing Education from 2006 to 2014: A Systematic Review of Research Publications. *International Journal of Mobile and Blended Learning*, 9(1), 16–33. doi:10.4018/IJMBL.2017010102

Assis-Hassid, S., Heart, T., Reychav, I., & Pliskin, J. S. (2016). Modelling Factors Affecting Patient-Doctor-Computer Communication in Primary Care. *International Journal of Reliable and Quality E-Healthcare*, 5(1), 1–17. doi:10.4018/IJRQEH.2016010101

Bailey, E. K. (2017). Applying Learning Theories to Computer Technology Supported Instruction. In M. Grassetti & S. Brookby (Eds.), *Advancing Next-Generation Teacher Education through Digital Tools and Applications* (pp. 61–81). Hershey, PA: IGI Global. doi:10.4018/978-1-5225-0965-3.ch004

Balasubramanian, K. (2016). Attacks on Online Banking and Commerce. In K. Balasubramanian, K. Mala, & M. Rajakani (Eds.), *Cryptographic Solutions for Secure Online Banking and Commerce* (pp. 1–19). Hershey, PA: IGI Global. doi:10.4018/978-1-5225-0273-9.ch001

Baldwin, S., Opoku-Agyemang, K., & Roy, D. (2016). Games People Play: A Trilateral Collaboration Researching Computer Gaming across Cultures. In K. Valentine & L. Jensen (Eds.), *Examining the Evolution of Gaming and Its Impact on Social, Cultural, and Political Perspectives* (pp. 364–376). Hershey, PA: IGI Global. doi:10.4018/978-1-5225-0261-6.ch017

Banerjee, S., Sing, T. Y., Chowdhury, A. R., & Anwar, H. (2018). Let's Go Green: Towards a Taxonomy of Green Computing Enablers for Business Sustainability. In M. Khosrow-Pour (Ed.), *Green Computing Strategies for Competitive Advantage and Business Sustainability* (pp. 89–109). Hershey, PA: IGI Global. doi:10.4018/978-1-5225-5017-4.ch005

Basham, R. (2018). Information Science and Technology in Crisis Response and Management. In M. Khosrow-Pour, D.B.A. (Ed.), Encyclopedia of Information Science and Technology, Fourth Edition (pp. 1407-1418). Hershey, PA: IGI Global. doi:10.4018/978-1-5225-2255-3.ch121

Batyashe, T., & Iyamu, T. (2018). Architectural Framework for the Implementation of Information Technology Governance in Organisations. In M. Khosrow-Pour, D.B.A. (Ed.), Encyclopedia of Information Science and Technology, Fourth Edition (pp. 810-819). Hershey, PA: IGI Global. doi:10.4018/978-1-5225-2255-3.ch070

Bekleyen, N., & Çelik, S. (2017). Attitudes of Adult EFL Learners towards Preparing for a Language Test via CALL. In D. Tafazoli & M. Romero (Eds.), *Multiculturalism and Technology-Enhanced Language Learning* (pp. 214–229). Hershey, PA: IGI Global. doi:10.4018/978-1-5225-1882-2.ch013

Bennett, A., Eglash, R., Lachney, M., & Babbitt, W. (2016). Design Agency: Diversifying Computer Science at the Intersections of Creativity and Culture. In M. Raisinghani (Ed.), *Revolutionizing Education through Web-Based Instruction* (pp. 35–56). Hershey, PA: IGI Global. doi:10.4018/978-1-4666-9932-8.ch003

Bergeron, F., Croteau, A., Uwizeyemungu, S., & Raymond, L. (2017). A Framework for Research on Information Technology Governance in SMEs. In S. De Haes & W. Van Grembergen (Eds.), *Strategic IT Governance and Alignment in Business Settings* (pp. 53–81). Hershey, PA: IGI Global. doi:10.4018/978-1-5225-0861-8.ch003

Bhatt, G. D., Wang, Z., & Rodger, J. A. (2017). Information Systems Capabilities and Their Effects on Competitive Advantages: A Study of Chinese Companies. *Information Resources Management Journal*, 30(3), 41–57. doi:10.4018/IRMJ.2017070103

Bogdanoski, M., Stoilkovski, M., & Risteski, A. (2016). Novel First Responder Digital Forensics Tool as a Support to Law Enforcement. In M. Hadji-Janev & M. Bogdanoski (Eds.), *Handbook of Research on Civil Society and National Security in the Era of Cyber Warfare* (pp. 352–376). Hershey, PA: IGI Global. doi:10.4018/978-1-4666-8793-6.ch016

Boontarig, W., Papasratorn, B., & Chutimaskul, W. (2016). The Unified Model for Acceptance and Use of Health Information on Online Social Networks: Evidence from Thailand. *International Journal of E-Health and Medical Communications*, 7(1), 31–47. doi:10.4018/IJEHMC.2016010102

Brown, S., & Yuan, X. (2016). Techniques for Retaining Computer Science Students at Historical Black Colleges and Universities. In C. Prince & R. Ford (Eds.), *Setting a New Agenda for Student Engagement and Retention in Historically Black Colleges and Universities* (pp. 251–268). Hershey, PA: IGI Global. doi:10.4018/978-1-5225-0308-8.ch014

Burcoff, A., & Shamir, L. (2017). Computer Analysis of Pablo Picasso's Artistic Style. *International Journal of Art, Culture and Design Technologies*, 6(1), 1–18. doi:10.4018/IJACDT.2017010101

Byker, E. J. (2017). I Play I Learn: Introducing Technological Play Theory. In C. Martin & D. Polly (Eds.), *Handbook of Research on Teacher Education and Professional Development* (pp. 297–306). Hershey, PA: IGI Global. doi:10.4018/978-1-5225-1067-3.ch016

Calongne, C. M., Stricker, A. G., Truman, B., & Arenas, F. J. (2017). Cognitive Apprenticeship and Computer Science Education in Cyberspace: Reimagining the Past. In A. Stricker, C. Calongne, B. Truman, & F. Arenas (Eds.), *Integrating an Awareness of Selfhood and Society into Virtual Learning* (pp. 180–197). Hershey, PA: IGI Global. doi:10.4018/978-1-5225-2182-2.ch013

Carlton, E. L., Holsinger, J. W. Jr, & Anunobi, N. (2016). Physician Engagement with Health Information Technology: Implications for Practice and Professionalism. *International Journal of Computers in Clinical Practice, 1*(2), 51–73. doi:10.4018/IJCCP.2016070103

Carneiro, A. D. (2017). Defending Information Networks in Cyberspace: Some Notes on Security Needs. In M. Dawson, D. Kisku, P. Gupta, J. Sing, & W. Li (Eds.), Developing Next-Generation Countermeasures for Homeland Security Threat Prevention (pp. 354-375). Hershey, PA: IGI Global. doi:10.4018/978-1-5225-0703-1.ch016

Cavalcanti, J. C. (2016). The New "ABC" of ICTs (Analytics + Big Data + Cloud Computing): A Complex Trade-Off between IT and CT Costs. In J. Martins & A. Molnar (Eds.), *Handbook of Research on Innovations in Information Retrieval, Analysis, and Management* (pp. 152–186). Hershey, PA: IGI Global. doi:10.4018/978-1-4666-8833-9.ch006

Chase, J. P., & Yan, Z. (2017). Affect in Statistics Cognition. In *Assessing and Measuring Statistics Cognition in Higher Education Online Environments: Emerging Research and Opportunities* (pp. 144–187). Hershey, PA: IGI Global. doi:10.4018/978-1-5225-2420-5.ch005

Chen, C. (2016). Effective Learning Strategies for the 21st Century: Implications for the E-Learning. In M. Anderson & C. Gavan (Eds.), *Developing Effective Educational Experiences through Learning Analytics* (pp. 143–169). Hershey, PA: IGI Global. doi:10.4018/978-1-4666-9983-0.ch006

Chen, E. T. (2016). Examining the Influence of Information Technology on Modern Health Care. In P. Manolitzas, E. Grigoroudis, N. Matsatsinis, & D. Yannacopoulos (Eds.), *Effective Methods for Modern Healthcare Service Quality and Evaluation* (pp. 110–136). Hershey, PA: IGI Global. doi:10.4018/978-1-4666-9961-8.ch006

Cimermanova, I. (2017). Computer-Assisted Learning in Slovakia. In D. Tafazoli & M. Romero (Eds.), *Multiculturalism and Technology-Enhanced Language Learning* (pp. 252–270). Hershey, PA: IGI Global. doi:10.4018/978-1-5225-1882-2.ch015

Cipolla-Ficarra, F. V., & Cipolla-Ficarra, M. (2018). Computer Animation for Ingenious Revival. In F. Cipolla-Ficarra, M. Ficarra, M. Cipolla-Ficarra, A. Quiroga, J. Alma, & J. Carré (Eds.), *Technology-Enhanced Human Interaction in Modern Society* (pp. 159–181). Hershey, PA: IGI Global. doi:10.4018/978-1-5225-3437-2.ch008

Cockrell, S., Damron, T. S., Melton, A. M., & Smith, A. D. (2018). Offshoring IT. In M. Khosrow-Pour, D.B.A. (Ed.), Encyclopedia of Information Science and Technology, Fourth Edition (pp. 5476-5489). Hershey, PA: IGI Global. doi:10.4018/978-1-5225-2255-3.ch476

Coffey, J. W. (2018). Logic and Proof in Computer Science: Categories and Limits of Proof Techniques. In J. Horne (Ed.), *Philosophical Perceptions on Logic and Order* (pp. 218–240). Hershey, PA: IGI Global. doi:10.4018/978-1-5225-2443-4.ch007

Dale, M. (2017). Re-Thinking the Challenges of Enterprise Architecture Implementation. In M. Tavana (Ed.), *Enterprise Information Systems and the Digitalization of Business Functions* (pp. 205–221). Hershey, PA: IGI Global. doi:10.4018/978-1-5225-2382-6.ch009

Das, A., Dasgupta, R., & Bagchi, A. (2016). Overview of Cellular Computing-Basic Principles and Applications. In J. Mandal, S. Mukhopadhyay, & T. Pal (Eds.), *Handbook of Research on Natural Computing for Optimization Problems* (pp. 637–662). Hershey, PA: IGI Global. doi:10.4018/978-1-5225-0058-2.ch026

De Maere, K., De Haes, S., & von Kutzschenbach, M. (2017). CIO Perspectives on Organizational Learning within the Context of IT Governance. *International Journal of IT/Business Alignment and Governance, 8*(1), 32-47. doi:10.4018/IJITBAG.2017010103

Demir, K., Çaka, C., Yaman, N. D., İslamoğlu, H., & Kuzu, A. (2018). Examining the Current Definitions of Computational Thinking. In H. Ozcinar, G. Wong, & H. Ozturk (Eds.), *Teaching Computational Thinking in Primary Education* (pp. 36–64). Hershey, PA: IGI Global. doi:10.4018/978-1-5225-3200-2.ch003

Deng, X., Hung, Y., & Lin, C. D. (2017). Design and Analysis of Computer Experiments. In S. Saha, A. Mandal, A. Narasimhamurthy, S. V, & S. Sangam (Eds.), Handbook of Research on Applied Cybernetics and Systems Science (pp. 264-279). Hershey, PA: IGI Global. doi:10.4018/978-1-5225-2498-4.ch013

Denner, J., Martinez, J., & Thiry, H. (2017). Strategies for Engaging Hispanic/Latino Youth in the US in Computer Science. In Y. Rankin & J. Thomas (Eds.), *Moving Students of Color from Consumers to Producers of Technology* (pp. 24–48). Hershey, PA: IGI Global. doi:10.4018/978-1-5225-2005-4.ch002

Devi, A. (2017). Cyber Crime and Cyber Security: A Quick Glance. In R. Kumar, P. Pattnaik, & P. Pandey (Eds.), *Detecting and Mitigating Robotic Cyber Security Risks* (pp. 160–171). Hershey, PA: IGI Global. doi:10.4018/978-1-5225-2154-9.ch011

Dores, A. R., Barbosa, F., Guerreiro, S., Almeida, I., & Carvalho, I. P. (2016). Computer-Based Neuropsychological Rehabilitation: Virtual Reality and Serious Games. In M. Cruz-Cunha, I. Miranda, R. Martinho, & R. Rijo (Eds.), *Encyclopedia of E-Health and Telemedicine* (pp. 473–485). Hershey, PA: IGI Global. doi:10.4018/978-1-4666-9978-6.ch037

Doshi, N., & Schaefer, G. (2016). Computer-Aided Analysis of Nailfold Capillaroscopy Images. In D. Fotiadis (Ed.), *Handbook of Research on Trends in the Diagnosis and Treatment of Chronic Conditions* (pp. 146–158). Hershey, PA: IGI Global. doi:10.4018/978-1-4666-8828-5.ch007

Doyle, D. J., & Fahy, P. J. (2018). Interactivity in Distance Education and Computer-Aided Learning, With Medical Education Examples. In M. Khosrow-Pour, D.B.A. (Ed.), Encyclopedia of Information Science and Technology, Fourth Edition (pp. 5829-5840). Hershey, PA: IGI Global. doi:10.4018/978-1-5225-2255-3.ch507

Elias, N. I., & Walker, T. W. (2017). Factors that Contribute to Continued Use of E-Training among Healthcare Professionals. In F. Topor (Ed.), *Handbook of Research on Individualism and Identity in the Globalized Digital Age* (pp. 403–429). Hershey, PA: IGI Global. doi:10.4018/978-1-5225-0522-8.ch018

Eloy, S., Dias, M. S., Lopes, P. F., & Vilar, E. (2016). Digital Technologies in Architecture and Engineering: Exploring an Engaged Interaction within Curricula. In D. Fonseca & E. Redondo (Eds.), *Handbook of Research on Applied E-Learning in Engineering and Architecture Education* (pp. 368–402). Hershey, PA: IGI Global. doi:10.4018/978-1-4666-8803-2.ch017

Estrela, V. V., Magalhães, H. A., & Saotome, O. (2016). Total Variation Applications in Computer Vision. In N. Kamila (Ed.), *Handbook of Research on Emerging Perspectives in Intelligent Pattern Recognition, Analysis, and Image Processing* (pp. 41–64). Hershey, PA: IGI Global. doi:10.4018/978-1-4666-8654-0.ch002

Filipovic, N., Radovic, M., Nikolic, D. D., Saveljic, I., Milosevic, Z., Exarchos, T. P., ... Parodi, O. (2016). Computer Predictive Model for Plaque Formation and Progression in the Artery. In D. Fotiadis (Ed.), *Handbook of Research on Trends in the Diagnosis and Treatment of Chronic Conditions* (pp. 279–300). Hershey, PA: IGI Global. doi:10.4018/978-1-4666-8828-5.ch013

Fisher, R. L. (2018). Computer-Assisted Indian Matrimonial Services. In M. Khosrow-Pour, D.B.A. (Ed.), Encyclopedia of Information Science and Technology, Fourth Edition (pp. 4136-4145). Hershey, PA: IGI Global. doi:10.4018/978-1-5225-2255-3.ch358

Fleenor, H. G., & Hodhod, R. (2016). Assessment of Learning and Technology: Computer Science Education. In V. Wang (Ed.), *Handbook of Research on Learning Outcomes and Opportunities in the Digital Age* (pp. 51–78). Hershey, PA: IGI Global. doi:10.4018/978-1-4666-9577-1.ch003

García-Valcárcel, A., & Mena, J. (2016). Information Technology as a Way To Support Collaborative Learning: What In-Service Teachers Think, Know and Do. *Journal of Information Technology Research*, *9*(1), 1–17. doi:10.4018/JITR.2016010101

Gardner-McCune, C., & Jimenez, Y. (2017). Historical App Developers: Integrating CS into K-12 through Cross-Disciplinary Projects. In Y. Rankin & J. Thomas (Eds.), *Moving Students of Color from Consumers to Producers of Technology* (pp. 85–112). Hershey, PA: IGI Global. doi:10.4018/978-1-5225-2005-4.ch005

Garvey, G. P. (2016). Exploring Perception, Cognition, and Neural Pathways of Stereo Vision and the Split–Brain Human Computer Interface. In A. Ursyn (Ed.), *Knowledge Visualization and Visual Literacy in Science Education* (pp. 28–76). Hershey, PA: IGI Global. doi:10.4018/978-1-5225-0480-1.ch002

Ghafele, R., & Gibert, B. (2018). Open Growth: The Economic Impact of Open Source Software in the USA. In M. Khosrow-Pour (Ed.), *Optimizing Contemporary Application and Processes in Open Source Software* (pp. 164–197). Hershey, PA: IGI Global. doi:10.4018/978-1-5225-5314-4.ch007

Ghobakhloo, M., & Azar, A. (2018). Information Technology Resources, the Organizational Capability of Lean-Agile Manufacturing, and Business Performance. *Information Resources Management Journal*, *31*(2), 47–74. doi:10.4018/IRMJ.2018040103

Gianni, M., & Gotzamani, K. (2016). Integrated Management Systems and Information Management Systems: Common Threads. In P. Papajorgji, F. Pinet, A. Guimarães, & J. Papathanasiou (Eds.), *Automated Enterprise Systems for Maximizing Business Performance* (pp. 195–214). Hershey, PA: IGI Global. doi:10.4018/978-1-4666-8841-4.ch011

Gikandi, J. W. (2017). Computer-Supported Collaborative Learning and Assessment: A Strategy for Developing Online Learning Communities in Continuing Education. In J. Keengwe & G. Onchwari (Eds.), *Handbook of Research on Learner-Centered Pedagogy in Teacher Education and Professional Development* (pp. 309–333). Hershey, PA: IGI Global. doi:10.4018/978-1-5225-0892-2.ch017

Gokhale, A. A., & Machina, K. F. (2017). Development of a Scale to Measure Attitudes toward Information Technology. In L. Tomei (Ed.), *Exploring the New Era of Technology-Infused Education* (pp. 49–64). Hershey, PA: IGI Global. doi:10.4018/978-1-5225-1709-2.ch004

Grace, A., O'Donoghue, J., Mahony, C., Heffernan, T., Molony, D., & Carroll, T. (2016). Computerized Decision Support Systems for Multimorbidity Care: An Urgent Call for Research and Development. In M. Cruz-Cunha, I. Miranda, R. Martinho, & R. Rijo (Eds.), *Encyclopedia of E-Health and Telemedicine* (pp. 486–494). Hershey, PA: IGI Global. doi:10.4018/978-1-4666-9978-6.ch038

Gupta, A., & Singh, O. (2016). Computer Aided Modeling and Finite Element Analysis of Human Elbow. *International Journal of Biomedical and Clinical Engineering*, *5*(1), 31–38. doi:10.4018/IJBCE.2016010104

H., S. K. (2016). Classification of Cybercrimes and Punishments under the Information Technology Act, 2000. In S. Geetha, & A. Phamila (Eds.), *Combating Security Breaches and Criminal Activity in the Digital Sphere* (pp. 57-66). Hershey, PA: IGI Global. doi:10.4018/978-1-5225-0193-0.ch004

Hafeez-Baig, A., Gururajan, R., & Wickramasinghe, N. (2017). Readiness as a Novel Construct of Readiness Acceptance Model (RAM) for the Wireless Handheld Technology. In N. Wickramasinghe (Ed.), *Handbook of Research on Healthcare Administration and Management* (pp. 578–595). Hershey, PA: IGI Global. doi:10.4018/978-1-5225-0920-2.ch035

Hanafizadeh, P., Ghandchi, S., & Asgarimehr, M. (2017). Impact of Information Technology on Lifestyle: A Literature Review and Classification. *International Journal of Virtual Communities and Social Networking*, *9*(2), 1–23. doi:10.4018/IJVCSN.2017040101

Harlow, D. B., Dwyer, H., Hansen, A. K., Hill, C., Iveland, A., Leak, A. E., & Franklin, D. M. (2016). Computer Programming in Elementary and Middle School: Connections across Content. In M. Urban & D. Falvo (Eds.), *Improving K-12 STEM Education Outcomes through Technological Integration* (pp. 337–361). Hershey, PA: IGI Global. doi:10.4018/978-1-4666-9616-7.ch015

Haseski, H. İ., Ilic, U., & Tuğtekin, U. (2018). Computational Thinking in Educational Digital Games: An Assessment Tool Proposal. In H. Ozcinar, G. Wong, & H. Ozturk (Eds.), *Teaching Computational Thinking in Primary Education* (pp. 256–287). Hershey, PA: IGI Global. doi:10.4018/978-1-5225-3200-2.ch013

Hee, W. J., Jalleh, G., Lai, H., & Lin, C. (2017). E-Commerce and IT Projects: Evaluation and Management Issues in Australian and Taiwanese Hospitals. *International Journal of Public Health Management and Ethics*, 2(1), 69–90. doi:10.4018/IJPHME.2017010104

Hernandez, A. A. (2017). Green Information Technology Usage: Awareness and Practices of Philippine IT Professionals. *International Journal of Enterprise Information Systems*, 13(4), 90–103. doi:10.4018/IJEIS.2017100106

Hernandez, A. A., & Ona, S. E. (2016). Green IT Adoption: Lessons from the Philippines Business Process Outsourcing Industry. *International Journal of Social Ecology and Sustainable Development*, 7(1), 1–34. doi:10.4018/IJSESD.2016010101

Hernandez, M. A., Marin, E. C., Garcia-Rodriguez, J., Azorin-Lopez, J., & Cazorla, M. (2017). Automatic Learning Improves Human-Robot Interaction in Productive Environments: A Review. *International Journal of Computer Vision and Image Processing*, 7(3), 65–75. doi:10.4018/IJCVIP.2017070106

Horne-Popp, L. M., Tessone, E. B., & Welker, J. (2018). If You Build It, They Will Come: Creating a Library Statistics Dashboard for Decision-Making. In L. Costello & M. Powers (Eds.), *Developing In-House Digital Tools in Library Spaces* (pp. 177–203). Hershey, PA: IGI Global. doi:10.4018/978-1-5225-2676-6.ch009

Hossan, C. G., & Ryan, J. C. (2016). Factors Affecting e-Government Technology Adoption Behaviour in a Voluntary Environment. *International Journal of Electronic Government Research*, 12(1), 24–49. doi:10.4018/IJEGR.2016010102

Hu, H., Hu, P. J., & Al-Gahtani, S. S. (2017). User Acceptance of Computer Technology at Work in Arabian Culture: A Model Comparison Approach. In M. Khosrow-Pour (Ed.), *Handbook of Research on Technology Adoption, Social Policy, and Global Integration* (pp. 205–228). Hershey, PA: IGI Global. doi:10.4018/978-1-5225-2668-1.ch011

Huie, C. P. (2016). Perceptions of Business Intelligence Professionals about Factors Related to Business Intelligence input in Decision Making. *International Journal of Business Analytics*, *3*(3), 1–24. doi:10.4018/IJBAN.2016070101

Hung, S., Huang, W., Yen, D. C., Chang, S., & Lu, C. (2016). Effect of Information Service Competence and Contextual Factors on the Effectiveness of Strategic Information Systems Planning in Hospitals. *Journal of Global Information Management*, *24*(1), 14–36. doi:10.4018/JGIM.2016010102

Ifinedo, P. (2017). Using an Extended Theory of Planned Behavior to Study Nurses' Adoption of Healthcare Information Systems in Nova Scotia. *International Journal of Technology Diffusion*, *8*(1), 1–17. doi:10.4018/IJTD.2017010101

Ilie, V., & Sneha, S. (2018). A Three Country Study for Understanding Physicians' Engagement With Electronic Information Resources Pre and Post System Implementation. *Journal of Global Information Management*, *26*(2), 48–73. doi:10.4018/JGIM.2018040103

Inoue-Smith, Y. (2017). Perceived Ease in Using Technology Predicts Teacher Candidates' Preferences for Online Resources. *International Journal of Online Pedagogy and Course Design*, *7*(3), 17–28. doi:10.4018/IJOPCD.2017070102

Islam, A. A. (2016). Development and Validation of the Technology Adoption and Gratification (TAG) Model in Higher Education: A Cross-Cultural Study Between Malaysia and China. *International Journal of Technology and Human Interaction*, *12*(3), 78–105. doi:10.4018/IJTHI.2016070106

Islam, A. Y. (2017). Technology Satisfaction in an Academic Context: Moderating Effect of Gender. In A. Mesquita (Ed.), *Research Paradigms and Contemporary Perspectives on Human-Technology Interaction* (pp. 187–211). Hershey, PA: IGI Global. doi:10.4018/978-1-5225-1868-6.ch009

Jamil, G. L., & Jamil, C. C. (2017). Information and Knowledge Management Perspective Contributions for Fashion Studies: Observing Logistics and Supply Chain Management Processes. In G. Jamil, A. Soares, & C. Pessoa (Eds.), *Handbook of Research on Information Management for Effective Logistics and Supply Chains* (pp. 199–221). Hershey, PA: IGI Global. doi:10.4018/978-1-5225-0973-8.ch011

Jamil, G. L., Jamil, L. C., Vieira, A. A., & Xavier, A. J. (2016). Challenges in Modelling Healthcare Services: A Study Case of Information Architecture Perspectives. In G. Jamil, J. Poças Rascão, F. Ribeiro, & A. Malheiro da Silva (Eds.), *Handbook of Research on Information Architecture and Management in Modern Organizations* (pp. 1–23). Hershey, PA: IGI Global. doi:10.4018/978-1-4666-8637-3.ch001

Janakova, M. (2018). Big Data and Simulations for the Solution of Controversies in Small Businesses. In M. Khosrow-Pour, D.B.A. (Ed.), Encyclopedia of Information Science and Technology, Fourth Edition (pp. 6907-6915). Hershey, PA: IGI Global. doi:10.4018/978-1-5225-2255-3.ch598

Jha, D. G. (2016). Preparing for Information Technology Driven Changes. In S. Tiwari & L. Nafees (Eds.), *Innovative Management Education Pedagogies for Preparing Next-Generation Leaders* (pp. 258–274). Hershey, PA: IGI Global. doi:10.4018/978-1-4666-9691-4.ch015

Jhawar, A., & Garg, S. K. (2018). Logistics Improvement by Investment in Information Technology Using System Dynamics. In A. Azar & S. Vaidyanathan (Eds.), *Advances in System Dynamics and Control* (pp. 528–567). Hershey, PA: IGI Global. doi:10.4018/978-1-5225-4077-9.ch017

Kalelioğlu, F., Gülbahar, Y., & Doğan, D. (2018). Teaching How to Think Like a Programmer: Emerging Insights. In H. Ozcinar, G. Wong, & H. Ozturk (Eds.), *Teaching Computational Thinking in Primary Education* (pp. 18–35). Hershey, PA: IGI Global. doi:10.4018/978-1-5225-3200-2.ch002

Kamberi, S. (2017). A Girls-Only Online Virtual World Environment and its Implications for Game-Based Learning. In A. Stricker, C. Calongne, B. Truman, & F. Arenas (Eds.), *Integrating an Awareness of Selfhood and Society into Virtual Learning* (pp. 74–95). Hershey, PA: IGI Global. doi:10.4018/978-1-5225-2182-2.ch006

Kamel, S., & Rizk, N. (2017). ICT Strategy Development: From Design to Implementation – Case of Egypt. In C. Howard & K. Hargiss (Eds.), *Strategic Information Systems and Technologies in Modern Organizations* (pp. 239–257). Hershey, PA: IGI Global. doi:10.4018/978-1-5225-1680-4.ch010

Kamel, S. H. (2018). The Potential Role of the Software Industry in Supporting Economic Development. In M. Khosrow-Pour, D.B.A. (Ed.), Encyclopedia of Information Science and Technology, Fourth Edition (pp. 7259-7269). Hershey, PA: IGI Global. doi:10.4018/978-1-5225-2255-3.ch631

Karon, R. (2016). Utilisation of Health Information Systems for Service Delivery in the Namibian Environment. In T. Iyamu & A. Tatnall (Eds.), *Maximizing Healthcare Delivery and Management through Technology Integration* (pp. 169–183). Hershey, PA: IGI Global. doi:10.4018/978-1-4666-9446-0.ch011

Kawata, S. (2018). Computer-Assisted Parallel Program Generation. In M. Khosrow-Pour, D.B.A. (Ed.), Encyclopedia of Information Science and Technology, Fourth Edition (pp. 4583-4593). Hershey, PA: IGI Global. doi:10.4018/978-1-5225-2255-3.ch398

Khanam, S., Siddiqui, J., & Talib, F. (2016). A DEMATEL Approach for Prioritizing the TQM Enablers and IT Resources in the Indian ICT Industry. *International Journal of Applied Management Sciences and Engineering, 3*(1), 11–29. doi:10.4018/IJAMSE.2016010102

Khari, M., Shrivastava, G., Gupta, S., & Gupta, R. (2017). Role of Cyber Security in Today's Scenario. In R. Kumar, P. Pattnaik, & P. Pandey (Eds.), *Detecting and Mitigating Robotic Cyber Security Risks* (pp. 177–191). Hershey, PA: IGI Global. doi:10.4018/978-1-5225-2154-9.ch013

Khouja, M., Rodriguez, I. B., Ben Halima, Y., & Moalla, S. (2018). IT Governance in Higher Education Institutions: A Systematic Literature Review. *International Journal of Human Capital and Information Technology Professionals, 9*(2), 52–67. doi:10.4018/IJHCITP.2018040104

Kim, S., Chang, M., Choi, N., Park, J., & Kim, H. (2016). The Direct and Indirect Effects of Computer Uses on Student Success in Math. *International Journal of Cyber Behavior, Psychology and Learning, 6*(3), 48–64. doi:10.4018/IJCBPL.2016070104

Kiourt, C., Pavlidis, G., Koutsoudis, A., & Kalles, D. (2017). Realistic Simulation of Cultural Heritage. *International Journal of Computational Methods in Heritage Science, 1*(1), 10–40. doi:10.4018/IJCMHS.2017010102

Korikov, A., & Krivtsov, O. (2016). System of People-Computer: On the Way of Creation of Human-Oriented Interface. In V. Mkrttchian, A. Bershadsky, A. Bozhday, M. Kataev, & S. Kataev (Eds.), *Handbook of Research on Estimation and Control Techniques in E-Learning Systems* (pp. 458–470). Hershey, PA: IGI Global. doi:10.4018/978-1-4666-9489-7.ch032

Köse, U. (2017). An Augmented-Reality-Based Intelligent Mobile Application for Open Computer Education. In G. Kurubacak & H. Altinpulluk (Eds.), *Mobile Technologies and Augmented Reality in Open Education* (pp. 154–174). Hershey, PA: IGI Global. doi:10.4018/978-1-5225-2110-5.ch008

Lahmiri, S. (2018). Information Technology Outsourcing Risk Factors and Provider Selection. In M. Gupta, R. Sharman, J. Walp, & P. Mulgund (Eds.), *Information Technology Risk Management and Compliance in Modern Organizations* (pp. 214–228). Hershey, PA: IGI Global. doi:10.4018/978-1-5225-2604-9.ch008

Landriscina, F. (2017). Computer-Supported Imagination: The Interplay Between Computer and Mental Simulation in Understanding Scientific Concepts. In I. Levin & D. Tsybulsky (Eds.), *Digital Tools and Solutions for Inquiry-Based STEM Learning* (pp. 33–60). Hershey, PA: IGI Global. doi:10.4018/978-1-5225-2525-7.ch002

Lau, S. K., Winley, G. K., Leung, N. K., Tsang, N., & Lau, S. Y. (2016). An Exploratory Study of Expectation in IT Skills in a Developing Nation: Vietnam. *Journal of Global Information Management, 24*(1), 1–13. doi:10.4018/JGIM.2016010101

Lavranos, C., Kostagiolas, P., & Papadatos, J. (2016). Information Retrieval Technologies and the "Realities" of Music Information Seeking. In I. Deliyannis, P. Kostagiolas, & C. Banou (Eds.), *Experimental Multimedia Systems for Interactivity and Strategic Innovation* (pp. 102–121). Hershey, PA: IGI Global. doi:10.4018/978-1-4666-8659-5.ch005

Lee, W. W. (2018). Ethical Computing Continues From Problem to Solution. In M. Khosrow-Pour, D.B.A. (Ed.), Encyclopedia of Information Science and Technology, Fourth Edition (pp. 4884-4897). Hershey, PA: IGI Global. doi:10.4018/978-1-5225-2255-3.ch423

Lehto, M. (2016). Cyber Security Education and Research in the Finland's Universities and Universities of Applied Sciences. *International Journal of Cyber Warfare & Terrorism, 6*(2), 15–31. doi:10.4018/IJCWT.2016040102

Lin, C., Jalleh, G., & Huang, Y. (2016). Evaluating and Managing Electronic Commerce and Outsourcing Projects in Hospitals. In A. Dwivedi (Ed.), *Reshaping Medical Practice and Care with Health Information Systems* (pp. 132–172). Hershey, PA: IGI Global. doi:10.4018/978-1-4666-9870-3.ch005

Lin, S., Chen, S., & Chuang, S. (2017). Perceived Innovation and Quick Response Codes in an Online-to-Offline E-Commerce Service Model. *International Journal of E-Adoption, 9*(2), 1–16. doi:10.4018/IJEA.2017070101

Liu, M., Wang, Y., Xu, W., & Liu, L. (2017). Automated Scoring of Chinese Engineering Students' English Essays. *International Journal of Distance Education Technologies, 15*(1), 52–68. doi:10.4018/IJDET.2017010104

Luciano, E. M., Wiedenhöft, G. C., Macadar, M. A., & Pinheiro dos Santos, F. (2016). Information Technology Governance Adoption: Understanding its Expectations Through the Lens of Organizational Citizenship. *International Journal of IT/Business Alignment and Governance, 7*(2), 22-32. doi:10.4018/IJITBAG.2016070102

Mabe, L. K., & Oladele, O. I. (2017). Application of Information Communication Technologies for Agricultural Development through Extension Services: A Review. In T. Tossy (Ed.), *Information Technology Integration for Socio-Economic Development* (pp. 52–101). Hershey, PA: IGI Global. doi:10.4018/978-1-5225-0539-6.ch003

Manogaran, G., Thota, C., & Lopez, D. (2018). Human-Computer Interaction With Big Data Analytics. In D. Lopez & M. Durai (Eds.), *HCI Challenges and Privacy Preservation in Big Data Security* (pp. 1–22). Hershey, PA: IGI Global. doi:10.4018/978-1-5225-2863-0.ch001

Margolis, J., Goode, J., & Flapan, J. (2017). A Critical Crossroads for Computer Science for All: "Identifying Talent" or "Building Talent," and What Difference Does It Make? In Y. Rankin & J. Thomas (Eds.), *Moving Students of Color from Consumers to Producers of Technology* (pp. 1–23). Hershey, PA: IGI Global. doi:10.4018/978-1-5225-2005-4.ch001

Mbale, J. (2018). Computer Centres Resource Cloud Elasticity-Scalability (CRECES): Copperbelt University Case Study. In S. Aljawarneh & M. Malhotra (Eds.), *Critical Research on Scalability and Security Issues in Virtual Cloud Environments* (pp. 48–70). Hershey, PA: IGI Global. doi:10.4018/978-1-5225-3029-9.ch003

McKee, J. (2018). The Right Information: The Key to Effective Business Planning. In *Business Architectures for Risk Assessment and Strategic Planning: Emerging Research and Opportunities* (pp. 38–52). Hershey, PA: IGI Global. doi:10.4018/978-1-5225-3392-4.ch003

Mensah, I. K., & Mi, J. (2018). Determinants of Intention to Use Local E-Government Services in Ghana: The Perspective of Local Government Workers. *International Journal of Technology Diffusion*, *9*(2), 41–60. doi:10.4018/IJTD.2018040103

Mohamed, J. H. (2018). Scientograph-Based Visualization of Computer Forensics Research Literature. In J. Jeyasekar & P. Saravanan (Eds.), *Innovations in Measuring and Evaluating Scientific Information* (pp. 148–162). Hershey, PA: IGI Global. doi:10.4018/978-1-5225-3457-0.ch010

Moore, R. L., & Johnson, N. (2017). Earning a Seat at the Table: How IT Departments Can Partner in Organizational Change and Innovation. *International Journal of Knowledge-Based Organizations*, *7*(2), 1–12. doi:10.4018/IJKBO.2017040101

Mtebe, J. S., & Kissaka, M. M. (2016). Enhancing the Quality of Computer Science Education with MOOCs in Sub-Saharan Africa. In J. Keengwe & G. Onchwari (Eds.), *Handbook of Research on Active Learning and the Flipped Classroom Model in the Digital Age* (pp. 366–377). Hershey, PA: IGI Global. doi:10.4018/978-1-4666-9680-8.ch019

Mukul, M. K., & Bhattaharyya, S. (2017). Brain-Machine Interface: Human-Computer Interaction. In E. Noughabi, B. Raahemi, A. Albadvi, & B. Far (Eds.), *Handbook of Research on Data Science for Effective Healthcare Practice and Administration* (pp. 417–443). Hershey, PA: IGI Global. doi:10.4018/978-1-5225-2515-8.ch018

Na, L. (2017). Library and Information Science Education and Graduate Programs in Academic Libraries. In L. Ruan, Q. Zhu, & Y. Ye (Eds.), *Academic Library Development and Administration in China* (pp. 218–229). Hershey, PA: IGI Global. doi:10.4018/978-1-5225-0550-1.ch013

Nabavi, A., Taghavi-Fard, M. T., Hanafizadeh, P., & Taghva, M. R. (2016). Information Technology Continuance Intention: A Systematic Literature Review. *International Journal of E-Business Research*, *12*(1), 58–95. doi:10.4018/IJEBR.2016010104

Nath, R., & Murthy, V. N. (2018). What Accounts for the Differences in Internet Diffusion Rates Around the World? In M. Khosrow-Pour, D.B.A. (Ed.), Encyclopedia of Information Science and Technology, Fourth Edition (pp. 8095-8104). Hershey, PA: IGI Global. doi:10.4018/978-1-5225-2255-3.ch705

Nedelko, Z., & Potocan, V. (2018). The Role of Emerging Information Technologies for Supporting Supply Chain Management. In M. Khosrow-Pour, D.B.A. (Ed.), Encyclopedia of Information Science and Technology, Fourth Edition (pp. 5559-5569). Hershey, PA: IGI Global. doi:10.4018/978-1-5225-2255-3.ch483

Ngafeeson, M. N. (2018). User Resistance to Health Information Technology. In M. Khosrow-Pour, D.B.A. (Ed.), Encyclopedia of Information Science and Technology, Fourth Edition (pp. 3816-3825). Hershey, PA: IGI Global. doi:10.4018/978-1-5225-2255-3.ch331

Nozari, H., Najafi, S. E., Jafari-Eskandari, M., & Aliahmadi, A. (2016). Providing a Model for Virtual Project Management with an Emphasis on IT Projects. In C. Graham (Ed.), *Strategic Management and Leadership for Systems Development in Virtual Spaces* (pp. 43–63). Hershey, PA: IGI Global. doi:10.4018/978-1-4666-9688-4.ch003

Nurdin, N., Stockdale, R., & Scheepers, H. (2016). Influence of Organizational Factors in the Sustainability of E-Government: A Case Study of Local E-Government in Indonesia. In I. Sodhi (Ed.), *Trends, Prospects, and Challenges in Asian E-Governance* (pp. 281–323). Hershey, PA: IGI Global. doi:10.4018/978-1-4666-9536-8.ch014

Odagiri, K. (2017). Introduction of Individual Technology to Constitute the Current Internet. In *Strategic Policy-Based Network Management in Contemporary Organizations* (pp. 20–96). Hershey, PA: IGI Global. doi:10.4018/978-1-68318-003-6.ch003

Okike, E. U. (2018). Computer Science and Prison Education. In I. Biao (Ed.), *Strategic Learning Ideologies in Prison Education Programs* (pp. 246–264). Hershey, PA: IGI Global. doi:10.4018/978-1-5225-2909-5.ch012

Olelewe, C. J., & Nwafor, I. P. (2017). Level of Computer Appreciation Skills Acquired for Sustainable Development by Secondary School Students in Nsukka LGA of Enugu State, Nigeria. In C. Ayo & V. Mbarika (Eds.), *Sustainable ICT Adoption and Integration for Socio-Economic Development* (pp. 214–233). Hershey, PA: IGI Global. doi:10.4018/978-1-5225-2565-3.ch010

Oliveira, M., Maçada, A. C., Curado, C., & Nodari, F. (2017). Infrastructure Profiles and Knowledge Sharing. *International Journal of Technology and Human Interaction, 13*(3), 1–12. doi:10.4018/IJTHI.2017070101

Otarkhani, A., Shokouhyar, S., & Pour, S. S. (2017). Analyzing the Impact of Governance of Enterprise IT on Hospital Performance: Tehran's (Iran) Hospitals – A Case Study. *International Journal of Healthcare Information Systems and Informatics, 12*(3), 1–20. doi:10.4018/IJHISI.2017070101

Otunla, A. O., & Amuda, C. O. (2018). Nigerian Undergraduate Students' Computer Competencies and Use of Information Technology Tools and Resources for Study Skills and Habits' Enhancement. In M. Khosrow-Pour, D.B.A. (Ed.), Encyclopedia of Information Science and Technology, Fourth Edition (pp. 2303-2313). Hershey, PA: IGI Global. doi:10.4018/978-1-5225-2255-3.ch200

Özçınar, H. (2018). A Brief Discussion on Incentives and Barriers to Computational Thinking Education. In H. Ozcinar, G. Wong, & H. Ozturk (Eds.), *Teaching Computational Thinking in Primary Education* (pp. 1–17). Hershey, PA: IGI Global. doi:10.4018/978-1-5225-3200-2.ch001

Pandey, J. M., Garg, S., Mishra, P., & Mishra, B. P. (2017). Computer Based Psychological Interventions: Subject to the Efficacy of Psychological Services. *International Journal of Computers in Clinical Practice, 2*(1), 25–33. doi:10.4018/IJCCP.2017010102

Parry, V. K., & Lind, M. L. (2016). Alignment of Business Strategy and Information Technology Considering Information Technology Governance, Project Portfolio Control, and Risk Management. *International Journal of Information Technology Project Management, 7*(4), 21–37. doi:10.4018/IJITPM.2016100102

Patro, C. (2017). Impulsion of Information Technology on Human Resource Practices. In P. Ordóñez de Pablos (Ed.), *Managerial Strategies and Solutions for Business Success in Asia* (pp. 231–254). Hershey, PA: IGI Global. doi:10.4018/978-1-5225-1886-0.ch013

Patro, C. S., & Raghunath, K. M. (2017). Information Technology Paraphernalia for Supply Chain Management Decisions. In M. Tavana (Ed.), *Enterprise Information Systems and the Digitalization of Business Functions* (pp. 294–320). Hershey, PA: IGI Global. doi:10.4018/978-1-5225-2382-6.ch014

Paul, P. K. (2016). Cloud Computing: An Agent of Promoting Interdisciplinary Sciences, Especially Information Science and I-Schools – Emerging Techno-Educational Scenario. In L. Chao (Ed.), *Handbook of Research on Cloud-Based STEM Education for Improved Learning Outcomes* (pp. 247–258). Hershey, PA: IGI Global. doi:10.4018/978-1-4666-9924-3.ch016

Paul, P. K. (2018). The Context of IST for Solid Information Retrieval and Infrastructure Building: Study of Developing Country. *International Journal of Information Retrieval Research*, 8(1), 86–100. doi:10.4018/IJIRR.2018010106

Paul, P. K., & Chatterjee, D. (2018). iSchools Promoting "Information Science and Technology" (IST) Domain Towards Community, Business, and Society With Contemporary Worldwide Trend and Emerging Potentialities in India. In M. Khosrow-Pour, D.B.A. (Ed.), Encyclopedia of Information Science and Technology, Fourth Edition (pp. 4723-4735). Hershey, PA: IGI Global. doi:10.4018/978-1-5225-2255-3.ch410

Pessoa, C. R., & Marques, M. E. (2017). Information Technology and Communication Management in Supply Chain Management. In G. Jamil, A. Soares, & C. Pessoa (Eds.), *Handbook of Research on Information Management for Effective Logistics and Supply Chains* (pp. 23–33). Hershey, PA: IGI Global. doi:10.4018/978-1-5225-0973-8.ch002

Pineda, R. G. (2016). Where the Interaction Is Not: Reflections on the Philosophy of Human-Computer Interaction. *International Journal of Art, Culture and Design Technologies*, 5(1), 1–12. doi:10.4018/IJACDT.2016010101

Pineda, R. G. (2018). Remediating Interaction: Towards a Philosophy of Human-Computer Relationship. In M. Khosrow-Pour (Ed.), *Enhancing Art, Culture, and Design With Technological Integration* (pp. 75–98). Hershey, PA: IGI Global. doi:10.4018/978-1-5225-5023-5.ch004

Poikela, P., & Vuojärvi, H. (2016). Learning ICT-Mediated Communication through Computer-Based Simulations. In M. Cruz-Cunha, I. Miranda, R. Martinho, & R. Rijo (Eds.), *Encyclopedia of E-Health and Telemedicine* (pp. 674–687). Hershey, PA: IGI Global. doi:10.4018/978-1-4666-9978-6.ch052

Qian, Y. (2017). Computer Simulation in Higher Education: Affordances, Opportunities, and Outcomes. In P. Vu, S. Fredrickson, & C. Moore (Eds.), *Handbook of Research on Innovative Pedagogies and Technologies for Online Learning in Higher Education* (pp. 236–262). Hershey, PA: IGI Global. doi:10.4018/978-1-5225-1851-8.ch011

Radant, O., Colomo-Palacios, R., & Stantchev, V. (2016). Factors for the Management of Scarce Human Resources and Highly Skilled Employees in IT-Departments: A Systematic Review. *Journal of Information Technology Research*, *9*(1), 65–82. doi:10.4018/JITR.2016010105

Rahman, N. (2016). Toward Achieving Environmental Sustainability in the Computer Industry. *International Journal of Green Computing*, *7*(1), 37–54. doi:10.4018/IJGC.2016010103

Rahman, N. (2017). Lessons from a Successful Data Warehousing Project Management. *International Journal of Information Technology Project Management*, *8*(4), 30–45. doi:10.4018/IJITPM.2017100103

Rahman, N. (2018). Environmental Sustainability in the Computer Industry for Competitive Advantage. In M. Khosrow-Pour (Ed.), *Green Computing Strategies for Competitive Advantage and Business Sustainability* (pp. 110–130). Hershey, PA: IGI Global. doi:10.4018/978-1-5225-5017-4.ch006

Rajh, A., & Pavetic, T. (2017). Computer Generated Description as the Required Digital Competence in Archival Profession. *International Journal of Digital Literacy and Digital Competence*, *8*(1), 36–49. doi:10.4018/IJDLDC.2017010103

Raman, A., & Goyal, D. P. (2017). Extending IMPLEMENT Framework for Enterprise Information Systems Implementation to Information System Innovation. In M. Tavana (Ed.), *Enterprise Information Systems and the Digitalization of Business Functions* (pp. 137–177). Hershey, PA: IGI Global. doi:10.4018/978-1-5225-2382-6.ch007

Rao, Y. S., Rauta, A. K., Saini, H., & Panda, T. C. (2017). Mathematical Model for Cyber Attack in Computer Network. *International Journal of Business Data Communications and Networking*, *13*(1), 58–65. doi:10.4018/IJBDCN.2017010105

Rapaport, W. J. (2018). Syntactic Semantics and the Proper Treatment of Computationalism. In M. Danesi (Ed.), *Empirical Research on Semiotics and Visual Rhetoric* (pp. 128–176). Hershey, PA: IGI Global. doi:10.4018/978-1-5225-5622-0.ch007

Raut, R., Priyadarshinee, P., & Jha, M. (2017). Understanding the Mediation Effect of Cloud Computing Adoption in Indian Organization: Integrating TAM-TOE- Risk Model. *International Journal of Service Science, Management, Engineering, and Technology*, 8(3), 40–59. doi:10.4018/IJSSMET.2017070103

Regan, E. A., & Wang, J. (2016). Realizing the Value of EHR Systems Critical Success Factors. *International Journal of Healthcare Information Systems and Informatics*, 11(3), 1–18. doi:10.4018/IJHISI.2016070101

Rezaie, S., Mirabedini, S. J., & Abtahi, A. (2018). Designing a Model for Implementation of Business Intelligence in the Banking Industry. *International Journal of Enterprise Information Systems*, 14(1), 77–103. doi:10.4018/IJEIS.2018010105

Rezende, D. A. (2016). Digital City Projects: Information and Public Services Offered by Chicago (USA) and Curitiba (Brazil). *International Journal of Knowledge Society Research*, 7(3), 16–30. doi:10.4018/IJKSR.2016070102

Rezende, D. A. (2018). Strategic Digital City Projects: Innovative Information and Public Services Offered by Chicago (USA) and Curitiba (Brazil). In M. Lytras, L. Daniela, & A. Visvizi (Eds.), *Enhancing Knowledge Discovery and Innovation in the Digital Era* (pp. 204–223). Hershey, PA: IGI Global. doi:10.4018/978-1-5225-4191-2.ch012

Riabov, V. V. (2016). Teaching Online Computer-Science Courses in LMS and Cloud Environment. *International Journal of Quality Assurance in Engineering and Technology Education*, 5(4), 12–41. doi:10.4018/IJQAETE.2016100102

Ricordel, V., Wang, J., Da Silva, M. P., & Le Callet, P. (2016). 2D and 3D Visual Attention for Computer Vision: Concepts, Measurement, and Modeling. In R. Pal (Ed.), *Innovative Research in Attention Modeling and Computer Vision Applications* (pp. 1–44). Hershey, PA: IGI Global. doi:10.4018/978-1-4666-8723-3.ch001

Rodriguez, A., Rico-Diaz, A. J., Rabuñal, J. R., & Gestal, M. (2017). Fish Tracking with Computer Vision Techniques: An Application to Vertical Slot Fishways. In M. S., & V. V. (Eds.), Multi-Core Computer Vision and Image Processing for Intelligent Applications (pp. 74-104). Hershey, PA: IGI Global. doi:10.4018/978-1-5225-0889-2.ch003

Romero, J. A. (2018). Sustainable Advantages of Business Value of Information Technology. In M. Khosrow-Pour, D.B.A. (Ed.), Encyclopedia of Information Science and Technology, Fourth Edition (pp. 923-929). Hershey, PA: IGI Global. doi:10.4018/978-1-5225-2255-3.ch079

Romero, J. A. (2018). The Always-On Business Model and Competitive Advantage. In N. Bajgoric (Ed.), *Always-On Enterprise Information Systems for Modern Organizations* (pp. 23–40). Hershey, PA: IGI Global. doi:10.4018/978-1-5225-3704-5.ch002

Rosen, Y. (2018). Computer Agent Technologies in Collaborative Learning and Assessment. In M. Khosrow-Pour, D.B.A. (Ed.), Encyclopedia of Information Science and Technology, Fourth Edition (pp. 2402-2410). Hershey, PA: IGI Global. doi:10.4018/978-1-5225-2255-3.ch209

Rosen, Y., & Mosharraf, M. (2016). Computer Agent Technologies in Collaborative Assessments. In Y. Rosen, S. Ferrara, & M. Mosharraf (Eds.), *Handbook of Research on Technology Tools for Real-World Skill Development* (pp. 319–343). Hershey, PA: IGI Global. doi:10.4018/978-1-4666-9441-5.ch012

Roy, D. (2018). Success Factors of Adoption of Mobile Applications in Rural India: Effect of Service Characteristics on Conceptual Model. In M. Khosrow-Pour (Ed.), *Green Computing Strategies for Competitive Advantage and Business Sustainability* (pp. 211–238). Hershey, PA: IGI Global. doi:10.4018/978-1-5225-5017-4.ch010

Ruffin, T. R. (2016). Health Information Technology and Change. In V. Wang (Ed.), *Handbook of Research on Advancing Health Education through Technology* (pp. 259–285). Hershey, PA: IGI Global. doi:10.4018/978-1-4666-9494-1.ch012

Ruffin, T. R. (2016). Health Information Technology and Quality Management. *International Journal of Information Communication Technologies and Human Development*, 8(4), 56–72. doi:10.4018/IJICTHD.2016100105

Ruffin, T. R., & Hawkins, D. P. (2018). Trends in Health Care Information Technology and Informatics. In M. Khosrow-Pour, D.B.A. (Ed.), Encyclopedia of Information Science and Technology, Fourth Edition (pp. 3805-3815). Hershey, PA: IGI Global. doi:10.4018/978-1-5225-2255-3.ch330

Safari, M. R., & Jiang, Q. (2018). The Theory and Practice of IT Governance Maturity and Strategies Alignment: Evidence From Banking Industry. *Journal of Global Information Management*, 26(2), 127–146. doi:10.4018/JGIM.2018040106

Sahin, H. B., & Anagun, S. S. (2018). Educational Computer Games in Math Teaching: A Learning Culture. In E. Toprak & E. Kumtepe (Eds.), *Supporting Multiculturalism in Open and Distance Learning Spaces* (pp. 249–280). Hershey, PA: IGI Global. doi:10.4018/978-1-5225-3076-3.ch013

Sanna, A., & Valpreda, F. (2017). An Assessment of the Impact of a Collaborative Didactic Approach and Students' Background in Teaching Computer Animation. *International Journal of Information and Communication Technology Education*, *13*(4), 1–16. doi:10.4018/IJICTE.2017100101

Savita, K., Dominic, P., & Ramayah, T. (2016). The Drivers, Practices and Outcomes of Green Supply Chain Management: Insights from ISO14001 Manufacturing Firms in Malaysia. *International Journal of Information Systems and Supply Chain Management*, *9*(2), 35–60. doi:10.4018/IJISSCM.2016040103

Scott, A., Martin, A., & McAlear, F. (2017). Enhancing Participation in Computer Science among Girls of Color: An Examination of a Preparatory AP Computer Science Intervention. In Y. Rankin & J. Thomas (Eds.), *Moving Students of Color from Consumers to Producers of Technology* (pp. 62–84). Hershey, PA: IGI Global. doi:10.4018/978-1-5225-2005-4.ch004

Shahsavandi, E., Mayah, G., & Rahbari, H. (2016). Impact of E-Government on Transparency and Corruption in Iran. In I. Sodhi (Ed.), *Trends, Prospects, and Challenges in Asian E-Governance* (pp. 75–94). Hershey, PA: IGI Global. doi:10.4018/978-1-4666-9536-8.ch004

Siddoo, V., & Wongsai, N. (2017). Factors Influencing the Adoption of ISO/IEC 29110 in Thai Government Projects: A Case Study. *International Journal of Information Technologies and Systems Approach*, *10*(1), 22–44. doi:10.4018/IJITSA.2017010102

Sidorkina, I., & Rybakov, A. (2016). Computer-Aided Design as Carrier of Set Development Changes System in E-Course Engineering. In V. Mkrttchian, A. Bershadsky, A. Bozhday, M. Kataev, & S. Kataev (Eds.), *Handbook of Research on Estimation and Control Techniques in E-Learning Systems* (pp. 500–515). Hershey, PA: IGI Global. doi:10.4018/978-1-4666-9489-7.ch035

Sidorkina, I., & Rybakov, A. (2016). Creating Model of E-Course: As an Object of Computer-Aided Design. In V. Mkrttchian, A. Bershadsky, A. Bozhday, M. Kataev, & S. Kataev (Eds.), *Handbook of Research on Estimation and Control Techniques in E-Learning Systems* (pp. 286–297). Hershey, PA: IGI Global. doi:10.4018/978-1-4666-9489-7.ch019

Simões, A. (2017). Using Game Frameworks to Teach Computer Programming. In R. Alexandre Peixoto de Queirós & M. Pinto (Eds.), *Gamification-Based E-Learning Strategies for Computer Programming Education* (pp. 221–236). Hershey, PA: IGI Global. doi:10.4018/978-1-5225-1034-5.ch010

Sllame, A. M. (2017). Integrating LAB Work With Classes in Computer Network Courses. In H. Alphin Jr, R. Chan, & J. Lavine (Eds.), *The Future of Accessibility in International Higher Education* (pp. 253–275). Hershey, PA: IGI Global. doi:10.4018/978-1-5225-2560-8.ch015

Smirnov, A., Ponomarev, A., Shilov, N., Kashevnik, A., & Teslya, N. (2018). Ontology-Based Human-Computer Cloud for Decision Support: Architecture and Applications in Tourism. *International Journal of Embedded and Real-Time Communication Systems*, *9*(1), 1–19. doi:10.4018/IJERTCS.2018010101

Smith-Ditizio, A. A., & Smith, A. D. (2018). Computer Fraud Challenges and Its Legal Implications. In M. Khosrow-Pour, D.B.A. (Ed.), Encyclopedia of Information Science and Technology, Fourth Edition (pp. 4837-4848). Hershey, PA: IGI Global. doi:10.4018/978-1-5225-2255-3.ch419

Sohani, S. S. (2016). Job Shadowing in Information Technology Projects: A Source of Competitive Advantage. *International Journal of Information Technology Project Management*, *7*(1), 47–57. doi:10.4018/IJITPM.2016010104

Sosnin, P. (2018). Figuratively Semantic Support of Human-Computer Interactions. In *Experience-Based Human-Computer Interactions: Emerging Research and Opportunities* (pp. 244–272). Hershey, PA: IGI Global. doi:10.4018/978-1-5225-2987-3.ch008

Spinelli, R., & Benevolo, C. (2016). From Healthcare Services to E-Health Applications: A Delivery System-Based Taxonomy. In A. Dwivedi (Ed.), *Reshaping Medical Practice and Care with Health Information Systems* (pp. 205–245). Hershey, PA: IGI Global. doi:10.4018/978-1-4666-9870-3.ch007

Srinivasan, S. (2016). Overview of Clinical Trial and Pharmacovigilance Process and Areas of Application of Computer System. In P. Chakraborty & A. Nagal (Eds.), *Software Innovations in Clinical Drug Development and Safety* (pp. 1–13). Hershey, PA: IGI Global. doi:10.4018/978-1-4666-8726-4.ch001

Srisawasdi, N. (2016). Motivating Inquiry-Based Learning Through a Combination of Physical and Virtual Computer-Based Laboratory Experiments in High School Science. In M. Urban & D. Falvo (Eds.), *Improving K-12 STEM Education Outcomes through Technological Integration* (pp. 108–134). Hershey, PA: IGI Global. doi:10.4018/978-1-4666-9616-7.ch006

Stavridi, S. V., & Hamada, D. R. (2016). Children and Youth Librarians: Competencies Required in Technology-Based Environment. In J. Yap, M. Perez, M. Ayson, & G. Entico (Eds.), *Special Library Administration, Standardization and Technological Integration* (pp. 25–50). Hershey, PA: IGI Global. doi:10.4018/978-1-4666-9542-9.ch002

Sung, W., Ahn, J., Kai, S. M., Choi, A., & Black, J. B. (2016). Incorporating Touch-Based Tablets into Classroom Activities: Fostering Children's Computational Thinking through iPad Integrated Instruction. In D. Mentor (Ed.), *Handbook of Research on Mobile Learning in Contemporary Classrooms* (pp. 378–406). Hershey, PA: IGI Global. doi:10.4018/978-1-5225-0251-7.ch019

Syväjärvi, A., Leinonen, J., Kivivirta, V., & Kesti, M. (2017). The Latitude of Information Management in Local Government: Views of Local Government Managers. *International Journal of Electronic Government Research, 13*(1), 69–85. doi:10.4018/IJEGR.2017010105

Tanque, M., & Foxwell, H. J. (2018). Big Data and Cloud Computing: A Review of Supply Chain Capabilities and Challenges. In A. Prasad (Ed.), *Exploring the Convergence of Big Data and the Internet of Things* (pp. 1–28). Hershey, PA: IGI Global. doi:10.4018/978-1-5225-2947-7.ch001

Teixeira, A., Gomes, A., & Orvalho, J. G. (2017). Auditory Feedback in a Computer Game for Blind People. In T. Issa, P. Kommers, T. Issa, P. Isaías, & T. Issa (Eds.), *Smart Technology Applications in Business Environments* (pp. 134–158). Hershey, PA: IGI Global. doi:10.4018/978-1-5225-2492-2.ch007

Thompson, N., McGill, T., & Murray, D. (2018). Affect-Sensitive Computer Systems. In M. Khosrow-Pour, D.B.A. (Ed.), Encyclopedia of Information Science and Technology, Fourth Edition (pp. 4124-4135). Hershey, PA: IGI Global. doi:10.4018/978-1-5225-2255-3.ch357

Trad, A., & Kalpić, D. (2016). The E-Business Transformation Framework for E-Commerce Control and Monitoring Pattern. In I. Lee (Ed.), *Encyclopedia of E-Commerce Development, Implementation, and Management* (pp. 754–777). Hershey, PA: IGI Global. doi:10.4018/978-1-4666-9787-4.ch053

Triberti, S., Brivio, E., & Galimberti, C. (2018). On Social Presence: Theories, Methodologies, and Guidelines for the Innovative Contexts of Computer-Mediated Learning. In M. Marmon (Ed.), *Enhancing Social Presence in Online Learning Environments* (pp. 20–41). Hershey, PA: IGI Global. doi:10.4018/978-1-5225-3229-3.ch002

Tripathy, B. K. T. R., S., & Mohanty, R. K. (2018). Memetic Algorithms and Their Applications in Computer Science. In S. Dash, B. Tripathy, & A. Rahman (Eds.), Handbook of Research on Modeling, Analysis, and Application of Nature-Inspired Metaheuristic Algorithms (pp. 73-93). Hershey, PA: IGI Global. doi:10.4018/978-1-5225-2857-9.ch004

Turulja, L., & Bajgoric, N. (2017). Human Resource Management IT and Global Economy Perspective: Global Human Resource Information Systems. In M. Khosrow-Pour (Ed.), *Handbook of Research on Technology Adoption, Social Policy, and Global Integration* (pp. 377–394). Hershey, PA: IGI Global. doi:10.4018/978-1-5225-2668-1.ch018

Unwin, D. W., Sanzogni, L., & Sandhu, K. (2017). Developing and Measuring the Business Case for Health Information Technology. In K. Moahi, K. Bwalya, & P. Sebina (Eds.), *Health Information Systems and the Advancement of Medical Practice in Developing Countries* (pp. 262–290). Hershey, PA: IGI Global. doi:10.4018/978-1-5225-2262-1.ch015

Vadhanam, B. R. S., M., Sugumaran, V., V., V., & Ramalingam, V. V. (2017). Computer Vision Based Classification on Commercial Videos. In M. S., & V. V. (Eds.), Multi-Core Computer Vision and Image Processing for Intelligent Applications (pp. 105-135). Hershey, PA: IGI Global. doi:10.4018/978-1-5225-0889-2.ch004

Valverde, R., Torres, B., & Motaghi, H. (2018). A Quantum NeuroIS Data Analytics Architecture for the Usability Evaluation of Learning Management Systems. In S. Bhattacharyya (Ed.), *Quantum-Inspired Intelligent Systems for Multimedia Data Analysis* (pp. 277–299). Hershey, PA: IGI Global. doi:10.4018/978-1-5225-5219-2.ch009

Vassilis, E. (2018). Learning and Teaching Methodology: "1:1 Educational Computing. In K. Koutsopoulos, K. Doukas, & Y. Kotsanis (Eds.), *Handbook of Research on Educational Design and Cloud Computing in Modern Classroom Settings* (pp. 122–155). Hershey, PA: IGI Global. doi:10.4018/978-1-5225-3053-4.ch007

Wadhwani, A. K., Wadhwani, S., & Singh, T. (2016). Computer Aided Diagnosis System for Breast Cancer Detection. In Y. Morsi, A. Shukla, & C. Rathore (Eds.), *Optimizing Assistive Technologies for Aging Populations* (pp. 378–395). Hershey, PA: IGI Global. doi:10.4018/978-1-4666-9530-6.ch015

Wang, L., Wu, Y., & Hu, C. (2016). English Teachers' Practice and Perspectives on Using Educational Computer Games in EIL Context. *International Journal of Technology and Human Interaction, 12*(3), 33–46. doi:10.4018/IJTHI.2016070103

Watfa, M. K., Majeed, H., & Salahuddin, T. (2016). Computer Based E-Healthcare Clinical Systems: A Comprehensive Survey. *International Journal of Privacy and Health Information Management, 4*(1), 50–69. doi:10.4018/IJPHIM.2016010104

Weeger, A., & Haase, U. (2016). Taking up Three Challenges to Business-IT Alignment Research by the Use of Activity Theory. *International Journal of IT/Business Alignment and Governance, 7*(2), 1-21. doi:10.4018/IJITBAG.2016070101

Wexler, B. E. (2017). Computer-Presented and Physical Brain-Training Exercises for School Children: Improving Executive Functions and Learning. In B. Dubbels (Ed.), *Transforming Gaming and Computer Simulation Technologies across Industries* (pp. 206–224). Hershey, PA: IGI Global. doi:10.4018/978-1-5225-1817-4.ch012

Williams, D. M., Gani, M. O., Addo, I. D., Majumder, A. J., Tamma, C. P., Wang, M., ... Chu, C. (2016). Challenges in Developing Applications for Aging Populations. In Y. Morsi, A. Shukla, & C. Rathore (Eds.), *Optimizing Assistive Technologies for Aging Populations* (pp. 1–21). Hershey, PA: IGI Global. doi:10.4018/978-1-4666-9530-6.ch001

Wimble, M., Singh, H., & Phillips, B. (2018). Understanding Cross-Level Interactions of Firm-Level Information Technology and Industry Environment: A Multilevel Model of Business Value. *Information Resources Management Journal, 31*(1), 1–20. doi:10.4018/IRMJ.2018010101

Wimmer, H., Powell, L., Kilgus, L., & Force, C. (2017). Improving Course Assessment via Web-based Homework. *International Journal of Online Pedagogy and Course Design, 7*(2), 1–19. doi:10.4018/IJOPCD.2017040101

Wong, Y. L., & Siu, K. W. (2018). Assessing Computer-Aided Design Skills. In M. Khosrow-Pour, D.B.A. (Ed.), Encyclopedia of Information Science and Technology, Fourth Edition (pp. 7382-7391). Hershey, PA: IGI Global. doi:10.4018/978-1-5225-2255-3.ch642

Wongsurawat, W., & Shrestha, V. (2018). Information Technology, Globalization, and Local Conditions: Implications for Entrepreneurs in Southeast Asia. In P. Ordóñez de Pablos (Ed.), *Management Strategies and Technology Fluidity in the Asian Business Sector* (pp. 163–176). Hershey, PA: IGI Global. doi:10.4018/978-1-5225-4056-4.ch010

Yang, Y., Zhu, X., Jin, C., & Li, J. J. (2018). Reforming Classroom Education Through a QQ Group: A Pilot Experiment at a Primary School in Shanghai. In H. Spires (Ed.), *Digital Transformation and Innovation in Chinese Education* (pp. 211–231). Hershey, PA: IGI Global. doi:10.4018/978-1-5225-2924-8.ch012

Yilmaz, R., Sezgin, A., Kurnaz, S., & Arslan, Y. Z. (2018). Object-Oriented Programming in Computer Science. In M. Khosrow-Pour, D.B.A. (Ed.), Encyclopedia of Information Science and Technology, Fourth Edition (pp. 7470-7480). Hershey, PA: IGI Global. doi:10.4018/978-1-5225-2255-3.ch650

Yu, L. (2018). From Teaching Software Engineering Locally and Globally to Devising an Internationalized Computer Science Curriculum. In S. Dikli, B. Etheridge, & R. Rawls (Eds.), *Curriculum Internationalization and the Future of Education* (pp. 293–320). Hershey, PA: IGI Global. doi:10.4018/978-1-5225-2791-6.ch016

Yuhua, F. (2018). Computer Information Library Clusters. In M. Khosrow-Pour, D.B.A. (Ed.), Encyclopedia of Information Science and Technology, Fourth Edition (pp. 4399-4403). Hershey, PA: IGI Global. doi:10.4018/978-1-5225-2255-3.ch382

Zare, M. A., Taghavi Fard, M. T., & Hanafizadeh, P. (2016). The Assessment of Outsourcing IT Services using DEA Technique: A Study of Application Outsourcing in Research Centers. *International Journal of Operations Research and Information Systems*, 7(1), 45–57. doi:10.4018/IJORIS.2016010104

Zhao, J., Wang, Q., Guo, J., Gao, L., & Yang, F. (2016). An Overview on Passive Image Forensics Technology for Automatic Computer Forgery. *International Journal of Digital Crime and Forensics*, 8(4), 14–25. doi:10.4018/IJDCF.2016100102

Zimeras, S. (2016). Computer Virus Models and Analysis in M-Health IT Systems: Computer Virus Models. In A. Moumtzoglou (Ed.), *M-Health Innovations for Patient-Centered Care* (pp. 284–297). Hershey, PA: IGI Global. doi:10.4018/978-1-4666-9861-1.ch014

Zlatanovska, K. (2016). Hacking and Hacktivism as an Information Communication System Threat. In M. Hadji-Janev & M. Bogdanoski (Eds.), *Handbook of Research on Civil Society and National Security in the Era of Cyber Warfare* (pp. 68–101). Hershey, PA: IGI Global. doi:10.4018/978-1-4666-8793-6.ch004

About the Contributors

Jan Olaf Blech is consulting major automotive companies in the field of innovation trends in software architecture. He was a research fellow in the Australia-India Research Centre for Automation Software Engineering at RMIT University in Australia. Further previous affiliations include fortiss GmbH in Germany, Verimag in France, TU Kaiserslautern, TU Berlin and the University of Karlsruhe in Germany. Dr. Blech has worked on several publicly and industry funded projects and collaborated with major industrial automation and automotive companies in Europe and Australia. His experience comprises research, consulting and technical project leadership roles. He has (co-) authored over 70 peer-reviewed scientific publications.

Claude Godart is a Professor at University of Lorraine, France. He has lead researches about business process management and Web services composition in complex settings: flexible process models, transactional processes, Web services composition and governance with QoS properties, trusted execution of processes in clouds. He is author and co-author of more than 200 papers, adviser of around 30 PhD theses, and participated in many industrial contracts. He is member of the editorial board of several journals (IEEE TSC, IJSC ...) and member of many conference program committees (BPM, ICWS, Cloud, SCC ...).

Georgia Kapitsaki is an Assistant Professor at the Department of Computer Science of the University of Cyprus (UCY) and faculty member of the Software Engineering and Internet Technologies (SEIT) laboratory in UCY. She received her PhD from the National Technical University of Athens (Greece) in 2009 and her M.Sc. degree in Technoeconomical Systems in 2008. Her research interests include: software engineering, service-oriented computing, open source software reuse and privacy enhancing technologies. She has published over 40 papers in international conferences and journals, has participated in conference organisation (e.g. ICSR) and has served as a TPC member and referee in repudiated journals and conferences. She has been involved in EU projects and has worked as a software engineer in the industry.

Koswatte R. C. Koswatte received the bachelor's degree in 2006 from Sri Lanka Institute of Information Technology, Sri Lanka. She completed master degree in Information Management in 2010 from Sri Lanka Institute of Information Technology, Sri Lanka and master degree in Computer Science and Engineering in 2015 from School of Computer Science and Engineering, University of Aizu, Japan. Her research interests include Semantic Web, Ontology Learning and ICT Education.

Banage Kumara received the bachelor's degree in 2006 from Sabaragamuwa University of Sri Lanka. He received the master's degree in 2010 from University of Peradeniya and Ph.D degree in 2015 from School of Computer Science and Engineering, University of Aizu, Japan. His research interests include Semantic Web, Web Data Mining, Web Service Discovery and Composition.

Angel Fernando Kuri-Morales is an Engineer in Electronics by the Universidad Anáhuac in Mexico City. He got a M.Sc. degree from the University of Illinois and a Ph.D. from Kennedy-Western University. He is the author or co-author eight text books and more than 100 articles published in international journals and conferences. He has thrice received the Merit Medal from the National University (UNAM) for his academic career. He has directed or co-directed over 40 Master's and Doctoral's thesis. His works have been cited in over 30 countries during the last 20 years. He has been a member of the National System of Researchers (SNI) (1999-2015). He has been included in "Who is Who in the World" in 1988, 1998, 2000, 2002, 2003 and 2007-2012. Won an international prize for the best solution to the "Iterated Prisoner's Dilemma" during the International Congress on Evolutionary Computation in 2000. He received the best paper award in the 7th Industrial Conference in Data Mining, Leipzig, Germany (2007); the second best paper award in MICAI (the Mexican International Congress on Artificial Intelligence) in 2013; the best paper award in MICAI in 2014. He has been president of several International Congresses, and invited speaker in many national and international scientific events. He belongs to the Evaluating Committee in the Area of Computer Science of CONACYT (the National Council for Science and Technology in Mexico). He was founding partner of Micromex, Inc. and IDET, Inc. and Director of Applied Research in the Center for Research in Computation of the National Polytechnic Institute. He is a Distinguished Lecturer of the Association for Computing Machinery (ACM) and member of the Scientific Committee of the World Scientific and Engineering Academy and Society (WSEAS). He was a member of the Board of IBERAMIA and President of the Mexican Society for Artificial Intelligence. The methodology he designed for the analysis and processing of large data bases has been adopted as a standard in a major international banking network. Presently he is Professor in the Autonomous

Technological Institute of Mexico (ITAM) and External Consultant for several Public and Private enterprises.

Cin-Hao Ma received the B.S. degree in electronic engineering from National Taipei University of Technology, Taipei, Taiwan, R.O.C., in 2012. He is pursuing the Ph.D. degree in computer and communication engineering at National Taipei University of Technology currently. His research interests include signal processing and multimedia applications.

Kashif Munir received his Ph.D. degree from University of Innsbruck, Austria in 2009. He was a post-doctoral researcher at IMT Atlantique (formerly known as Telecom Bretagne), France from February 2011 to December 2012. He is working as an Associate Professor in the department of Computer Science at National University of Computer and Emerging Sciences (NUCES), Islamabad, Pakistan. His areas of research include admission and congestion control, quality of service for bulk data transfers, performance modeling of computer and communication systems, high-performance computing, and mobility cost analysis. He is a reviewer of Computer Networks (Elsevier), Telecommunication Systems (Springer), Cluster Computing (Springer), Concurrency and Computation (Wiley), Journal of Network and Computer Applications (Elsevier), International Journal of Computer Mathematics, and Journal of King Saud University-Computer and Information Sciences. He is an author of numerous peer-reviewed conference and journal publications.

Incheon Paik received the M.E. and Ph.D. degrees in Electronics Engineering from Korea University in 1987 and 1992, respectively. Now he is an associate professor in the University of Aizu, Japan. Research interests include Deep Learning, Semantic Web, Web Services and Their Composition, Web Data Mining, Awareness Computing, Security for e-Business, and Agents on Semantic Web. He served several conferences as a program chair and program committee member for numerous international conferences. He is a member of ACM, IEEE, and IPSJ.

Olivier Perrin (full professor, Université de Lorraine) has an expertise in Business Process Modeling for virtual organizations; Web services compositions, workflow management, and enterprise application & data integration, covering the process life cycle from modeling to execution including compliance purposes. He proposed the DISC event-oriented framework which was a unified declarative framework designed to reconcile the process design, verification and monitoring of services compositions. DISC provides a flexible and highly expressive composition design that can accommodate various aspects such as data relationships and constraints; services dynamic binding, compliance regulations, security or temporal requirements.

312

He is currently working on enhacing security aspects (authentication, authorization and trust management) within a open Platform as a Service in order to allow collaborative activities and services to be handled between various partners. Olivier Perrin has published several articles in international journals (Data & Knowledge Engineering, Distributed and Parallel Databases, Journal of Data Management...), and conferences (World Wide Web, ICSOC, WISE, CAiSE, BPM, ICWS, SCC, CoopIS...), international workshops and he was involved in many international and European projects. He has been recently Program Committee member of several conferences (BPM, ICSOC,...), and he is a regular reviewer for IEEE Transactions on Services Computing, IEEE Transactions on Software Engineering, IEEE Transactions on the Web, Web Services Handbook, Journal of Intelligent Information Systems, and Software and Systems Modeling journals.

Wei-Ho Tsai received his B.S. degree in Electrical Engineering from National Sun Yat-Sen University, Kaohsiung, Taiwan, in 1995. He received his M.S. and Ph.D. degrees in Communication Engineering from National Chiao-Tung University, Hsinchu, Taiwan, in 1997 and 2001, respectively. From 2001 to 2003, he was with Philips Research East Asia, Taipei, Taiwan, where he worked on speech processing problems in embedded systems. From 2003 to 2005, he served as a Postdoctoral Fellow at the Institute of Information Science, Academia Sinica, Taipei, Taiwan. He is currently a Professor in the Department of Electronic Engineering & Graduate Institute of Computer and Communication Engineering, National Taipei University of Technology, Taiwan. His research interests include spoken language processing and music information retrieval. Dr. Tsai is a life member of ACLCLP and a member of IEEE.

Zhitao Wan is the Chief Technology Officer of Ge Lian Corporation. He was a senior researcher at Siemens and assistant professor in Computer Science at Nanjing Audit University. His research interests include blockchain, services computing and many-core processors. He received his PhD degree from Peking University.

Yilong Yang received the B.S. degree in Computer Science from China University of Mining and Technology, China in 2010. The M.S. degree from the Guizhou University, China in 2013, and he was a follow in United Nations University - International Institute for Software Technology, Macau. His research interests include automated software engineering and machine learning.

Ehtesham Zahoor has been affiliated with National University of Computer and Emerging Sciences (NUCES), Islamabad, Pakistan as an Assistant Professor. He is also heading the Secure Networks and Distributed Systems (SENDS) Research Group. He received his Ph.D. degree from Université de Lorraine, France for the research work he carried out at Lorraine Research Lab in Computer Science and its Applications (LORIA/INRIA). Before joining NUCES, he was working as an ATER at Université de Lorraine, France. He has been an active researcher in the domain of large scale distributed systems and author of numerous peer reviewed conference and journal publications. He also has vast experience of working in the software industry.

Index

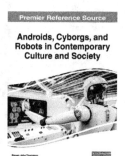

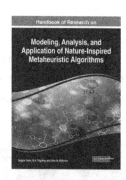

Ensure Quality Research is Introduced to the Academic Community

Become an IGI Global Reviewer for Authored Book Projects

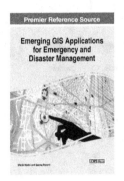

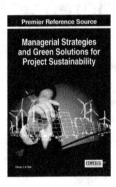

The overall success of an authored book project is dependent on quality and timely reviews.

In this competitive age of scholarly publishing, constructive and timely feedback significantly expedites the turnaround time of manuscripts from submission to acceptance, allowing the publication and discovery of forward-thinking research at a much more expeditious rate. Several IGI Global authored book projects are currently seeking highly qualified experts in the field to fill vacancies on their respective editorial review boards:

Applications may be sent to:
development@igi-global.com

Applicants must have a doctorate (or an equivalent degree) as well as publishing and reviewing experience. Reviewers are asked to write reviews in a timely, collegial, and constructive manner. All reviewers will begin their role on an ad-hoc basis for a period of one year, and upon successful completion of this term can be considered for full editorial review board status, with the potential for a subsequent promotion to Associate Editor.

If you have a colleague that may be interested in this opportunity,
we encourage you to share this information with them.